We're All From Somewhere Else

First Printing, 2015
ISBN-10 1490387803
ISBN-13 978-1490387802

LaHara Publishing International
4951 Arroyo Lindo Ave
San Diego , California 92117

This memoir is a work of creative nonfiction, subject to the limitation of ancient recollection. All names of potentially living persons (except my immediate family) and some street names have been changed to protect potentially sensitive sensibilities.

Inquiries may be directed to the author at rickahill77@yahoo.com

WE'RE ALL FROM SOMEWHERE ELSE

A Southern California Childhood, 1953–1965

by Rick Hill

CONTENTS

ACKNOWLEDGEMENTS

Thanks to Abby Lemon and Will Olliff for copyediting; also much gratitude to Will for crucial editorial suggestions. Thanks also to Kevin Heath, Nick Hill, Ray Jones, Robin Lang, Pete Barnett, and Aura Talbott for reading early drafts and providing valuable feedback. And special thanks to Tim Britain for layout expertise and a sharp eye on everything. Finally, supreme appreciation to my wife Judy for all the above (except layout expertise) plus loving and unflagging encouragement through the long haul.

Dedicated to the memory of my always-loving parents, no matter what names they were using, and to Pete and Ray, who lived the same timeline but didn't know me yet.

INTRODUCTION

During my childhood in the late 1950s and early '60s, it really did seem that everyone in Southern California came from somewhere else. This phenomenon wasn't new: from the 1849 Gold Rush on, immigrants to California outnumbered the native born. But with the influx of Dust Bowl refugees and war workers in the 1930s and '40s, the gap widened dramatically.

Twenty-first-century tourists find relics of this demographic history at Hollywood souvenir shops, where racks of nostalgic postcards portray such midcentury wonders as orange groves, extinct amusement parks, and gridlocked 1950s freeways stretching out from L.A. like glorious rushing rivers—or sinister, smoggy tentacles, depending on your point of view. Each bulbous car in those photos is a droplet in the multi-generational flood of dreamers, go-getters, black sheep, and miscellaneous drifters who poured into Southern California after World War II. Examine the antique freeway postcard through a magnifying glass and you can almost make out my mother, first stepfather, infant sister, and me in our '49 Plymouth with Alabama plates, arriving just in time for the big bang of West Coast Culture.

While most memoirs skip childhood altogether or fast-forward to adolescence, my story focuses on twelve formative years in Southern California's last golden age. Highlighting vintage backdrops and interesting supporting characters, I attempt to sort out certain cultural assumptions along the way and provide a subjective look at my parents' post WWII generation as they finagled their way in and out of prosperity. My hope is that readers who join me, especially those from pre- or post-My Generation, will enjoy the view of one young passenger on that freeway from Somewhere Else.

— Rick Hill, May, 2015

PROLOGUE

~ Southern Gothic ~ Guns and Liquor ~ School and Jail ~ Hollywood 1940s
~ "Through These Portals Pass the Most Beautiful Girls in the World"
~ Mexico Mania ~ Dancing in the Sticks ~ Family Complications ~ One Way Ticket

Although Bessemer, Alabama, provided all the classic features of American small town life in the 1930s, Jane Ross was not blessed with a stable upbringing. Alcoholism and violence ran in her family, especially on the paternal side. To illustrate: one afternoon in 1935 Uncle John Ross, a local bootlegger, came home in a drunken rage and shot his wife Ethyl (pronounced Ee-thil) in the stomach. Their also-drunk, grown son Albert (nicknamed Heavy) pulled his own gun to retaliate. Though mortally wounded, John managed to return fire, and Heavy went down. While John rummaged the kitchen cupboards for a last drink, Ethyl, holding her stomach with both hands, staggered up Exter Avenue, also known as Ross Hill because so many Rosses lived on it. Eight-year-old Jane came forth to investigate the noise, just in time to see her aunt collapse and die on the sidewalk.

Jane ran downtown to find her daddy, Elijah Ross, or "Lige" as friends and family called him. Lige worked as a deputy sheriff and strove to be a loving parent, but after a few drinks, he too followed the family predilection to homicidal blackouts. One day in 1918 while drunk on duty, he shot and killed a suspect, although no particular crime was suspected. Fortunately for him, the U.S. had recently entered World War I, and City Hall permitted Deputy Ross to join the army instead of going to trial. A year later, upon return from Over There, the brave soldier resumed his role as town peace officer.

Lige remained a bachelor until his mid-thirties. Then in autumn, 1924, while on patrol in front of Bessemer High School, he met Hazel

Parsons, age seventeen, daughter of Thomas and Nancy Parsons, both Bessemer natives and Baptist Church elders. A few months later the whole town expressed shock when timid little Hazel wed the middle-aged black sheep of the Ross family.

Despite widespread predictions that Hazel would regret the marriage, everything seemed idyllic at first. Lige reduced his drinking episodes to once or twice per year, and fathered four children: Elijah Jr. (called "Son"), Jane, Kirby, and Don. But when Son died of diphtheria at age five, Elijah Senior began arriving home from work muttering and waving a pistol. Sometimes he would fire a few rounds into neighboring houses. Once he put a bullet between Hazel and baby Kirby when they were lying a foot apart on the bed.

After such incidents, the local equivalent of the SWAT team (usually police friends of Lige), would usually appear. But no one in town dared enter the house when Deputy Ross had imbibed heavily, except for his little daughter Jane. The record is unclear whether the policemen actually encouraged Jane to go in while they waited behind the garage with guns drawn or if she independently crossed police lines, but officially or otherwise, she always served as their chief negotiator.

"Here, let me get you a piece of pie, Daddy," she'd say. "Now let's lay down and take a nap." Once Lige was resting comfortably, Jane would bring an armload of guns out to the police, who then sounded the all-clear through the neighborhood.

After several harrowing years with Lige, Hazel fled the marriage and Alabama. At first she lived with one of her cousins who had migrated to Los Angeles a few years before with ambitions to break into show business. Hazel left her three children with her mother, Nancy, the only person in town who didn't fear the bereft father. Nancy had mixed feelings about the arrangement, and she expressed them as an old-fashioned disciplinarian: when Kirby, Don, or Jane misbehaved, they were ordered to "cut me a switch" from the privet hedge. If the switch were not thick enough to draw welts, she sent the child back to cut another one. Don later reported he would sometimes climb a tree to avoid this treatment while Grandmother Nancy stood below, throwing rocks to dislodge him.

Lige called Nancy "The Hell Cat" and avoided confrontations with her even when intoxicated, a state he now found himself in most of the time. Soon after the separation with Hazel, he shot and killed a deaf man who didn't obey an order to "Halt or I'll shoot!"

With the country between World Wars, the military option wasn't available; instead he drew a three to five year sentence in State Prison at Montgomery, a hundred miles south of Bessemer. Jane and her brothers visited him there one Sunday every month.

By the time Lige made parole, Jane had begun attending Bessemer Junior High. On his first day home he bought her a pearl-handled .22 pistol, complete with shoulder holster, and she wore the ensemble to school until an elderly teacher noticed it under her jacket. Convinced that the daughter of the infamous Lige Ross planned to murder her, the poor woman screamed and ran from the room. But in those days Jane had only to apologize and promise to leave the gun at home.

Despite these and more Southern Gothic episodes, Jane and her brothers did live the small-town life as best they could. Grandfather Thomas Parsons sold popcorn and candy from a stand outside the Bessemer Theater. Movies were popular during the depression, so, as Don reported later, "We always had enough to eat and plenty of candy besides." They attended church picnics, listened to the radio every night, and were active in school theatre and sports.

All three siblings did well in their studies, for the Ross family valued education. Jane's cousin Barbara Ross, who later became a teacher at Bessemer Junior High, began practicing for her career at age six. Barbara held daily sessions, imparting to five-year-old Jane everything the first-grade teacher had taught earlier in the day. The elder cousin was a strict and exacting instructor, once reportedly burning Jane with an iron when she didn't learn her daily lesson fast enough. But Barbara did such a fine job overall that when Jane took her school entrance tests the next year, the authorities "skipped" her to second grade.

This head-start served her well when, a few years later, she missed an entire year of school due to scarlet fever, a severe offshoot of strep throat and a frightening epidemic in the days before antibiotics. The county health authorities quarantined Jane, making the act official with a large "DANGER! KEEP OUT!" sign on the front door. She spent most of the year in an upstairs room, reading travel books and movie magazines her father brought her. Daddy Lige was the only one who entered the room, always disinfecting himself coming and going. And he didn't drink at all that year.

To balance her interests in guns, travel, film, and hostage negotiation, Jane kept active in the Baptist church. At eight or nine years old, she sang and danced in local talent contests, and by high school she swam on the girls' varsity team and excelled in jitterbug dancing. Extended trips to visit her mother in Los Angeles added to Jane's local glamour. In the late 1930s and 40s, film stars actually did live, shop, and work in Hollywood. The famous Red Car trolley took passengers anywhere in the city for a nickel; beaches were pristine; nightclubs unparalleled.

But life with Mother was sometimes difficult. After escaping from Alabama and her alcoholic husband, Hazel began to take a drink herself now and then. She veered wildly between late-blooming, roaring-twenties flapper and serious, church-going penitent. In Jane's later visits, Hazel was between congregations, working at the Broadway Crenshaw department store by day and carousing by night with her boyfriend John (aka Johnny) Chittum. Johnny, a fortyish World War II sailor who had served in the army during World War I, kept up with her drinking and then some. Difficult as it must have been for a young girl to live down an ex-convict father, Jane suffered even deeper embarrassment when police jailed her mother for drunk in public, which became an alarmingly regular occurrence during Hazel and Johnny's courtship.

Once on coming home from tenth-grade classes (she always attended school on her extended visits to Los Angeles), Jane found Hazel missing. "That was strange," she said in telling the story later. "When I left in the morning, Momma was in bed with a cold."

A local fireman called soon to clear up the mystery: according to his report, officers observed an intoxicated Hazel wandering down a residential street, completely nude and incoherent. Someone called the fire department, which raises an interesting question — was the LAFD the municipal agency responsible for women inebriates in those days? In any case, the hook-and-ladder crew apprehended Hazel, wrapped her in a blanket, and put her in an equipment closet at the firehouse until she sobered enough to give them her home address.

A few such instances, combined with Johnny's habitual leer at her developing figure, probably convinced Jane to return to Bessemer for eleventh grade in fall 1943. On her first weekend home she dated Pat, a young man who had graduated and spent the summer working for his parents' mortuary business. Pat had enlisted in the army a few days previously, and following the patriotic custom of the times, the youngsters were married a week before he shipped out. This development marked the end of Jane's high school career.

She later reflected that she didn't actually love Pat—she liked him, but gaining independence and the opportunity to show off for the other girls provided her main motives. In any case, within a few months the marriage ended in either divorce or annulment and she booked passage on a Greyhound bus back to Los Angeles.

Soon after she arrived, Jane accompanied a girlfriend to an audition for the Earl Carroll Review. Located somewhere on the entertainment continuum between elegant musical showcase and tawdry exploitation of the female form, the Earl Carroll Theatre was one of Hollywood's most popular nightspots. Over its entrance hung the legendary sign *"Through these portals pass the most beautiful girls in the world."* At the audition, one of the directors saw a statuesque young woman in the audience. He introduced himself and she charmed him with her southern accent. He asked this "Miss Ross" to try a dance routine, and in a true-life scene straight from a forties musical, he hired her on the spot.

Jane soon established herself as a professional showgirl, and her credentials expanded to international status when she joined a dance troupe bound for Mexico. During the war years Europe couldn't export live acts, so a mania for South American music swept the entertainment industry: Carmen Miranda, Xavier Cugat, Desi Arnaz, and other immigrants led the Yankees in mambos, congas, rumbas, and cha-chas as the Latin beat echoed through popular music and movies well into the 1960s. The leisure class in Mexico became as enamored with Hollywood as Hollywood enthused over everything Latin, so the several weeks the troupe planned to spend in Mexico stretched into eighteen months. Jane danced in the finest Mexico City and Acapulco nightclubs and played small parts in several Mexican films[1]. She also appeared in a dance scene in *Fiesta*, a Hollywood movie filmed on location, featuring Esther Williams, a former national competitive swimmer and star of many MGM musicals. In another film the versatile Jane reportedly doubled in a dive scene for Esther, then nursing an ear infection.

But something happened to derail Jane's show business career. Fifty years later, she told female relatives the story of an agent who assured her she could go far if she were willing to travel by casting couch—look how well it worked for Marilyn Monroe! But

---

[1] *Hay Muertos que no Hacen Ruido*, with Mexican comedian Tin Tan, is, as of this writing, available for viewing on YouTube. Jane dances with Tin Tan about fifty minutes into the film.

Jane declared herself unwilling. Instead, for the next few years she alternated between modeling jobs in Hollywood and short visits to Bessemer. In late 1951, perhaps recovering from a love affair, she rode a sleeper coach train across the country and moved into a two-bedroom apartment with her father. The next day she answered a newspaper advertisement for instructors at an Arthur Murray dance studio in Birmingham. She took a bus from Bessemer for the interview, turning local heads with her newly dyed red hair and tight calf-length skirt, the latest in West Coast fashion.

Al Landry, manager of the studio, resembled TV personality Steve Allen with his horn-rimmed glasses and dark, wavy hair. Extreme nearsightedness kept him out of the service; he spent the war years teaching dancing in Manhattan. When peace came Al seized an opportunity to run his own Arthur Murray franchise, even though it meant moving way, way down in the sticks. Perhaps he comforted himself with the knowledge that Birmingham drew mention in the famous Erskine Hawkins song "Tuxedo Junction," as popularized by the Glen Miller band. In any case, Al bought a home in the suburbs, where he lived with his wife and four children as New Yorkers in exile. Besides excelling in all the ballroom and Latin routines, Al kept up with the latest innovations. In her scrapbook Jane saved a clipping from a write-up in the style section of the *Birmingham News* which features photos of Al, in sharp suit and hand-painted tie, spinning a lady reporter through the proto-Rock and Roll dances of the early fifties.

The studio did moderately well under Al's management, but business boomed after he hired Jane. An Arthur Murray instructor's salary depended on convincing customers to purchase more lessons, and lonely men by the dozen were soon buying long-term memberships from Jane. Before long Al too became smitten with his number-one dance instructor and somehow talked her into moving into a spare room in his family home. That way, he explained, she would be closer to work and could avoid riding the crowded bus from Bessemer every day. Al's wife seemed less than thrilled with the arrangement, but the children were enchanted by this tall, vivacious young woman who listened to their problems and gave them fashion tips.

When she told family stories later, Jane always skipped over details of her relationship with Al. But one thing apparently lead to another, and by the middle of 1952, she found herself pregnant. In those days, marrying the father, better late than never, remained the only hope possible for a decent girl in such a predicament. Al seemed agreeable at first, but then he balked at leaving his family. Instead, he gave Jane enough money for a one-way Greyhound bus ticket to California and a couple of hundred dollars to tide her over. It would be interesting to be privy to Jane's thoughts on the long ride across the country. Could she possibly have kept up the optimism and self-confidence she was known for?

Hazel met her at the downtown LA station. Jane's mother lived in a one-bedroom apartment in Hollywood and still cavorted nightly with Johnny Chittum. Having no choice, Jane made herself a bed on the convertible sofa, by the closet which stored her two boxes of memorabilia from her Earl Carroll days and the years in Mexico: show programs, glossy headshots, inscribed photos of Mexican movie stars, ("Jane! Mi amour! Mi Corazon!"), letters from stateside old flames, and pay stubs for vast sums of pesos.

So at twenty-five years old, a high school dropout and soon-to-be unwed mother, virtually penniless and unable because of her "condition" to act, dance, or otherwise charm herself into an independent living situation, Jane settled in to wait for her baby.

I arrived on April 2, 1953, right on time to experience childhood in perhaps the most interesting decade-and-a-half in modern history.

Jane Ross, ca. 1948

PART I: 1953–1959

Hollywood, Bessemer, Central L.A., San Pedro, Van Nuys, Northridge

Tuba and Tractor 1956

Guns and Daddy 1956

Swords and Friend 1957

On the Road 1957

CHAPTER ONE

~ Hollywood Promenade ~ Back to Bessemer ~ Whiskey Men
~ Firehouse Dental ~Sweet Teeth ~ Crowded Conditions
~ Switchboards ~ School Days ~ By the Toe

My world debut in 1953 coincided with a watershed in popular culture: I was born the same week that the first issue of *TV Guide* went on sale nationally.[2] My grandmother Hazel didn't have a TV in her small Hollywood apartment, but on her days off from the Broadway Crenshaw department store, she joined forces with Jane to promenade their little Ricky. From my stroller I observed scenes now viewable only through the time machine lens of early-fifties film. The palm-lined Hollywood streets teemed with bulbous Ford Mercuries and DeSoto Firedomes, sleek Cadillac Coupe deVilles and Studebaker Starlights, huge Hudson Hornets and Packard Clippers. Hollywood and Sunset Boulevards, running parallel through the heart of town, were parade routes of fast-fading glamour: Grumman's Chinese theatre, Schwab's drugstore, the Brown Derby restaurant. Blind veterans sold pencils and plastic carnations on street corners; kids hawked newspapers. Out-of-town tourists lingered for photos at Hollywood and Vine, gawking at celebrities who drove in from Beverly Hills to dine at the Derby and be seen at the Coconut Grove. Electric buses, called "trolley coaches," crackled down the middle of less-famous avenues south and east, disgorging men in double-breasted suits and women in tight calf-length skirts and Robin Hood hats.

All so lovely, thick smog notwithstanding, and no one seemed to care if Jane's left hand bore no wedding ring. (I called my mother

---

[2] In an interesting coincidence, the first *Guide* cover story featured another Little Ricky, child of Lucille Ball and Desi Arnaz, stars of the number-one sitcom *I Love Lucy*.

"Mom" from my earliest memory till her last days, but for narrative clarity I will use "Jane" throughout this account.)

She had everything a single mother with show business aspirations could want: anonymity, sundress weather, palm trees, and proximity to the heart of the entertainment industry. So it is one of the unsolved mysteries of my family history that sometime in 1955, she returned to Alabama.

How could the scandalous Jane Ross dare come home when everyone in town knew she'd had a child by a married man? And why, after the social ordeals of her childhood, would she move into a Bessemer apartment with her unstable father and her fatherless son, those twin emblems of societal shame? No one will ever know the complete answer, but from overheard bits of conversation it seems likely that Jane fled something in L.A., probably another love entanglement.

Back in 1954, after I grew old enough to be left for a few hours with my grandmother Hazel (or "Nanny" as all the grandkids called her), Jane attempted to renew her show business connections. At one of her old aspiring-actor hangouts she met and dated a tall, lanky southerner named Fess Parker. Parker later became a celebrity when he won the role of Davy Crockett in the popular *Disneyland* series. As the family story goes, he became infatuated with Jane, but she finally rejected him. So what could she have been thinking a couple of years later, in the humid Bessemer evenings in Daddy's apartment while she read her toddler son the *Little Golden Book* story of Davy Crockett? Disney's illustrator drew Davy as Fess Parker, so every time she opened the book, Jane saw page after page of her old boyfriend. But when asked forty years later why she and Parker didn't get more seriously involved, she shrugged and said, "He was too tall."

Our return to Bessemer invites speculation that the breakup was more traumatic than Jane cared to admit. But possibly she came back hoping to reunite with my father, Al Landry, who still ran the dance studio in Birmingham. Sometime in spring 1955 Al brought his official children to Bessemer for a get-together. The visit took place before my first conscious memories and I never saw any of them again, but a photo from the event features Lige (whom I always called "Daddy—like Nanny, he couldn't bear to be called anything with "grand" in it), Al, his two girls, his older son, and me.

My half-brother, who looks around seven, is outfitted in a tie and knickers, an ensemble straight from a 1930s photo. My half-sisters, approximately ten and twelve years old respectively, wear matching dresses with Peter Pan collars. Al took off his horn-rimmed specs for the photo, and his resemblance to me at age forty is striking. But various queries arise from the photo. What did Al's wife have to say about the reunion? And what did Daddy think about this casual visit from the married man who compromised Daddy's little girl?

And yet another question from the 1955-56 period: if Al were back in Jane's sights, why was she socializing with her younger brother Don's wild Southern-boy crowd? Certain events pertaining do register in my earliest memories. After Daddy left the apartment for his night watchman patrol at the local iron mine, I'd wake up to the sound of one or another of these young fellows laughing in the living room. When I climbed down my bunk bed ladder and padded down the hall, I would find my mommy sitting on the couch by some smiling big man. Both would be smoking cigarettes and drinking from funny-smelling glasses and both seemed delighted to see me, though I had trouble understanding what they were saying.

Friendly as these evenings were, it probably worked out for the best that Daddy didn't return from work early enough to meet any of these guests. After he finished his parole in the late 1930s, he never again ventured outdoors unarmed—he even carried his pistol on airplanes. And even at age 65, he remained a formidable character, still known to shoot first and ask questions later. While we lived with him he foiled at least one armed robbery attempt at the iron mine office and suffered a gunshot wound in the process.

My favorite Daddy story is more about general toughness than violence: the time when, having begun to have considerable dental troubles in his early fifties, he decided to have his dozen or so remaining teeth removed to make way for a set of dentures. In his estimation, he had suffered through too many expensive visits to the dentist already, so no sense throwing good money after bad. Instead he called on his old friend Fred at the Bessemer fire station. I met Fred when Daddy took me to visit at the station a few years later, so I can imagine the dental consultation.

"See these teeth, Fred?" says Daddy. "They got to come out. You got a pair a pliers?"

"Yessir, I believe I do."

And after sharing a few nips of liquid anesthesia with Daddy, Fred goes to work, yanking teeth until his unflinching friend's gum line is clear for brand new upper and lower plates.

For all such idiosyncrasies, Lige had a reputation for being kind to all and loved by most—when sober. The Daddy I knew was a patient rock of love who called me "Buddy"; who taught me the parts of a gun at age two and took me shooting before I turned four; and who, on his night watchman salary, bought me more Christmas presents (full cowboy suit with hat and twin sixgun cap-shooters, ride-'em tractor, rocking horse, kid-size tuba) than any kid outside of Beverly Hills or the Bessemer equivalent could expect. And when we drove to the downtown Walgreen's in Daddy's '51 Ford, I was always granted license to sit on his lap and help him steer the car.

Daddy saw me as the reincarnation of Lige Junior, a blessing from heaven never to be corrected or discouraged. Jane generally agreed with this view and kept the vow she made to herself as a youngster to reject all child-rearing strictures practiced by her grandmother Nancy. With Daddy's compliance, she ventured well beyond the permissive approach of Dr. Spock, midcentury's bestselling child psychologist. Nobody stopped me from pounding nails in the apartment wall—wasn't it cute how well I used a hammer? And when I missed the nail and whacked a large hole in the plaster, then yelled, in emulation of Daddy, "HOT damn, I missed it!" Daddy just laughed and Jane shrugged and canceled plans to have me baptized the next Sunday. She didn't want any trouble when the pastor sprinkled me with the holy water.

Throughout their childhoods, Mama Nancy gave Jane and her brothers a choice: either eat everything on their plates or go out and cut a switch. As a result, Jane never forced me to ingest anything I didn't want. What I *did* want was plenty of sugar. For my first few years, my caloric intake consisted almost entirely of Sugar Pops, Sugar Frosted Flakes, chocolate donuts, chocolate ice cream, frosted cinnamon rolls, Hostess Cupcakes, and Snowballs plus daily doses of Hershey's kisses and Reese's peanut butter cups, all washed down with Dr. Pepper, Kool-Aid, milk with Bosco chocolate syrup, and two-for-a-penny wax cylinders full of artificially-colored, concentrated-sugar solution, the intensity of which I didn't encounter again until I took a hypoglycemia test in my twenties. Oh, and a peanut butter, banana, and mayonnaise sandwich now and then.[3] I ate so much sugar and so little of anything else in those pre-school years that I developed a mild case of rickets (according to a doctor who examined me later) and needed oral surgery to remove my two-year molars before I turned three. And, as noted by the county dentist who examined my teeth in first-grade, eight more cavities appeared in the next few years.

In the idyllic days before Jane went to work, I would wake up to Captain Kangaroo at nine and play with my abundant toys until *The Mickey Mouse Club* came on at three. At five the William Tell Overture, theme song for the *Lone Ranger* TV show, signaled the appearance of that iconic masked western hero and his faithful Indian companion, Tonto. I named my rocking horse Silver, like the Ranger's famous steed, and nightly Jane would rock me on his saddle until I nodded off and she could carry me to bed. On Saturdays, Mighty Mouse and other cartoon reruns supplemented the entertainment.

In the afternoons before Daddy left for work, I chatted with him as he put on his uniform and loaded his .38 pistol. I would accompany him to his car, and then roam the vast Cloverdale apartment domain (which has since shrunk mightily, as I found when I stopped by few years ago). I remember eating ants at the bigger kids' direction and collecting fireflies when they came out at dusk. While the big kids were at school, I could sit by the creek and listen to the high school marching band practicing on the other side. One of my earliest longings was for a gleaming, golden tuba to parade with, and in anticipation I practiced on the plastic model I received for my third Christmas.

My toddler idyll ended in early 1956 when Jane found a switchboard operator job at a busy Birmingham office. For the benefit of those who haven't seen that long-gone-to-automation occupation in old movies, the role of switchboard operator involves the manual transfer of outside phone calls to and from the many offices in the building. The operator sat in front of a large, perforated panel, from and to which she pulled and plugged colored telephone jacks corresponding with different phone lines.

---

[3] The only other place I have seen this Southern staple food combination mentioned is in Elvis Presley biographies. Elvis reportedly liked his peanut butter and banana sandwiches Mississippi style: bread spread with butter on the outside, then fried like a grilled-cheese sandwich. Alabamians preferred the health food version: the mayo, peanut butter, and banana mashed together and spread on untoasted white bread.

Until the beginning of this employment, I had been the center of Jane's universe. But she somehow made it clear that, even though she'd rather stay home with me, she must go to work. I took this news with equanimity at first, for I assumed Daddy would be my daytime companion. But, as she explained, Daddy had to sleep all day after his night watchman job. So I would get to go to school like a big boy. I wasn't convinced that this idea was sound, but just before my third birthday I began all-day attendance at a daycare (or "nursery school" as they called them then) run by two old-maid sisters in their ancient house on the far side of Bessemer.

Typing the words "nursery school" conjures painful visions of the first day of my 18-month sentence in that institution. In one of my oldest memory films, Daddy's 1951 Ford comes into view, with Jane driving and me standing up in the front seat, balancing as best I can. If I bounce a bit, the top of my head touches the headliner. Fifty years later, a mother would be cited (or perhaps jailed) if caught transporting a toddler in this manner, and Jane does suggest that I "Sit down, Honey." But I perceive that she feels guilty for abandoning me, so I ignore her in frigid dignity.

As this early memory continues, we pull up next to a commercial panel truck driven by a young fellow in bow tie and military cap. He is on his regular route, selling bread, donuts, cookies and pies. The breadman is a nationwide phenomenon in the fifties and will be a common sight for another ten years or so, when he will follow the iceman, the milkman and the switchboard operator into occupational oblivion.

Jane leans across the seat and smiles out the window: "Hi! Can you tell me where Orchid Street is?"

"Uh, Sure, Ma'am. Turn left at the corner and two blocks over." Only in the South can a young fellow address a woman his age as "Ma'am" while leering at her. I recognize the general expression from the whiskey men in the living room.

Unfortunately, this fellow's directions prove accurate. My memory cuts to a driveway of an old house with a four-foot-high chain link fence around the front yard, behind which children move about listlessly. Suddenly everything seems to go in fast motion: Jane lifting me out of the car; strange big people crowding close, a hurried conversation. I find myself surrounded by complete strangers, sobbing bitterly as my mommy drives away. She couldn't really be leaving me here! She has always done exactly as I'd wished, and I emphatically wish to be far, far away from this place. I am marooned at the Alamo with the armies of Santa Anna closing in and no Davy Crockett to save me.

Unfortunately, my initial dread proves prescient. The twenty or so pupils in attendance spend most of their days playing in forced near-silence on the linoleum floor of a large dining room. For amusement we have ancient blocks for the boys, used to make forts which larger boys scatter the instant they are raised to smashable height. These swaggering five-year-olds periodically make a break for the halls, to run around mindlessly until herded back into the dining room. The girls play jacks, bouncing small rubber balls and picking up metal tokens in prescribed bunches. During good weather mornings we are allowed an hour in the back yard to take turns on the two-seat swingset or dig in the red Alabama clay that shows through the patchy grass. On warm afternoons we are permitted to mill about in the front yard, where passersby view the young inmates, all yearning through the chain links for parents to return. About once a week we take a walk around the neighborhood in junior military formation, with one old lady in the front and one policing the rear. But as a rule we stay in the house and keep quiet.

Should any of us become too rambunctious, everyone in the malefactor's vicinity is put to task scraping gum off the floor with butter knives. Since gum is strictly forbidden at the school in our era, I imagine the crusty grey stuff as leftovers from tribes of Indians who inhabited the room before settlement by the Prune sisters. That's what my five-year-old mentor Rudy calls the old ladies; he said their faces looked like prunes. The very mention of prunes is hilarious, since Rudy told us prunes made you go poop.

If a child talks at all during the punitive gum-scraping sessions, the meaner sister swoops down, snatches him or her roughly by the shoulder and places a grim face in close proximity.

"Straighten up! Look at me!"

Her visage is indeed prune-like, her expression pitiless.

"Put out your hand! Open it!"

She brandishes one of those little paddle toys with a small red ball attached by a rubber band, but her paddle has no attachment. Maintaining her pitiless gaze, she raises the paddle dramatically and brings it down on the little outstretched palm before her. Two spanks are standard. If you jerk your stinging hand away at the first strike, her stringy talon forces your palm back into position for the second blow, then a third for flinching. Apparently Dr. Spock's gospel is not yet universal.

One day I get several harder-than-usual spanks and am sentenced to stand in the corner for what seems like hours. In a persona poem I wrote some thirty years later featuring Steve LaHara, a frequent alter-ego, I describe the scene fairly accurately, coming to some conclusions about innocence and blame:

Reflections of Steve LaHara Upon Losing his Job and Having a Fight with his Girlfriend Trudy

Now my whole life of trouble ain't nature, it's nurture —
I'm a circumstance victim, a martyr to virtue.
And I can't help but think (with my trusty glass raised)
that the trouble all started in nursery school days
when a jug-eared just-four who looked just like me
got himself all mixed up in some bad company.

My friend Rudy is five. He can fight. He ain't scared
of old Prune Face who watches us. Rudy says
the red Alabama dirt we spoon up by the swings
is devil's clay. I can feel it getting hotter as we dig.
This morning in the long first hour after Mama
dropped me off, Rudy gives me an inkpen tattoo
big as his — Cheerios, like on the commercial.
They get bigger when we make our muscles.

Rudy points at two girls sitting across from us.
One is tall as him. She's four and a half,
with braids and a big smile. The other one is three.
She looks like that baby next door who don't like me.

I want to play cars, guns, something else, but Rudy says,
"Let's get em!" "Uh-uh," I reply. "Let's play airplanes."
"No! Let's catch em, kiss em! Then they'll be our girlfriends!"
So we chase them down the hall, screeching through the
    kitchen,
Through Corina's big brown legs, and on to the bathroom

To trap 'em by the tub and slam the door behind us.
Rudy pushes the big girl down, kisses her lips.
She's laughing and slaps at him. I trip Babyface,

but she don't laugh. She bumped her head
on the cold floor and stares up, big eyes and dry lips.

I want her to laugh now. I want to yell "Laugh! Laugh!
You're supposed to be my girlfriend!" My girlfriend,
like Mama with those big whiskey men in the front room,
always laughing, laughing, like Rudy is laughing now —

I scramble up, stumble back through the kitchen
and go flying down the hall, face all hot and stomach
    swirly —
Mama, Mama, Mama, I want my Mama —
then I hear my girlfriend's cry like the peep-peep-peep
of an Easter chick right behind me as I round
the corner and slam right into old Prune Face.

It's funny what comes up when you slow down and think;
how the muddy past clears when you've had a few drinks —
Hurt's whole enchilada, pain's whole panorama,
winds back to a preschool in north Alabama.
All these hassles at work and squabbles with Trudy,
these dumb tattoos, even — it's all your fault, Rudy.

I based the "Corina" in the poem on a black maid who worked
at the nursery school. Contrary to our TV-induced popular culture
conception, many mothers — white and black — worked in the fifties.
Were there nursery schools for little African American kids, too? More
likely they were left home with infirm grandparents or unemployed
siblings old enough to watch them. And most post-toddler black kids
went to work early in Alabama. The grocery boy, perhaps the first
non-white male I remember seeing, couldn't have been more than
ten. He came to our building almost daily, carrying in the basket
on the front of his bike a bag's worth of staples: milk, eggs, bread,
Hostess cupcakes, Hershey bars and Dr. Pepper.

"Corina" was perhaps forty, her youngest children probably
already grocery boys or apprentice maids. As she worked, she usually
paid little attention to the kids always underfoot. But one day Rudy
provoked a response by dancing around in front of her, blocking
her way, chanting "Eeney, Meeny, Minie Moe, catch a nigger by the
toe!" Soon all of us were chanting it, jumping up and down in our
excitement. "Eeney, Meeny, Minie Moe, catch a nigger by the toe!"

"Ain't nobody gon' catch me by my toe," she said with an odd smile.

We kept up the chant, and she repeated, with a broader smile this time, "Ain't nobody gon' catch me by MY toe!"

We continued to dance around, shouting the song even louder. Suddenly she pushed past us, shaking her head, this time muttering. "Ain't NOBODY gon' catch me by MY toe!"

Even such mild defiance was rare in the Alabama where Corina spent her life. But nearby Birmingham became a battleground of the civil rights war that began in earnest around the time we left. Perhaps currents of the movement were already roiling within her. The Southern Christian Leadership Conference was formed early in 1957, with young Martin Luther King as its first president. The group organized bus boycotts in Birmingham as well as Montgomery, where only a year before, Rosa Parks refused to give up her seat and thereby brought the struggle to nationwide attention. Ahead were beatings, church bombings, dogs, fire hoses, and hysterical pronouncements. In March of 1957, probably around the time of the incident with Corina, Birmingham adopted an official ordinance declaring it "henceforth unlawful for white and colored persons to play together, or, in company with each other…in any game of cards, dice, dominoes, checkers, pool, billiards, softball, basketball, baseball, football, golf, track, and at swimming pools, beaches, lakes or ponds or any other game or games or athletic contests, either indoors or outdoors."

Black citizens were moving from passive acquiescence to organized defiance, but as late as 1967 I saw residual evidence of the old attitudes. During a short return to Bessemer from California (see the epilogue), I happened to be strolling down a sidewalk on the outskirts of town early one Sunday morning. A group of tough-looking black teens approached from the other direction, all walking abreast on the otherwise deserted street and blocking my path. Too frightened to alter my course, I kept walking toward them. To my astonishment, they all stepped into the street to let me, a scrawny thirteen-year-old, have the sidewalk to myself.

But a change was coming. I'd be reaching too far to put thoughts in "Corina's" head, but even at four—and this isn't merely retrospective memory—I detected defiance and resolution in her face as she pushed past us.

But for me that day counted as just one more in an indeterminate sentence. Jane's later recollection had me enjoying nursery school after the first few weeks. If so, the happy memories have faded; but in any case, deliverance was at hand and great changes in store. Soon I would take my place in the immigrant flood homing in on California from all parts of the nation.

CHAPTER TWO

~ New Family Members ~ Off the Wagon ~ Sans Freeway ~ Locusts
~ Tongue Sandwiches ~ Passing the Inspection ~ Home at Last

MapQuest figures 2,050.71 miles from the Cloverdale complex on West Twelfth Street in Bessemer to Hazel and John's old house on the 4200 block of Kenwood Avenue in South Central L.A. The current driving time is listed as thirty hours. But in 1957 traveling cross-country was a more complex and time-consuming endeavor.

The difference can be attributed to the U.S. Interstate Highway system, a heretofore utopian dream of early twentieth-century motorcar pioneers. President Eisenhower signed the dream into law in 1956, only a year before we started for California. Back in 1918, Eisenhower led an army motorcade across the continental USA in an expedition that took two months. Then, in Germany after World War II, Ike saw the autobahn and the future of American auto travel. That future was now, November 1957. Jane and me, plus two hangers-on (my new step-father Luke Langston and new sister Patricia), were on the road.

Luke first appeared at our apartment in late 1956. Age 22 and fresh out of the army, he was one of the whiskey men who met Jane through her younger brother Don. Born in 1934, Luke was a contemporary of Elvis Presley, the national show business sensation and a demigod among Luke's peers in the South. Elvis's clothes, his hair, and his whole polite-but-smoldering persona set the style for the new Southern manhood. The honky-tonk sound of fellow Alabamian Hank Williams (who had passed away only three years before) became passé: when farm boys like Luke went to town, they danced to "All Shook Up" instead of "Hey, Good Lookin'." These Hillbilly Cats actually did wear blue suede shoes, and they wouldn't let a hat, cowboy or otherwise, within three feet of their delicately constructed pompadours.[4]

Luke had an easy-going personality and an Elvis smile, complete with dimples and perfect teeth, plus a just-out-of-the service physique and paratrooper tattoo. Combine these charms with Jane's bigger-than-Bessemer glamour and add the family penchant to throw caution to the winds after a few drinks, and the two of them were involved fairly quickly, even by Ross standards.

One rainy afternoon a month after Jane met Luke, I accompanied them on a drive to his family's house in the country. The vehicle, his father's torpedo-body 1949 Plymouth, featured a cavernous interior, windshield wipers in the back, and robe rails on the rear seats. As we clanked and bumped down the muddy red roads of Northern Alabama, I stood up in the rear footwell, holding on to the upholstered ropes and imagining pirate ships and war movie tanks.

Details of this formal visit have faded with the years, but I do recall an old steel-string acoustic guitar, brought in from the porch on account of the weather. It was the first full-size instrument I ever picked up, though I did own a Mickey Mouse ukulele. The guitar stood tall as a standup bass would to me now, but I hoisted it onto my lap and began to strum. That year Elvis appeared on all of TV's major variety shows, so I'd had the opportunity to study his technique. I'm not sure to what extent my act broke the ice for the adults at their awkward meeting, but I know I managed to get everyone's momentary attention, for I remember delighted faces and exclamations: "Look a' that! Look at lil' Elvis!"

What happened after this event raises yet another question for this murky part of my early history: why did Jane get so involved with Luke Langston, who, despite the abovementioned attributes, remained a country boy to the bone and a scandalous seven years younger than she? Decades later, when I asked her a more diplomatic version of the question, Jane replied simply, "I must have been out of my mind."

A practical reason for Luke's upcoming role as stepfather was provided by Jane's pregnancy. Soon afterward, the expecting parents drove to Mississippi for a quick wedding—no blood test or waiting period required—and Luke moved into the apartment.

[4] A source for Elvis biographer Peter Guralnick reported that the King required three different hair oils for his elaborately constructed coiffure: regular-strength grease for the sides, thicker still for the back, and a lighter weight to get the front wave just right.

Since he found only sporadic work on construction jobs, he had leisure for some step-fatherly overtures, including taking me along when he and his younger brother Bubba went squirrel hunting and frog-gigging.[5]

Jane quit the switchboard job when the new baby became imminent, and thus, like a Siberian prisoner released from the gulag for complex political reasons beyond his understanding, I found myself freed from the Prune Sisters' nursery school — one day scraping gum with smarting palms, the next in the bosom of my family, luxuriating as of old to Captain Kangaroo episodes and tuba music from across the creek.

But this idyll, or at least the outdoors part of it, was short-lived. An afternoon in mid-October found me galloping along the sidewalk in front of the apartments, lost in a Lone Ranger fantasy. I remember looking down and enjoying the sight of ground rushing under my feet. Suddenly I slammed into the heavy chrome bumper of a car parked across a driveway. The blow opened a gash in my forehead, but I continued, neither much-pained nor overly perturbed, to run toward home with my head down, dripping blood on the sidewalk in an interesting pattern.

Jane saw me coming from the living room window. Nine months pregnant, she dashed downstairs, snatched me up and drove frantically to the hospital. The doctor complimented me for holding still like a big boy while he sewed up the wound, and the stitches in my forehead looked good for Halloween, which arrived shortly afterward. But following the accident Jane became more nervous in general, especially about me. I wasn't allowed to go outside again until we moved several weeks later.

Three adults and a homebound child crowded the two-bedroom, one-bath apartment, and steady work continued to evade Luke. Perhaps like me getting out of nursery school, he felt no enthusiasm for daily contact with authority figures once he left the army. He did make some effort, even going so far as to cut his Elvis hairdo much shorter, but steady employment continued to elude him.

Living space became even tighter when Patricia (hereafter called

---

[5] A passage laden with "Luke," "Bubba," "squirrel hunting," and "frog gigging" could lead jaded readers to conclude the story is fabricated from bad sitcoms — the kind in which synthetic Southerners say things like "Kiss my grits." But I hereby affirm that all cited names and events are factual. Furthermore, we probably did have grits for our pre-hunt breakfast.

by her family nickname "Trish") arrived in early November, 1957. As Jane balanced care for her new child and new husband and a not-quite-five-year-old reluctant to give up his place at the center of her life, she began a series of brief conversations with her mother in California—brief because long distance calls then cost two dollars for the first three minutes. Nanny, eager to see her grandchildren, assured Jane that L.A. was booming. If they moved out there, she would see to it that John secured Luke a job on one of the glazier (window installer) crews he supplied. "Plenty of work, Darlin'! You come on ahead and bring those babies out here!"

One morning, soon after Jane spoke with Daddy about the possibility of moving to California, he stumbled into the apartment. I watched from the kitchen as he staggered through the living room. Puzzled that he hadn't acknowledged my greeting, I followed down the hall and found him sitting unsteadily on his bed in the room we shared. He began to dismantle his gun for its daily cleaning, but he was squinting one eye and then the other and seemed to have trouble seeing anything clearly.

"Hi, Daddy," I said, looking at him curiously.

Still holding the gun, he grabbed me in a bear hug. I hugged him back and he kept mumbling, "Oh, Buddy. Oh, Buddy."

I recall vividly the reek of whiskey mixed with his old man smell, his confining grip when I tried to wriggle away after a minute, the gun parts falling onto the linoleum floor when he bumped the night table. I looked up to see Jane in the doorway. She was tense and wary of alarming him, but stood ready to rescue me if necessary.

Daddy finally let go and fell backward on the bed, mumbling incoherently. Jane led me to the kitchen for a peanut butter and banana sandwich. As she mashed the bananas with a fork, the frown line between her eyes looked deeper than I'd ever seen it.

Jane's always restless itch to start fresh, the crowded conditions, and the childhood memory of Daddy in a blackout, shooting within inches of her baby brother Kirby's head—all the above must have contributed to the final decision made soon afterwards. We left Bessemer right before Thanksgiving, 1957, when Trish, three weeks on the planet, was deemed old enough to travel. Luke packed us into the '49 Plymouth, either a wedding gift from his daddy or a case of over-extended car borrowing by a grown child (a not unusual practice in our family as the years unfolded), and we set out for California.

A modern interstate freeway driver may fall into a peaceful, almost hypnotic state, auto-correcting the steering but otherwise free to dissolve into reverie and/or satellite radio as the miles fly by. But in the fifties, the way west followed empty stretches of poorly maintained two-lane road. Radio reception faded in and out. Night driving meant staring into the bright lights of oncoming traffic. Passing or being passed by another car presented another nerve-wracking challenge: as any reader of Road novels is aware, one might suddenly overtake an Okie family in an ancient truck going twenty-five miles an hour, or be overtaken at ninety by a beat-up new Hudson Terraplane full of bennie-crazed hipsters bound for San Francisco.

The state highways were punctuated by congested small towns, each with zealously enforced twenty miles per hour speed limits and unsynchronized traffic lights. Nowadays those little Mississippi or Louisiana or Texas hamlets barely register as off-ramp signs to the modern traveler zooming by at eighty. But each town then meant a half-hour, bumper-to-bumper zigzag through city traffic, repeated every hour or so along the road. Once in a town, a driver might come to a traffic light on, say, Main Street and Commerce Avenue, and see before him several wooden posts covered with a confusing hash of route numbers and arrows. Turn left on Commerce for Routes 12, 32, 40, & 82; go right for 3, 17, 41, and 78; continue on Main for another ten or so route numbers which will eventually lead north, south, east, and west. The small municipalities would have seemed less congested with better city planning, but in the 1940s and '50s the national feeling celebrated plentiful expanses and happy expansion.

Motels along the way cost from two to six dollars per night, but Luke and Jane couldn't afford such expense on a routine basis. Most nights they took turns driving, pulling over to sleep in the car when both were too tired to go on. Baby Trish rode in her bassinet in the front seat beside them; I sat in the back among luggage and cardboard boxes, craning my neck to stare out the window, daydreaming *Lone Ranger* episodes or imagining myself a giant, chewing telephone poles like toothpicks. These days, media players with separate screens for each child are standard middle-class family travel equipment, but not even the motels had TVs then.

Not that we weren't up to date with road gear. Jane had invested in the latest travel-generation gadget, a baby bottle warmer that plugged into the Plymouth's cigarette lighter. She also brought a box of what were then considered emergency-use-only disposable diapers, which she disposed of by tossing them out along the road between towns. Before the relentless "Don't Be a Litterbug" campaign of the sixties, few motorists thought twice about throwing trash out of their car windows. Moreover, municipal agencies and volunteer businesses had not yet organized to pick up litter, so thousands of roadside miles were covered in tons of waste paper, broken glass, crumpled cigarette packs, and rusty steel beer cans, with plenty of old tires, stripped cars, iceboxes, and dead animals chunked in.

The Plymouth's radio quit working somewhere in Mississippi, so except for Trish's occasional crying spells, our interstate passage remained quiet. Luke and Jane exchanged minimal conversation; perhaps she already realized how little they had in common.

We rolled on through Louisiana and East Texas, stopping only for gas. The first motel stay stemmed from an emergency of sorts: somewhere mid-Texas we ran into a locust swarm. Billions of three-inch-long grasshoppers covered the land, a literal cloud of them.[6] Eerie yellowish light filtered through the swirling mass, making the afternoon seem like twilight. Baby Trish began to cry, and I leaned against Luke's army duffle bag and closed my eyes, listening to the locusts bouncing off the car. Jane, who happened to be driving at the time, pulled into the first gas station/motel combo she saw. A local denizen ambled out to fill the tank, ignoring the locusts crawling over him. He showed dark brown teeth when he grimaced into the car.

Jane opened the window a crack. "How long does this go on?"

He shrugged. "Dunno. You want a room?"

Jane handed over four dollars and we made a run from the car to a low adobe building. Our kitchenette unit included a double bed, end-table with ceramic lamp and large ashtray, and wooden table with a two-burner hotplate on top. Grasshoppers clicked incessantly against the window. Jane heated some baby formula in a tin saucepan. Luke used a rolled-up towel to stuff the gap at the bottom of the door, then sat under a bare bulb to study the map. I fell into an uneasy sleep on the end of the bed.

At dawn, Jane carried me at a run to the Plymouth and Luke followed with the baby. Only a few locusts smashed against the

---

[6] Such phenomena are now rare; the swarming locusts that plagued the west in the 1860s to 1880s were supposed to be extinct by the turn of the century. But they came again during the dust bowl years, and apparently that corner of the southwest sheltered their last remnants.

windshield as we pulled out with the red sun rising behind us. By New Mexico, towns nestled farther and farther apart and the terrain began to resemble what I'd seen on the TV westerns. Somewhere in Arizona we stopped at a gas station and "Trading Post." Indians in authentic moccasins ran the store, but none of the braves wore long hair or headdresses. For twenty-nine cents, Jane bought me a little drum decorated with feathers. She also purchased a can of beef tongue, a loaf of bread and some bottles of Coca-Cola in the original 6 ½ ounce size.

We ate beef tongue sandwiches as I watched The West out the Plymouth's back window. Jane told me the big Saguaro cactuses were full of water, and people stranded in the desert could cut them open and drink their fill. On a lonely mid-Arizona highway we stopped for sheep crossing the road, shepherded by a short haired, cowboy-booted Indian on horseback. Two dogs looking more like wolves stood on either side of the road stripe, facing the traffic and barking until all the sheep had crossed.

The next night we were driving through Kingman, near the California border, when the headlights began to dim. When we pulled into a station for gas, the car wouldn't start again. We waited two days for a rebuilt generator, and the repair cost a ruinous eleven dollars, parts and labor, plus eight dollars for two nights in the nearest motel. That outlay all but obliterated the remaining funds that Nanny advanced for the trip.

Back in '57, thick adobe walls and small electric fans battled the heat in scores of little court motels that lined the old highway in Kingman. In recent travels I found that a few of these almost-time-capsules remain in business half a century later, but the mostly (East) Indian proprietors have added to each unit a small refrigerator, color TV and large air conditioner. Trish became feverish during our second night in the motel. Jane bathed her with tepid water from the bathroom sink, but she cried for hours, then brought forth green diarrhea, a phenomenon which stoked my ongoing wonder at everyone's solicitude toward the noisy little creature. When we finally left town, we spent a couple of the few dollars remaining on a canvas "Original Desert Waterbag" to hang on the front of the radiator. "Adds you some extra cooling power," said the portly fellow in the Stetson hat who sold it to us. "And you gonna need it in that desert if you don't wait till night to start out."

Until well into the 1960s, travelers considered a daytime desert crossing, even in the late fall, a risky venture. But as we were behind schedule and out of money, we set off among the trucks and newer cars on the near-empty stretch to Barstow. Nowadays the state border inspection station is situated far inland and cars merely slow down as they pass the usual "No inspection today" sign. But back then everyone had to stop, and uniformed inspectors were almost as serious as airport security workers are today. Commercial fruit, especially citrus, constituted a major state industry, and officials took great precautions to stave off contamination from insects and plant diseases.

"Where you folks from?"

"Any fruit or vegetables to declare?"

The officiousness also extended to further inspection—perhaps as a holdover from attempts to limit immigration by Okies in the thirties, or perhaps they had seen all the film noir movies of gun-crazy gangsters crossing into California to wreak havoc.

"What brings you to California?"

"Please open your glove box, sir."

"May I take a look in your trunk?"

Remembering that Daddy always kept a pistol in his glove compartment, I felt nervous—what if Luke also carried a gun at all times? Would there be a shootout? But somehow we passed the inspection.

California seemed at first even more desolate than the Southwest desert, but after a few hours the dry country faded into scrubby meadows, cows, and oil wells that resembled giant grasshoppers. We passed the turnoff for San Bernardino as traffic increased. I dozed for a while; when I woke up, smoking factories and countless billboards lined the roadways. Jane read a smaller sign among them: "Los Angeles County Line." Like so many other rootless refugees from all corners of the nation, we had made passage to the Promised Land.

CHAPTER THREE

*~ L.A. Lingua Franca ~ Shoe Precision ~ My First Job ~ Demographic Transition
~ Brothers ~ An Incongruous Grandma ~ Easy Payments*

The massive influx from Somewhere Else pushed Southern California into rapid transition on many fronts, from environmental to racial to socioeconomic, as presently I would begin to see from a child's-eye view.

We stayed with Nanny and John in south central Los Angeles for six weeks or so, until sometime in late January 1958. The afternoon we arrived, I lay on the kitchen table while John, with Luke and Jane's assistance, took out the stitches from the cut I'd gotten running head-on into the parked car a few weeks before. While serving in the army in World War I and the Navy in WWII, John had learned some first-aid basics. Using tweezers, he carefully picked out the threads. Luke, the Korean War Vet, dabbed at the spot with hydrogen peroxide. Jane applied hot compresses. As when the doctor put the stitches in, I followed orders and didn't move my head a bit. From the early days in nursery school on through my childhood, I rarely sobbed, whimpered, or flinched in public. John remarked on my fortitude, then said, "Should've come out sooner. Look, the flesh is starting to grow over and mortify." When a year or so later I began watching the Three Stooges on TV and heard Curly exclaim, "Am I mortified!" I remembered John's comment and felt a certain kinship with my favorite stooge.

At age four I found Nanny's house cavernous and fun to explore, but I liked John's garage even better. It smelled of old grease and cheap whiskey, and in the dim light of a bulb hanging from the ceiling I could see naked ladies smiling down from dozens of calendars tacked to the walls. Since John usually suggested I go elsewhere whenever I ventured in, I spent more time in Nanny's back yard, climbing the fig tree, peeking out into the dirt alley, and chasing Nanny's grey cat Missy through last summer's overgrown vegetable and flower garden.

By the back fence I found a fascinating cement monolith with an elongated chimney and thick steel door, behind which I discovered a compartment full of ashes. Nanny called it "the incinerator," but it reminded me of a Davy Crocket Little Golden Book illustration depicting a riverboat belching smoke and flame.

I inquired further, imagining the fun I could have playing boat captain as someone stoked the next fire. But sadly I had arrived a month or so after such opportunities ceased. For many years, incinerators had been standard home equipment in Los Angeles. Plumes of whitish smoke rose at all hours from hundreds of thousands of backyard units and blended in the atmosphere with black effusion from a million citrus grove smudge pots. A further intermingling of raw car exhaust, factory smoke, and oil refinery emissions created an eye-watering grey cloud over most of Southern California. In order to curb the rising "smog" (a term coined in London at the turn of the century), L.A. had recently banned incinerator use and instituted curbside trash collection.

No doubt the new anti-pollution ordinances saved the city from incidents like the famous 1952 smog in London that killed 4000 people.[7] But as I contemplated the cold ashes of Nanny's final backyard fire, the passing of incinerators seemed a tragedy probably brought on by the same sort of people who fought Davy Crockett at the Alamo. What fun it would have been to have a campfire in the back yard every day, like in the cowboy shows! But all that was gone now. At age four-and-a-half, I felt my first melancholy twinge at being born too late.

The racial makeup of Los Angeles was also in transition, as I began to discover during our first week of residence. John came through with the glazier job for Luke, and since Luke took the car to work, Jane and I set out by bus to visit Nanny at her department store. We had left an Alabama in racial turmoil over segregated busses, but Los Angeles public conveyances were legally integrated. On the first leg of our journey, I saw more African Americans in close proximity than I had ever observed before. As we waited in line at a transfer point, Jane sat on the bench and I stood beside her. She seemed to

---

[7] For a gripping account of L.A.'s war on smog, see "Early Smog Control Efforts" at www.aqmd.gov/home/library/public-information/publications/ 50-years-of-progress

be in deep thought, and as our next bus approached, she placed her hands on my shoulders and spoke quietly.

"Honey, out here people don't call colored people 'niggers' like we do in Alabama. Out here they call them Negroes."

"Negroes?" I'd never heard the term before.

"Yes, Honey. 'Negro' is what they call colored people out here. You should never say 'nigger.'"

We stepped onto the bus and as we moved down the aisle, I saw a large black woman ahead. "Look, Mommy!" I shouted, "A Negro!"

Except for Jane, all passengers in the vicinity, black and white, rumbled with indulgent laughter.

But I was indignant. "Why are they laughing?" I demanded. "I didn't say nigger!"

The laughing ceased abruptly, and Jane spent the rest of the ride looking intently out the window.

We finally arrived at The Broadway Crenshaw department store, a palatial edifice accented with palm trees. The air inside felt cool and diffused a pleasant, leathery smell. When we found Nanny in the children's shoes division, she dropped everything to measure my feet in a complex-looking metal device designed to determine exact width and length. In those days, shoe stores were ostentatiously meticulous about the precision of their measurements; today's discount stores full of imported plastic shoes in approximate sizes would have seemed an abomination to the technicians of that era. Until recently, some upscale stores had featured the zenith of modern shoe science: x-ray machines set at foot level. In my research of this fascinating topic I found the following copy in a magazine ad:

> **They'll Need Their Feet All Through Life.** Guard their foot health carefully through correctly fitted shoes. To help ensure better fit, leading shoe stores use the ADRIAN X-Ray Machine. The ADRIAN fluoroscopic x-ray picture illustrated above clearly shows correct or incorrect fit in an instant. Shoes that are too short or too long, too wide or too narrow, or even too pointed, are immediately indicated in an easily viewed, instantaneous picture. You **SEE** your child's foot **IN THE SHOE.**[8]

---

[8] See www.orau.org/ptp/collection/shoefitting fluor/shoe.htm for more info and photos of the machine.

Later investigations determined that shoe stores administered these x-rays in huge, unshielded doses which contributed to various cancers. The machines were outlawed in the U.S. beginning in 1957, right before I had the opportunity to be properly fitted.

About the time Nanny left for work at The Broadway, John would, if he were not occupied with serious drinking in the garage, go out in his glazier supply truck to construction sites all over the city. He usually returned by noon, then spent the next few hours puttering around the house or sitting in his breakfast nook office, where, during a one-sided conversation, I discovered a treasure trove of wire recorders (a forerunner of the tape recorder that used spools of thin wire instead of tape), stamp pads with different colored inks, and adding machines with mechanized keys and handles on the side. Also scattered about were miscellaneous three-cent stamp dispensers, blank billing sheets, glue, index cards, and many other items fascinating to a not-quite-five-year-old. Throughout the house and garage John also stored cases full of watches in various states of repair, boxes of books, and countless antique tools. I lost no time in covering numerous note pads with stampings, unwinding spools of wire, jamming the keys on several adding machines, and scattering tools all over the back yard.

To distract me, John provided my first work for pay. He took me to his bedroom (he and Nanny both snored mightily, so they slept at separate ends of the house), where he placed on his bed large containers of screws and nuts and a cardboard box full of small cellophane baggies. "You count out a pile of twenty screws," he said. "Then put them in the little bag. Fold the bag like so and put 'em in this box."

"What for, John? What do you do with the little bags?"

"Sell 'em to the glaziers and get rich." He promised that if I did a good job, he'd take me with him one morning to the construction sites he visited. And to sweeten the deal he said, "I'll give you a penny a pack for every pack you fill."

For an undisciplined first child, I could focus pretty well with something interesting at hand, and money had begun to interest me. By the time I turned four I could count to twenty; now I put my skill to work for hours at a stretch, sitting on the edge of John's double bed with the hardware and little bags before me. After a couple of days Jane put a stop to the child labor, but I had already earned thirty-eight cents. John told Nanny it was the best thirty-eight cents he ever spent.

That afternoon I went forth to explore the neighborhood. Until the early 1950s, various written and unwritten policies kept L.A. largely segregated, and the Vermont and Vernon area remained all white. But the Catholic Church, which owned Nanny and John's house and a dozen more on the street, began to purposefully ignore all such strictures. By late 1957, the racial makeup of Kenwood Avenue stood at 70% white and 30% black. The neighborhood soon had several empty houses as well; for every African American family moving in, two white families moved out.

This white flight accelerated when real estate speculators began to sell one black family a home in a white section at a reduced value; then, as white neighbors panicked, the developers bought their homes at cut-rate prices to rent or sell to other blacks at a premium. By 1962, the South Central racial percentage had changed to approximately 85% Black and 15% Caucasian, with most of the whites elderly long-time residents. By 1967, two years after the Watts riots, Nanny and John were among only a handful of non-African Americans living within a several mile radius of the action. They stayed on until 1970, when the church sold all its Kenwood properties.

Within the first few days at Nanny's I met two friends, brothers aged eight and five, who lived a few houses up the street. When I showed them the money I'd made working for my grandpa, they led me to the little store up on Vernon, where I reciprocated their kindness by treating them to gum and swigs from my soda. The store was well stocked with indigestible items within my budget, including many varieties of penny candy and even two-for-a-penny candy hats with the consistency of today's Gummy Bears. Generic sodas of carbonated, vaguely fruit flavor were available for nine cents in a no-deposit/no return bottle. A regular Coca Cola or Dr. Pepper, or a Royal Crown Cola in the magnificent sixteen ounce size, could be enjoyed for ten cents plus two cents bottle deposit.

I first discovered Bazooka bubblegum at that little store: one penny bought a double chew plus a folded-around-the-gum comic strip. Comics star Bazooka Joe, in his skewed baseball cap and pirate eyepatch, was obviously no Little Golden Book hero. Joe's sidekick Mort pulled his turtleneck sweater up over his nose like an outlaw, and all the characters seemed free of adult strictures. I would have to wait until I learned to read to fully appreciate the strip's humor, but I vaguely understood its counterculture stance as art that mocked and resisted the adult world. The comics were probably produced by middle-aged men with families and mortgages; still, the irresponsible teen sensibilities of Joe and his gang were a nice contrast to the impeccable goodness of the Lone Ranger and Mighty Mouse.

I don't remember my friends' names, but we played together regularly for the month or so we lived at Nanny's house. I have a photo of the older brother and me sword fighting with a plastic fencing set I received for Christmas. The equipment included protective face masks, but you couldn't see much through them, so we wore them on top of our heads, like hats.

One sunny day a week after Christmas the brothers took me to meet their great-grandmother, who lived at their house. "Come see Granny. She older'n anybody and white." the younger brother announced, and sure enough, the lady was definitely the oldest person I'd seen to date and several shades lighter than her great-grandchildren.

Both brothers gave me a look of smug triumph, as if to say, "You thought you were the only one with old white folks at your house, huh?" From this experience I reasoned that perhaps race occurred randomly, like hair color. Trish had been born white, but perhaps my next brother or sister would be black. When I asked Jane about this possibility, she smiled and said, "Luke might not like that."

The same day she announced, in the first of a long series of such proclamations in the next few years, that we would be moving soon. Flush with a month's earnings from Luke's first real job, they went shopping in one of the cut-rate credit furniture emporiums springing up in Southern California. After arranging easy credit payments on a "starter family" package, they found their first real home together, an apartment in San Pedro, near Luke's current worksite. Within the week the furniture store would deliver a deluxe ensemble of modern no-slat beds, adjustable crib, trapezium-shaped couch, Formica table, and black-and-white console TV with rabbit-ear antenna.

My Southern California childhood—with its fourteen schools in six years and twelve residences, with its routine evasions of landlords and creditors, its near-poverty alternating with middle-class opulence, its two stepdads and three last names—had reached the launching pad.

CHAPTER FOUR

~ Worker Housing ~ Tonsil Crackdown ~ Learning by Experience ~ Leisure
~ Amnesia and the Toy Box ~ Wheeling and Dealing

The community of San Pedro, still pronounced "San Peedro" even by many of its older Hispanic residents, sits at the hilly end of the Palos Verdes Peninsula in South L.A. County. Originally a fishing village and later a major commercial port, the town's waterfront provided atmosphere for hundreds of Hollywood films. Channel Heights, the worker-housing megacomplex where Jane and Luke set up housekeeping, put us close enough to the harbor to hear the foghorns in the morning. Here I would dwell from February 1958 until November 1959. The larger world saw rapid change during that period: The Cold War looked better, then worse. Russian Premier Nikita Khrushchev had recently sent monkeys and dogs into space, a challenge which goaded Congress into spare-no-expense NASA mode. Among other milestones, the U.S.A. added two remote states, the South descended into civil rights Götterdämmerung (at least on TV), and a Midwestern immigrant to California invented the microchip. But for me that eighteen months provided the longest duration without major changes in domicile and/or family and the nearest thing to stability that I would experience in the next several years.

Conceived by prominent modern architect Richard Nuestra in the early 1940s to serve wartime shipyard workers, the Channel Heights housing project epitomized the New Deal obsession with "planned communities" that Tom Wolfe skewers in his book From Bauhaus to Our House. Wolfe critiques the built-in condescension of the "worker housing" concept, but by today's low-income dwelling standards, the two-bedroom apartments were roomy and even stylish, more like modest townhomes in overall design. Our street traversed a long, steep slope from the main avenue above to a cul-de-sac below.

Each unit had a small lawn in front and another in back, bisected by straight walkways from the parking lot to each unit door. Nowadays it is difficult to imagine apartment dwellers taking time to groom a community lawn, even a section directly in front of their unit. But back when most working men still put in six-day weeks, many of them dispatched themselves on their day off to the maintenance office, checked out a push mower from the attendant, and did just that.

According to contemporary news stories, Nuestra designed Channel Heights not only to last, but to be major maintenance-free for fifty years or more. But Southern California is the land of impermanence. In a recent search of the San Pedro Historical Society's files, I discovered the entire carefully-planned masterpiece had been razed in the early sixties to make room for discount tract homes. The same upward aspirations which prompted the newest wave of California immigrants to mow lawns that weren't even theirs also inspired them to scrimp, save, and finally abandon Nuestra and Co.'s benevolent patronization for homes of their own. I would here opine that the demolition of Channel Heights marks an architectural tragedy, but to look back with nostalgia in a land where rapid change is the norm only invites heartache.

Fathers in the complex generally worked in construction or manufacturing, and almost all had recently immigrated from other states and countries. Some mothers stayed home, but most supplemented the family income as clerks or cannery workers. Three- to six-child families were the norm, and ratio of kids to adults presaged trouble for the sixties when we would all become teenagers.

On weekend and summer days, children generally followed orders to stay out of the small apartments when not eating or doing chores. Yet at any given time, around 15% of the youth population could be found indoors, still wearing pajamas and watching TV. The explanation for this mysterious statistic is medical: the indoor percentage had recently undergone tonsillectomies, an operation which for a few years seemed to be an almost universal rite of passage, as the ear tube insertion procedure became a generation later and the head-shaping helmet for babies seems to be becoming in this era. Fortunately I was too young when the tonsil removal craze hit its peak; its hapless participants were the same slightly older kids who a decade later also had the ill-luck to be draft age at the height of the Vietnam War. Those born in 1952 became the last to be conscripted en masse, so I missed compulsory service by the same few months that spared me a tonsillectomy.

I initially felt deprived by this reprieve. Not only did some tonsil surgeons present their young patients with the offending organs preserved in a jar for display, but they also authorized all the ice cream desired, with unlimited TV privileges as a default bonus. Unfortunately, reality failed to match the advertising. The post-ops stared at their TVs while enduring throats so raw they couldn't talk or even eat much ice cream, though they tried their level best. Gradually I began to understand the tonsillectomy dream as another adult ruse, like when they told us we could catch a bird by putting salt on its tail. I only hoped that Santa Claus and the Tooth Fairy didn't fall into this category.

In spring 1958, most of us not recovering from surgery hunted the boxwood clover bushes of the complex. We set forth, glass jars at the ready, to catch honey bees. Big-game hunters stalking elephants in Victorian India learned to distinguish between varieties of pachyderm, lest the unprepared sahib be trampled by a sex-crazed young bull in the throes of "musth." Similarly, according to older boys recognized as experts, so-called yellow bees could be caught safely by hand and transferred to our jars, while all but seasoned hunters avoided black bees. Unfortunately, no bees were exclusively black or yellow; only the experts could tell which color predominated.

One day in the heat of the chase, I asked one of the experts about a particular target. "Hey, Billy! Zata[9] yella bee or a black bee?"

"Yella bee," he intoned with certitude.

"Okay!" I grabbed and could feel the little creature buzzing in my cupped hands.

"No, wait! Black bee!"

I instantly opened my fingers, but too late—the bee departed, leaving his stinger in my palm. Experience, as I had begun to learn, is the only reliable teacher.

Two levels up the hill from our apartment a resident had installed a swing set, complete with a teeter-totter. There I learned the California variation of "Eeney Meeny Minie Mo," the invocation

---

[9] Linguistic note for non-California residents: by spring 1958 I had progressed rapidly in jettisoning my Alabama drawl, replacing it with the distinctive Southern California front-drop slur: "Is that a" becomes "Zata"; "Let's go eat" becomes "Squeet"; "It's not too early" becomes "Snot twirly," etc.

used in choosing someone in a group for a particular delight or disappointment as the case may be. In the Alabama version of the chant, one would "catch a nigger by the toe"; in California, it became a tiger who, when captured, was required to pay fifty dollars every day if he hollered. Further embellishment sometimes accompanied the incantation: "My mother told me to pick the very best one and you are it." Or, to add suspense, "My mother told me to pick the very best one, and the one who is the dirty dish is out, and O, U, T, spells out, and that is — you!"

Most kids eventually understood this judicial tool could be easily manipulated by adding a word or two. If you employed the method to decide, say, who would have the next turn on the teeter totter, and you preferred a particular candidate, you could drop or add modifiers to fix the game: "My mother told me to pick the very best one and you are NOT it." Thus the desired result could be achieved under a cover of impartiality, and we received an early introduction to practical politics.

As for commerce, every boy under thirteen and even some of the girls owned a bag of marbles, which we carried with us at all times. To show off one's cats-eyes, puries, steelies, pee-wees, boulders, and spaghettis (the swirled-color orbs that actually seemed to be made from marble) provided great satisfaction. Rarity was the mark of worth; for example, odd-sized specimens, somewhere between regular and boulder circumference, were prized jewels rarely traded. Cat's-eyes, so called because of their clear outside and colored pattern inside, were widely available in stores, so a serious trader would usually have to offer two or three cat's-eyes for a purie. For tyros who wanted to look like high rollers, a bag bulging with cat's-eyes with the rarer marbles strategically placed on top made the same impression as did, in more mature gaming circles, a bankroll of one-dollar bills topped with a hundred dollar note.[10]

Across the street and down a level, a big fifth-grade girl (practically a grown-up of serious mien and "pixie-cut" short hair) had dug an elaborate marble-playing field on one of the more unkempt back lawns. Her design resembled a miniature baseball diamond with four holes for bases, but with added traps and sanctuaries for the marbles as they made their way around the course. Games at this site

---

[10] Around this time, in an opening monologue of Red Skelton's popular weekly TV show, Red noted a distinction between the "Kansas City Bankroll" (a hundred dollar bill wrapped around a roll of one-dollar bills) and the "Arkansas Bankroll" (a one-dollar bill wrapped around a turnip).

could be for "fun" or "keeps." In keeps games, you could literally lose your marbles, for those who shot into all the holes and returned to home base became "poison" and could go hunting backwards along the base line, winning and appropriating every competitor's marble they hit.

Toward the bottom of the cul-de-sac lay the domain of third and fourth graders who, disdaining "kid games," gathered between two buildings to shoot straightforward circle-in-the-dirt marbles. The rules were simple: if on your turn you knocked a marble out of the ring, you won that marble and shot again. This game was always for keeps, and the players hunched over the ring like old hands around a craps table, candy cigarettes clenched between their teeth.

Bicycle riding was also a popular pastime. Afternoons and all day weekends, packs of boys would pedal down the hill, straining to achieve as much speed as possible while avoiding at the last instant a crash into the apartments at the bottom. The race leaders of summer 1958 were three brothers resplendent in Mohawk haircuts. Twenty years before punk rockers appropriated the style, the Mohawk became the rage when the weekly *Disneyland* TV show adapted Conrad Richter's colonial Indian adventure novel *The Light in the Forest.*

Meanwhile over on somebody's porch, future *Popular Science* subscribers experimented with the latest "Think Toys." Most popular was Silly Putty, a chemical goo packaged in a plastic egg. This little flesh-colored blob cost a whole dollar—but you could bounce it, stretch it if you pulled it apart slowly, break it if you snapped it fast, and even flatten it over a Sunday comic and pick up the image, which could then be stretched entertainingly. Confirmed neighborhood nerds of the fifties also loved Slinky, a high-tech spring that likewise cost a dollar. With Slinky, by holding one end in each hand and watching the rings follow one another inexorably when each hand rose slightly in turn, you could prove a scientific principle (Gravity? Newton's Third Law?). You could also give the thing a start downstairs and it would robotically complete the journey all by itself.

Slinky and Silly Putty had been around for years, but they took off in 1957 with heavy advertising on the children's shows—promoters had begun to realize the unparalleled sales bonanza the era's youth population explosion could provide. Fortunes multiplied right through the sixties on quick production of everything from Howdy-Doody hats to replicas of the little square sunglasses popularized by Jim (aka Roger) McGuinn of the Byrds rock group.

Back in 1957, the front yards of the apartments provided the war zones. Some troops owned toy rifles; some made do with sticks. Pretend grenades, designated "pineapples" (American) or "potato mashers" (German) depending on the army represented, were also popular. All soldiers could execute the proper sound effects for every weapon in the arsenal, and we all knew the rules: if you fall in battle, you must lie and wait until a survivor of your army circles back to touch you and pronounces "New man!" At that point you had authorization to rise from the dead and wage more war.

During peacetime, kids traded briskly in Zorro and baseball cards, usually specializing in one or the other. Like most younger kids, I preferred Zorro, a Batmanesque Disney hero with exploits set in Colonial California. The cards provided exciting pictures and plot synopses from the series. I couldn't decipher these yet, but Jane would read them to me if I didn't ask her to read too many in a row.

My longing for these tokens led to a falling out with my friend Bear, who lived at the bottom of our street, directly in the bicycle race line of fire. Bear (real name Harlan Defries), a skinny kid from Indonesia, didn't fit his nickname, except perhaps for his deep brown coloring. Our dispute occurred one Saturday afternoon at the local market while we operated a gumball-style machine that dispensed Zorro and baseball cards for one cent per card. Cards also came five for a nickel in a pack which included a stick of usually stale gum, but these penny machines catered to those of us with more limited means.

With seven or eight pennies left of my twelve-cents-a-week allowance, I had a revelation while standing behind Bear, then busy feeding the machine. In a flash of certainty I realized that the cards did not distribute randomly as we'd assumed—rather they alternated with perfect regularity between Zorro and baseball. I stepped in quickly when Bear paused to dig another penny from his jeans. Inserting my coin and extracting a Zorro card, I said officiously, "Okay, now your turn."

Bear stepped up and the machine gave him a baseball card.

My turn again—another Zorro.

"You lucky duck!" Bear exclaimed. His next penny brought forth another baseball card. At this point he finally began to catch on.

"Hey, wait! Gimme another turn—I want a Zorro!"

"You just went!" I insisted with Machiavellian logic. "So now it's MY turn!"

"No, wait, this is a…a…" Bear wasn't familiar with the term "fixed game," but he knew a scam when he saw one. "MY turn!"

"Uh-uh!" I shoved him aside. "No cuts! It's MY turn."

Bear then entreated me to trade him at least one of my Zorros for one of his baseball cards. I refused, citing ethics and fairness; as a result, our friendship remained strained for at least a week. But I always remembered Sandy Koufax, the odd named player he wanted to trade. Koufax, a young pitcher for the Los Angeles Dodgers became a baseball superstar of the early sixties. When I checked recently, a Koufax rookie card in mint condition is worth around $1000 and the soon-after cards we discharged for a penny are worth around $400 each. If Bear has held onto his two Koufaxes all these years, he's achieved the last laugh, for in 2014, an entire set of 88 Zorro cards was available on EBay for less than $500.

Trading was universal on the street; girls as well as boys bartered cards, marbles, candy, and toys. Thus we learned supply-and-demand psychology and practical math on the fly. In late 1958 or early '59 the yo-yo craze began to take off with a massive TV campaign. On-air spots featured the Duncan Yo-Yo Man and a cadre of kid experts doing the sleeper, walk the dog, cat's cradle, and other amazing tricks. To acquire such skill seemed the height of worldly achievement. In the heat of the yo-yo frenzy, a neighborhood girl showed me a beautiful Duncan Imperial model acquired from her grandfather. I fervently believed, as do most of my adult golfer friends nowadays, that top-of-the-line equipment dramatically increases one's skill level. The girl affected a serene unwillingness to barter for the Imperial, but I hurried home to rummage through my possessions, hoping I could find something to tempt her.

At the bottom of my toy box I discovered a number of prehistoric relics—items I didn't recall at all, since everything before age two-and-a-half had departed my conscious memory. Deep in the pile I found an amber heart about the size of an apricot, with a gold loop on top to string a chain through. It could have been one of Jane's more extravagant pieces of costume jewelry, something she gave me when it caught my toddler eye. I strained unsuccessfully for some recollection of ownership. However, the item occupied my toy box, so it must be mine. I took it back across the street to the girl with the yo-yo.

"How 'bout this?" I held up the heart enticingly, in the manner of a jeweler showing a five carat diamond engagement ring to a debutante. Her eyes grew large. She reached for it and cradled it in her palm, then pressed it to her chest where it would hang with a chain. Without a word of the extended bargaining that usually took place in such transactions, she handed over the Duncan Imperial. I yo-yoed away, my satisfaction tempered by the feeling I could have done better. From her rapt expression, I sensed she probably could have been inveigled into throwing in some marbles on the deal.

My land-of-the-black-sheep social development was proceeding apace.

CHAPTER FIVE

~ You Can't Go Home Again ~ Practical Jokes ~ Hide-and-Go-Seek
~ The Other San Pedro ~ Who Needs Kindergarten?
~ An Unexpected Celebration ~ Two Rites of Passage

During the second summer of the San Pedro epoch, I accompanied Nanny on a visit to Alabama. Beginning when she began to earn paid one-week vacations at the Broadway, she returned to her homeland every few years to see her brothers Red and Charlie and visit any recent grandchildren. To my delight, we flew both ways on a real airplane, bigger by far than the one on the Sky King TV show. The terminals seemed less crowded in those days, and most passengers dressed in their best clothes, for flying brought forth a sense of ceremonious danger. Relatives accompanied departees to the gates, embracing as if this might be their last time together. Many travelers (or their relatives) purchased flight insurance from vending machines near the terminals.[11] Passenger aircraft in the fifties used propeller power, and though the trip took a bit longer and the flights were relatively more expensive, the cabins were roomier than in modern jets. Fliers enjoyed comfortable seats and free meals, with cigarettes in sample-size boxes provided gratis. Long distance flights featured a lounge area in the back, complete with a horseshoe-shaped couch.

After a connection in Dallas, we arrived in Birmingham, where

---

[11] Those vending machines have since disappeared from airports, perhaps due to two famous cases in which bombers purchased the maximum insurance, and then placed explosives in suitcases checked onto the aircraft. One case involved a suicide bombing to provide for a depressive's family; the other a matricide that also killed 43 others on the flight. The latter bomber, Jack Gilbert Graham, was captured and convicted. Queried before his execution as to whether he felt remorse for the other people he killed, Graham replied, "I don't. I can't help it. Everybody pays their way and takes their chances. That's just the way it goes." See Field, Andrew J. Mainliner Denver: The Bombing of Flight 629. Boulder, Colorado: Johnson Books, 2005.

my grandfather picked us up in his '51 Ford. Daddy still lived in our old apartment, and Uncle Don now occupied the room Luke and Jane vacated. Nanny slept at Uncle Kirby's down the street; he had recently moved his family into the Cloverdale complex.

During the visit I slept in my old bed in Daddy's room, tried on his World War I gas mask again, and helped him clean and reload his snub-nose pistol, which he did each evening. I caught fireflies in a jar in the steamy summer evenings and made a clay snake (with a bobby pin from Nanny for the forked tongue) that worked admirably to scare my three-year-old cousin Sharon. While the grownups marveled at my cousin Nancy (Uncle Kirby's newest daughter) I turned on Kirby's TV. Spinning channels, I found a kid show featuring Popeye cartoons—but it was hosted by a different sailor-suit clad emcee than Tom Hatten, the "real" Popeye host back in L.A. The Alabama show came on at a different time, too. Aunt Jo Ann also informed me that the people set their clocks two hours earlier in California—something about the sun and the earth revolving. The whole business seemed eerie to me.

A you-can't-go-home-again feeling suffused the short visit. Daddy remained inarticulately glad to see me, but I wasn't the same person I'd been at four and a half, and our conversation didn't flow as in the old days. One more emotionally uncomfortable story from the Alabama visit dovetails better with events chronicled in the next chapter, but suffice to say now that the feeling of estrangement lingered when I came home to San Pedro.

I have traced my lifelong abhorrence of practical jokes to the day John picked up Nanny and me from the airport and drove me back to Channel Heights. After enduring Jane's endearments and remarks at my growth, I wandered outside. The neighborhood seemed oddly quiet and void of acquaintances. I ended up in an empty yard across the street, wondering what to do with myself.

Suddenly a portly kid I knew only peripherally came running down the embankment from the next building up. "Hey! Hi!" he shouted from halfway down, smiling broadly as he came. "You want some gum?" He stood before me, panting and holding out a pack of Doublemint, with a single piece sticking out from the pack.

This display of spontaneous generosity lifted my spirits a bit. "Thanks." I smiled and pulled at the gum. With a loud snap, a spring-loaded trap came down on my finger. It hurt enough to bring tears, but the kid's look of sadistic glee seemed worse. I brooded at the depths of human duplicity as I exited this ignominious scene. Likely my little cousin Sharon felt a similar disillusionment when I pulled my clay snake ruse back in Alabama, but I didn't make the connection until some years later.

Youth is resilient, and any lingering alienation I might have felt wisped away in the long summer evenings of my first week home. The hide-and-go-seek season had reached its peak, with thirty or forty kids of all ages participating every night. Some of the otherwise dour parents raised in the thirties and grandparents who remembered the game from their childhood at the turn of the century smiled from their porches and called the game "Kick the Can" even though we used no can. But somehow they seemed to understand the magic of it all, letting us stay out till 9:30 or even 10, reveling in the excitement of running around outside after dark.

One night in the hushed conversation before we finally returned to our houses, we who had lived outside of California (which included almost all of us) agreed that the only missing component for the perfect summer evening was fireflies. The West had nothing comparable to those improbable insects. I reported my recent attempt to import some specimens, but unfortunately the subjects had died in the jar even before our plane took off from Alabama.

My life also had an entirely different dimension in 1958–59, a weekday world beyond Channel Heights which I entered through economic necessity. Luke's salary, though relatively substantial for a blue collar worker, remained insufficient to keep up payments on the new furniture and their recently purchased late-model Ford Fairlane. So when Jane found a job at a cash register factory in Long Beach, she placed Trish and me in the charge of Bert (possibly short for Roberta), one of Luke's second- or third-cousins who had migrated from Alabama. Bert was probably in her early forties, a tall, stooped, taciturn lady who wore dentures and looked sixty by today's standards. Her family lived in a large rented house when we first met them, but a temporary layoff at her husband's factory had forced them to move to a smaller, more affordable place fronting an alley. The $20 per week Luke and Jane paid for babysitting provided a welcome boost to their family finances.

So, less than four months from my reign as an only child, I not only had a younger sister, but found myself surrounded by a huge family. I bonded most closely with Linda, age 9, and Robbie, 10. Jerry, 17, and Dennis (aka Dent), 16, each had sideburns and a hot rod.

Luanne, 18, a high school student when I met her, began working at the Terminal Island tuna cannery the day after she graduated. I don't remember the name of Bert's husband, whom I rarely saw after his reinstatement at the factory, or the names of their two other sons: an introverted thirteen-year-old and a grown-up twenty-year-old who lived with his wife and child in a downtown San Pedro apartment. This older son owned a hot rod even louder than Dent's or Jerry's, and his wife had worked at the cannery since their hasty marriage at seventeen.

Everyone in the family had been born in Alabama, and everyone except the thirteen-year-old spoke with at least a trace of Alabama inflection, even Robbie and Linda, who came as toddlers and had been subjected to California TV and radio since they began talking. Despite the influence of Jane and Luke, I was losing my accent quickly among the polyglot of Channel Heights, but most of Robbie and Linda's friends on this side of town also sprung from families recently immigrated from Alabama, Tennessee, Mississippi and Georgia to find work in local shipyards and factories.

Jane would drop Trish and me at Bert's by seven a.m., and we'd be there until dinner or beyond if the cash register factory decreed mandatory overtime. Bert managed to fit my general care plus three-months-old Trish's feeding, diaper changing, and bathing into an already busy day. She rose at dawn to make breakfast and fill lunch pails for eight people. When everyone had departed for work or school, she gave the house a thorough cleaning, made all the beds, washed clothes and hung them on the line, and then ironed everything (including the sheets). She cooked dinner every day from scratch, which involved peeling potatoes, snapping beans, shelling peas and the like, and also baked a daily cake for the family, with alternating lemon and chocolate icing.

With her demanding schedule, Bert wasn't one for idle chitchat and it never occurred to her that adult caregivers should provide entertainment for children. For better or worse, children today seem to expect more-or-less constant attention, especially, it would seem, during adult conversations ("Look what I'm doing now, Mommy!" "Will you play with me, Daddy?"), whereas my generation, like countless who came before, avoided adult notice if at all possible. As the saying goes, children were seen but not heard. But we preferred to not be seen, either.

Thus Bert and I usually went about our respective business until she called me for lunch, usually a bowl of Campbell's tomato or chicken noodle soup and a lunchmeat sandwich on Wonder Bread, with a glass of Kool-Aid to wash it down. Mealtime coincided with Sheriff John's lunch brigade, a fixture on KTTV Channel 11. I could see the TV from the dining room by looking sharp left while I ate. This arrangement seemed entirely satisfactory, but our mutual taciturnity was interrupted one day after lunch — on April 2, 1958, to be exact — when Bert entered the dining room from the kitchen carrying a cake with five lit candles on it. I suppose the adult equivalent would be if a hardbitten old waitress at a frequented coffee shop somehow found out your birthday, baked a cake, and delivered it, candles blazing, to your place at the lunch counter. Bert watched me stare at the cake for a few seconds, then said, "Well, happy birthday."

As a Sheriff John Lunch Brigade watcher, I knew the protocol: make a wish and blow out the candles. The good Sheriff sang about it every day on his show with a self-penned composition called "The Birthday Cake Polka" full of pie, sandwiches, kids playing and singing together, and a fine understanding for the youngsters' thrill at growing another year older.

Bert and I became warmer associates afterward, and when she had time, we spoke more often. She did, in my estimation, over-react one day when, after concentrated trial and error with different instruments, I managed to poke a hole in Trish's water-filled teething ring. Squeezing the ring then produced a pleasant geyser and a severe scolding: "You shouldn't ought to be mean to your sister — if your mama don't whip you, I will!" But Bert never followed through with the threat, and I didn't hold her antipathy to scientific experimentation against her.

Sometimes I'd go in the kitchen to watch her work for a few minutes, usually about the time she crafted the daily cake. She appeared closest to serenity when she frosted, handling the flat knife like an artist as she arranged the stuccoesque swirls. I would make myself as conspicuous as possible until she'd take the hint and let me scrape the cake batter and icing from the eggbeater and bowls.

Soon after my fifth birthday celebration, I passed two other milestones. First came riding a bike without training wheels, a rite of passage each child in my culture had to accomplish before age six or face maximum social ostracization.

Although I knew by observation that traveling by two wheels was possible, the act seemed to contradict physics as I understood them. Perhaps this intellectual stubbornness held me back; in any case, whenever I had tried riding big kids' bikes I always fell over immediately. The catalyst for change came one Saturday at a neighborhood birthday party when I observed Timmy, a month younger than me, demonstrating his prowess on his two-wheeler, a hand-me-down from his big brother. I resolved not to be left behind by such a baby. While the other party-goers played pin-the-tail-on-the-donkey, I borrowed Timmy's bike and pushed it down the street. Twice I climbed on the seat, braced myself for peddling, and fell over immediately. What secret of elementary science had I overlooked?

Then came a flash of inspiration. I took a *running* start, leapt on the seat, and began peddling. The first time I actually stayed upright for several yards. The second attempt I peddled half a minute and even steered round a corner before I crashed into a tree. I kept at it and improved after each fall. Timmy's bike had taken a beating, but nothing actually fell off, so he complained less than Jane did when she saw me after the party with my best pants ripped at one knee and my scraped elbow dripping blood onto my white shirt. (Kids dressed up for social occasions in those days.) But I paid little attention to her remonstrance as I recalled the moment that the birthday party attendees saw me return in triumph astride the bike, my expression a study in nonchalance. I had made the transition from babyhood to boyhood.

But not quite. As a junior member of Channel Heights male society, it was high time I heard my first dirty joke. A comedian named Ronnie, a second-grader who lived two doors down in my building, did the honors. Even without this distinction, Ronnie stands out in my mind because his parents gave him and his four siblings a generous twenty-five cents a week allowance. The catch was, they had to save *all* of it in their bank accounts. If Ronnie did extra chores, he might get to keep a nickel.

Perhaps bitterness at this economically despotic regimen led Ronnie into pornography. In any case, he contributed "Johnny Fuckerfaster," a classic shaggy dog joke, to my cultural education. The art of the shaggy dog story consists of piling on more and more details and postponing the weak punch line as long as possible. Thus Johnny tells his next-door neighbor, "Take off your left shoe," and she replies. "If you give me a cookie."

"Okay," Johnny continues. "Now take off your right shoe." No matter what Johnny requests, she always replies, "If you give me a cookie," and complies when he produces the goods. The buildup is stretched through every possible item of clothing until the girl is naked. Then, after a dramatic pause, the joke-teller relates that Johnny's mom enters the room. Scandalized, she intones the lad's full name: "Why, Johnny Fuckerfaster!" And at last comes the anti-climactic punch line, "I'm fuckin' her as fast as I can, Ma!"

I didn't understand the point of this "fuckin'" activity, but it seemed rather unsavory. "Rubber balls and liquor," the second dirty joke I heard, was at least shorter: a participation exercise wherein the listener is instructed to repeat the tag line "Rubber balls and liquor" after each question asked. "What'd you have for breakfast?" "What'd you have for lunch?" "What'd you have for dinner?" "What're you gonna do with your girlfriend tonight?" I snickered appropriately at this one, but I remained confused. Did girls have "balls?" I thought those items were exclusive to boys' anatomy. And what about this "lick her" business? None of it made much sense at age five. Another repeat-after-me joke seemed much more humorous to me: a participation exercise in which you instruct your victim to say, "My father works in the shipyard" while holding his tongue between thumb and forefinger. Now *that* was funny.

CHAPTER SIX

~ Walking in the Fog ~ Elvis and Pat ~ Novelty Songs
~ Clay Balls and Steel Balls ~ Ogre Attack
~ Don't Remind Me of Chickens ~ Trash Picking

Even in today's regimented society, sending one's child to Kindergarten remains legally optional in California, though virtually every parent exercises the option. But in the 1950s the brief morning or afternoon sessions were an inconvenience for many working parents, mine included, so I remained at Bert's when school took up in September. Not that I wasn't receiving early childhood education: when Jane dropped me off each morning, I would have breakfast with the family, then begin my studies by climbing into the recliner in front of the TV in time for Chucko the Clown. Chucko began at eight a.m. on KABC Channel 7, and *I Married Joan* reruns followed immediately. Next I would switch to KNXT Channel 2 for recycled episodes of *I Love Lucy* and *December Bride*. I could spin the channel wheel like a safe-cracker, precisely to the desired station. At home, stepdad Luke maintained that rapid station-changing somehow damaged the television, but what did Luke know about TV, except for how to get the rabbit ear antenna fixed just right for *Wagon Train*?

Bert usually appeared after *December Bride* with her big Hoover vacuum cleaner. "Get on outside, now," she'd say, and usually add, "You'll lose both your eyes lookin' at that thing." I took this pronouncement with a grain of salt, but as I left the house I always checked the mirror by the sink in the back utility room to confirm that my eyes remained firmly attached.

Once in the open air, I could roam the cluttered alley behind Bert's house, or contemplate the junk-lumber chicken coop which housed the suppliers of family eggs, or pretend to drive Dent's or Jerry's car when one or both of those teenager jalopies were grounded for repair in the dirt driveway. No one locked cars in those days.

When I had a nickel or dime, I journeyed to a little market a few blocks away. This side of San Pedro seemed more historic than the Channel Heights side. I walked to the store through a 1910 time capsule of two-story wooden houses punctuated by vacant lots, all set between narrow streets and long alleys. Every house had elaborate porches and yards full of overgrown grass and wildflowers: daisies, poppies, black-eyed Susans, snapdragons, and more. The whole neighborhood seemed perennially damp from the thick coastal fog which usually lifted at midmorning, but sometimes didn't lift at all. On those days, the walk seemed a sort of mystical passage: nothing visible ahead but a bank of grey as the line of sight opened ahead and closed behind.

In that era no one worried about youngsters roaming their neighborhoods, drinking from garden hoses, or sharing sodas indiscriminately. Most of us ate regularly from neighborhood fruit trees; I'd already learned to enjoy oranges in Channel Heights and figs from Nanny's back yard. So one day when I discovered a huge avocado tree a few houses down the alley from Bert's, I confidently picked up and bit into one of the odd-looking fruits littering the ground. The result was memorable: I gagged and spit convulsively, then ran for the nearest water hose. That rotten avocado remained in my memory as the most disgusting thing I'd ever tasted, and I didn't eat another one until I became a teenage vegetarian a decade later.

After my adventures abroad, I'd come back to Bert's for lunch and Sheriff John. Bert then shooed me outside again in good weather; on rainy days I'd listen to the radio in oldest girl Luanne's room until four or so, when everyone came home from school. Sometimes I'd watch *American Bandstand* with Luanne and the thirteen-year-old brother whose name I can't remember. His moody air seemed out of place in the Bert family, and he rarely talked except to say, "Quit looking at me!" in an effeminate voice. Bert took me aside later and explained, "He's got teenage pimples and don't like nobody to stare at him."

I did occasionally stare at him, but *American Bandstand* commanded the bulk of my attention. Dick Clark, the George Washington of teen TV hosts, appeared to be the same age as the older boys on the dance floor, only they wore sports coats and he wore a shiny suit. The dancing fascinated me, and I showed an early interest in song lyrics. Perhaps because the title seemed particularly funny to a five-year-old, I vividly recall the show featuring the world premiere of the single "Bony Maronie."

Most of my favorite tunes of this era were novelty items: "Witch Doctor" by David Seville, who also created the hit-making Chipmunk vocal sound by electronically altering the pitch of normal singers to make them sound like rodents; Shep Wooley's "Purple People Eater" (which also incorporated a chipmunk voice at the end, since that gimmick was selling so well), and "Please Mr. Custer," a number-one hit by Larry Verne.[12] In the latter song, a reluctant private under General Custer's command foresees trouble in the coming battle at Little Big Horn. He opines in a comic hillbilly accent that, because he quite naturally wishes to avoid being killed or scalped, he is unfairly branded a coward. Grad students in American Studies might in this lyric detect postwar cynicism as it bled through to pop culture, heralding the 1960s attitude that cowardice in battle is the stuff of light humor while bravery is at best stupid and unimaginative. In any case, I considered the "Mr. Custer" song pretty funny.

But novelty songs weren't all I took seriously. After two-plus years at the top of the country, R&B, and pop charts, Elvis remained King of the radio, and I liked his songs, even the slow ones. He had been drafted and reported for duty on March 24, 1958, but RCA timed a steady release of singles he'd recorded before his induction. Luanne had most of these and dozens of photos of him tacked to her walls, with more in stand-up frames on her orange-crate vanity table. In the months prior to her high school graduation and career at the tuna cannery, I first heard Elvis and other popular singers via 45 rpm singles on her little record player.

All of Luanne's high school girlfriends crocheted octopus doilies that year and sometimes they'd come over and work on their projects to music. When I wandered in, the girls would cluck over me and comb my hair like Elvis's. I usually acquiesced, especially after I discovered I could make them laugh with my imitation of Elvis's crooked smile. Pat Boone and Elvis were considered dark

---

[12] I originally planned to quote memorable song lyrics as my memoir unfolded, but obtaining permission to do so is prohibitively expensive and hampered by extensive red tape. The good news is that all the lyrics I would have quoted are available on the Internet, as are other illustrations of cultural phenomena cited in this chronicle. Furthermore, YouTube is a treasury of vintage video clips of popular songs mentioned herein, and I heartily encourage readers to view them all, starting with Larry Verne lip-syncing "Mr. Custer." Those who wish to pursue further research may also access its little known sequel, "Please Mr. Sitting Bull."

and light rivals, roles the Beatles and Rolling Stones would assume a generation later. Boone wore signature white buck shoes, and I had a scuffed pair like them. With my Boone footwear and Presley coiffure, I had a foot in both camps.

I enjoyed these precocious teen activities, but I remained closest to Linda and Robbie, who often took me along on their neighborhood adventures. The building boom that would eat Los Angeles had begun to roar on this side of town, too, and we played in the construction sites, pretending to drive the tractors and patiently removing all the single tissues from the porta-potties. But the wilderness remained available: canyons with catchable horned toads, little creeks swarming with crawdads, and trees full of birds and squirrels, those handy targets for slingshots. Robbie and pals made their weapons from whittled tree branches, then attached strips cut from unpatchable bicycle tubes and a middle piece of old leather, exactly the right size for the smooth stones they always looked out for. Each boy kept his best missiles handy in an exclusive, quick-draw "rock pocket."

The slingshot whittling had more to do with poverty than pride; any boy Robbie's age would have instantly traded his handmade weapon for a store-bought Whammo® model. Robbie became the first of his crowd to achieve this dream, using money he earned selling flower and vegetable seeds door to door. He would go out peddling on Saturdays and an hour or two in the evenings after his chores and homework. A few years later I follow the same path to self-employment. The seeds sold retail for ten cents per package, and the seller earned three to five cents per pack, depending on sales volume. If Robbie's experience matched mine, the seeds moved slowly at best, and earning the price of the slingshot probably took weeks of neighborhood slogging. But Robbie's happy day finally came, and he granted me permission to accompany him to the sporting goods store.

"Help you, son?" The clerk seemed polite, but must have been skeptical of any significant business from the two lads before him: the elder one breathing down on the glass counter as he stared intently at the treasures within, and the younger squinting directly into the case from the front.

Robbie pointed resolutely at the weapon of his dreams. "That one."

"You want just the slingshot or the deluxe package?" The latter came with custom ammo, around thirty marble-size clay balls and a dozen or so stainless steel balls for hunting big game.

Robbie, usually laconic in the extreme, realized his moment of long-deferred gratification had come. He straightened to his full height, grinned wide, and found his voice. "The whole shebang!"

Outside the shop with the new slingshot in hand, Robbie laughed, beamed, and sparkled with joy. Until today the shyest kid in town, he actually broke into a spontaneous little dance, singing "Oh, I've got clay balls and steel balls!"

We then went in search of Robbie's peers to show off the amazing acquisition. The older neighborhood boys never knocked on a friend's door; instead they would stand across the street from the house, cup their hands, and holler "Hoo-Woo! Hoo-Woo!" until the friend appeared. This method had probably carried on generation after generation since young Davey Crockett whooped for his friend George Russell in the Tennessee settlements, but it apparently didn't survive the 1960s.

When Robbie was busy with chores, homework, or other obligations I'd go along with Linda, who also possessed an adventurous spirit.[13] I've never met a Linda I didn't like, but this one was extra-special, with a warm, crooked-tooth smile and a maternal nature. She always wore her dirty-blonde hair in a ponytail and had attained such height and slimness that her big brothers Dent and Jerry called her "Bony Maronie" after that haunting ditty made the Top Twenty.

Linda and I explored the neighborhood, prowling through the construction sites and checking for dimes in return slots of corner phone booths. She always looked out for me at busy crossings and, on one memorable day, rescued me when a huge ten-year-old girl took offense at me stepping on her lawn when, in some reverie, I had wandered off the sidewalk.

"Get OFF my property!" The girl standing in front of me, arms akimbo, looked closer to Robbie's age and height. She leaned down to scream in my face. "You hear? GET OFF MY PROPERTY!"

I froze, too stunned to move. To a child of five, a ten-year-old is proportionately much bigger than the largest threatening stranger

---

[13] Linda became the official most popular girl's name through the 1950s and early 1960s. An International "Linda Club," based wryly on the ubiquity of the name, still holds yearly conventions (see www.lindaclub.org). But two generations later, that pleasant appellation is rarely if ever bestowed on newborns.

ever encountered by a grown-up. Suddenly she rushed at me, the relative size-equivalent of a crazed, eight-foot tall, six-hundred pound ogre from the storybooks—only this one was alive, spitting unintelligible words, and grabbing at me.

Linda had walked ahead to pick wildflowers from a vacant lot. Now she looked back in time to see the behemoth throw me to the ground and begin kicking me. Terrified, I instinctively curled up and covered my head. Suddenly the kicking stopped, and as I scrambled to my feet I saw Linda pushing the bigger girl away from me. The girl was a head taller than Linda, but my champion stood between us, eyes flashing and yelling at full volume: "Quit it! Why don't you pick on someone your own size? It's not FAIR!"

The ogre gave ground before Linda's moral onslaught, but she glared with naked hate as Linda hurried me away. A hundred yards down the block I risked a furtive glance back. She stood in the middle of the street with her hands on her hips. When she saw me looking, she screamed, "YOU STAY OFF MY PROPERTY!"

We hurried on. I was shaken, but I didn't take the attack as an affront to my manhood. True, a girl overpowered me and another girl had rescued me. But considering the situation and size differences of the participants, the experience seemed more like being an intrepid South American explorer attacked by an incidentally female Bigfoot monster, then succored by an Amazon warrior (I was, of course, familiar with all these icons from my TV watching).

But no Amazon is honored in her own country. Linda, baby of her household until I came along, drew the lowly chore of looking after the family's little flock of chickens, including cleaning out the coup. She met this task with her usual equanimity, and as she scattered the feed or collected the eggs, she'd tell me all about the hens' habits and peculiarities. One afternoon, she dragged me away from *American Bandstand* to see a chick pecking its way out of an egg. She bubbled with excitement and wonder at the glories of nature, but I showed less enthusiasm than she hoped I would, for I felt a certain sensitivity on the subject of baby chicks.

This sensitivity dated from the recent trip to Alabama with Nanny. While there we had visited relatives on a farm out in the country. The woman of the house served chicken and dumplings with sweet potatoes and peas for lunch, and berry pie for dessert. Minding my own business, I applied myself to the meal. I liked to start with the starch, then eat the vegetables, then proceed to the meat. After a few minutes, one of the old great-uncles noticed me eating one food at a time. With a serious expression (after, perhaps, a surreptitious wink at the other grownups), the old man told me the "real way" to eat: take a bite of one food, then take a bite of something else. "You ought t' mix it up, son. Nobody with sense eats like you been doing."

He grinned round the table, but I felt too overwhelmed by unfamiliarity to appreciate his humor. It seemed to me I had a right to eat however I wanted without ridicule or having my intelligence questioned. I said nothing and ate no more.

After lunch the grown-ups remained at the table, drinking coffee and smoking cigarettes, grinding out the butts in their saucers. I stepped outside, feeling lonesome and homesick for California. Soggy clouds hid the summer sun and the humidity felt oppressive as I walked slowly down a gravel driveway toward a weathered barn. On the way I came upon a henhouse with dozens of chickens pecking and clucking outside. Using the skills I developed while hunting horned toads, I crept up slowly on some baby chicks and caught one. The mother hen squawked and ruffled her feathers, but then ran to gather up the other babies.

The chick's high-pitched peeps clearly sounded its distress, but the warm and fuzzy little body felt good in my hands. As I walked back out to the gravel driveway, I started tossing the chick up and catching it, gently at first. Then I threw it higher and caught it. Then I threw it again and missed.

The little chick lay there in the gravel, its neck broken. Suddenly the thick air seemed hard to breathe. I picked up the chick again, and its little neck lolled over the edge of my hand. I looked around wildly, then tossed the body into a bush.

As I hurried back to the house I must have been the picture of furtive guilt. I couldn't go tell old uncle what's-his-name who'd been so mean to me for eating one food at a time. I couldn't tell Nanny, who'd hold herself responsible for bringing the murderer to the farm. I couldn't even tell Linda, months later when she showed me her chickens. Only now, after passage of more than fifty years, am I able to confess my shame and guilt, though, in an interesting display of human-nature compartmentalization, I continued to eat chicken and eggs with gusto for years afterward.

I escaped from Linda's egg hatching demo as soon as I could, but continued to share many of her interests. She reigned as family champ at Parcheesi, and when the hula-hoop craze reached mass hysteria in summer 1959 and the populace rushed to purchase more than 25 million of the devices, Linda became an expert. She patiently taught me the basic motions to keep the hoop spinning around the waist and also how to roll it along the ground with a backward spin that causes it to return like a boomerang.

One spring day I tagged along with Linda and a couple of her friends for my first venture at the neighborhood kid pastime called "trash pickin'. We crisscrossed the neighborhood from garbage can to garbage can, up and down all the alleys. That day the loot included a Chinese checkers set and several naked dolls, but I took most pride in a plastic space helmet. Space toy interest and production had ramped up since the advent of Sputnik and other interstellar probes, and this one had only a little crack in the top and a couple of scuffs on the face plate.

Occasionally one of what seemed like a neighborhood army of ragged men came shuffling down the alley, most of them lugging cloth sacks over their shoulders. These fellows, often old sailors lost to drink, had few if any teeth and a trembly, whipped-dog air about them. They hurried by, looking wistfully at the cans we rummaged through. Linda and her girlfriends called these men "hobos" and said they dug their food and clothes from trashcans.

As the day unfolded, I resolved to be a hobo myself after serving what I understood to be an obligatory stint in the navy. In a state of near-euphoria brought on by sudden wealth, general tiredness, and being the center of attention, I began singing the lyrics to the Popeye theme song, "I'm strong to the finich, 'cause I eats me spinach; I'm Popeye the sailor man!" over and over. Popeye had become my favorite cartoon character, and (unlike most children I knew) I actually liked the taste of spinach, so I felt a special bond with the famous sailor. For variety's sake, one of Linda's friends taught me an additional unauthorized verse to the song: "I eat all the worms, and spit out the germs; I'm Popeye the sailor man!" and I sung this one with gusto. In hindsight, I experienced that day perhaps the most pleasant and carefree afternoon of my early childhood.

CHAPTER SEVEN

~ Boat Building ~ Inspiration at the Dump ~ Creation ~ Acclaim ~Revenge ~ Infamous

Speaking of Popeye, Linda always stopped in our neighborhood rounds to call on a retired San Pedro fisherman who lived across the alley, an old fellow who bore a striking physical resemblance to the cartoon sailor, right down to the squinty eyes and pipe. We would usually find him in his garage, building a small fishing boat he had started from scratch. In subsequent weeks I visited him almost daily on my own, and mightily did I itch to join the construction.

"I can hammer nails!"

"Not around here."

"Can I rub the sandpaper on this part?"

"Nope. Stand aside there, boy."

"I painted a bird house with my mom when I was only four."

"This here's marine paintin'. Gotta have a union card."

Before he shuffled away to his lonely dinner, the old man would meticulously sweep the concrete floor with a push broom and then haul his scraps to the vacant lot across the street from Bert's. The lot also served local handymen and shadetree mechanics; almost everyone in those days considered any unimproved property a legitimate dump site. One afternoon I wandered across the street to look over the neighborhood refuse. As I gazed upon the variety of interesting scrap, something momentous started to stir in my mind. I may have been inspired by the old man's industry, or perhaps I experienced an early visitation of the muse. In any case, I kept busy for the next few hours with my first major act of artistic creation.

To understand that vacant lot brainstorm, we must backtrack to early 1957 during Luke and Jane's courtship in Alabama. One night they brought me along on a movie date at the Bessemer walk-in theatre. I had ambivalent feelings toward this big stranger Mommy seemed to like so well, but he did buy me some popcorn and I soon lost myself in the screen action. During the climactic scene, a berserk robot (played by an actor in an aluminum suit) clomps around a soundstage. From what appears to be an automobile headlight on its chest, the mechanical monster shines a death beam on the puny humans trying to stop him. Despite extensive research, the title and further particulars of this film remain obscure, but the scene provided memorable terror to a four-year-old, and I longed to have a robot of my own. Unfortunately, toy companies had yet to manufacture such unedifying items — even the morbid Crashmobile cars were several years in the future.

Surveying the dump in San Pedro a year or so later, with an Idea! lightbulb practically visible over my head and the manic focus which occasionally came upon me, I realized I could build my own robot. Like a junior Victor Frankenstein combing the charnel house, I surveyed the materials at hand. First I laid out a rectangular plywood body; then I found another triangle of plywood to serve as a head. From a pile of roofing scraps came some twisted rain gutter pieces for legs and arms, but I found no way of cutting them to size. However, some fragments of an old grape trellis proved serviceable: I could lay the trellis pieces over a rusty iron post and stomp them to fit. My shoe wouldn't work for a hammer, but a fist-size piece of cement served to first straighten, then pound bent, rusty nails as I attached head and legs to the torso.

Humming the first bars of the Popeye song over and over, I tried bending nails into makeshift staples to affix a rusty chrome headlight gasket to the creature's chest. The nails weren't long enough, so using a stub of thick carpenter's pencil I carefully sketched a double circle on the plywood torso to represent a death ray. I hesitated before drawing the face. I'd been doing pencil portraits of Superman lately, but I usually did the body, complete with cape and a big, sometimes backward "S" on the chest, and then asked Jane to draw the head. I wished I'd had more practice with eyes and mouths, but I needn't have worried. The creature's expression came out precisely as I wanted it: inhuman and pitiless.

I worked until almost sunset without a break. Finally, with mounting excitement, I raised my killer robot to its feet. My creation towered over me, but I managed to half-walk, half-drag it back across the street and around to the back yard, marveling at the long shadow we cast.

Robbie had been hoo-wooing for me in the neighborhood while Linda searched the construction sites. Bert assumed I had accompanied one of them, so no one in authority showed alarm as yet. We all returned to the house about the same time, in the lull before dinner. Bert's husband, just arrived from the factory, stood with his older sons around the raised hood of Jerry's Ford, with its air cleaner and other parts laid out on the front fender.

The teenagers usually noticed me about as much as they'd notice a stray cat, and adults in those days didn't make a point of inflating children's self-esteem with loud praise for the slightest accomplishment. But as I approached, all of them, even Jerry and Dent, looked my way with heightened interest. Bert's husband actually smiled, and Dent stepped back in exaggerated astonishment. "Bo', that mo-sheen is twice your size!"

"Yeah, man," said Jerry, straightening up from his position over the Ford's engine and lighting a cigarette. At seventeen, he had a five o'clock shadow and his hairline had already started to recede. "Dent ought to hire you to fix up his sorry Chevalay!"

Dent grinned, showing a gap between his two front teeth. "Least my Chevalay is running."

Robbie looked the robot over carefully and patted me on the back in mute respect. Linda laughed delightedly and danced around. Someone brought Bert out to see. She shook her head and sighed, but she smiled after the sigh.

Jane pulled in the driveway a few minutes later from her job at the cash register factory. She looked tired; there had been mandatory overtime at the factory all week. But she roused herself to a proper level of enthusiasm and agreed to take my creation to our house if we could fit it in the car. Dent and Robbie helped maneuver the robot in the back seat, putting down some newspapers so the splinters and nails wouldn't tear the cloth upholstery and rolling down the back window for the head to peek out. Jane propped baby Trish in the front seat between us and drove home. The day had been long and productive. I kept turning to look at the Robot as I burned with the sublime thrill of artistic accomplishment.

Years later I wrote an account of the incident as an ersatz nursery rhyme, using artistic license on some details:

NURSERY RHYME

Young Ricky was a babysitter's dream
When Mummy dropped him off at Sal's, at seven:
He never whined; he'd watch the Zenith screen
Dry-eyed and unmoving past eleven.

Avenger Androids, Interstellar Andy,
Frankenstein on Mars, then Rocket John —
Till Sally roused him with a piece of candy,
Shooed him out and switched her Hoover on.

Out through the backroom, past the rabbit pens,
Past baby chicks who hid from sticky hands,
Past jealous mother cat who scratched, and then
He passed the gate where outer-space began.

Behind a tree hung thick with avocados
(No one picked them back in fifty-eight),
He hid from hobos — hacking, always blotto —
Who combed the alley's rubbish cans and crates.

A dried-out garden next: potato bugs,
Limp snapdragons, earwigs, wormy pears,
Black-edged lettuce, weeds, tomato slugs,
And stickers climbing in his underwear.

But past the caved-in fence, a wondrous shed
With paint-stiff brushes, car parts, holey pails;
Fluorescent bulbs to balance on his head,
Plywood scraps, a hammer, rusty nails —

Creation! Sheetrock torso, arms stuck sideways;
Aluminum molding legs bent into place;
Nailed to her chest, a headlight gasket death ray;
A frown scratched on her jagged plywood face.

I raised her up. I hardly reached her tummy.
I dragged her in the gate, through Sally's backroom
Across the threshold, Rocket Rick's new Mummy,
To save my Zenith from that snarling vacuum.

The poem, with all its darkish psychological nuances, won an award at the Iowa Writer's Workshop in 1988; but alas, the original robot was ill-fated. All seemed well at first. I showed it around the Channel Heights neighborhood, and almost everyone admired Robbie, the name I'd given it on Jane's suggestion. She wasn't thinking of Bert's son, but of a robot in *Forbidden Planet*, a big-budget 1950s science fiction film I didn't see till much later. "Robbie the Robot" seems in retrospect a triple winner: the name of a real movie robot, a tribute to surrogate big brother Robbie, and some nice alliteration to boot.

But some people just don't appreciate art. For instance, when I unloaded the robot at home, I saw Peter, a big Channel Heights first-grader, hanging out in the parking lot with a couple of friends. He strutted over to see my creation, and when my mom stepped out of earshot, he snarled, "Piece a junk!"

Before going in for the evening, I stood Robbie against the storage locker outside our apartment's back door. He looked pleasantly pitiless when we left the next morning for Bert's. Upon our arrival home, I dashed from the car, anxious to walk my creation around the neighborhood again. But then I stopped short halfway across the yard. Robbie's torso lay decapitated in the trampled grass. I found his head in the next yard over. His trellis legs and arms had been splintered beyond repair.

My face burned. The fruit of my toil and imagination, destroyed by mindless vandals. Or vandal. I knew who did it. And I would have my revenge.

Jane stood at the stove, boiling a jar of baby food and opening cans for dinner. I passed without a word and climbed the stairs to my room. Thanks to Uncle Bubba, I owned a three-inch pocket knife that featured two dull blades and a bottle opener. He presented it to me on one of the Navy leave weekends he came to spend with us. I suspect that after we'd moved out West, Bubba joined the Navy to be near the big brother he idolized. From his base in Long Beach, Bubba would hitchhike to our place when he could secure a weekend pass. He slept in my room those Friday and Saturday nights, and I remember him exuding a calm, un-patronizing friendliness. He gave me one of his sailor hats, too, and it fit me perfectly — at ages five and twenty-one, we shared the same hat size.

The hat could be folded down to achieve a mask-like disguise, but I gave no thought to concealment. I proceeded directly to the cigar box in which I kept my treasures—my rarest marbles, a silver dollar from Daddy, some Indian head pennies from Nanny. And the knife. It felt good in my hand. I opened it and closed it a few times, then marched back outside.

My enemy lived in an apartment one level above. I made my way up the footpath through the hillside ice plants, and as I approached the building, I heard Peter's querulous voice among a dozen or so children frolicking in the dusk. I stepped through the boxwood hedge into the clearing and opened the knife. In as deep a voice as I could manage, I yelled "Peter!"

He turned and looked at me. Then he saw the knife, and his pudgy face froze. His guilt showed plainly in his expression, and I began to move forward. I had no plans to actually stab anyone; I only wanted to make this vandal crawl and beg for his life, as seen on TV crime shows. I moved toward him, imitating the most menacing look I could recall from TV juvenile delinquents who always seemed to be threatening peaceful citizens with switchblade knives.

As I closed the gap, the thought occurred that Peter might not be so scared after all, might not believe I would actually stab him. What if he merely laughed, or became furious and beat me up? If he screamed for his parents, would they call the police? I had a vision of the coppers hauling me off in handcuffs to a movie prison scene, like the one I'd seen recently on Saturday afternoon TV starring Edward G. Robinson. When the coppers nailed you, it was curtains. The rubber hoses! The rockpile!

Suddenly Peter bolted for his apartment. In what seemed like less than a second the whole mob of boys and girls panicked and followed suit, slamming their wooden screen doors behind them.

I stood alone in the clearing, now eerily quiet, brandishing my knife. Coolly surveying the windows full of observers, I folded the blade and made a slow turnabout to step through the bushes and down the trail. Returning to my yard, I carefully picked up the scraps of robot and carried them to the communal trash site, a cluster of heavy round cans in the days before apartment dumpsters. If it had been possible to burn Robbie in a solemn funeral pyre ceremony, I would have done so.

A few of the witnesses must have squealed to their parents, but, hard as it is to believe a half-century later when little boys are suspended from school for drawing pictures of guns or sent to therapy for pointing a popsicle stick at a playmate, no repercussions were forthcoming. When I saw Peter on Saturday by the bushes where the kids hunted bees, he kept his distance. But I heard him whining to another boy, trying to work up his anger.

"That little kid is crazy! He pulled a knife on me!"

I looked at them both coldly and they edged away. I couldn't have felt happier, even if I'd still had the robot.

CHAPTER EIGHT

~ The Crown Prince ~ Cruising Hollywood ~ Luke's Middle Age
~ A Digression on Beaches ~ Show-Up Poker

I have outlined my San Pedro double life between the Channel Heights apartments and Bert the babysitter's, but if my regular days with my grandmother are taken into account, I actually had a *triple* life in progress. Nanny had Wednesdays off from the Broadway department store, and she devoted them to me. As a five- and six-year-old, I commanded little respect at either end of San Pedro, and between the brusque older marble shooters at Channel Heights and Bert's large family, I learned how to be a (slightly) less-spoiled only child. But Wednesdays with Nanny undid most of the lessons. I served as her Crown Prince and she my ticket to big-city glamour.

Jane would dress me extra-carefully those mornings: white shirt buttoned to the top, a sweater vest in the winter, and always my best Buster Brown shoes. By age five I balked at the bow tie and fedora I had been subjected to in previous years, but nonetheless I remained quite the young dude.

Nanny would pick me up at Bert's around eleven in her 1953 baby-blue Buick convertible which Jerry and Dent, those connoisseurs of automotive beauty, so rightfully admired. In her early fifties, Nanny cut a slim and stylish figure, with faded red hair and elegant clothes bought with her Broadway discount. But she was even older than Bert and so seemed ancient in my young eyes. Though she could be sharp with her husband ("John, you are acting like a TWO-year-old!"), her manner with me was diffident, almost timid. Still, she had a fine dry sense of humor. She called anyone assuming unwarranted authority "The Kingpin," and she'd say "Back in '91" when she caught herself talking about the good old days. Years later, I gathered that the latter had been an expression she and her fellow teenagers used in the 1920s to make fun of old folks reminiscing about the 1890s. She also said, "Leave it to beaver!" when she made a mistake, so I surmise that the expression had been ancient before the *Leave It to Beaver* TV show revived it.

On some of our days together, we'd drive first to downtown L.A. for lunches at Clifton's cafeteria, an eatery that made frequent use of daytime TV advertising. My sixth birthday fell on Thursday in 1959, but Jane took the day off on Wednesday, April first, so she and Nanny could take me to Clifton's. I specifically asked to have luncheon there because, according to their commercials, they presented kids celebrating birthdays with a special treasure chest. I don't remember the prizes living up to their advertising hype, but I nonetheless found it exciting to eat in a place actually shown on TV.

More often Nanny would drive us straight to Hollywood, and the Buick seemed right at home on the Boulevard. Stars and famous names imbedded the sidewalks and interested viewers could just make out the big H-O-L-L-Y-W-O-O-D letters up on the smoggy mountain. The new Capitol Record building resembled a stack of records, and it also featured a HOLLYWOOD sign in red lights visible to passing aircraft.

Several large, comfortable, well-maintained cinema palaces dating from the twenties and thirties beckoned between Vine and Highland. Nanny was amenable to any movie I wanted to watch, so I've always wondered why we didn't see *Sinbad the Sailor*, a stop-action pioneer with sword fighting skeletons, when it premiered. She may have been on one of her periodic binges, or perhaps we were visiting in Alabama during the run of the picture.

After the movie we would stroll, with me dashing ahead to look in shop windows and Nanny clipping along behind me in her high-heeled shoes. Somewhere along Hollywood Boulevard a novelty store beckoned, full of the gags usually seen only in comic book advertisements, wondrous items like X-ray specs, whoopee cushions, and flies in fake ice cubes. We could also stop in Walgreen's drug store, with its old fashioned soda fountain featuring hot fudge sundaes in ornate glassware. Nanny wouldn't hesitate to splurge on my slightest whim.

Daddy and Nanny had taken divergent life paths, but they shared two things: attraction to drink and a fierce affection for me. Daddy flew out to San Pedro for a week or so sometime during that period, primarily to see me. Jane was either between jobs or taking a few days off, and I stayed home from Bert's. In the evenings Daddy cleaned his pistol as of old, and he sat out on the porch every afternoon, smoking cigarettes and whittling scrap wood swords for me. We didn't talk much, and after a while I'd get restless and run off to play with friends. Looking all of his 68 years, Daddy seemed impossibly ancient. He had been my age in 1895, before planes, cars, and home electricity, not to mention TV and rockets. If an historical Methuselah had actually lived 963 years, he wouldn't have experienced nearly as many societal upheavals and rapid innovations in the slower days of early civilization as Daddy saw in his exciting lifespan.

Luke bore extended visits from his father-in-law and little brother with equanimity, and he made no complaint when Jane quit her factory job in late summer of 1959 to attend a trade school for grocery checker training. Checkers were considered skilled workers then; they had a strong union, Local 770, run by an East coast goodfella named DeSilva, who had negotiated previously unheard of money and benefits. The grocery business promised to be a good career move, and with Luke's steady glazier work, they could afford to live on one paycheck for the six weeks until Jane earned her certificate. Plus, since I would start first grade in September, they wouldn't have to hire Bert to watch me.

In his mid-twenties, Luke had already settled into the workingman rut. He remained good looking, but he'd gained twenty pounds in two years, mostly around his middle. He wasn't a big drinker, but he usually sipped his way through a quart of Brew 102 brand beer every night, and he loved fried food and desserts. The resulting middle-twenties waist expansion would probably have happened to Elvis if he'd stayed a truck driver. Luke enjoyed TV enormously; after dinner he always studied "the TV log," as he called *TV Guide,* to plan his evening. The Three Stooges and Laurel and Hardy were enjoying a renewed popularity on the small screen, but as a back-country child without access to the town theatres, Luke had never developed an appreciation for these stars in his formative years. And the musicals, doctor shows, and crime dramas Jane preferred only bored him — he liked Westerns, of which there were plenty, including *Wagon Train, Have Gun Will Travel, Sugarfoot,* and *The Rebel.*

Except for shopping trips, Luke and Jane rarely ventured forth on the weekends. He had no hobbies and took no regular exercise, though I do recall one fairly strenuous beach hike with him and Bubba. We began in a bay at low tide, climbing around rocks in our bare feet with our long pants rolled up. The brothers joked with one another like Robbie and his friends, paying little attention to me. I remember collecting some starfish—or "sea stars" as they are currently referred to in elementary school textbooks in order to distinguish them from actual fish. These interesting creatures were abundant in Southern California waters then. I also recall trying to keep up along a narrow path on a sheer cliff face. Allowing a five-year-old to make this climb today would bring forth lifeguards, police, and child protection agency officers, but I struggled to the top with the big boys for a panoramic view of the old commercial fishing ship grounded in the bay.

Southern California beaches bore little resemblance fifty years ago to those now managed currently by city, county, and state agencies. On the plus side, some shorelines were accessible and unspoiled; anyone could build a fire, camp out for days or weeks, never pay a dime for parking, and never feel crowded. Seals, lobsters, tuna, and tide pools abounded, enough to make the modern oceanography museums with interactive displays for kids completely unnecessary. When I read *Cannery Row* at age fourteen or so, I caught the feeling of my early beach trips in John Steinbeck's portrait of the California coast in the nineteen-thirties. Main character Doc drives to San Diego to collect marine specimens, and the plentitude of crabs, octopi, starfish (sea stars), anemone and more in the account seems much exaggerated. But the shore actually did teem with sea life until, beginning in the sixties, the coastline population and waste water disinfection chemicals exterminated most of the minor players in the food chain.

On the non-nostalgic side, with the exception of a few oases like Santa Monica and Santa Barbara, most beaches lacked the cleanliness and safety of today's super-regulated coastal preserves with protected "public access." Much of the shoreline was privately held, either by the military, the oil companies, or the wealthy. However, since winters were damp, the salt air ate up cars, and the general miasma caused diphtheria and other bugaboos (or so went the current wisdom), rich people only came to the shore in the summer. Thus stretches of shoreline architecture were given over to ugly low-rent bungalows and fishing shacks. Until the early sixties, people who wanted to *save* money could move to the coast.

Since no multi-million dollar programs were yet in place to replace sand washed away by tides, far fewer sandy stretches existed. But citizens smoked freely on open beaches and dumped refuse with impunity—everything from miscellaneous garbage to old cars and rotted hulks of boats. Most beaches where people congregated collected even more litter than the open highways. And of course flies and mosquitoes abounded, along with plenty of garbage, dead fish, dead seals, and thick carpets of rotting seaweed.

To add to the non-picturesqueness of the scene, oil wells— especially the smaller kind that resemble robot insects—were ubiquitous, right on the beach in some places and planted randomly all through towns up and down the coast. Long Beach, hundreds of square miles of it, steeped in the oil aroma. Other beach towns stank of oil whenever the air grew still. As an ocean lover and surfer stereotypically irritated by crowds, pompous, lifeguards, and the patronizing attitude of costal regulators, I would, if given the choice and a time machine, probably opt to go back to the uncrowded beaches of the fifties—but I'd go with no delusions of picturesqueness.

Exploring the cliffs and tide pools with Luke and Bubba remains a delightful memory, and the Langston brothers also seemed to enjoy themselves, even though we all came home with sunburns and lacerated feet. More often Luke spent his leisure time in sedentary pursuits, none too social, but once or twice in the years we lived in the apartments, buddies from work came over on a Sunday afternoon to drink beer and play penny-ante poker. All of these fellows had accents—mostly southern, but I heard an occasional east coast twang. None seemed to be married—or if they were, they didn't bring their wives.

During one such party I asked Jane between poker hands to draw a head on one of my pre-drawn Superman bodies. One of Luke's pals, feeling magnanimous after winning a two dollar pot, smiled at me and flicked a silver Ben Franklin half-dollar across the table. "Here you go, Sport—I'll stake ya. Let the kid sit in on a hand of Show-Up."

Neither Luke nor Jane objected, so I cashed in my half-dollar for nickels, dimes, and pennies and took my first fling at gambling. Show-Up Poker is a game of chance and blind nerve where you're dealt five cards face up with betting after each card. I called all raises and won over a dollar in one hand of cards, an event I found delightful and which fueled a continuing childhood interest in poker.

But as Jane made known later, attending gatherings with Luke was no fun. For such an otherwise pleasant and personable fellow, he showed a tendency to morbid jealousy and would become uncomfortable to the point of rudeness if she chatted politely with one of his friends. This trait may have accounted for their stunted social life, and his insecurity seemed to increase with time. Jane called the family shots on most things, but in this area Luke remained unmovable and unreasoning. To maintain the peace, she learned to keep her eyes on him whenever answering questions put to her by any male between the ages of twenty and sixty. But she remained unbowed, as we shall see.

Unaware of this growing family strain, I entered first grade in September, 1959. A week before opening day I went to Bert's for the last time. I had no idea that the end had come—I understood I would no longer make regular visits to their house, but there had been breaks in the routine before. So the last day with them unfolded with so little drama that I don't remember any details.

Those good folks, especially Linda and Robbie, served as my surrogate family for a significant part of my early childhood, but I have no photos nor hope now of tracking them—I don't even remember their last name. Bert and her husband are surely gone. Jerry and Dent, the hot rod teens, are in their seventies; I hope they're among the grizzled old American Bandstand generation, proudly showing off lovingly-restored fifties hot rods at the classic car shows. If Robbie is still alive, he has reached retirement age; and Linda, that shining example of female goodness, recently arrived there, too. Does she wonder now and then in reverie what ever became of the little boy she rescued from a neighborhood ogre, and in the process demonstrated the power of moral courage? Does she remember the child to whom she showed the mysteries of nature and taught, beyond how to spin a hula hoop, the principles of fair play in games? Does she recall the self-centered lad to whom she never showed the slightest impatience? That was me, dear Linda, and in my reverie I'm still following you down the 1958 alleys in a cracked space helmet.

CHAPTER NINE

~ Demographics ~ First Grade Mosaic ~ Dick & Jane: Subjective Groupings
~ A Portentous New Career ~ Sudden Upheavals

Opening day of first grade at Park Western Elementary School confirmed something I'd already begun to notice since returning from Alabama almost two years before: practically everyone in Southern California came from somewhere else. The demographic tide was still rising in 1959, with plenty of growing pains. I would attend eighteen schools in Los Angeles and Orange counties over the next several years, observing teachers and administrators, many themselves black sheep, go-getters, failures, dreamers and refugees from other states, doing their best (or not) to cope with the chaos.

Classrooms often packed in forty or more and sometimes met in split morning and afternoon sessions. Park Western didn't have double sessions in 1959, but they did use the A and B system, a way in which enrollment could be staggered over the year. I began my academic career as a "B-1" in an extremely full class. About half the students were slightly older "A-1s" who had started first grade at midyear the previous January.

In a series of photos taken by Jane and Nanny on that foggy San Pedro morning, my first teacher, Mrs. Hedgecock, looks like a severe, old maid type from B-movie central casting. But she turned out to be a warm sort of boot camp sergeant. As we left our family members outside and filed into the classroom, she directed us B-1s to sit on the big rug. The A-1s sat at the scaled-down tables, looking down upon us with jaded condescension. Teacher sat herself on her high stool at the front of the room. "My name is Mrs. Hedgecock," she said drily. Then she smiled. "I know it's a funny name."

We B-1s tittered nervously; the A-1s looked supremely bored. Mrs. H continued, "It's all right if you call me 'Teacher' if you want.

I'm from Kansas. Came to California during the war. My husband worked in the shipyards and we lived right here in the Channel Heights. Where are you all from? Let's go 'round the room. If you were born in California, say where your parents are from. Kevin, you want to start? You're from a fine state, aren't you?"

Kevin, an A-1, said he hailed from Kansas, too. I understood Teacher had chosen him on purpose, and I began to dial in to her sense of humor. The girl to his right claimed Michigan roots. The next girl named another California town as her birthplace, but her older brothers and parents migrated from New York. So it went, around the room. Only two identified as natives of the Golden State, one a Japanese girl who looked four or five years old. Her parents, she said, had also been born in California. In her ruffled skirt, patent leather Mary Janes, white gloves, and air of self-possession, she seemed more adult than child.

My friend Bear, henceforth on school grounds called by his real name, Harlan Defries, was born in Indonesia, controlled by the Netherlands until 1949, only ten years before. I had heard Bear talking in a different language with his parents, but he had no accent when he spoke English. He now announced himself as "Dutch," which prompted Mrs. Hedgecock to praise him as our farthest world traveler.

Later Teacher organized the B-1s into three groups, each assigned a red, green, or blue primary reader. The red book proceeded slowly with much repetition of one and two word sentences; the green book advanced more rapidly, and the blue book introduced several new words and longer sentences with each chapter. Eschewing today's extensive scientific testing, Mrs. Hedgecock simply called out students' names for each group and we started right in.

The grouping seemed to be based on appearance. Four Mexican boys went to the red book with Bear, who had even darker skin than theirs. Rougher-looking white kids (mostly boys with shaggy haircuts, ringworm spots on their faces, and old jeans) rounded out the slow readers. The green group had the largest population, about half and half boys and girls, all plainly but neatly dressed, all occidental except for a Japanese boy. Besides one other boy, the Blue group to which Teacher assigned me consisted of females coiffed as if for church, and all Caucasian except for the little Japanese girl.

I could compete in the same fashion league as the rest in my group; Jane and Nanny had outfitted me as if for a 1940's juvenile musical audition. My blonde hair had been oiled and parted ruler-straight and my face scrubbed pink. I wore a dress shirt with Mr. B collar buttoned tightly to my neck and a checked Eisenhower jacket sans lapels with two buttons at the bottom. A stylishly thin alligator belt secured my severely creased dress pants, and mirror-sheen Buster Brown oxfords, fresh from the Broadway department store box, adorned my size-one feet. So I was a shoe-in, as it were, for an initial assignment to the top reading classification.

Such racial and social profiling would not be tolerated today, but Mrs. Hedgecock had no one to answer to in 1959. While she did subsequently make a few adjustments from her initial intuitive mix, I stayed in the blue group and Bear stayed in the red. He was a good-natured fellow, but he found sitting in class tedious. Already the fastest runner in the neighborhood, he picked up the ball game "two-square" so rapidly that after only a week on the playground he could hold his own with the A-1s and even some of the second graders.

I too liked recess and became reasonably adept at ball games, but I felt comfortable enough indoors and enjoyed most learning activities without benefit of a head start in Kindergarten. I started to forge ahead in the reading book, sounding out new words before the group reached them. I liked the positive feedback from Teacher, and when I began to read signs around the neighborhood and along the roads, I received much encouragement from Jane, Nanny, and even Luke.

In the first few weeks we practiced our letters and learned how to write numbers all the way to twenty. For science lessons, we planted sweet potato vines using water glasses and toothpicks. We had a fifteen-minute recess in the morning and a longer playtime after lunch, followed by a short rest on the rug. My favorite school activity came two or three days a week when we worked on our wooden model boats. The educational goal was to give hands-on practice with tools while using the results to help us learn about shipping and harbors. The nautical component would be capstoned with a walking field trip to the actual San Pedro harbor, only a few blocks away. Meanwhile several kids started tugboats; the Japanese girl began building the Queen Mary; most of us boys constructed freighters. With satisfaction I remembered the old man across Bert's alley and the little pleasure boat project he wouldn't let me help with. Well, I was older now and no such small-time builder as he — my freighter even had smokestacks.

Since creating my killer robot I'd been itching to work with tools other than rocks and shoes. Mrs. Hedgecock taught us how to use bit and brace drills, hammers, and handsaws, with particular emphasis on safety. To this day when I use a handsaw, I first mark my cut with a pencil, then, as she demonstrated, draw the saw teeth backward with the three careful strokes (never two or four) along the line in order to give the saw a sure start.

On school mornings I'd walk with the army of kids heading in the same direction. The boys bunched together, carrying the latest in colorful super-hero lunchboxes with matching thermoses, mostly Cliff Canaveral, Zorro, and Superman. Children of more frugal parents hauled their dads' hand-me-down grey round-top lunch pails, or, if their parents were poorer yet, recycled paper bags with their name written on the sides. Packs of girls, usually ahead of the malingering boys, primly clutched their neatly-rolled lunch bags or square lunch boxes painted in pink with doily patterns.[14] All of us meandered to the school gates in a loose flow, then funneled down to tighter organization as the monitors herded us into the playground. At the first bell, we lined up by classroom in designated areas of the blacktop; when the bell rang again, we marched into our rooms.

Since first grade classes were dismissed an hour earlier than the others, the after-school walk proceeded with less crowding. Jane remained home the first few school days of September, but with the advent of her grocery checker job, I became what has in recent years been designated a latchkey kid. Of course in those days no latchkey was necessary; they simply left the door unlocked.

Jane's new position came as a result of her rigorous trade school training. She had been the best student in the grocery checker class, and her teacher, an avuncular retired store manager, became so dazzled by her aptitude and other attributes that he felt moved to contact a friend who managed Fox Market in the San Fernando Valley. The friend happened to have an opening for an apprentice checker, and Jane took the job, beginning a pattern of long commutes she would continue for much of her working life.

Like most families then, we had one car, which Luke usually drove to work. But Jane's instructor also knew two former students who lived in Long Beach and commuted to stores even farther than

---

[14] The iconic Barbie doll made her debut in toy stores in 1959, but according to a brief note on the Smithsonian website, the Barbie lunchbox began production in 1962. Had I known then that I would eventually write this socio/historical account, I would have paid more attention to girls' lunchboxes, especially since the official history of them is so spotty.

Fox Market. In exchange for gas money, Jane secured rides with her fellow checkers and managed to make her scheduled shifts. At five-thirty each morning, having already gotten me up and laid out my clothes and packed lunch for everyone, Jane would walk up the hill to meet her ride at the corner. If I were quick to dress, I'd accompany her. After watching the car disappear into the gloom, I'd walk back down the hill and eat some cereal with Luke in the dim morning light. We didn't talk much—he never inquired about school, and I wasn't one to volunteer information.

To be clear, Luke never showed hostility towards me, and he went out of his way to be generous at times. As noted, he took me hunting and to the movies during his courtship of Jane. The day he began his career as a glazier, he gave me a glass cutter tool. And aware that Nanny had started me on a coin collection, he presented me one morning in fall 1959 with two brand new Lincoln pennies he'd acquired as change. These sesquicentennial celebrations of Abe's birth had the Lincoln memorial stamped on the back to replace the stalks of wheat featured there since 1909, and the historical importance of the commemoration duly impressed me. But other than these thoughtful acts and some carping about changing the TV channels too fast, I don't remember much interaction with Luke during the two and a half years we'd been living together. He became even more reserved when Jane started working. We both missed her at the breakfast table, and in another sense of the word, we both also missed any signs of the great changes already under way.

The revolution officially began one Monday morning in November, two years after we migrated from Alabama. Luke left for work a few minutes after 6:00. Jane had announced at dinner the night before that she'd been scheduled for next Saturday and so had the day off. When I came downstairs around 6:30, she said, with an inscrutable expression, "You don't have to go to school today."

I sat at the table, feeling a pleasant sense of adventure. I asked if we would be meeting Nanny and going to Clifton's Cafeteria again. But Jane only said, "We're going to go somewhere for a while" before returning to whatever she had been doing upstairs. As I ate my Cheerios with four spoons of sugar, I heard her moving things around in her room. Then came a knock on the back door. I opened it to find Fran Faye, Jane's old friend from Alabama, looking like a movie star in red capris, gold sandals, and boat neck sweater. In a southern accent like Jane's, she chirped, "Hi, Ricky, is your mamma home?"

Fran, a few years younger than Jane, had been a Bessemer High school classmate of Uncle Don's. In her early teens she followed Jane's career, resolving to come to California herself. Upon arrival in L.A. in the late 1940s, she immediately located her mentor. Apparently they had had many single-girl-in-Hollywood adventures, some sketchy details of which I learned forty years later. Leading the way into scandal, Fran had borne an out-of-wedlock daughter, Melinda, before she landed Dan Faye, a successful businessman twenty years her senior. They now lived in a huge suburban dream house in Northridge, at the far end of the Valley.[15]

Jane shouted, "Just a minute, Fran," then called me upstairs, where I found her in my room. She had pulled my toy box from the closet, and she told me now to put in everything I really, really wanted to keep.

"Are we going back to Daddy's?"

"You'll see, Honey. Just pack up as fast as you can."

She seemed so serious that I didn't ask more questions. She and Fran loaded the car swiftly, Jane's clothes on hangers and mine and Trish's in cardboard boxes Fran had brought with her. I had packed my keepsakes in the wooden toy box: the white plastic table radio I'd gotten for Christmas and four volumes Nanny had given me of the 10-volume, 1923 edition of readings for youngsters called *Journeys to Bookland*. Of my Little Golden Books I only retained Davy Crockett, my first acquisition. I put my favorite toys on top: marbles, plastic Prince Charming sword (a tie-in to the new release of the Disney *Sleeping Beauty* movie) and a few other priceless items I've now forgotten. I held my cigar box of real treasures (knife, coins, glass cutter, etc.) in my lap when we set off.

Through the oil stench of East San Pedro, the sea breezes of Santa Monica, and seemingly endless miles of Sepulveda Boulevard snaking north, I stared out the window in the pleasant trance that long car rides always provided. Two-year-old Trish babbled in the seat up front between Jane and Fran as the older girls chatted in conspiratorially low voices.

That morning I had planned on school as usual. I had had every

---

[15] Desi Arnaz and Lucille Ball owned a five acre orange ranch close by. According to Desi's autobiography, they bought the ranch for $10,000 in the early forties; today the land is worth many millions. Fran and her husband missed their chance for prime land at such low prices; Dan lamented he had been gouged $20,000 for their ranch style home on an acre-size lot, with pool and walnut orchard.

reason to believe I would be forging ahead in my reading group, playing with Bear and my other friends, and continuing construction on my wooden freighter. But now it began dawning on me—I would probably never see Park Western Elementary School again. Or Channel Heights. As an avid TV watcher, I had been exposed to many dramatizations of marital discord and had heard phrases like Seven-Year Itch and Quickie Divorce. So now I began to get the picture: Jane had left Luke. The poor old country boy was history.

CHAPTER TEN

~ The Old SFV ~ Frogs and Toads ~ Toilet Paper and Tomato Crackdown ~ In Stir
~ A Life-Defining Discovery ~ The Long Dead Past ~ On Down the Rapids

The morning of our flight from San Pedro introduced me to the smoggy bowl of the San Fernando Valley, where I would dwell periodically until young adulthood. Since around 1915, the Valley had been "the country" to denizens of L.A. Like Manhattanites coveting rural getaways in New England, Angelinos dreamed of owning a chicken ranch or horse property in the still smogless expanse north of the city. Both Bing Crosby and Roy Rogers took up the theme in the forties with Gordon Jenkins's hit song "San Fernando Valley," stressing the Valley's mild weather and the romance of the authentic country life right over the mountain from Hollywood.

We drove for over an hour to a rural area, mostly fields and swampy ground in those days. At one point toward the end of the journey, Fran turned around in the seat and said, tangential to a remark about babysitting fees, "You'll like it, Ricky; she's really nice."

I had been picking up snatches of the conversation up front and understood dimly that I would soon be left with a caretaker I had never met. Before my assignment to Bert, we had paid a formal call first. I had been introduced to Robbie, Linda and the rest and had looked forward to great adventures with personable big kids. The arrangements this time didn't feel quite as promising.

I could see Jane's eyes on me in the mirror. We turned onto a little street and parked. Fran continued talking as she shut off the engine…Mary ADORES children, and I know you'll just love her."

Jane was talking at the same time, and suddenly I became the center of attention: "… only for a few days, and I'll call every day…"

I made no reply. All this verbiage called up feelings of such dread and resentment that I avoided taking Jane's hand as we made our way up the front sidewalk.

An old woman opened the door before we stepped onto the porch. Previously identified as "Mary who ADORES children," she gave me a tight, perfunctory smile and fell into conversation with Jane as we all entered the house. The talk centered on Trish; at not quite two-years-old, my little sister had become extremely mobile and needed constant attention.

"Oh, I've been through it, Mrs. Ross, with Mrs. Faye's children when they were babies. And of course my own baby boys, but they're all grown now."

What was all this talk of babies? My indignation rose. Who did the old woman think she was dealing with here?

Jane—somehow reinstated, I noted, to "Mrs. Ross"—began to discuss tedious technical details: feeding, diapers, and such.

No one seemed to be paying attention to me, so I stepped back outside to survey the neighborhood. Wherever we had landed was definitely out in the country. I saw a brown horse in a corral across the street, and a little brook in the middle of a mowed field, its course marked by longer and lusher green grass. As I approached this curiosity, I spied a frog sitting beside a flowering hydrangea bush. The local kids later corrected me: all such creatures around the neighborhood were toads, not frogs. But I found out recently in my exhaustive research for this book that toads are actually a subset of the vast frog genus. My mood lightened instantly as I began to creep up upon this specimen of the Bufonidae, or "true toad" family (containing over 300 species). But before I could pounce, Jane called me inside. Everyone stood near the door except Trish, who lay asleep on the couch, clutching a doll. After an awkward moment in which I refrained from looking at anyone, Jane kissed me and bade me be a Good Boy. Then she drove off with Fran Faye.

Since my emotional breakdown upon being left at nursery school, I had picked up the notion that males who deserved respect— Western heroes like the Lone Ranger, or Popeye, or Bazooka Joe's gang—all took misfortune without a whimper. So I put on my stoic best as Mary showed me around the house. I don't remember much of the first couple of days in exile except my disappointment that the home had no TV. I talked to Jane on the phone the second day, but she spoke only vaguely about when she planned to return. I had been out of school only half a week, but San Pedro already seemed like a lifetime ago.

My resolution to hang tough soon met the challenge of two

dramatic scenes with old Mary, followed by a momentous turning point in my life. All three events took place on the third day of my incarceration. The first began when I came in around ten after a brisk workout with my new Prince Charming sword upon hoards of imaginary enemies. I parked the weapon inside the back door and proceeded to the bathroom. After taking a seat I began, in my imaginary Prince Charming alter ego, to daydream a battle with the dragon alter-ego of Maleficent, the movie *Sleeping Beauty's* frightful female villain.

Suddenly the door opened.

Even in the mists of time before my earliest memories, the bathroom had been a private sanctuary for me. According to Jane, when she would place me on the child holder that fit over the regular toilet seat, I always insisted that (a) she exit the bathroom immediately, closing the door behind her and (b) she refrain from re-entering the room until I called her to assist my descent from the throne. But now old Mary stood in the doorway like Maleficent herself, *looking* at me on the toilet and yammering something about me using too much toilet paper.

This affront was not to be borne. I stood up and with both hands pushed the door shut, then clicked the lock. I could hear her muttering on the other side of the door, but I refused to be rushed. I used my customary amount of toilet paper, and as usual, her decrepit toilet had to be flushed twice to finish its job.

The harangue continued when I came out. "Flushing twice takes water and you could stop up the bowl putting in so much paper!"

Not deigning to answer, I made a regal exit, sword in hand. To take my mind off the shocking breach of dignity I'd suffered, I began to search the yard for toads and their offspring. In the little creek swam pollywogs enough to fill many jars, and in sweeps through adjacent yards and grassy lots, a hunter could collect dozens of slow grownups, especially in early mornings and around dusk. I had previously investigated the fenced-in horses and had taken the walk across the huge open field to Callahan Street School, where, yet unbeknown to me, I would soon enroll. In addition to the horse lots, the neighborhood homesteads featured rabbit pens, chicken coops, and large vegetable gardens. Except for the mountains in the near distance, the countryside had the general features I would observe years later in rural Midwestern states.

If the reader will pardon a slight digression for an epiphanic moment, a startling turn of events some years later brought the above scene vividly to mind. The epiphany took place during the winter of 1972 when, as a nineteen-year-old slacker, I found a temporary job as a San Fernando Valley ice cream man. One late afternoon as my converted mail truck blared "Yankee Doodle" (the company theme song), I turned off Reseda Boulevard and slowly cruised a suburban neighborhood in Northridge I hadn't explored yet. One lucky street full of children could boost the day's profits considerably, but unfortunately these avenues and cul-de-sacs featured tightly packed, uniformly landscaped tract houses seemingly devoid of any humans younger than forty.

With a shrug, I turned off the loudspeaker, stepped on the gas, and headed back for the main thoroughfare. Passing an elementary school, I idly read the name set in metal letters on the side of the front building: CALLAHAN STREET SCHOOL.

I stopped the truck, backed up, and stared. It couldn't be — this simply could not be the same school I remembered across the big open field from old Mary's rural neighborhood with its horse corrals and huge trees. But here it was. The school board wouldn't give the same name to two schools in the Valley. But... but...the very topography had been bulldozed by developers and reshaped beyond recognition — even the little brook had disappeared. The passage of time since the little toads hopped here so freely seemed more like a half-century than little more than a decade.

It struck me then that in my long-ago youth of thirteen years before, I'd seen the last remnants of an era. Apparently too many people heard Roy and Bing's siren song about the Valley, and the whole RFD scene had been engulfed. The twentieth-century metamorphosis from rural/small town to suburban/urban happened all over the country, but the change seemed most rapid of all in Southern California. At nineteen, conversant with all the sordid urban features of what the SFV had become, I felt a familiar nostalgic ache at time's inexorable passing.

Returning to the more concrete concerns of a memorable day in 1959, I quickly forgot the morning's bathroom invasion as I focused on the toad hunt. Gathering a quantity of the ugly little fellows, I deposited them in the middle of an old truck tire. After waiting stolidly for me to leave, they would rouse themselves and hop away, climbing over each other to escape. But plenty more hopped the grounds where those came from.

At lunch time hunger prompted me to let bygones be bygones with old Mary. When she brought my plate, I classified the peppered raw tomatoes next to my tuna sandwich as some kind of decorative garnish, like sprigs of parsley on restaurant platters. No one I knew ever ate a salad in my presence. I had tried a raw tomato once and found it revoltingly slimy. I finished everything else and reached for my sword, but the local Maleficent blocked my path.

"You'll have to clean your plate before you're excused," she announced.

"I hate tomatoes," I explained.

"Tomatoes have good vitamins. They keep you regular and you won't have to use so much bathroom paper."

I bristled. Just what did she mean by regular, and what did all this have to do with toilet paper?

She then proceeded to add injury to insult by announcing I would either eat the tomatoes or take a nap.

This encounter had begun to try my patience. "I'm not sleepy," I said evenly.

She declared she would call my mother if I didn't comply, but this threat didn't frighten me; I knew Jane would probably take my side in this dispute. My mom may have abandoned me from time to time, but she had never made me eat anything I didn't like. But it occurred to me that my dignity as a Western hero would be at stake if I brought a mother into this situation. No, I would handle it myself.

"I hate tomatoes," I reiterated with patient restraint.

The old lady stiffened. "You can eat your good tomatoes or take a nap."

I chose to stand on principle. So in the middle of a perfect afternoon for further swordplay or toad gathering, the old lady imprisoned me in a different back room than the one I slept in. Furthermore, she ordered me to recline on one of the twin beds for an hour. For an active six-year-old, an hour in bed roughly equaled a month in solitary at a maximum-security prison for an adult. In what I perceived as a particularly cruel and unusual addition, she drew the curtains and switched off the light before leaving.

But I would not be cowed. After a minute, I sat up, swung my legs, and dropped from the bed, my Buster Brown shoes resounding on the hardwood floor. As if on cue, the old woman opened the door. "You get back in that bed, now! You need to calm down."

I resented her implication that I was less than calm, but said nothing. As she closed the door, I noticed a bookshelf by the dresser. I waited another minute, then slipped off my shoes and tiptoed to investigate, squinting at the shelves in the dim light through the curtained windows. At first I saw only dusty old grownup tomes with no pictures. But on the bottom shelf I found an illustrated volume of stories that must have been a third- or fourth-grade reading textbook from the 1940s, when the old lady's two now-grown sons were young.

Taking the book back to the bed, I reclined against the headboard, examining my find. Every page had five times more words than Dick and Jane paperbacks, and some pages had no pictures at all. The title page featured a drawing of people wearing clothes like on the Davy Crockett shows. A boy in the foreground held a musical instrument that looked like a small guitar. I'd heard the term fiddle on TV, but I'd never seen one in person or seen the word in print. Yet the f sound and short i, the two d's and the l clearly said "fiddle" as I sounded it out. I still didn't understand the "silent e" teacher had talked about in reading group, but there, beyond doubt, I perceived the word corresponding to the object.

Encouraged, I made out several more words I'd never seen before, words no grownup had introduced. I had previously guessed from context on street signs, but now, with the sort of focus applied to law studies by heretofore uneducated criminals facing long prison terms, I began to apply basic phonetics and deductive reasoning. The boy played the fiddle, and he entered a "fiddling bee." I'd heard of spelling bees from Jane, who had won one when in her school days, so I made the contest connection. The boy seemed to have no hope of prevailing, but the young girl had a faith in him. Sure enough, he played so well that even the older kids who'd previously scoffed all cheered him when he won the prize.

Suddenly I became aware of reading a "real" book. Almost every word! A book more advanced than anything the A-1s were tackling back at Park Western Elementary, and I could read it!

When the old lady came in to check on me some thirty minutes later, I forgot my resentment and began babbling about the story. She didn't order me to go to sleep. In a matter-of-fact voice, but with an oddly tender smile, she said I could read it any time. And I could also go play whenever I was ready.

Did she say play? The spell shattered; I grabbed my sword and sallied forth to capture more toads. But I read for a while each day afterwards, voluntarily retiring to the back bedroom in the late morning or after lunch and working methodically through the several long stories listed in the book's table of contents.

So, thanks to some tomatoes and an irritable old lady, I found, earlier than I might have otherwise, a pastime which heralded my future career. I seemed to be moving rapidly toward whatever future lay in store, for by the time I finished the storybook a week or so later, I lived in a new apartment, attended a new school, and had a brand new stepdad.

CHAPTER ELEVEN

~ Enter Jay ~ Love Conquers All ~ Working the System ~ Cottage Cheese and the
First Grade Outlaw ~ May I Be Excused?

"Why didn't you ask your mom why she left Luke?" wondered my wife when she first heard the story of the San Pedro evasion. "And how come you didn't ask her why she dumped you at a strange babysitter's for a week, and with no warning at all?"

I initially replied, "I'm not sure," and after much reflection, my answer stands. As a youngster I was neither particularly shy nor submissive, but it didn't occur to me until much later to question my parents' often-inexplicable behavior. However, in bits and pieces picked up over many years, I did learn the underpinnings of our new family dynamic. Jane had started her job at Fox market in the San Fernando Valley a month or so before. She enjoyed the work, but she stood out among the other female checkers like an orchid in a bed of daisies. She treated the male employees, all decidedly invigorated by her presence, with the distant charm she managed so well. But Jay, the assistant manager ("second man" in retail terminology) proved harder to discourage.

An assistant manager is like an executive officer on a ship, troubleshooting stock shortages, fielding customer complaints, filling in wherever necessary to keep the shoppers moving through the checkout lines. Jay seemed to hover at Jane's register often, bagging for her and helping with prices. She couldn't help but notice his easy authority among the checkers, and his skill at all store tasks. When he operated the register, his fingers danced over the keys, and boxboys marveled aloud at his bagging speed.

Under his Fox apron Jay always wore a starched, tab collar shirt and a Windsor-knot tie. He sported French cuffs with links and deep-shined his shoes. A heavy smoker, he nonetheless had fine teeth, and he took care of his fingernails. His dark hair had begun to recede, but he disdained the comb-over look and brushed it straight back from his forehead. Premature balding and rough skin saved him from being a too-handsome fellow; as Jane said later, she'd seen enough of those in Hollywood. Nonetheless, Jay had the air of a dashing but tough-as-nails leading man. He could have played Humphrey Bogart's younger brother in a forties film-noir thriller.

At the beginning of Jane's second day at work, Jay struck up a conversation in the break room. How would she like to go to lunch? "There's an Italian place just down Ventura Boulevard that serves *real* Italian, not like all these pizza joints."

She demurred. "Thanks, but I ate my lunch at the break."

But when he asked again the next day, she decided that talking to a man without having to endure Luke's jealous steaming would be a pleasant change. Over the lunch special and house wine, Jay showed himself as a natural charmer, with the sort of charisma that gave those around him the feeling of membership in an exclusive circle, superior yet tolerant of those outside. Quick-witted and a good-natured teaser, he pretended to misunderstand her accent, called her "Bubbles," and scoffed when she suggested they had better get back to work. But he made it plain he found her fascinating.

After a few lunch dates their conversation became more intimate. She revealed that she was married but not altogether happy with the union. He understood, since he had been divorced a year ago. He too had children, whom he loved as dearly as she loved her Ricky and Trish. They also shared interests in movies and fine dining. Both had left school before graduating—she before twelfth grade to get married, he in ninth grade to be an apprentice butcher—but they both read avidly and always had a paperback or two going. And when she told him about her professional dancing—

"No kidding! I taught dancing in my early twenties. Arthur Murray studio, in Burbank."

"I worked for Arthur Murray's in Alabama! Do you dance a lot now? I hardly ever get the chance—my husband doesn't like to go out."

The jukebox played romantic Italian songs, and the restaurant had a tiny dance floor. But he shook his head, dismissing the obvious romantic opportunity. "I like nightclubs, the ones with class, but dancing usually seems too much like work after teaching it."

Nonetheless, the attraction deepened and events began to move.

No more than three weeks after they met, sometime in late October or early November, Jane skipped her ride home from work and joined Jay for drinks and an overnight assignation. The excuse she gave Luke involved the market's monthly inventory, which paid time-and-a-half for overtime. She assured Luke that she could sleep at Fran Faye's in the Valley, and Fran would drive her to work in the morning. The deception worked well enough, and another such late night followed. Jay plied her with liquor on the next date and she became argumentative when he contradicted himself on some element of his past:

"You need to get your stories straight, Mister."

They had a spat and Jay left her at the motel. He didn't come to work for two days. When he returned, he showed a charming contriteness. The next day she consented to a long lunch with wine at the Italian place.

After some banter to demonstrate how much he missed her, Jay confessed he had not exactly divorced his wife.

"To tell the truth, I wasn't even separated until the last few days. I had to get away—I couldn't go back to her after being with you."

She understood and also agreed that she could no longer stay with Luke. Clearly this love transcended petty considerations. They decided that they needed to act, and act boldly. Over the weekend and through several clandestine pay-phone communications, Jane arranged to borrow a hundred dollars from Nanny, who took an advance on her department store salary. Jane also enlisted Fran Faye, who lived in the Valley, knew a reliable babysitter, and also relished participation in such a dramatic intrigue. Jane made her move the following Monday, dropping off Trish and me at Mary's. She stayed with Jay in a Sepulveda motel while they looked for an apartment.

When Luke found Jane gone, he called his mother-in-law for information. But Nanny had left her own excitable husband in Alabama and had plenty of experience in covering tracks. No, she didn't know Jane's whereabouts or even at which store Jane worked. "Didn't she tell *you?*" she asked Luke.

"Uh, naw—guess I never asked."

Well, Nanny didn't think the store name was Lucky's or Vons when he suggested these.

"How 'bout Piggly Wiggly? Or Fox?"

No, those didn't sound familiar either.

"Well, what about that friend of hers—that Fran what's her name—where's she live?"

Nanny said she hadn't seen Fran in years. She had just sent another fifty dollars to Jane care of Fran, but Luke hadn't exactly asked for her address.

Fortunately for Jane and Jay, Luke showed no inclination to get drunk, buy a gun, and start searching the Valley, market by market. He continued going to work and coming home to an empty house, probably until the month's rent came due. I see him in my mind's eye, sitting in front of *Wagon Train* or *Have Gun, Will Travel*, drinking his quart of Brew 102 alone.

Thus Jay's dashingly romantic plan came off with no discernible hitches. Within four days they had rented a furnished one-bedroom apartment in Van Nuys and bought a TV on credit. As Jane came to learn, Jay had a way of managing credit history when he put his mind to it. The lovers showed up at old Mary's house four days later. In relative time, those days lasted somewhat longer for me than for her; but here she was, as promised.

Jane chatted with the old lady about Trish's ongoing colicky stomach for a while; then she said we'd better be going. She picked up a stack of folded laundry. "Open the door for me, Honey."

I did so, and then followed her outside. As we approached a car I hadn't seen before, she said, "Sit up in the front seat a minute. I'll get Trish and be right out."

The car, a 1954 Chrysler, had been backed into the driveway and the trunk and passenger door stood open. Through the windshield, I could make out someone behind the wheel. I slid in, darting a quick glance at the driver. Jane closed the door and leaned in the window, smiling as if nothing odd at all were going on. "Ricky, this is Jay."

In the greenish dash light I could just make him out: thin, hunched over, smoking. He said "Hi" and nodded, then looked back down. Jane returned to the house. Several awkward, silent minutes passed during which time I fairly accurately surmised the situation with Jane and this Jay guy. No big deal; I'd gone through the business of getting a new stepdad before. This one seemed as quiet as the last one, a good sign—we'd see how it went. Meanwhile, I felt glad to see my mom, glad to get away from the old lady and her tomatoes.

Part two of the master plan for new romance called for Trish and me to continue staying with Mary on weekdays. We would sleep in our new apartment on Tiara Street in Van Nuys, and Jane would drive us across the Valley every morning. Jay had gotten them both jobs as checkers at a different market in Sepulveda (in case his wife, or Luke, or both became too energetic), but they didn't always work the same hours. Sometime in the evening, either Jane or Jay would pick us up, depending on the schedule.

Enrolling me at the school across the field from Mary's house seemed most convenient for the situation. The difficulty lay in that L.A. schools strictly adhered to district boundaries in those crowded days, and a request for a Van Nuys resident to attend a Northridge school wouldn't even be considered. So Jay patiently explained to Jane how to circumvent the rules. "Just give the old woman's address," he said. "They won't check."

"You mean lie to them?"

"You're catching on fast, Bubbles."

Jane indeed became an apt pupil. Asking to use Bert's address so I could go to kindergarten had never occurred to her the year before, but now, after charming Mary into going along with the ruse, she took me to the school and invented whatever information the registrar requested. The next Monday I enrolled at Callahan, and, in the first of many episodes casting me as an accomplice to one of Jay's circumventions, he admonished me to not tell *anyone* I lived in Van Nuys.

The new location made a promising first impression: Callahan was more modern than Park Western, the Valley sunnier than San Pedro, and my new teacher's classroom, with its big windows overlooking the playground, much brighter than Mrs. Hedgecock's. New teacher Mrs. Washburn assigned me to group two in reading, the default for entering students. But when my turn came I read with such authority that she made a field promotion, advancing me to the top group as soon as I finished my paragraph.

The first day proceeded pleasantly. Most of the boys in class played two-square or kickball during morning recess, but Callahan had a large sandbox, a delightful novelty for me. The box featured deluxe monkey bars, but I preferred to carve out a corner for myself and spend the breaks making castles and roads.

The morning of the second day unfolded well enough at first. After recess I discovered that instead of building boats with tools, first-graders here painted on easels and modeled in clay. The current project was handprint ashtrays. When a student finished an ashtray and signed it with a toothpick, teacher baked it in a kiln shared by the two first-grade classrooms. I appreciated the new art and craft opportunity, but as I worked on my handprint, I suddenly missed Park Western. By now Mrs. Hedgecock had probably thrown my freighter away. I wouldn't be there for the field trip to the harbor. I wondered if Bear even remembered me.

The lunch bell interrupted this emotional letdown. Park Western's limited its food service to hot dog day on Fridays, but Callahan had a cafeteria where, for twenty-five cents, students could purchase a daily hot meal with milk. We sat tightly packed at long tables, assigned by classroom. As students finished eating, they raised their hand and the teacher on cafeteria duty nodded approval to leave for lunch recess.

The first day I methodically cleaned my plate and proceeded to the sandbox. But Tuesday's menu included cottage cheese. I'd never seen the stuff before, and it looked repulsive. With some foreboding, I ate all other food and then raised my hand. The monitor looked over and shook her head. A few other students finished and left. I raised my hand again. The monitor walked over and bent down, smiling officiously. "You're a new boy, aren't you? Well, we have to leave a clean plate."

"I don't like that stuff," I explained, pointing at the cottage cheese. A camper might have used the same gesture to indicate an engorged tick pulled from a companion's scalp and flicked in the dirt.

"When you finish *all* of your food, you may be excused." She smiled again and nodded another student to freedom.

My face grew hot. Bad enough that everyone from babysitters to schools in this oddly sunny foreign place served disgusting food, but where did they get off with edicts about consuming substances one found repulsive? I took pride in being a good eater. I usually took pride in eating everything on my plate. I could eat TWO plates if they didn't put inedible stuff on them!

Soon I sat alone, the only student at the table, as recess slipped away. Perhaps cottage cheese wouldn't taste as bad as it looked. I took a deep breath, then a small bite, then gagged and convulsively spit out the vile stuff. It tasted sour, like throw-up with horrid lumps, even worse than tomatoes.

The monitor stood behind me again, but this time she wasn't smiling. "We do *not* play with our food here."

The *monstrous* unfairness of it all! Somehow I kept my composure. More minutes passed, and finally the monitor dismissed me with a parting threat to report my behavior to the authorities. I walked out numbly. Yes, I had prevailed, but my triumph was a Pyrrhic victory. Now only a few minutes of recess remained; no time for the sandbox. I slumped down, my back against a classroom building.

A boy came running by. Without any conscious thought, I stuck out my foot and tripped him. He performed a spectacular half-somersault and landed hard on the asphalt. He had just begun to wail when a teacher on playground duty jerked me to my feet. She commenced scolding and shaking me. Another teacher helped the kid up. He sobbed mightily and held up a bleeding elbow for all to see.

The powers that be — the yard teachers, the stern-faced male vice-principal to whom they marched me, and Mrs. Washburn when she answered the office summons — began the interrogation.

"You maliciously tripped that boy! How *could* you do such a mean thing?

"I don't know."

I spoke the truth. There was no why to it I could hope to articulate. So I came off as sullen and unrepentant. From then on Mrs. Washburn seemed decidedly cool toward me, and classmates gave me a wide berth at the sandbox.

At least the incident remained on campus. The vice-principal threatened to call my mother, but for obfuscation purposes she had listed no phone contact at all. Between the overcrowded school and overworked staff, my case fell through the administrative cracks. But unfortunately my mealtime troubles weren't quite over for the week.

Dinner at home featured the usual fried meat and canned vegetables. I ate hastily, eager to be finished in time for the start of *Lassie*, starring the famous collie genius.

I jumped up and started for my usual spot on the floor in front of the set. But Jay, who sat at the table smoking and reading a paperback western, said, "Hold on, Pal" and pointed to my seat.

Puzzled, I sat back down. I'd known Jay for a week now, and he seemed like a decent fellow. He had demonstrated a friendlier nature than Luke's by wrestling with me and giving me and Trish rides on his back. He didn't drink much, but had the sweet tooth of a child, so he could be depended upon to bring home plenty of Hershey bars and brownies from the store.

But now he looked stern. "Before you leave the table, you ask to be excused."

"Huh?" What was he talking about? "How…?"

"Say, 'May I be excused.'"

This was becoming asinine. You couldn't sit down to a meal anymore without some stranger demanding you eat something disgusting or jump through an arbitrary hoop. At home with Luke, we always timed dinner before the good shows, and when you finished eating, you simply got up and watched them. And Nanny had TV trays at her house: you ate right in front of the set and didn't have to get up at all.

Well, I wouldn't participate in this pointless little charade. I felt confident that Jane would intervene if I showed the firmness I had maintained at the school lunch table. She had bristled at Luke when he so much as told me to stop turning the TV channels so fast. But now she said, "Go ahead, Honey. It's okay to say, 'May I be excused.'"

So now everyone presumed upon my good nature, even my own mother. I heard Lassie's theme music swelling behind me. The poignant, whistling melody borrowed from an Irish folk song seemed to call up all the pain of love betrayed, as only a dog could understand. Tears welled up and I fought to keep them back, sitting resolutely until the Lassie episode concluded. But even then Jay wouldn't let me go unless I uttered his hateful little phrase. I could throw a tantrum, cry and scream "I hate you" to both of them, but such drama would lose me my self-respect as sure as giving in would. And self-respect was all I had left.

But the grownups I'd been thrust among had worn me down. They had worked seemingly together for more than a week, timing the psychological blows for maximum effect. I held out for another half-hour; finally I mumbled, "Canabecused." Jane had been watching me anxiously the whole time; now she looked vastly relieved. Jay nodded from his paperback western, with no hint of triumph.

I walked slowly down the short hall. Trish and I slept in the bedroom; Jane and Jay shared a living room couch that converted to a bed. In the room I lay awake for a long time, playing with the electric blanket control and sinking a little deeper into the only truly private corner of the universe: the one between my ears. The third grade reader featuring the fiddling bee story hadn't included any Russian novelettes; if it had, I wouldn't have been much impressed. Tolstoy's Ivan Desonovitch had nothing on me.

CHAPTER TWELVE

~ Rehabilitating Drop Drills ~ Cafeteria Gourmet ~ Literary Discussion and Conflict
~ Bowling Pins and Rabbits Feet ~ Learning How to Lie ~ Interstate New Year

Popular media has reduced the fifties to cartoon images, and no modern film, feature article, or TV pop history of the era would feel complete unless it ridiculed the era's nuclear-preparedness "drop drills." I first experienced these much maligned training sessions at Callahan Street School. We'd be in reading group or doing arithmetic or block printing exercises, and Mrs. Washburn would say, "Drop!" in a loud, clear voice. This was our cue to immediately, with great kicking over of chairs and drumbeat of knees on hardwood, crawl under our desks and curl up, knees to chest, hands covering our necks.

The teachers took the drills seriously, but they didn't regale us with stories of annihilation and nuclear winter as became popular in subsequent generations. After a minute we'd get back up and return to our class work, feeling, if anything, refreshed by the change of pace. I also remember regular fire drills and extensive instruction on traffic and railroad track safety, but somehow, according to history from the sixties on, the school drop drill belonged in a ridiculous and/or terrifying class by itself.

When I became a teenager, I signed on to the progressive catechism that any attempt to survive nuclear attack amounted to useless nonsense, since everyone would be disintegrated and the whole planet devastated no matter what we did. But if one cares to do a little research, the picture was less bleak. Certainly, the kids at, say, Loma Portal school in San Diego — a mile from the juicy target of the Nuclear sub base at Point Loma — had something to worry about. When they assumed the drop position under their desks, they might as well, as the poster with mock instructions said in the sixties, "kiss their asses goodbye." It's also true that radiation would have made ground zeroes uninhabitable for many years to come, and a nuclear war would have killed several million citizens (in a total population of 179 million according to the 1960 census).

But in most of the country, including the mostly rural area around Callahan School, the immediate danger of even the mightiest nuclear blast on a military or large city target came down to imploding windows. Of course radiation sickness would claim more lives after the blast, but the first order of business was to survive the flying glass. Since stowing kids under desks with their faces covered put them in the best position to avoid that particular danger, the drills were arguably practical.

As for the supposed psyche scarring suffered by citizens of my era, my recollection is that most people took the Cold War with an equanimity seemingly unthinkable today. Current commentators jump to the conclusion that war anxiety left people in the fifties and early sixties psychically crippled. But by then, war had been an almost constant state for three generations, and we'd survived as a nation. Almost everyone's grandpa had served in World War I. Most of our fathers had fought in World War II. A few years later brought 37,000 more American casualties in Korea, and immediately after that we began fighting another war, a "cold war" so called. We figured Russia would probably sneak-attack us someday, as Japan had sneak-attacked Pearl Harbor. On TV we saw Khrushchev, the shoe-pounding Communist bully, declaring, "We will bury you."

But kids who noticed such things weren't brought to the highest pitch of anxiety or terror. We'd won all the previous wars and we'd win the next one somehow, H-bombs or no H-bombs. We had God on our side, apparently, as Bob Dylan would soon sarcastically put it. But the threat of nuclear war incapacitated few grownup psyches outside of Greenwich Village, as we will see later when I recount my experience with the Cuban Missile Crisis. Not to belabor a point, but the popular historical template is sometimes less than accurate. With their distorted focus on a few elements and artifacts of the fifties, most commentators at-distance haven't discerned, much less conveyed, the real gestalt of the decade.

At any rate, most students seemed to take the drop drills at Callahan School as another school regimen, like lining up after lunch to go back to the classroom. We also learned the pledge of allegiance through daily repetition and, through song rotation every day after the pledge, memorized the lyrics to "America the Beautiful," "My Country Tis of Thee," and "The Star Spangled Banner," which I sang without the faintest stirring of rebellion in my proto-hippie soul. Perhaps I liked old tunes more than most kids; in any case the songs from the thin music books we opened once or twice a week — "Ah, Lovely Meadows," "Take Me Out to the Ball Game," "Yellow Bird," "Dr. Iron Beard," "Sidewalks of New York," "John Henry," "White Choral Bells" and other classics — made more of an impression on me than Khrushchev the iconic villain.

Moving along to other under-discussed cultural phenomena, I began at Callahan to appreciate the distinctive lunch repasts offered daily. I attended a dozen more schools in Southern California in the next few years, and they all seemed to have the same recipes, probably dispatched from civil service dietitians in Sacramento for consumption by students from Crescent City to San Diego, from Catalina to Needles. Intellectual alarm at such mass planning probably brought on books like *The Organization Man*, but I have pleasant sensory memory of cubed turkey with gravy over thin mashed potatoes; of overcooked spaghetti with the sauce stirred in and cheese caked on top; fish deboned and reconstituted as "fish sticks"; soupy, lightly-spiced chili; hamburgers tenderized with grain filler and served on heavily buttered buns, and many more unique treats available no matter which school in California I found myself. True, cottage cheese sometimes marred the universal dining experience, but not every school insisted on the clean plate. In institutions that did insist, a weekly menu provided advance notice when the abomination made an appearance, whereupon I exercised the option of bringing a baloney sandwich and cookies from home and buying a five-cent milk carton from the window by the cafeteria.

Despite the turbulent beginning at Callahan, I soon settled in to my new environment. After-school care from the old lady babysitter lasted only a couple of hours per day. This modified arrangement did not include meals, so raw tomatoes ceased to be an issue. I also encountered no further trouble on the school playground. In class, I showed up every day, shouted "Aqui!" when Teacher took attendance ("Yo!" "Present!" and "Here!" were also acceptable answers, and after several drafts completed my clay handprint ashtray and put it in the long line for kiln firing. Though Jay and Jane lived close to the margin, they gave me two dollars for the official Callahan School sweatshirt when teachers and administration began shamelessly promoting that line of local apparel.

I made no close friends at Callahan, but at home in Van Nuys I fell in with several companionable boys my age. A tall first-grader whose name I've forgotten shared my interest in reading. One day the two of us discovered that in our different schools we were reading the same story in the same Dick and Jane book. These topical stories of an ideal suburban family are rarely praised as good literature today. One Amazon.com reviewer of a reprint collection wrote, "Dick and Jane books have no cohesive plots. They are just repetition." This same critic also wrote, "I doubt if Dick and Jane ever saw an African-American on their block or knew what a Buddhist was."

I suspect this reviewer may be also be retroactively concerned about the shadow of nuclear war on fifties children, but in any case, my tall friend and I somehow managed to enjoy the stories. I remember one late afternoon, the two of us standing on the corner, hands in pockets, hunched against the December wind as we earnestly discussed the latest episode:

"That was funny when Dick got the footprints all over the kitchen."

"Yeah! And when Sally made the train with the wagon and rode Spot and Puff around!"

"Yeah, that was funny!"

Unfortunately, as do many literary critics for reasons not always connected with literature, my tall friend and I had a falling out. One Saturday found me returning from the little store a few blocks away with my hands full. Celebrating my allowance raise to twenty cents a week, I had paid a dime for a blue rabbit's foot, bought a balsa wood airplane kit for eight cents, and spent the change on two Bazooka Joe bubble gums. I also carried a Mars Bar because, when I said I planned a trip to the store, Jay, who had been home more often lately, had given me an extra dime to pick one up for him.[16]

The tall kid had always seemed mature and reasonable before, but for some reason he now blocked my way on the sidewalk, playfully at first, then more aggressively. I felt frustration from the beginning—it's difficult to keep up one's end in a "playful" shoving match when one's hands are full. He escalated the frustration by grabbing at my rabbit's foot, which made me drop the airplane. Then he stepped on the plane.

As I heard the crunch, I dropped everything else and dived at him, knocking him to the ground. We wrestled on the grass near the

---

[16] Mars Bars were exotic concoctions featuring white nougat and nuts. At ten cents a bar, my age group considered them expensive adult fare.

building's rock-bordered walkway. In sudden inspiration I grabbed up one of the football-size decorative rocks with both hands and raised it over my head as if to smash it down on his face, meanwhile twisting my expression into a Richard Widmark, psycho-movie criminal leer.

My opponent immediately stopped struggling. He watched wide-eyed as I slowly lowered the rock closer and closer. Finally I touched it to his forehead; then relaxed my grip to let him feel some of the weight of it. Then I tossed it aside.

He lay as if paralyzed as I scrambled up, picked up my items, and walked off without looking back. Jay's Chrysler wasn't parked at the curb, which probably meant he'd gone to pick up Jane at work, taking Trish along. As I entered our place on the second floor, my feeling of dramatic psychological triumph in the recent battle gave way to consternation: I discovered that, in addition to the plane being cracked and covered with mud, the Mars Bar had also been smashed and dirtied in the scuffle.

I sat on the still-unfolded couch bed to weigh my options. I looked at the Mars wrapper clotted with grassy mud. One end had torn, exposing the candy. Jay probably wouldn't want to eat it. But would he be mad and want me to pay back the ten cents he'd given me? I slowly tore off the wrapper as I considered the best course of action. Meanwhile, I ate the Mars Bar. Chewing the last of it, I formulated a plan.

I betook myself back across the street and disposed of the candy wrapper in a dumpster behind a building. On the way back I saw a few previously unnoticed cars parked along the curb and I stopped to copy down the license numbers from their black-on-yellow California plates, using a pencil stub that fit in the spiral binding of my pocket notebook. All the boys on the block carried notebooks in emulation of TV detectives, and I had made my mark in law-enforcement with the neighborhood's longest list of licenses.

Jay had returned home when I came in. When he asked for his Mars Bar, I gave him a short version of the tall kid's perfidious attack and the ensuing fight, and then showed him the damaged airplane. I said the candy had been stomped into the mud and I'd already thrown it away across the street.

"That was fast. You didn't eat it?"

"No, it got all mashed up."

"You sure?"

I beamed wounded innocence. "It was all covered with dirt!"

"Okay. But open your mouth and let me see."

For all I knew, my teeth and tongue remained coated with chocolate and the game was up; but there seemed nothing to do but go through the motions and hope for the best.

Jay examined my mouth and seemed satisfied. Then he helped me fix the plane by carefully taping the cracked wing with a thin piece of scotch tape he cut with a grocery box opener. He said that in his youth, the balsa wood came in rectangles with the plane's outline traced on the wood. "We had to cut out all the pieces of the plane with an Exacto knife. You ever see an Exacto knife?"

I hadn't. I also had to ask his help again when I bought my next plane, for though I liked free form construction, mechanical instructions have never been my strong suit. But one thing did stay with me from the Mars Bar incident: one could avoid consequences by lying, remaining calm, and sticking to the lie even when all seemed lost. This knowledge would stunt my character growth over the years, but it seemed like a fine life tool at the time.

In addition to detective work, literary criticism, and street fighting, I participated with my Tiara Street peers in bowling pin collecting, a local craze made possible by a factory dedicated to the manufacture of these fascinating items which was conveniently located behind the apartments on the next block over. Bowling pins are usually perceived in groups and seen from afar, but up close they are individual gems — large wooden gems weighing several pounds each. On any given day a small pile of cosmetically-marred, factory-rejects would be piled on the tarmac right over the six-foot chain link fence separating factory Van Nuys from residential Van Nuys.

The bigger kids would climb the fence and hand over enough pins to share among us. Then, in the hard-packed dirt around the unobtrusive side of one comrade's apartment building, we'd set them up in official triangle formation. But since we couldn't talk any of the kids whose dads had bowling balls into borrowing, the displays were purely artistic.

As Christmas approached, each Callahan Street School class collected canned food for the poor, wrapping the cans in festive tissue paper. I had always assumed that if you worked in a food market, all merchandise would be free for the taking, and Jay seemed to think so, too. So, since we had a good supply of canned goods at home, I brought several to school. On the Friday before Christmas vacation,

Callahan held its Christmas assembly. The sixth graders enacted the manger scene, and we all put our cans for the poor around a big decorated tree in the auditorium. We sang "Rudolph the Red Nosed Reindeer," a Gene Autry song Jane had already taught me, and "Silent Night," a new one. Many Jewish families lived in the Valley, mostly immigrants from New York and the east coast, so we also sang

> *Oh Hanukah oh Hanukah, come light the menorah*
> *Let's have a party; we'll all dance the Hora.*

After the Christmas assembly, school dismissed for two weeks, and at first Jane said I didn't need to go back to old Mary's during vacation. Jane and Jay both remained home, too, though one or the other of them seemed to always be at the corner phone booth. The next Thursday we drove to Nanny's where, at Jay's suggestion, we began the family tradition of opening presents on Christmas Eve. This innovation saved parents from having to get up Christmas morning and gave kids a head start on playing with their new toys, a win-win. I had discarded my belief in Santa Claus by this time and had no objection to jettisoning outmoded tradition if it meant getting at those presents sooner.

Some of the other nonbelievers on Tiara Street were confident that their parents would bless them with new bikes for Christmas, and I mightily hoped to be among them. But when I asked about the possibility, Jane said, "We're pretty broke this year, Honey."

This seemed hard to believe when she and Jay presented me a card containing the vast sum of five dollars cash. Trish got some Tinker Toys, which I helped her play with, and both Trish and I also received our usual new shoes and slippers from Nanny. Later I saw Nanny give Jane some money I assumed was also a Christmas present.

We drove back to Van Nuys late, but I woke up early Christmas morning and roamed the neighborhood most of the day, trying out the new toys my friends had gotten and casually showing off my five-dollar bill. I held onto my riches for almost a week, during which time I spent a couple of days at Mary's after all. Jay and Jane drove us there late mornings; they seemed to be on some kind of vacation schedule, too.

Back home for the last afternoon of the year and the decade, I became bored at having to read lips on the TV while Jane vacuumed. I decided to go to the store and finally break my five-dollar bill (or "fin," as Jay called it). In California's early winter twilight I returned with my purchases — a green rabbit's foot, a Milky Way bar, and a Dr. Pepper. The street was deserted but I could hear the hiss of cars up on Van Nuys Boulevard. Walking slowly, I contemplated the mystery of time. When I returned to Mrs. Washburn's class next week, I'd be writing 1960 on my papers instead of 1959. Did the measured pace of hours ever stop or go any faster? Could someone in real life break the time barrier, like Superman, to go forward or backward at will?

Coming out of these deep meditations, I found myself in front of our building, where I noticed the smallest enclosed U-Haul trailer I'd ever seen. It had an Arizona license plate I hadn't yet chronicled in my detective work, so I took down number by the light of a streetlamp. When I opened our front door, I saw our living room full of cardboard boxes, and Jay and Jane busy filling them. I strolled to the window and looked out. Sure enough, the trailer with the Arizona plates attached to Jay's 1954 Chrysler. We were moving. No more Tiara street. No more Callahan. It seemed odd that they hadn't mentioned their relocation plans, but as I would learn in subsequent evasions, a family had to maintain security when dodging potential hazards such as overdue rent, unpaid babysitters, and ex-wives or husbands.

Jane said with a bright smile that we would be taking a long drive through the desert. "You remember the desert, don't you, honey?"

"Are we going back to Alabama?"

Jay hefted a large box, pushing it up with his knee. "Not a chance, pal. One of those "way-ell shut mah mouth" accents is plenty for me." He grinned at Jane, then back at me. "Here, you want to follow me with one of those little boxes?"

"Okay. Are we going to see those big cactuses full of water?"

"Probably. Come on, I'll show you how to pack a load."

And so around two a.m. in the first hours of the nineteen-sixties, we crossed the Nevada state line, leaving behind a memorable decade as well as everything else that wouldn't fit in a small trailer, including my bowling pin collection.

PART II: 1960

Las Vegas, San Pedro Again, Burbank, Central L.A., East L.A.

Vegas

Langston Siblings October 1960

Wyvernwood Apartments

CHAPTER THIRTEEN

~ Oscar Nails It ~Primordial Vegas ~ The Old Soul
~ Valentines Under Construction ~ Regrouping

According to Oscar Wilde, "The mystery of love is greater than the mystery of death." I tend to concur with Oscar, especially when I consider Jane and Jay's early months together. The events of that period provided many opportunities to observe the enigmatic chemistry of attraction as it meets the prosaic world.

Of course my access and insight were limited then, but over many years and conversations, I pieced together the background to our Las Vegas evasion. The tentative plan began to shape itself about two weeks after Jay and Jane secured the Van Nuys apartment and found jobs in Sepulveda. Jay had had an altercation with the new store manager and resigned on the spot. He made it a point of pride throughout his life to suffer no highhandedness from an employer, or anyone else for that matter, and his resignation explained why I had noticed him around the apartment so much in the weeks before we left town.

Jane continued to work at the store, not the last time she would be employed when Jay was not. A week or so before we left, she happened to be in the break room when a small but fierce-looking Mexican woman stormed into the manager's office. Through the open door, Jane could hear the woman shouting, "Where's Jay Hill? WHERE'S MY HUSBAND?"

"It's a damn good thing you weren't around," Jane told Jay when she returned home afterward, "And that the boss didn't point me out as your new girlfriend."

"Why, Bubbles?" Jay asked, lighting a cigarette with his silver Zippo. "Were you scared?"

"Scared I'd have to snatch her bald-headed."

Behind her bluster, Jane felt profoundly embarrassed. Further embarrassment lay in store. When she followed her report with some pointed questions, Jay revealed he had not been divorced as he'd told her when they met. Neither was he separated and seeking a divorce as he'd amended the story later. Actually, he'd left his wife and children on the same day Jane had left Luke, also without discussing it beforehand.

Jane had also recently discovered Jay had never been an Arthur Murray dance instructor as he'd claimed; in fact, he could barely dance at all. Other disappointing revelations probably surfaced during the post-honeymoon period, but the most important concern, and another catalyst for the move, involved finances. They'd managed to scrape enough to rent the furnished apartment back in mid-November, but most of their weekly paychecks after living expenses had gone for repairs to Jay's aging Chrysler, the weekly TV payments, and food he couldn't make off with at the store. They'd paid the old babysitter regularly until the last week, but now owed her $30. Also on the debit side, the rent had come due on December 15 and the excitable landlord had visited twice since then, demanding immediate payment.

After discussing their options, Jane and Jay decided the solution for these difficulties would be immediate relocation to Las Vegas. Vegas happened to be much in the public eye around then: Howard Hughes investing lavishly in casinos, Frank Sinatra playing the Sands regularly, and a spectacular murder case filling the headlines. But the most compelling reason for the move might have been that in that up-and-coming town they could both secure quick divorces, then get married after six weeks' residence. Meanwhile, they would get jobs and settle in the area, safe from (1) all their creditors (2) Luke, who continued to call Nanny regularly, and (3) Jay's ex-wife, whom, he assured Jane, would not easily give up on finding him.

So off we sallied on New Year's Eve, all our possessions in the small U-Haul trailer with Arizona plates. Trish and I were asleep when they finished packing; Jay carried her, and Jane led me in my pajamas to the car. I woke up to the New Year's Day sun rising over the desert. By sundown we had established Vegas residency in an ancient, one-bedroom over-under duplex on a dirt lot. Almost immediately I discovered the most interesting feature of the place in its detached laundry room. Over a rusty sink perched the first electric clothes wringer I'd ever seen, a working antique from the thirties or earlier.

Jane remembered this contraption from her childhood. The next day she demonstrated how to take each item from the washer and feed it through the wringer, a process designed to squeeze out a prodigious amount of water and cut clothesline-drying time by half or better.

The device was the 1920 timesaving equivalent of the microwave oven, but it could be dangerous. With labor-saving tools like electric wringers, electric fans with no screens, and electric heaters with no grills, the emergency rooms and children's hospitals earlier in the century must have done a good business. A few days after we arrived, Jane put her fingers too close to the roller and ran her hand through it. She then calmly hit the reverse button and ran it through again backwards to free herself. The hand remained unusable for a week, and Jay made a sling for her to wear. Despite the pain, Jane treated the whole incident as a joke, and except for one tense moment toward the end, I don't remember her being anything but cheerful during the whole Las Vegas period.

Vegas itself seemed, despite all the optimistic reports, decidedly uncheerful. Throughout January a bitterly cold wind brought clouds of choking dust. Huge tumbleweeds blew across desolate empty lots, and I saw ice in the gutters on the two-mile walk to the elementary school, the walk made necessary because the school implemented no bus service. Occasionally Jane would drive, but Jay would walk me most mornings to save gas.

The part of downtown Las Vegas I saw in the daytime seemed like any dusty little burg in Texas or New Mexico we'd seen on our trip from Alabama, except for the slot machines in grocery stores and gas stations (penny, nickel, and dime slots predominated, with a few quarter units for the high rollers). But the town was definitely growing, for the school ran double sessions with forty to a classroom in each session. I attended the morning first-grade class, eight to noon, with a fifteen-minute recess at 9:30 and no lunch period. The teachers were allowed an hour off, and then taught the afternoon session from one to five.

Recess took place in a gravel area about half the size of Park Western or Callahan's playgrounds, so crowded I found it impossible to run without crashing into someone. The few balls available didn't bounce well on gravel. Playground equipment included a swing set, some tetherball poles, and one of those industrial steel, push-power merry-go-rounds responsible for an alarming number of gravel-scraped hands, elbows, and faces as kids were flung outward by centrifugal force or tripped and dragged under while attempting to push the thing. We were not allowed to stay in the classroom or hallway during breaks, so I spent most recesses in the doorway, trying to keep out of the cold wind. Holding my position presented a challenge, since the one rule of the building seemed to be "Keep the door clear!"

The classroom featured a triple row of long tables, each furnished with workbooks for block printing, lined paper, blank drawing paper, pencils, and crayons. We didn't do the pledge of allegiance or sing any songs, and Teacher held few if any whole-class teaching sessions. She would meet with reading groups for twenty minute intervals. Apparently she had conducted some reading instruction before Christmas, but now the sessions consisted of reading book passages as a group, followed by individual turns at reading out loud. Teacher would correct any mistakes, order the mistake-maker to pronounce the word again three times, and then proceed with the reading. She looked at her wristwatch often.

On my first day in group as a new kid, I took my turn and read my assigned paragraph with no mistakes. As a result, I had no further reading interaction with the teacher during my time at the Vegas school, a relief to both of us. In her short breaks between groups, she would come around to check our printing workbooks. Here I did attract her attention: she instructed me to make my letters larger so they would match the size of the workbook examples. She admonished me about this more than once and never seemed to remember that she'd done so already. I continued to judge the examples as ridiculously large — no grownup printed letters that size.

When not participating in our reading groups, we were required to stay in our assigned chair at our designated table, but as long as we remained seated we could do anything reasonably productive and even talk quietly. So I spent around three hours a day chatting with — actually, mostly listening to — the two girls across the table. While socializing, I also worked on my drawings of a house, or more precisely dozens of studies of the same house. I would first draw a three-dimensional box, a skill I had recently acquired at Callahan. Then I'd add a peaked roof, a chimney, a door, two windows, and a walkway. These features were standard on every house I produced, always in the same proportions. I would then accessorize the houses with snowmen, flowers, bare or leafed-out trees, and other icons of the seasons. It wasn't that I couldn't draw other things (I had been drawing Superman for years); I had simply entered the House period of my artistic career. Interestingly, this phase synchronized with pop art currently in vogue — Andy Warhol's silk screen subjects also repeated obsessively in varied colors.

The winter weather rarely allowed outside play, so during afternoons and weekends, two or three neighborhood kids about my age gathered at Marshall's house. Marshall, a short, slight, sad-eyed boy old enough for second grade, had never attended school. His mother taught him at home, but she welcomed neighborhood playmates. Marshall could write and draw well, on reflection no surprise since his mom could give him more instruction in an hour than the local school kids received in a month. She spoke forthrightly about Marshall's special needs and proscriptions. "Marshall is a hemophiliac, that's HE-mo-FEEL-ee-ack. It means he can't bump around with you because he starts bleeding easily and doesn't stop bleeding once he starts."

I understood her concern and offered a solution. "If you put a Band-Aid on him, the blood will go away." I showed her the scar on my forehead as proof.

She assured me that in Marshall's case the blood would keep coming. Marshall also suffered allergies to almost everything: cats, dogs, rubber, plastic, dust, milk, meat, and wheat. His mom fed him all sorts of odd concoctions, and I tasted my first vegetarian sausage at his house. It didn't make a good first impression.

Marshall weighed only forty pounds, so I felt downright burly at fifty-three when his mother weighed us all on the doctor's scale she stood her son on every day. Despite Marshall's small size and various limitations, all the kids liked him. He owned an erector set and other interesting toys, and one afternoon he taught me checkers. Marshall never showed anger or irritation, even when he lost a game. With his faraway eyes and quiet smile, he might have been deemed an "old soul," if anyone had so described anyone in those days.

As Valentine's Day approached, most of the kids began to bring dime-store valentine cards to school, the kind featuring sayings like "Bee my valentine" illustrated with a cartoon bee. These cards came in packs, with small envelopes included. In order to collect Valentines, each of us made a suitably decorated manila folder (mine featured my standard house with hearts growing on the lawn), and Teacher showed us how to staple the sides to make a pouch. We thumb-tacked our pouches to the bulletin board by the coat racks, and the cards began to accumulate.

I knew funds were low at home because neither Jay nor Jane had a job or seemed to leave the house much lately. Something happened to Jay's car, and he spent a couple of days underneath it, lying in the icy gravel in his oldest white shirt and slacks. The money Nanny had given them ran out, and they eked a few dollars from a pawn shop downtown, first with their wedding rings, then with items of more dubious value. But despite our obvious poverty, I didn't want to be the only kid who didn't bring Valentine cards to school. When I asked Jane about the possibility on the day before the holiday, she looked grim and said we'd see.

After our pork and beans and canned spinach dinner, I asked if I could be excused and started playing marbles on the floor. I'd been an avid television fan all my life, but the house got poor TV reception, so I'd gotten out of the habit even before the rental TV they'd brought from Van Nuys followed the rings to the pawn shop along with their electric blanket and suitcases. Jay pulled his shoeshine box from under the bed. It had a wooden foot on top to step on, like at a real shoeshine stand. Inside were brushes and several kinds of shoe polish with the kiwi bird logo on them. Jay started working on his black slip-ons, and, when I showed interest, he gave me a lesson on how to use the brush. I heard the expression "elbow grease" for the first time while he explained the necessity of brushing the backs of shoes carefully. Some people, he averred, always look at the back of your shoes to see if you have class. "Guys with class," he said, "pay as much attention to the backs of their shoes as they do to the front."

When the mood seemed right, I asked him if I could get some Valentines. He lit a cigarette and glanced over at Jane, who sat at the table reading a paperback science fiction book she'd brought from Van Nuys and read twice already.

"Well, Charlie," Jay said, "we're pretty broke right now."

Jane put down the book and looked pointedly at Jay. "Ricky's still wearing the same school clothes I bought last year, and he's getting too big for them."

Jay grinned at her. "Well, he's eating enough for a grown man."

"Uh-huh. Pork and beans and canned vegetables."

The canned goods came from the cases Jay had brought home from work back in Van Nuys — the same stock that supplied the Christmas-wrapped cans I'd brought to school for poor people. As I sat there contemplating our own poverty, the irony wasn't lost on me.

Then I had an idea. "I can use my Christmas money for the Valentines. I got four dollars left." Besides buying a twenty-five cent pack of cats-eye boulder marbles when we first arrived, I hadn't spent any money since the last night in Van Nuys.

"We may have to borrow some money from you, pal," said Jay, with a serious look. Somehow the look conveyed that if I consented to the loan (somehow the necessity of my consent was implied), I would be instrumental in our survival.

I didn't know what to say. Jay looked at me closely. "Listen," he said, "do you have to have cards for all the girls, or is there one real special one?"

"Uh, just one, I guess." Convention called for exchanging cards with all classmates, but I cared only for Star, the girl who sat directly across from me at the classroom table. She garnished her long, light brown hair with spitcurls at the ears, and her face reminded me of Alice Cramden, TV wife of Jackie Gleason on the *Honeymooners*. As best I can remember, Star was the first girl who interested me in any sort of romantic way.

"Okay, we'll make her a nice card." Jay stabbed out his cigarette. "She'll like it; trust me." I felt embarrassed by admitting I liked a girl, but Jay seemed to be taking it in stride in this one-man-of-the-world-to-another exchange. He pulled out a big envelope full of art pens, T-square, and ruler from when he had done the print ads for one of the stores. Jane found the scissors and dug up some white paper and a red flyer for a real estate company printed only on one side. In the next half-hour, Jay created a card resplendent with hearts, rococo lettering and other artistic trimmings. It looked fine enough to overcome my natural child tendency to want the cheap, packaged Valentines that conformed to what everyone else in class had been handing out. Then I remembered another detail I absolutely must conform to. "I need a envelope," I said. "We're supposed to put the cards in envelopes."

Jay smiled. "No sweat, Charlie." And he proceeded to make a perfectly serviceable envelope from a blank sheet of paper, skillfully cutting, folding and pasting it as if he made hand-crafted envelopes for a living.

The final product turned out bigger than the cards the other kids gave, but the next morning, pride overcame apprehension when I put it in Star's valentine pouch. She was too shy to comment, and I too shy to ask how she liked it, but I did catch her giving me quizzical but not disapproving looks across the table.

The above scene took place on Friday. Saturday night I came home from some kind of funny-tasting soup for dinner at Marshall's, where I had an open invitation. You never could tell what you'd find on your plate there, but I had grown tired of pork and beans and was usually willing to take a chance. Jay's car, which he'd gotten running again, backed up close to the front door. I entered the house to find boxes packed all over our living room.

"We're going back to California!" Jane said brightly. But she looked like she'd either been crying or would begin to do so soon.

I began to gather my treasures, but first I glanced through the valentines I'd brought home. In upper elementary grades I would see scrawls of "Your Friend," "I.L.B.C.N.U.," "D-liver D-letter, D-Sooner D-Better" and more), but in first grade most kids simply printed their names in block printing under "Bee my Valentine." I looked at the one that said "Star" for a few seconds, then threw them all in the wastebasket and started packing my cigar box.

Then I stopped. I felt no great fondness for Las Vegas—it had never seemed anything like home to me—but I didn't feel up to moving again. I had a mild headache, probably from the cold and dust, and it struck me that if I were sick, we wouldn't be able to go. I called Jane in and exaggerated the headache considerably. She looked worried and consulted with Jay. He felt my forehead and said I did seem to have a temperature, always the gold standard for him in questions of illness. After counting change in the doorway, he left the house. I felt a twinge of guilt mixed with excitement—my plan seemed to be working. Jay returned with a small tin of Bufferin and gave me two tablets. Then he and Jane left off packing and sat down to have a cigarette. I could hear them murmuring in the living room and thought I heard the word "doctor."

Sometime later, Jane came to my bedside. "How's your headache, now, Honey?"

"It's okay." It now seemed likely that if I continued my charade, they would drive me to the doctor. But what good would a doctor do? I knew they cost money, and nobody had any except me.

Come to think of it, I was ready to go. I assumed we'd be staying with Nanny and John for a while, as we did when we moved from Alabama. I could play in the big back yard, look up my friends, and go to the little store.

We left Vegas after dark, this time with no U-Haul trailer, only Jay's old Chrysler stuffed tight with boxes. When we stopped at a gas station outside the Vegas city limits, Jane borrowed my four dollars, almost enough to fill the tank. I stayed up pretty late, watching Joshua trees, power poles, and tumbleweed bushes go by in the moonlight before I fell asleep again. We crossed into California on the early morning of Valentine's Day—Jay seemed to have a penchant for skipping town on holiday eves.

It is lost to history whether Jay and Jane carried out particular arrival plans they made ahead of time, or if whatever plans they had made were abruptly changed after an argument on the road. In any case, they weren't talking much when we arrived at Nanny's in the early morning. In the kitchen, Nanny stood by nervously as Jane heated Trish's bottle. Jay unloaded most of the boxes into the middle of the living room floor, then drove away. I was out back, sitting in the lower branches of Nanny's fig tree, and didn't see his departure.

Nanny gave me a half-dollar later that afternoon, and I sought my friends, the brothers with the white granny. Their mom said they were visiting relatives down south, but I found the little store they had introduced me to. I purchased a Dr. Pepper, a Superman comic book, and several candy bars and strolled down Kenwood Avenue, enjoying the comparatively balmy weather. People seemed to be out and about, but I didn't see a single other white person except the eighty-year-old lady who lived next door. I spent the evening watching wrestling and roller derby on Channel 5. At bedtime, Jane tucked me in on the trundle bed in the living room. Jay had not returned, nor did he appear for breakfast the next morning. Once again I enjoyed the luxury of eating all my meals in front of the TV with John and Nanny. Jane didn't join us for lunch or dinner; she stayed on the phone in Nanny's room most of the day.

That evening the doorbell rang and Jane moved quickly to answer it. As I walked up behind her, I heard a familiar voice. There, framed in the doorway and looking thinner than I'd last seen him, with a little more uncertainty in his handsome smile, stood Luke Langston. After playing briefly with baby Trish, Luke began loading the boxes from the living room floor into his car. By midnight we were back in the apartment in San Pedro.

CHAPTER FOURTEEN

~ Dawn of the Sixties ~ A Brief Interlude of You Can't Go Home Again
~ Ping Pong to Burbank ~ Banana Splits and Apricots

A few years ago one of my son's professors at UC Berkeley told the class about the Sixties. The whole cultural history of the decade, he declared, could be found in Beatles songs, specifically from their *Revolver* album forward. That prof is probably around my age, and he agrees with most scholarly pop culture in thinking the Sixties actually began after mid-decade. But a closer look at the slow, inexorable buildup of my generation's pre-adolescence in the early sixties reveals 1960–65 as perhaps even more interesting than the more flamboyant second half.

In any case, the sixties began inauspiciously for me. At the end of February, Jane, Trish and I had returned to San Pedro for an episode of my childhood so murky I'm not even certain how long it lasted. When I asked Jane about that period a few years ago, she recalled less than I did. I attempted to jog her memory with the story of leaving Vegas with Jay and moving back in with Luke.

"We landed back at Channel Heights," I prompted. "With Luke. And I went back to the same school. How long were we there?"

"I'm not sure. It was short."

This exchange illustrates how the process of researching history from oral accounts is a game of win some, lose some. But it seems reasonable to assume Jane's story to Luke about her whereabouts and activities since she'd left him didn't include another man and six weeks in Vegas. I didn't volunteer any information about Jay, either, and apparently little sister Trish, who had begun to talk nonstop by then, didn't make any embarrassing pronouncements. To Luke's credit, he didn't interrogate or otherwise try to pump either of us. In fact, I don't remember talking to him much at all. He seemed somehow even less there than he had been before.

I was not feeling altogether there, myself. After two major moves in only four months, I had returned to the Channel Heights neighborhood where I'd felt more at home than any place in my life. But now it seemed as if I'd gone back to a parallel universe, though I hadn't heard that term as yet. Turnover in those apartments always ran high; now the booming economy allowed many working families to upgrade to the tract house developments springing up in all over L.A. Several friends (including Bear) had moved between school terms. The kids I had known before saw me as some variety of Rip Van Winkle, for I had become hopelessly out of step with the latest cliques and pastimes. No one cared for bowling pins around here or seemed impressed that I had collected them. Zorro cards had disappeared from the gum machine. In the dusk of early evenings, kids played street baseball instead of hide-and-go-seek.

The feeling of disorientation continued when Jane took me back to Park Western Elementary. Escalating enrollment had thrown the school's administration into mindless bureaucracy mode. Instead of placing me back in Mrs. Hedgecock's room as would have been both humane and logical, the officials shuffled me across campus to a hastily-constituted first grade class made up of new kids and behavioral problems culled from other classes. The teacher, who looked like she had been a veteran educator when Mrs. Hedgecock was still a schoolgirl, must have been coaxed out of retirement.

Any six-year-old could see that the old lady should have stayed home. I don't remember her providing instruction beyond some vague life lessons delivered in rushed recitation: "…And so boys and girls Mary found out from her experience with the little Scotty dog that it is always proper to tell the truth and nice little girls should always respect their parents and never tell a lie because once you tell a lie you have to tell another one and pretty soon …"

The dispenser of this wisdom was one of those thin, birdlike ancients who talked without stopping for breath when nervous, and she always seemed to be nervous. When the class became fidgety, she kept us in our seats with no reading group breaks, nap time, or drawing paper. We were supposed to remain quiet while she rattled on, but of course whispering and horseplay broke out regularly. A cycle of whining and scolding would follow, and tension rose swiftly.

As noted, students with behavior problems made up a substantial portion of our class population, but in those days a behavior problem meant someone who couldn't sit still, or scuffled at recess. Kids in every class committed all sorts of surreptitious infractions, but I had never seen anything even approaching open defiance until the old teacher pushed a kid named Raymond too far.

It happened at least three weeks after I'd been assigned to the old lady's classroom. Most of us were sitting numbly as she prattled. From a million miles inside the private realm of my brain, I detected her voice rising, so I returned to the surface to investigate. I remember the time was 9:50, because I had recently mastered the art of clock reading. I'd missed out on formal time-telling lessons in the shuffle from school to school, and as I began reading clocks on my own, I latched on and held stubbornly to the idea that if both hands on the twelve meant twelve o'clock, then both hands on the three had to be three o'clock, and so forth. Until I noticed my TV shows followed the other way, no one could convince me that my more logical configuration wasn't the best method. Now as I came out of my trance, I looked at the classroom clock with some resentment. Both hands on the ten meant ten minutes longer until lunchtime than it would have been under my system.

But here was something diverting: the old teacher standing over Raymond's seat, clutching his arm in her stringy claw. He squirmed as she berated him about leaving class to go to the bathroom. All the emphasis missing from her usual monologues now came out in force: "You KNOW better, young man! You MUST not leave your seat unless you raise your HAND and receive EXPLICIT permission!"

Raymond obviously belonged to the advanced group of problem children. It wasn't his grown-out butch haircut, his old cuffed jeans and worn hightop tennis shoes; those were standard fashion for the majority of students at Park Western. But Raymond also had ringworm splotches on his face and severely crooked teeth, and he always seemed to be hunched over like a cross between a hooligan in a cheap film noir and a street mutt who'd been kicked once too often.

Suddenly he jerked violently and broke free. The old lady stepped back as if he'd struck her; then she lunged forward to grab him again. He dodged and stood up, then ran to the far end of the room.

"Young man! You come back to your seat! Raymond, instantly return to your seat!"

He didn't move except to back up slowly. Through gritted teeth, with a crazed look of a lifer who's just killed a prison guard, he shouted "NO!"

Blatant disobedience! None of us, probably including the old teacher, had ever beheld anything like this. She began to totter toward him and he sprinted to another corner of the room, where he turned, breathing heavily, to face her. We were all wide awake now; watching intently. The old lady was a posse in a TV western moving in on a cornered criminal. Would he go down in a hail of bullets or jump off the roof of the saloon?

Suddenly the old lady turned and scurried from the classroom. If possible, her exit shocked us even more than Raymond's actions. She had deserted her post! No teacher in the room at all! Raymond watched her go and shifted uneasily on his feet. Then he moved uncertainly toward the windows. We all knew something bad was about to happen.

Within two minutes the old lady came back, followed by the only male instructor in the school. Tall, husky, fiftyish, this teacher had the walk and steely eye of a combat Marine sergeant in a war comic book. Planting himself inside the doorway to block the only exit, he glared at Raymond. "All right, Mister! March yourself over here!"

Raymond didn't move.

"NOW!"

The lip with the chronic cold sore began to tremble as Raymond's head drooped. Then he raised it and met the irate adult glare. "NO!"

Now, Raymond had been only two years old when *Rebel Without a Cause* debuted in theatres. The film hadn't made the late show yet, so he couldn't have copied from James Dean the existential angst, the deep-psychological-wound, the creature-driven-past-all-endurance-but-still-defiant anguish he managed to get into that "NO!" Yet in one word he matched all the agony of Dean's "You're tearing me apart!" speech. Ten or twelve years later when I finally saw the film, I remembered Raymond.

In a few quick strides the teacher closed in and collared the boy—literally jerking him to his tiptoes by his shirt collar. Then he grabbed both of Raymond's shoulders and shook him until the boy's neck seemed likely to snap off, shouting, "What do you MEAN, disobeying your teacher! You are a DISGRACE to this class! You are a DISGRACE to Park Western School! SIT DOWN!"

He pushed Raymond into an empty chair and continued to roar at him in front of the whole class—"JUST WHO DO YOU THINK YOU ARE!? STAND UP!!" The big man jerked the little boy back to his feet, bent down to snarl in his face. Then shoved him back onto the chair. Raymond, all the fight out of him, suddenly went limp and broke into choking sobs.

The teacher's performance may have been calculated, but his rage seemed genuine to the other students as we sat there like rubbernecks at a train wreck. Who would he turn on next? Finally he dragged Raymond roughly from the room. According to the old teacher, who monologued on the topic the rest of the day, he would spend the rest of the afternoon in the principal's office and be suspended from school—or more probably expelled.

My general outlook on education changed that day. Like many youngsters, I began to see school as a prison, the teachers as guards, the principal as the warden. I sympathized with all troublemakers and rebels, and reveled in any disruption of normal school business. Thus are outlaws and their fellow travelers initiated.

I don't know if Raymond ever came back, because within days I was gone myself. Luke and Jane's second honeymoon reunion hadn't turned out so well. I didn't find out until much later, but Jane was pregnant, most likely with Jay's baby. She had convinced Luke that he had fathered the child, giving him some variation of the classic: "As soon as I found out, I realized I really loved you and came back!"

But the timing was dicey. The absolute latest Jane could have become a mother-to-be with Luke would have been early November, timing that would put the latest normal delivery date around the first of August. But since the new arrival could take place as late as November if the baby were Jay's offspring, some sticky questions might lie ahead.

Always the bold opportunist, Jane kept improvising, taking things a day at a time, meanwhile holding Luke at arm's length when he sought to resume normal marital relations. Naturally, such a situation couldn't last. No longer than a few weeks after Luke brought us back to Channel Heights, we washed away from San Pedro in yet another tide of grownup drama. Luke left for work as usual one morning, and when he came home, he had become a bachelor once more.

My recollection is likewise foggy on details of the evasion, much more so than about anything else in this chronicle. But it's a good bet Nanny and Fran Faye once again facilitated. I have a dim recollection of Trish and me with the old lady babysitter (who would have seemed like an ingénue after the old lady teacher) for a few days. In any case, we soon rejoined Jay.

It will take several chapters to sketch a bare outline of what an enigmatic fellow Jay was. He had been blessed with charisma and intelligence, a combination that usually spells success—but only when those so-gifted actually follow through. In Las Vegas, we experienced what happens when they don't. Jay had jettisoned his family and a couple of jobs to win Jane; he'd put everything in motion for the divorces, marriage, and resettlement; he'd launched a complex plan, and arranged everything to insure the venture's success. Then he froze up and did absolutely nothing. He quit working and went starving broke, to the point where Jane actually had to leave him to feed her kids.

A clue to the enigma may be that psychologists today would classify Jay as an Adult Child of Alcoholics. Those who fit this profile often carry much negative emotional baggage from their unstable childhoods. According to the experts on the syndrome, its common symptoms are impulsive behavior, fear of failure, fear of success, problems with authority, mood swings, depression, and general emotional instability.

In any case, Jay always seemed to need a jolt of reality before he could begin to pick up any pieces he'd scattered. Jane's exit finally broke the spell. Back in effective-person mode, it took him only a short time to find a job. He saved his money for a couple of weeks, secured a loan from the Local 770 credit union, paid a month's rent on a furnished house in Burbank, and got back in touch with Jane. Naturally (for she was an Adult Child of Alcoholics herself) she decided to give him another chance, and Luke once again found himself in the dust heap of history.

The first morning after Jay and Jane reunited fell on a Saturday. I ran about in the overgrown back yard of the big house, trying out a new ball and bat Jay had brought me from work. He came out dressed in the skilled-worker, day-off uniform of the fifties and sixties: short sleeved white shirt open at the neck with crew-neck tee shirt underneath, older suit pants, white socks, and well-seasoned slip-on shoes. His day-off slip-ons always had a small hole punched over the little toe of the right foot because the toe splayed crookedly and rubbed painfully when he wore regular shoes. He said he had broken the toe in his youth jumping off a garage roof while emulating Superman.

He began to pitch me slow ones, squinting into the morning sun, cigarette in the corner of his mouth. While we played ball, Jane drove off with Trish to pick up more of our belongings from Nanny's. We were tired of the game before they returned.

"Wanna go for a walk, pal?" Jay offered.

"Okay."

We ambled up our street, turned left, and headed for uptown Burbank. Only six or eight weeks before, he had walked me to school in the bitter wind and frozen rain of Vegas, but it seemed we had leapfrogged to summer. We strolled about eight blocks, enjoying the lack of cold wind and tumbleweeds. The apricot and plum trees in almost every yard we passed had leafed out and set fruit. Burbank and Glendale were still garden spots then, in slow transition from an area of world-renowned salubrious climate to the smog-alert-daily pit it would become by the end of the sixties.

Our destination turned out to be a studio apartment he'd rented by the week while gearing up to win back Jane. A Spartan place, it featured a Murphy bed, something I'd only seen in a Laurel and Hardy movie. Paperback books and men's magazines (*Stag*, *Man's World*, etc.) all with brilliantly lurid covers, scattered among empty cigarette packs, candy wrappers, and paper cups. Jay began to pack shirts, ties, and his shoeshine equipment in a cardboard box, meanwhile making more conversation than usual.

With his contagious smile and jokes pitched right at my level, and especially his knack for making me feel like another adult, I couldn't help but warm to him again. Somewhere in the course of the packing, he gave me the rules, man to man, on wearing white socks: "Never with a suit or after dark, and never at a job interview. Everybody'll think you're a farmer. And no farmer knots—always tie a Windsor." While the advice may have been a tad premature, I appreciated his thoughtfulness. We had made a good start in take-two of our stepfather/son relationship.

The next Monday I enrolled in Franklin Elementary School, six blocks away and right over the Glendale border. Built around the turn of the century, Franklin had roomy, high-ceilinged classrooms, inside hallways, and huge trees on the playground. The teacher, a tall, slightly stooped woman, reminded me of Bert in looks if not temperament. She enthused about our newest states, Alaska and Hawaii, and communicated a real sense of the country expanding, getting bigger and better all the time. Though I hadn't experienced much in the way of learning for a while, I managed to catch up with the class within a few weeks, and the kids seemed nicer here, or at least more relaxed.

A barber shop operated across the street from the school, and in my second week at Franklin, Jay gave me money for the final haircut I endured without protest for many years. "Regular boys' cut" I ordered, with what I hoped sounded like man-about-town firmness. On the way home I passed a soda shop where one could sit at a counter and order a banana split, like in the Andy Hardy movies, or pick from a wide array of candy. Unlike most children I know now, I liked the taste of fruit almost as much as I liked candy, so Burbank proved to be a fine town for a sweet tooth. When my allowance ran out, I could always climb in any of dozens of apricot or plum trees in the immediate neighborhood and gorge myself for free. As a general rule, homeowners tolerated kids in their trees, just as most of them tolerated birds and squirrels.

Overall, Burbank in 1960 provided a fine place and time to be a child, but the area wasn't absolutely safe, wholesome, and fruit-tree centered. Only a few days after we moved in I managed in one day (with some outside coaching) to do more malicious damage, commit more outright crimes, and face more danger than I had in my life up to that point.

CHAPTER FIFTEEN

*~ The Outlaw ~ Trial by Ordeal ~ Windows, Forts, and Free Drinks
~ Bussing ~ Just Around*

My crime spree began the second Saturday after we moved to Burbank. While exploring an apartment construction site on our block, I saw a boy about my age standing in the framework of the second story. He noticed me and clambered down. "Hey," he said. "I'm Andy. I'm in third at Saint Mary's." Small for his eight years, Andy wore a flat-top and had dimples in both cheeks, like an all-American-boy advertisement in a Sears ad. I felt encouraged that a third-grader would talk to me and confessed myself a mere first-grader at Franklin.

"Yeah, I know. Watch this." In those days off-duty construction workers simply left everything on the job when they quit for the weekend. Andy grabbed a large, commercial grade lawn roller and showed me how he could squash snails with it. Then he dug an odd-looking key from his pocket and demonstrated how he could open the porta-potty toilet paper dispenser. Next he spread the tissues on the ground and, producing a book of paper matches with a restaurant logo on the cover, lit a small fire. I looked around nervously, but appreciated his expertise, having burned myself once while experimenting with those hard-to-manage paper matches.

Fire is somehow more fascinating when grown-ups aren't around. For a minute we both stared at the small blaze, then Andy stomped it out and said, "C'mon. I'll show you something." His smile seemed both friendly and challenging.

"Okay." I hurried to catch up as he set off at a fast walk. We made a few turns before coming to the end of a dead-end street sealed off by a chain link fence. I had never understood the supposed deterrent of chain-link fences; they seem to be made for climbing. I followed

Andy over this one and jumped to the ground from halfway down the other side like he did; only I didn't stay on my feet when I landed.

Andy helped me up and we stood on the edge of one of the cemented-in riverbeds crisscrossing L.A., each one locally known as "the wash." During heavy rains the washes fill up, and all city kids are under strict parental orders not to go near them. Now only a thin trickle of water in the middle of the concrete, surrounded by a larger stripe of green slime, marked the man-made waterway.

I looked down at the sheer drop of about thirty feet to the concrete river bottom, assuming this was the neat thing Andy had wanted to show me. But instead of climbing back over the fence, he stepped down onto a narrow black pipe a foot below the concrete lip of the precipice. The pipe spanned the wash, and the distance to the other side brought to mind a tightrope across Niagara Falls I remembered from a circus movie. Holding his arms out like a tightrope walker, Andy quick-stepped forward and stood over the abyss about ten feet from the edge. Then he turned his head and grinned back at me. "C'mon," he said. "There's some neat stuff on the other side."

Beginning around five years old, there's nothing some young boys can do in the face of a dare by an older kid but go forward. If you die, you die — but you can't back down. No doubt a few boys in those days had more sense than to subscribe to such a code, but I was not one of them. And yet I wasn't completely in thrall to peer pressure. One step on the narrow, slippery pipe convinced me I would not be dancing across as Andy seemed to be doing. He waited on the other side while I slowly lowered myself and straddled the pipe, then began scooting across a few inches at a time. My fear mounted with each scoot, but under Andy's cool gaze I kept moving. Halfway across, my thighs holding the pipe in a death grip, I had a moment of silent terror. Equidistant from both sides, too scared to go forward or back, I looked desperately at Andy, safe on the foreign shore. He watched me closely, his expression impassive but somehow encouraging.

I kept moving forward. When I made it across, he reached out his hand to help me up on the bank. "Nobody else on the block ever followed me across before," he said. "They're all babies."

Full of fresh courage, I followed Andy into the unknown land. After crossing a deserted street, we entered an abandoned industrial area, all empty factories and piles of rubble. Without a word, Andy began throwing rocks at the second story of the old factory before us, shattering the lumpy, opaque windows. When the rocks hit, big chunks of glass would break loose, tumble down the sides of the building, and land with a satisfying crash in the rubble below.

As deer instinctively bolt at the faintest footfall, young ballplayers and rock throwers learn to run at the first tinkling of glass. But here we could smash away with impunity. My literary imagination had called up my favorite moment from *Pinocchio*, the Disney film which had been periodically released in theatres since its premier in 1940. In the Pleasure Island scene, the carnival barker declared the "model home" now "OH-pen for destruction, boys!" And in this similar opportunity, we had no annoying little Jiminy Cricket conscience around to interrupt the fun.

I had just picked up another missile when Andy said, "S'go." He took off at a fast walk down the street. I hurried to catch up as he cut over one block and up two more until we returned to civilization. After a quick reconnaissance, he led me into the garage area of a gas station on the corner. He knew right where to find the switch to raise the hydraulic car lift, and we took turns giving each other elevator rides until the mechanic came in from pumping gas. "Hey!" he yelled at Andy. "Geddaoughtahere! Didn't I tell you to never come back again?"

Andy didn't bother to answer as we sprinted away. A block or so later, he darted into a Baskin Robbins Thirty-One Flavors ice cream shop. I was thirsty and hoping he had money to buy us some treats, but to my disappointment, he only grabbed a handful of straws and dashed out again before the counter girl noticed us. A block down the street he gave me two of the straws and bade me to keep following.

Andy marched us confidently into a big, gloomy warehouse, and then led me to an old-fashioned coin soft drink dispenser, the kind that resembles a large home freezer. He opened the lid and I could see the bottle tops of different brands of drinks, including Coca Cola in the small bottles, 7-Up, Orange Crush, and Vernors, all lined up in rows and held by their necks in narrow steel runways. To buy a soda, you slid the one you wanted by its top to the end of the row. Inserting a dime and a nickel opened a one-way slot the bottle could be pulled up from.

Andy smiled. "What kind you like?"

Okay, now he would buy me something. "Vernors!"

He reached in his jeans pocket, but instead of coins he pulled out one of the era's ubiquitous "church keys" that opened cans with the sharp side and bottles with the blunt side. He popped the top of a Coke at one end of the cooler and a Vernors at the other, then stuck a straw into the Coke, leaned over, and began drinking.

I looked around quickly. A couple of men in work clothes stood at the far end of the warehouse, but they paid us no attention. I inserted one of my straws and drank the soda nearly to the bottom in straight gulps. I could smell refrigerant and spilled soda, and the cold air felt refreshing as it welled up from the bottom of the unit. Andy popped another couple of caps and we drank down two more bottles. I started laughing and the raw ginger taste fizzed into my nose.

Andy had been smiling between gulps, but suddenly he looked up, fully alert. "C'mon," he said, "and don't look back." We walked quickly toward the door. My heart began to race and I expected a hand on my shoulder any second.

Andy relaxed when we reached the sidewalk. We sauntered a couple of blocks to a main avenue and stopped in front of a movie theatre to view the Now Playing posters for a double feature: army and western.

Now Andy seemed to be looking all directions at once. He said, "You ever been to a movie by yourself before?"

I shook my head.

"I seen both of these," said Andy. "They change pictures on Wednesday. I can get us in next Saturday without paying." He started walking again, then stopped in front of a liquor store. "Want some candy?"

"Uh, sure." I answered warily, but more curious than afraid.

"I'll get it. Just go back to the comic books and start reading. When the old man throws you out, I'll meet you at the next corner."

I sauntered in and found the comic book rack in the back of the store. I barely had time to thumb through the latest issue of *Hot Stuff* ("*The 'Lil Devil*") when the proprietor appeared, a grizzled old fellow exuding maximum huffiness. He immediately began reciting his variation of the script used by liquor store clerks everywhere, the one that always includes "This ain't a library!"

I made a mental note to never buy comic books at this place, assuming I could ever find it again. I walked out, the picture of affronted dignity, but I didn't see Andy. It dawned on me that, without him, finding my way home from here would prove difficult.

I hurried to the corner he'd indicated, and to my great relief saw him walking rapidly down the side street. I hurried to catch up.

We made a more few quick turns as I belatedly tried to pay attention in case we became separated. Soon we arrived at a large automotive sales lot with red and yellow canvas flags flying, only this lot sold travel vehicles instead of cars. Andy led me to the back row of cab-over campers, the kind that slide into pickup truck beds. Each unit now perched about three feet off the ground on large wooden sawhorses. We ducked underneath one in the middle of the row. Andy pushed aside a plywood trap door and I followed him through the opening.

Clubhouses, tree houses, forts, and other hideaways from adult supervision are prime childhood real estate. When my head popped up inside the camper I saw immediately that we occupied the movie star mansion of hideouts. Furnishing included a table and padded benches that converted into a bed, a countertop, stove and ice box. Above us another bed filled the cabover part, with keep-a-lookout windows on both sides.

We sat at the table and Andy grinned as he emptied his pockets. Like a hand of cards he fanned out five assorted candy bars. I understood he'd snatched them while the liquor store guy yelled at me in the back, but it seemed impossible he could have gotten them so *fast*.

Did I feel any remorse as we sat there at the table gorging on stolen merchandise and keeping watch out the windows? I don't remember any, but as Andy began recounting harrowing adventures: stealing money, setting fires, climbing on fire escapes of tall buildings and more, I did have a growing sense I might be playing out of my league.

"Did you ever get caught?" I ventured.

"Yeah. Stealing from a store downtown a couple months ago." Running fast had always saved him before, but one of the store clerks — "He had these long, long legs, like a giraffe or something" — chased and caught him. The police released him to his parents, and his dad had first beat him with a razor strop, a thick, hard canvas belt used by barbers as the final step in sharpening straight razors. Then the old man ordered Andy stay in his room for a week, with no lights and the first two days on bread and water.

I had watched a movie with prisoners on bread and water, so this aspect seemed particularly fascinating. I had also seen cartoons wherein characters starved in interesting ways. "Did you get so hungry you started seeing sandwiches in the air and stuff?"

"Nah. My mom snuck me some food." Andy continued with other tales. As a result of his adventures and transgressions, no kid on the block was allowed to play with him, and one boy's parents ordered their son to not be caught on the *same side of the street* as Andy. Andy chuckled dryly as he told that one. He had been expelled from two public schools for stealing and fighting and had reached his last chance at the Catholic school. "I ditched twice this week, but my cousin is a grown-up and I talked her into writing me a phony note for school cause she don't want my dad to beat me again. She hates my dad."

As an adult I've met a few so-called career criminals who, upon leaving jail on strict probation, proceed to rob and pillage and party until apprehended again. Then they bide their institutional time until the next release and more of the same. Andy may have been one of those fellows in training, and as it turned out, everything I'd marveled at so far that day was merely a warm-up.

We lounged around a while longer, containing our giggles as a salesman walked from the small office building through the lot and came within a few feet of our headquarters. Once the coast was clear, we headed out to the street. Andy said something about a bus, but he passed several thinly-populated bus stops until we came to one on a main street with a crowd waiting. "When I go," he murmured, hardly moving his lips, "follow me quick."

The next bus pulled up and passengers began disembarking from the rear door. Quickly Andy snaked through them with me in his wake. If that move weren't audacious enough, Andy then made his way through the people standing in the aisles and asked the driver for two transfers. The driver handed them over without looking. A mile or so later we used the transfers on another bus to take us downtown somewhere, perhaps into Pasadena or Glendale, but in any case well beyond the outskirts of Burbank I'd visited with Jay.

Hopelessly lost now, I stuck to Andy like a shadow. We roamed from street to street, dodging between the grownups. They looked busy, harried, with set destinations. But we sauntered along, window shopping the war surplus emporiums and gazing at the movie theater posters. At some point we entered a department store and walked through mazes of aisles. I felt tired now; the whole scene had taken on an edgy dreaminess. After glancing over some car models,

I looked up and Andy had disappeared. I began to panic, searching up and down aisles at random, but just as suddenly he reappeared, wearing a peculiar smile, and led me out of there.

A block or so down the street he turned into an alley, then stopped behind the first trash can. "Lookit this," he said casually. From his jeans he pulled an expensive and complicated-looking fishing reel, a shiny black model with five or six chrome buttons. He held it in his palm for inspection like a pirate showing a handful of doubloons.

I said, "Uh, d'you like to go fishing?"

He shrugged. "My old man took me once." He remained calm, grinning, and seemingly alert to his surroundings, but somehow the only one who could get me home looked to be in some other world.

Since we'd left the store I'd been wondering what I'd do if he disappeared again. Coming from school, I could find the new street I lived on and then get to my house, but I didn't remember the name of the street. I could only hope Andy wouldn't leave me behind. I stuck with him doggedly as we walked many blocks. Finally he knocked on an apartment door. "My cousin lives here," he said. "She's a grown-up, but she's okay."

The door opened and a young woman stood in the threshold. Probably in her early twenties and short for an adult, she had made herself up like a movie star. In retrospect she resembled a cocktail waitress about to go on shift. She smiled at Andy and gave me a puzzled look.

"New friend of mine," explained Andy as he nudged me inside. The cousin asked him about school. I guessed that she had been the one who composed the phony notes.

Andy flopped down in an overstuffed chair. "Got any Cokes?"

"Sure." She tapped off in her high heels. While she bustled around in the kitchen, Andy did a lightening search through drawers and under couch cushions. He found another pack of the restaurant matches I'd seen him with earlier, and pocketed something else so fast I didn't register what it was.

When the cousin returned, she started to ask about his parents. I gathered she didn't care for her aunt and uncle.

"Everybody's fine," he cut her off. "Can you lend us busfare?" He jerked his head in my direction. "He's gotta get home or he'll get in trouble."

"You're the one who needs to stay out of trouble," she said, with a look both scolding and indulgent. She brought her purse out from the kitchen and gave Andy two quarters.

We gulped down our cokes and ten minutes later were riding in an almost empty bus. Andy kept the change the driver gave him for the two quarters. As we left the downtown area, he pulled out his fishing reel and looked it over. We didn't talk much on the ride to our neighborhood. Darkness had fallen when we exited at the first familiar corner I'd seen in many hours.

"Well," Andy said. "Let's go see what the old man has to say." He took off in his fast walk I already knew so well, throwing the fancy reel up in the air and catching it. I could see the glint of the streetlights on the chrome buttons as he made his way down the street.

I found the family at the kitchen table. Jane had just begun to serve dinner, Jay squinted at a paperback book, and baby Trish gurgled in her highchair. She turned to smile at me. Usually I ignored her, but now I gave a weak smile in return.

From my experience and observation over many years since my day with Andy, it would seem a general rule that parents know more about their children's activities outside the home than children think their parents know. But it's also true that parents know much, much less about their children's activities outside the home than they (the parents) think they do.

"I was starting to get worried," Jane said, as she moved a pan of roast and potatoes from stove to table. "Where've you been?"

"Nowhere." I yawned. "What's for dessert?"

CHAPTER SIXTEEN

~ Collecting Paper ~ The African Princess ~ Refugees Like TV
~ The Last Time I Saw Andy ~ Another Backward Loop

"Step right up on the scale here, little lady, and tell us your name!"

"Mary."

"Look, boys and girls! Mary weighs 52 and her load total is 208 pounds! Exactly FOUR TIMES her weight in newspapers! Here's your slip, dear. Just step over to the table for your prize!"

I watched this triumph from the outdoor school lunch tables at Franklin Elementary. Along with scores of other students, I had showed up on a sunny spring Saturday afternoon for the annual paper drive. The proceeds of the event would supplement the school budget, apparently gaining quite a boost in revenue even if recycled newspapers were worth only a few dollars a ton. Teachers, parents, and fifth- and sixth-grade upperclassmen had decorated the lunch area like a carnival. The principal was in his glory, shouting through the microphone sideshow barker-style. Sixth-grade boys unloaded stacks of newspapers from flexible flyer wagons as students, including a few grownup-looking junior high schoolers, rolled up to the industrial scale in front of the lunch tables. Each wagoner received an official weight slip, redeemable for cherry snow cones, lemonade, and various prizes, large and small.

I looked down at my slip. Forty pounds. No chance for one of the transistor radios or other big awards. I'd have to settle for a yo-yo and a snow cone, but I vowed that next year I would out-collect everyone—knock on every door in Burbank, bring in 500 pounds, maybe a thousand. A surge of what I assumed must be school spirit coursed through me as I followed the crowd to the auditorium for the grand finale of the drive: a personal appearance by Tom Hatten, host of KTLA Channel 5's afternoon Popeye show.

In his tee-shirt and sailor hat, Hatten reminded me of good old Uncle Bubba, only more talkative and artistic. He would invite members of his studio audience to join him on camera, and he gave the same show at this personal appearance. I wished I could go up on stage, but a functionary picked the participants from the first few rows of kids who'd thought ahead and stationed themselves early. Using a black crayon, each kid drew a "squiggle" on a big drawing pad, one of several on the easels spaced across the stage. Without hesitation, Hatten moved from easel to easel, incorporating the squiggle thereon into a larger picture: pirate, steam shovel, elephant—no one could stump him by drawing a squiggle he couldn't work with, but they all received prizes anyway.

Not counting my adventure day with Andy, the paper drive probably accounted for the biggest excitement in the Burbank period. I do remember a few other highlights, including a classmate's birthday party at Travel Town in nearby Griffith Park, where you could run through antique rail cars and cabooses and even pretend to steer the engine. Closer to home, for about a week the entire neighborhood hunted the vacant lots for horny toads, and we fought several apricot- and plum-throwing wars. When I lived in San Fernando and Simi Valley a few years later, the wars still raged, but with oranges and avocados for missiles. All over southern California in the fifties and early sixties, boys pelted each other with assorted fruits, until the bulldozers uprooted the last of the small-orchard trees.

I hadn't seen my old partner in crime for weeks after our adventure. Then one day as I passed by Andy's house, he hailed me from over his side gate. His update on adventures since our last meeting had the same sense of detached wonder at himself I'd noticed before. He reported that when he'd tried to sneak the fishing rod up to his room, it had fallen out of his shirt and bounced down the stairway right at his dad's feet. With a rueful smile, he said, "My old man knocked me down, then belted me and grounded me to my room. I couldn't come out except to take a pee or a crap."

"How long did you get grounded?"

"Three weeks in my room. And he says I can't leave the yard all summer." Andy shrugged like the crooks in the movies who say, "Ten years? Hell, I can do ten standing on my head."

I admired his outlaw spirit, yet it seemed strange to me even then that Andy, so cool and resourceful in his criminal endeavors, had been suddenly clumsy when he faced the greatest danger. His behavior seemed to fit the quasi-Freudian "criminal always returns to the scene of the crime" and "criminals secretly want to fail" psychology intoned by the grizzled police commissioner in cops and robbers movies of the fifties.

Now he opened the gate. "My old man is at work," he said. "C'mon in; I got something to show you."

The spacious back yard contained a smaller house (the kind known in real estate parlance as a "granny unit") set among several mature trees. In his confinement Andy had climbed a huge oak and hung a rope from which one could swing from the second-story roof edge of the main house to the flat roof of the smaller house. He demonstrated his expertise with gusto, yelling like Tarzan as he swooped high above my head.

It looked fun, all right. I ended up with rope burns on my hands and on the side of my neck (the latter can be seen in the school photo taken soon after), but somehow I escaped more serious injury. That may have been the last time I saw Andy.

Shortly after my family moved in, our neighborhood enjoyed an infusion of wider world culture. Through a church program, a local family adopted two young refugees from the Eastern Europe zone then referred to as "behind the Iron Curtain." Both boys were extremely thin, with prominent cheekbones and butch haircuts. Neither could speak English at first, but they picked up the language quickly. Most evenings after dinnertime they would make the rounds, knocking on doors up and down the street. When a door opened, they'd say, with polite, crooked-toothed grins, "TV?"

With few exceptions the householders would usher them in to join the family evening activity. The brothers liked to make themselves comfortable on the living room floors, as close to the television as possible. Then, until they were ushered out at bedtime, they would watch everything on the screen intently, even the commercials. These neighborhood mascots eventually enrolled in school and were placed in grades appropriate for their ages. The school provided no extra tutorials, but within a month they could communicate in English. Out on the playground, some of the boys would recite strings of swear words at the brothers, and then steer them to where the girls played jump rope. There the foreigners would dutifully repeat the words and smile delightedly at the ensuing giggles and screams.

One of those jump-ropers became my second love interest.

On reflection, my eclectic appreciation of women began early, for Yvonne was pleasingly plump with dark, thick hair. She bore no resemblance at all to Alice Kramden, and so was as different from Star, my love interest in Las Vegas, as a girl could be.

Yvonne's walk home took the opposite direction from campus as mine, but we would talk by the gate after school let out. She told me about living in South America, and I told her all about my travels in the Western states and life in Alabama and Nevada. We discussed geography in general, and commented on Alaska and Hawaii, those new additions to the United States mentioned recently by the teacher, and how we'd like to visit both.

"But not Alaska in the winter," she cautioned. Even Burbank seemed cold to her after her years near the equator.

"Nah," I agreed.

But our families' penchant for traveling, which provided such a fine conversation opener, would also doom our romance. One afternoon Yvonne told me with some excitement tinged with wistfulness that, immediately after school let out for the summer, she would accompany her parents to Africa to be missionaries. With summer only a few weeks away, I lamented the capriciousness of fate. How unfair to meet someone so fascinating, only to have her torn from me.

Yvonne wore the standard mid-calf little-girl dresses, and I noticed during an early conversation that she had little wisps of downy dark hair on her legs. In a rare talkative mood, I told Jane about this phenomenon one afternoon and added that Yvonne would be moving far away. She repeated the story to Jay, and at dinner he teased me about "the girl with hairy legs" going to Africa. "Those monkeys over there have hairy legs, too, pal." The teasing seems mild enough in retrospect, but that was probably the last information about girlfriends I volunteered to parents until adulthood.

As it turns out, my first true romance would have been doomed even if Yvonne's parents weren't dedicated missionaries. When the end of the school year arrived after five surprise moves and five teachers, I had finally made it through first grade and felt settled in Burbank. About a week into summer vacation, I came home from a cap gun fight (a variation of the standard war game, only set in the old west). A couple of kids had employed the Mattel Fanner 50 sixgun, an innovative weapon capable of shooting plastic bullets and popping Greenie Stickum caps at the same time. The effect made a strong impression, and I planned to discuss with the authorities the possibility of my acquiring that cutting edge armament. But upon entering our house and finding the living room full of moving boxes, I knew instantly there would be no Fanner 50, no triumph for me at the paper drive next year, and no birthday party at the trains.

Later as I filled a moving box in my room, I recalled several foreshadowing events. For instance, a couple of weeks before I had been bouncing a ball against the side of our house in an intricate solitaire game of my own invention. At some point the ball escaped and rolled across the street into a neighbor's driveway, and when I ran over to pick it up, I saw what looked like half of a five dollar bill on the ground.

I doubted half a bill would be worth anything...but maybe I could get a quarter for it? I reached for the half-bill. It was a folded-over whole bill! No, it was... TWO bills! Two folded-up FIVE-DOLLAR BILLS!! I threw the ball in the air and raced home, waving the greenbacks as I burst through the front door.

To my profound disappointment, Jane said that since the windfall came from the neighbor's driveway, I'd better go back and let them know I found it. Seeing my distress, she smiled kindly. "They might give you a reward."

I trudged back across the street, sick at heart. "Rewards" to kids in those days, for services like rescuing cats from trees and errands like going to the store with a note for cigarettes, usually involved nickels and dimes. But perhaps the neighbors wouldn't be home. It seemed vaguely logical to me that if they didn't answer when I knocked, then they should forfeit all rights to the money. But my luck held even better than I'd hoped—not only were they absent from home, but a look through the uncurtained window revealed an empty house! They had moved! I took the money home, and with Jane's blessing, put it in my big plastic hound dog bank, which had contained mostly pennies and nickels until then.

That jackpot ties in to the first real inkling that things weren't so stable in Burbank. One night a week or so before the day of moving boxes, I was perusing a comic book in the room I shared with Trish. I could hear Jane and Jay in the living room, talking louder than usual. Then Jane appeared at the door.

"Can I borrow some of your money, Honey?" she said, putting on a bright smile. "I'll pay you back."

"Uh, okay," I said. Her credit was currently good; soon after we moved to Burbank, she'd returned the four dollars they'd borrowed in Vegas. Now, using a butter knife, she fished my two fives from the hound dog bank, leaving a dollar, two quarters, and some pennies and nickels.

The next portent followed immediately: Jay sometimes worked the swing shift, so I might not see him for a day or two, but he didn't seem to be around at all for a couple of days, and Jane took frequent walks to the corner phone booth. So when I came in and discovered her packing, the situation all fell into place. Or so I thought— for one more surprise lay in store.

Jane seemed preoccupied and provided no further information beyond the basic moving announcement. Jay returned and they packed together in silence. The atmosphere seemed too tense for questions, but I began to form an idea of what might be happening next when Nanny arrived. She stood around looking worried while Jane and Jay loaded our few boxes into the giant trunk of her '53 Buick. Jane put Trish and me in the backseat, where we burrowed in among more boxes. Then she sat in the front seat beside Nanny. Jay stayed on the porch as we drove away, smoking a cigarette and looking anywhere but at the car. So he was out of the picture. Again.

For the next week or so, Trish and I returned to Nanny's and Jane disappeared, providing no details when she kissed me goodbye and told me to be a good boy. Nanny took a few days off and had her hands full with Trish, which left me to my own devices. I was in an odd mood I couldn't articulate, even to myself. The neighborhood kids on Kenwood Avenue were all black now and mostly older. No one acted menacing or even unfriendly, but neither I nor they made any attempt to integrate their neighborhood pastimes. I spent most of those days in Nanny's back yard, imagining myself an outlaw, a combination of Andy and several movie prisoners I'd seen. I spoke from the side of my mouth to imaginary companions and threw dirt clods at Missy, Nanny's old grey cat.

When Jane came back she had no news, but I felt a sense of foreboding. Then she left again. I watched TV in the mornings, and then wandered out to throw figs at the gate and break bottles in the alley. I tried to fix a rope swing to the highest branch of the fig tree, but the wide branches interfered with the trajectory, and there was no place to swing to anyway. The next day I found a half-pack of Jane's Tareyton cigarettes (the brand with the "I'd rather fight than switch" slogan). I took one of them and a book of paper matches to a dirt alley down the block. After burning myself slightly, I managed to get the cigarette lit, but it tasted terrible. I had more fun lighting the whole book of matches and dropping it quickly when it flared up.

I vividly remember my return to the house, walking idly down quiet Kenwood Avenue. As I approached Nanny's, I saw a new 1960 Dodge Dart parked in the driveway. I looked it over and noted the paper license plate. When I heard the door open, I ducked behind the holly bush. Jane came out carrying a box; she was followed by a tall, thickset man in a short-sleeve sports shirt with the sleeves turned up, his muscles bulging under the weight of three boxes stacked up to his forehead. I couldn't make out his face at first, but his back looked familiar. Sure enough; when he turned, I saw good old Luke Langston.

CHAPTER SEVENTEEN

~ Disneyland Is My Land ~ Wyvernwood and Austrada ~ With Friends Like These ~ Cooties and Bedbugs ~ Haute Couture 1960

During the next few days of family reorientation, I visited the bachelor pad Luke had established with his brother Bubba after Jane left the second time. Bubba had completed his Navy enlistment and Luke had brought him in on the glazier crew. As Luke briefly outlined all this on the way over, he also said he had won a goldfish at a carnival, and told me I could have it.

But when we arrived, Bubba had bad news. He said, approximately: "'At crazy Lou-sana gal? Brung her home last night and she run off while I was sleepin'. Cleaned out my billfold, and own 'er way out she poured a whole bottle a chrome polish own the fish."

Sure enough, the water in the fish bowl on top of the new TV looked like grey soup with a chromed goldfish floating on top. But I felt glad in any case to see Bubba again. Both brothers now earned good wages in the ever-expanding L.A. building boom. Luke had not given up on Jane during her absence; he had established credit and began making payments on the new Dodge Dart and the top-of-the-line TV set we saw before us. Thus when Jane made her desperate phone call, he had fully equipped himself to make marriage work, if she would only tell him what it took to keep her from running off again. He then proved his sincerity by taking us all to Disneyland, the latest wonder of the world.

Fifty-plus years later, the expensive theme park outing is still de-rigueur for new stepfathers and newly-divorced dads. I can't speak for anyone else then, now, or in-between, but I stood willing to give the benefit of the doubt to any man who financed a trip to Disneyland. It's difficult to express in the twenty-first century without seeming flippant, but when a family made its pilgrimage to the Magic Kingdom in 1960, they reaffirmed, all in one day, their faith in the American Frontierland spirit, the Look Ahead to Tomorrowland spirit, the Doughty Adventureland Spirit, the Fantasyland Sense of Wonder and Celebration of Childhood spirit, and the American Main Street Ethic that Made America Great.

See? It does sound flip, but for all the requisite cynicism of my generation, and despite the unsavory stories about Walt's fascistic tendencies, and regardless that his security detail kicked me out in 1966 for too-long hair (at the time "too long" meant about the length of Jimmy Carter's when he ran for president ten years later), and even though security guards ejected my friends and me in 1968 and 1973 for certain highjinks other institutions might have been more tolerant of, and notwithstanding the current obscene admission fees, and even considering the greediness inherent in the current practice of crowding the place to near gridlock when they could instead make the Magic Kingdom a much more pleasant experience by selling a finite number of tickets through advanced reservations—despite all these contradictions, I say, I'll stand by my appreciation for the spirit of the place.

I felt definitely appreciative as the reconstituted Langston family walked under the admission tunnel and looked out at Main Street. Other than touring Hollywood with Nanny, I had never been close to any of the Southern California tourist attractions. Jane and Luke had taken me once each to the beach when we lived in San Pedro, and we'd been to the movies once or twice as a family with Jay, but otherwise Jane and her consorts were the homebody types: readers, card players, TV watchers.

But good old Luke rose to the occasion and seemed to have an endless supply of legal tender in his wallet. We used all the tickets in our deluxe fifteen-ticket books[17] and purchased the Mickey Mouse hats with embroidered names AND the helium double balloons with the Mickey Mouse ears on the inside. We saw the cowboy shootout in Frontierland; consumed hamburgers, fries, giant dill pickles, ice cream, cotton candy, fudge, fried chicken, and innumerable soft drinks; stood in the front row for a parade, and toured the House of the Future. Jane's heart presumably quickened at the microwave oven in the future kitchen, and Luke and I gaped at the impossibly

---

[17] The deluxe 15-ticket book plus admission cost $3.95 in those days, comparable $87 admission and unlimited attractions in 2006, the last time I took my granddaughter there. With today's crowds, getting to fifteen rides in a long day is usually the outside limit under the "unlimited" plan.

huge flat screen TV on the wall (as Walt so confidently predicted, I saw a remarkably similar giant HD 3-D flatscreen on sale recently at Costco).

When we finally staggered to the parking lot, Trish lay asleep in Luke's arms and I half-dozed on my feet with one hand in Jane's and the other clutching my balloon. Life with Jay seemed long ago and far away.

Jane's feelings probably remained more tentative, but she had practical concerns, the main one being that she was now six or seven months pregnant with the child Luke presumed he had fathered. While waiting until the first of July to move into our new family apartment, Trish and I continued to sleep at Nanny's, while Bubba made a quiet exit from the place in North Hollywood and Jane spent most evenings there. On weekends the reunited lovebirds bought furniture on credit. Acquisitions included many staples in this era's rage for "mid-century" furniture: a modern uncomfortable couch, a sling chair, two or three blonde coffee tables, a rubber plant, and the latest in gigantic ashtrays. And of course a complete layette for the impending baby. All of this treasure stacked up in Luke's apartment while they searched for a two-bedroom rental.

At last they settled on the Wyvernwood Garden Apartments in East L.A. Unlike obliterated Channel Heights, the complex continues as a going concern, housing one of the toughest Hispanic enclaves of East L.A. But in 1960 the federal Fair Housing Act was still eight years in the future and Wyvernwood remained an all-white, segregated island in the middle of an ethnic ocean. The management simply refused to rent to blacks or Latinos; they marketed to Anglos determined to stay in L.A. rather than follow the white flight to the suburbs. According to a helpful website:

[J]ust two miles east of downtown Los Angeles [Wyvernwood] was constructed in 1938 and 1939 [...] The property included 1,102 apartment units on 60 acres when it was initially conceived. Nine new buildings were added in the 1960's for a total of 1,175 units [...] It was designed as a self-contained community with a business district, school, play areas, recreational facilities and housing [...] The site plan segregated auto and pedestrian traffic, clustered buildings together around courtyards, and created large areas of open space. The architectural style is Minimal Traditional. This property has been formally determined eligible for listing in the National Register of Historic Places by the California Office of Historic Preservation. [18]

Most of the recreational facilities and business district didn't progress beyond the planning stages, but it's nice to see Wyvernwood might make it to the Register of Historic Places anyway. The judges probably took the historic worth on trust, for it is difficult to imagine an official of the California Office of Historic Preservation showing up in person to search for the recreational facilities nowadays, even in broad daylight.

I fell in love with the complex the first time I saw the pirate bridge. Merely a small, decorative wooden structure over a low spot in the huge grassy area ringed by the apartment buildings, the bridge nonetheless fired my imagination and seemed to embody all the magic of Disney pirate films. For my first act as a new Wyvernwood resident, I went forth with wooden sword and Jane-drawn skull and crossbones on my chest. On the little bridge I enacted pirate adventures for about fifteen minutes and then never played there again. As I learned fairly quickly, I lived in a different sort of neighborhood now.

The counterpoint to Caucasian Wyvernwood could be found in an adjacent area called Austrada, probably 75% Hispanic, 20% black, and 5% "other," excluding whites. An unplanned community, Austrada contained within its sprawl everything from decrepit shotgun shacks to newer apartments as nice as anything in Wyvernwood. For white kids, Austrada served as the Forbidden Zone, never to be entered lest savage ethnic tribes maim or kill the pale trespasser on sight. Likewise, brown or black faces were rarely seen in Wyvernwood, probably for fear of bodily harm or instant arrest.

But one day a black kid, probably nine or ten years old, rode deep into Wyvernwood on his bike and stopped near a crowded play area. Perhaps he came on a dare or as a gang/club initiation; in any case, he soon became surrounded by curious white boys and girls. He didn't seem frightened by the crowd, but stared back at us defiantly, an unlit cigarette dangling from his lips. Someone's dad broke the standoff by approaching to investigate. The black kid

---

[18] See home.earthlink.net/~perroudburns/ Lincoln Place Significance. htm. Initially finding Internet background information on this fascinating complex proved difficult because I typed in "Wyvenwood," without the r. All residents pronounced it that way in my day, as all denizens of San Pedro called their town "San Peedro."

threw down the cigarette, turned the bike, and pedaled furiously away. The dad asked a few questions, scowled in the direction of the kid's departure, and returned to his football game. We all pushed forward and made a circle around the cigarette. Standing closest, I could see its Winston label, as in "Winston tastes good like a cigarette should," a jingle so ubiquitous it had already spawned a parody: "Winston tastes bad like the last one I had No filter, no flavor, just old toilet paper!"

Suddenly Carey Muheler, the first friend I had made at Wyvernwood, scooped up the cigarette and threw it at my face. The Winston bounced off my lip and everyone howled with glee.

"Ewww — he got nigger cooties!"

"Cooties! Cooties!"

"Nigger lip! Nigger lip!"

Carey laughed the loudest. Though my age, he was huskier and tougher in a way I hadn't encountered before. Where Channel Heights and Burbank youth had been mostly innocent and open, the typical Wyvernwood personality seemed more like the movie version of New York's East Side kids. Wyvernwood boys assumed in advance that each interpersonal encounter would come to a conflict. All friendships remained superficial: it was every man for himself and watch your back.

In consequence, wariness, truculence, and false bravado were standard, and Carey, born and bred in Wyvernwood, embodied them all. He had a flat-top-with-fenders haircut, missing front teeth from which he could spit with fine precision, and an exaggerated swagger. Most boys get into scuffles from time to time; Carey picked fights almost daily. He often played "jokes" on me like the one with the cigarette, but he became infuriated the only time I tried one on him. As a result I lost the first fight of my career (actually, the fight with the tall kid in Van Nuys was the only one on my resume thus far), but it would not be my last defeat at Wyvernwood.

When his older friend Billy could come out and play, Carey had no time for me. The first afternoon I found them together, they teamed against me, using the whipsaw technique wherein if either one of them insulted me, the other laughed appreciatively at the brilliance of it; if I retaliated, they both agreed I wasn't funny or I'd gone too far:

Billy: Ricky is so low, he's gotta look up to see down!
Carey: (with delighted laughter) That's choice! Chop you so low, Ricky!
Me: Well, uh, Billy is so low, he's lower than a pregnant ant!
Billy: Huh? You talking about my aunt? I like my aunt!
Carey: (frowning and shaking his head at me) That's low, talking about a guy's family. What's wrong with you, bo'?

In fairness it must be said that, compared to some of the seriously abrasive kids in Wyvernwood, Carey came off as relatively personable. One day we ran a Kool-Aid stand and made over a dollar profit after paying my mom back for the Kool-Aid packets (she threw in the sugar gratis). Carey may have been brutish, slow at counting, and less imaginative in advertising than I, but I laud him as an undeniably wonderful cultural reference. In a lull between customers, he taught me a song so brilliant I memorized it instantly and for life, and I've passed it on to my children and granddaughter:

> *One morning when I woke up, I looked up on the wall*
> *The cooties and the bedbugs were havin' a game of ball*
>
> *The score was one to nothin', the cooties were ahead*
> *The bedbugs hit a home run, and knocked me out of bed*
>
> *I went downstairs to breakfast, the toast was very hard*
> *The bacon tasted like tobacco juice, the coffee tasted like lard*
>
> *The Joneses had a baby, they named him Tiny Tim*
> *They took him to the bathtub to teach him how to swim*
>
> *He drank up all the water, he ate up all the soap*
> *And now the Joneses baby knows how to float*
>
> *He floated up a river, he floated down a lake*
> *And now the Joneses' baby has a tummy ache*
> *Thanks to the bedbugs ... quartet![19]*

---

[19] The last line is sung to the tune of "Shave and a haircut ... two bits!"

Billy's parents kept him grounded most of the time, so Carey and I played together often through the summer. We had rock fights with other boys and threw dirt clods at girls whenever we sighted them. We hopped on the back bumper of the ice cream truck and rode it a block into Austrada, then ran for our lives back to the allied zone. We experimented with cigarette lighters and matches and told each other all the dirty jokes we'd heard so far. I soon picked up his style, including the flat top with fenders, and his generally belligerent demeanor. When I lost my front baby teeth, I assiduously practiced my spitting, and I adopted a milder version of his swagger.

Second youngest of five brothers and sisters, Carey belonged to the sort of classic mid-century American Catholic family that Pat Buchanan describes in his autobiography. With the blessing of the parents, the several siblings took turns inviting friends in a sort of old-fashioned "we're poor, but we have enough to share" hospitality and I joined them as a guest on two occasions. They said long, strange prayers at dinner under the stern eyes of their dad, and they seemed cowed by their God and somewhat restive under the iron rule of their religion.

By contrast, I had never been to church. The general feeling around my extended family placed religion as a good thing — Jane had gone to Baptist services regularly in her youth, and Nanny had had bouts of born-again fervor after she left Lige — but we never got around to actually praying, talking about spiritual matters, or attending services. I knew the baby Jesus story from Christmas songs and had seen several movies with religious people either portrayed as very good or very bad; otherwise, I had no background and little interest in the topic.

The Muheler's dinners were heavy on noodles and potatoes, and they never ate meat on Fridays (I had to take this last on trust, as non-Catholics never attended Friday dinners). Instead of the chocolate milk I preferred, they drank ice water with their meals, a practice I privately considered unsophisticated, if not downright barbarous. Another practice I hoped wouldn't catch on at my house consisted of the younger kids jumping up to clear the table and wash dishes after meals. Their dad, a full-time factory worker, also had a second job selling Dishmaster faucet units. These were fancy appliances indeed, with a space-age joystick for the temperature and pressure and a separate, soap-dispensing scrub wand. He had installed an employee-discount model in their apartment sink, and while he washed dishes, Carey demonstrated it to me with the same sort of pride I exhibited while showing off my family's new Dodge Dart.

Speaking of the Dart, the car became instrumental in an adventure even more thrilling and dangerous than the felonious day with Andy back in Burbank. At age seven, I would soon meet and become intimate with the first in a lifetime series of brilliant, long-haired, free-spirited young women.

CHAPTER EIGHTEEN

~ Enclave of the Gifted ~ Early Summer of Love ~ Flip Flops and Gull Heads
~ What Bozo Didn't Suspect

Despite tensions inherent in Wyvernwood's survival-of-the-fittest milieu, I felt at the same time a delicious sense of summer 1960 as it passed slowly, a golden interlude with nothing to do but whatever I wanted. I wouldn't have used the term "consciousness expanding" then, but fueled by daily doses of baloney with extra mayonnaise on Wonder Bread and quarts of red Kool-Aid, I absorbed influences and kept myself poised for new experiences, which usually involved elements no parent would approve. In short, my seven-year-old frame embodied the sixties state of mind well before the 1967 youth revolution, and I accomplished that embodiment with no help whatsoever from the Beatles or my son's professor at Berkeley.

In the expansion process, I became acquainted with the free-spirited California girl mentioned in the last chapter long before such demi-goddesses became idealized and/or notorious in my young male circles. One perfect July day, after donning my summer uniform (cut-offs, flip-flops, and tee-shirt), then carefully combing my flat top's fenders, I stepped out our back door and surveyed my domain. On the other side of the small strip of grass we shared with the next apartment, I saw a girl standing in the three-ring plastic blowup pool, holding a book close to her face with both hands. I had heard from Jane (who knew the mom next door from clothesline conversation) that this girl's name was Linda, and I noticed she looked vaguely like my old friend Linda, Bert's daughter from the San Pedro era. But since in those days every third girl between five and twelve years old in Southern California was thin with dirty blonde hair and named Linda, I don't remember any intense wonderment at the resemblance.

I studied this Linda for a minute before she noticed me. Her pink flip-flops lined up evenly beside the pool, and she wore the standard one-piece sun suit with spaghetti straps. She didn't look particularly smart—no horn-rimmed glasses or anything—but Jane had relayed the story of Linda already skipping twice and entering fifth grade in the fall. She would be the first of two brilliant kids I met at Wyvernwood. Perhaps, like the Bronx in the nineteen twenties, the East L.A. low-rent apartments of the sixties spawned physicists, famous authors, and philanthropists as well as a goodly number of ne'er do wells and twisted sensibilities and an interesting combinations of both extremes.

When the local Linda sensed my presence, she looked up from her book with a smile that considerably brightened her otherwise plain face. The gap between second and fifth grade (or between seven and eight years old for that matter) is immense to kids, but she seemed friendly enough. "Hi," she said. "Are you Ricky?"

"Yeah."

"Do you like to read?"

"Uh, Yeah."

She held up her book. "Have you read *Onion John*? It got a Newberry. It's kind of a boys' book."

I mumbled something to the effect that I hadn't gotten around to *Onion John* yet. She then announced she had read the entire Nancy Drew series by Carolyn Keene. I confessed unfamiliarity with that author, but Linda didn't hold my ignorance against me. "Nancy Drew is for girls. Have you read the Hardy Boys series?"

I'd never heard of the Hardy Boys, though I became a fan two years later. I sidestepped the question by telling her I could read a fourth grade book while still in first grade and modestly admitted my high standing in all reading groups thus far. "I went to five schools in first grade," I added, marking the first time I'd thought to brag about that feature of my academic record.

Linda seemed interested. She had a level gaze, for a girl. "You want to walk over to the store?" she asked. "I've got a quarter."

"Okay. We can look for bottles, too." I had been having good bottle luck lately.

As we strolled through the complex chatting, I found Linda straightforward and unaffected, an interesting conversationalist and a good listener. She told me she lived with her divorced mom and her dad lived in Massachusetts. "Mom has a boyfriend who stays over sometimes," she said, grinning. "And Dad has LOTS of girlfriends."

We moved from literature to music, and she taught me a racy variation of the Chiquita Banana song:

> *I'm Chiquita Icecube and I'm here to say*
> *If you want to get your boyfriend up early today*
> *Just stick an ice cube in your boyfriend's pants*
> *And watch your boyfriend do a hula dance!*

At that point we were walking by the rows of one-car garages. I stopped before ours and, demonstrating my manly strength, pulled then pushed the spring-loaded door up to reveal our new Dodge Dart.

She smiled politely. I sensed a lack of enthusiasm, but I pressed on. "Want to see something really neat?"

"Sure," she smiled a bit more warmly. I pulled the garage door down from the inside, and we stood in near darkness, with the only light from under the door and two mesh vents in the side wall. The car doors had been left unlocked as always, and we slid in the front seat. The Dart held its new car smell, and the squarish steering wheel, pushbuttons for the Torqueflight transmission, and buttons for almost everything else, suggested the cockpit of a rocket ship. I pushed a few transmission buttons, explaining how they made the car go forward and back.

"What's this one?" She pointed to the cigarette lighter.

"Careful!" I brushed her arm as I pushed in the button. When the lighter popped out, I held it up so she could see the red-hot filament. I picked up a scrap of Kleenex from the seat, twisted the end, and applied it to the heat. It began to smoke, then smolder. A tiny flame arched up. I pinched it out with my fingers and threw it out the window.

I looked back at her with my version of a devil-may-care expression, and in the dim light, I could see her staring at me in what seemed an odd way. "Did you ever..." she leaned in close, almost whispering, "Did you ever see a girl with all her clothes off?"

I felt a not altogether comfortable stirring, but somehow I kept my cool demeanor. "Uh, sure," I said. I spoke truth: I'd seen my little sister naked plenty back in the days when Jane used to diaper her.

Linda smiled, then opened the passenger door and stepped from the car. After a brief pause I slid across the seat and out to face her. We were standing between the side of the Dodge Dart and the stucco wall, and she was already slipping off the straps of her sun suit. Soon she stood naked, looking pretty much like my little sister looked without clothes, only taller.

This turn of events had begun to remind me of something, but I couldn't quite make the connection. Overall, I had mixed feelings. On the one hand, it felt exciting to be doing something so potentially dangerous, for as a Wyvernwood acolyte, I had begun to develop a taste for misbehavior for its own sake. On the other hand, this girl had suddenly usurped the daredevil role I'd established with the car and the lighter. In any case, following her lead seemed like the next right thing to do, so I took off my cutoffs and tee-shirt. Another brief pause, then I stepped out of my underwear. We examined each other without touching or speaking for a few seconds. Then, having achieved partnerhood in crime, we dressed in silence.

When we left the garage, we continued to the store. On the way I led the search for deposit bottles, looking under all the bushes. My luck persisted: we found five, enough to cash in for two candy bars and two gums at the new exchange rate of three cents per bottle. With the change and her quarter, we bought two Dr. Peppers. The store housed a sort of mini-mall, with a barbershop, ten-cent store, and bakery under the same roof. Each store had a distinct fragrance — the hair tonic from the barber's seemed particularly rich as we watched a young sport get a trim. Then the aroma from the bakery drew us to the window, and I spent a thus far hoarded dime on two fresh brownies. We munched them while trying on flip-flop sandals back in the ten-cent store. She called them "go-aheads," but I heard it as "gull heads." The store kept them in a huge bin, in all colors and sizes, priced at nineteen cents per pair.

Eventually we walked home, chatting away. Neither of us made any reference to our intimate encounter, but the next day when I saw Linda sitting under a tree reading a thick book, her first words were, "You want to go to the garage?"

We saw each other (as it were) almost every day that week, and we began to talk of intimate matters. She told me that when she'd first moved in a few months ago she'd had a sleepover with her friend Martha, the nine-year old sister of another boy I knew in the apartments. Martha had impressed me as a quiet type, but from what Linda said, I concluded that looks can be deceiving. After some hushed remarks about Martha's wide experience doing "nasty things" with boys and girls, Linda said, "Martha showed me how girls can fuck themselves."

I'd heard the word "fuck" many times by now, but had never

heard a girl say it. Clearly she had much more experience with this secret stuff than she'd let on.

Arranging her discarded sun-suit like a beach towel on the cement floor, she began to demonstrate what Martha taught her. The performance definitely intrigued me, but—though I couldn't put it into coherent thought—I also had the feeling that the action had gotten perhaps a bit too clinical. Sex as I knew it so far had been all about dirty jokes and furtive meanderings. She seemed so serious and focused.

After a minute or so she stopped and looked at me intently. Then she said, "Do you want to fuck me?"

Of course I didn't know it yet, but at age seven Fortune had presented me with a dream scene from a thirteen-year-old's wildest sex fantasy. Later as a young teenager, I would remember the moment and wish I had said, "Sure, Baby," and proceeded, thereby establishing myself as the undisputed earliest-lost-virginity champ of all my pals in the seventh grade.

But at the time, I could only think of what all this reminded me of…Yes! … Johnny Fuckerfaster! The first dirty joke I'd heard back in San Pedro, and one I'd recently repeated to Carey. Only in this real life version, the girl led the boy from event to event.

The reply I made to her offer still puzzles me. If I didn't have a distinct memory of the incident, I would have sworn that at age seven, I had only the vaguest notion of the sex act and how couples performed it, and an even murkier idea of how babies were conceived. But apparently I've forgotten some wisdom from someone, for I answered, "Nah. You might get pregnant."

Did I really think there was a danger? I don't know, but in any case I realized doing what she wanted could be big-time trouble, worse than playing with matches, worse than stealing from a department store. More importantly, and to put it bluntly, I didn't trust her. Many years later when grownup girlfriends told me tales of their friends' deepest sex confidences (which the friends would be mortified to learn I knew), I wondered the same thing about my confidence-breaking girlfriends that I wondered about Linda: if she told me the intensely private stuff Martha had confided to her, what would she tell Martha about what *we* had been doing?

In any case, I gave up an opportunity to lose my innocence (assuming we could have actually consummated the act), an opportunity that would not present itself again until my mid-teens.

Linda didn't insist. She gave me an inscrutable look and began putting on her sun suit and flip-flops. She spoke not a word as we walked back to our shared yard.

I wasn't sure what to do next, but she solved the problem for me. "S'long," she said. "I've got to read my new library book." For the rest of the summer we greeted one another sociably when we saw each other around the apartments, but we never returned to the garage nor walked around together again. And when we started school, she entered a different world among the exalted fifth graders.

Thus unfolded my first experience with an older woman. But an interesting postscript occurred a year or so later, after we were long gone from Wyvernwood. One afternoon I saw Linda's friend Martha on TV — in the studio audience of the Local KTTV Channel 5 *Bozo the Clown* show.

For my taste, Bozo, though an energetic entertainer, compared unfavorably with Chucko when it came to wit and urbanity, and I only watched because his show came on after Popeye. Bozo did go Chucko one better in self-marketing by showing cartoons starring his animated alter ego. But these cartoons, which featured a sidekick the animated Bozo called "Butchy Boy," seemed more irritating than entertaining. In any case, while watching the show in a desultory way one winter afternoon, I suddenly recognized Martha from Wyvernwood in the front row of the studio audience.

I felt strangely excited — I'd never seen anyone I knew on TV before. I called Jane to see. "Look! There's my friend's sister! Her name's Martha."

As we watched, Bozo walked over to the girl I was pointing to. "What's your name, Sweetie?"

"Martha."

"See! It's her! She went to my school!"

Jane seemed suitably impressed, even though she'd had plenty of experience in show business herself.

Martha and Bozo had a short conversation. I watched, fascinated as she smiled and chatted into the microphone. I knew her, had actually spoken with her! I felt like a real insider, but even more so than Jane could ever know. For as Bozo asked Martha to introduce a cartoon, and she smiled nervously, looking wholesome in her Brownie uniform, I reflected that the dumb clown had no idea, no inkling whatsoever, of what manner of wanton he was dealing with.

CHAPTER NINETEEN

The seemingly endless summer days remained long and warm as the 1960 Labor Day weekend ushered in the back-to-school shopping season. I accompanied Jane to Sears for jeans bought large to accommodate "growing into," a look that presaged oversized fashions decades later. En route we visited Nanny at work so she could supply the new shoes that felt so odd on feet gone bare or in gull heads for months. In the store parking lots I noticed Kennedy and Nixon posters for the first time. Suddenly all grown-ups seemed to be talking about the contest. JFK became the first Catholic since Al Smith in the twenties to run for president, and the Muehlers were among his most fervent supporters. In their living room, a Kennedy poster appeared on the wall right next to the Sacred Heart of Jesus painting. But other friends' parents were wary of a Kennedy presidency, since, according to them, all Catholics took their orders from the Pope.

A few weeks before the first presidential debate, Jane (who supplied Kennedy with at least one lapsed-Baptist vote) registered me at the school straddling the border between Wyvernwood and Austrada. We officially resided in the L.A. inner city now, with large enrollments and split sessions at the elementary schools. The harried office assistant assigned me to a morning-session second-grade class where 35 or more students sat in alphabetical order at long tables. My friend Carey and I (Langston and Muehler) could sit close and chat, with only a Lopez between us.

This Lopez, perhaps feeling left out of the conversation, interrupted to say he would beat us up one at a time after school. Furthermore, if we both jumped him at once, he would recruit the whole population of Austrada to destroy us.

With icy contempt, Carey assured him in neighborhood patois that if he brought his puny reinforcements, we would enlist all of Wyvernwood in the battle, and Austrada would be decimated. To this brinksmanship, I assented with a hearty "Yeah!"

Having discussed mutually-assured destruction with as much seriousness as the presidential candidates were about to display in the debates, we had no further friction with Lopez. Our teacher did her best to foster integration, but her charges roundly ignored her efforts. At recess the White, Mexican, and Black scholars self-segregated as faithfully as inmates in any California prison.

With school so crowded and school days so short, I don't remember more than cursory attention to formal reading, writing, or arithmetic in the three months I spent there. However, we did take regular field trips. After a unit on dairy farming, we rode a bus to an actual dairy somewhere east of the city. There I saw my first milk cow up close, a black and white model I knew to be Holstein from drawings we'd seen in a picture book.

The excursion undoubtedly met some educational rationale, but seemingly anything would do for a field trip. Looking back, I wonder if the principal kept a certain percentage of the school population off campus in case the city fire inspectors came and noticed how overcrowded we were. One morning we walked a few blocks as a class to witness the demolition of the old high school building, a three-story brick monolith from the turn of the century. As we watched the edifying spectacle of a gigantic iron wrecking ball smashing down walls, a fellow student sang a song which seems to me almost as lyrically inspired as the "Battle Hymn of the Republic," from whence it borrowed its structure and melody:

> *My eyes have seen the glory*
> *Of the burning of the school*
> *We have tortured every teacher*
> *We have broken every rule*
> *We've hung the principal*
> *Until his faced turned blue*
> *And there ain't no school no more!*
>
> *Glory, glory hallelujah*
> *Teacher hit me with a ruler*
> *Hit her in the bean*
> *With a rotten tangerine*
> *And there ain't no school no more!*

The repressed hatred of all authority expressed by the unknown author struck a revolutionary chord in all of us. Even if we only doodled around in half-day sessions, school boiled down to regimentation, patronizing teachers, and involuntary confinement. But we would overcome some day.

And so continued my drift into outlawhood, aided further by a lack of parental supervision in the lengthy afternoons following our noon dismissal from school. Luke worked six day weeks and Jane was kept busy with Trish and seeing her doctor regularly. He estimated the new baby's due date for August, but the little dickens insisted on being late — or so the story went. She welcomed any due date complication that could provide a convenient means by which Jay's baby could become Luke's baby.

In any case, my preoccupied parents left me to my own devices. One afternoon I joined forces with another classmate to set a fire in the bushes. A French lad about twelve years old (actually named Pierre, like all the Frenchmen on TV) happened by just in time. Pierre was born to be a gendarme: if he saw any violation of apartment rules, safety, or common sense, he would inevitably intervene. True to form, Pierre now stomped the blaze, yelling what I presumed were French expletives. My fellow arsonist had the presence of mind to run immediately, but I hesitated long enough for Pierre to grab me by the arm. As I struggled, he demanded, "Where do you leef? Who is your mudhare?"

Setting fires, like sex play, came under the classification of serious juvenile crime. So I struggled and begged in a manner unbecoming an outlaw, and Pierre finally let me go. "No eve-air set zee flame agane!" was his approximate admonishment, and I ran away, forever cured of fire-starting. Vive Le France!

Not long after this incident, I learned yet another important life lesson when my short, Carey-influenced career as a bully led me into neighborhood difficulties. One afternoon a boy in a cowboy hat ran away with a deposit bottle I had seen first. I gave chase, but lost him in the buildings. The next day, I saw two boys walking ahead of me, and I thought I recognized the one with the cowboy hat as the thief from the day before.

I hurried to catch up, and without preamble shoved the hat-wearer hard against his companion. He turned to face me and I immediately realized that we a case of mistaken identity had occurred. But he looked small and wore glasses, so I pushed the hat over his eyes and laughed exactly as Carey would have.

The little fellow took off the hat and gave me a cool appraisal. Then he removed his glasses and handed them to his friend. "Hold these, Bobby," he said, "while I take care of this guy."

I felt moved to laugh again, but suddenly the runt exploded with lightning fast left and right punches to my midsection. Completely unprepared, I doubled over in great pain. He replaced his glasses and hat, and then turned away without looking back, resuming the conversation I'd interrupted. I ran home, still doubled over, as shocked and baffled as the clueless Neanderthal in the William Golding novel *The Inheritors* when the little Homo Sapiens shoot arrows at him. That a kid almost a head shorter than I could be deadly with his fists and comport himself without any hint of swagger contradicted every bit of Wyvernwood street smarts I'd picked up so far.

On the way back from the store a few days later, I saw the same kid. He grinned at me and pointed to the comic book I carried under my arm. "Whatcha got there? New Superman! Lemme see."

I nodded dumbly and handed it over. He gave me an appraising stare through his glasses. "I just want to check it out. You like monster mags? Come on to my house and I'll show my collection."

I nodded again and followed, but remained apprehensive. He introduced himself as Eddie, and as we made our way to his apartment, it became apparent that he belonged, like Linda the literate nymphomaniac, to the ultra-bright set. He told me about books he had read lately (young adult novels I'd never heard of, though the title of one, *Huckleberry Finn*, stuck with me) and a couple of jokes I hadn't heard. He asked if I played draw poker, then offered to teach me when I said I had played the kind where everyone sees all the cards.

"Oh yeah, showdown poker. Kid stuff. You got a piggy bank? We can play penny-ante draw, jacks to open."

He revealed that his mom and dad were "lushes" and divorced. He hadn't seen his dad in years. His grandpa, "a rich guy in Santa Barbara," paid for a private school but wouldn't give Eddie's mom a dime otherwise. Eddie had only recently turned eight but had skipped third grade. "I'll go to college by the time I'm sixteen. My grandpa says a couple years of law school and I'm Perry Mason, only not so goody-goody."

I recognized Perry Mason as a lawyer on TV, but the rest of the discourse skimmed over my head. Chatting rather one-sidedly, we entered his apartment. A woman I presumed to be his mom sat drinking a beer in the kitchen. Eddie passed by as if he didn't see her. As we continued to his room (as an only child he had one all to himself, an almost unique situation at Wyvernwood), he kept up a running monologue. He showed me his monster magazine collection, his model cars, and three *Stag* Magazines. "Check this; you can almost see her nipples!"

I recognized *Stag*; Jay had bought it regularly, along with *Popular Mechanics* and paperback westerns. Each monthly issue featured an extravaganza of crime stories, World War II adventures, exposes of big city mobs and Hollywood call girl rings, cannibal islands, nudist camps, and Nazis, all of which Eddie seemed to know everything about. Conversation with Eddie became more and more disorienting — he talked like a grownup in a little kid's body. Occasionally he would cock his head and ask me questions: what I thought about this or that movie or record or TV show, even politics. "I'm for Nixon," he said. "My grandpa says Kennedy's just a pretty boy. My mom likes him, so there you go. What do you think?"

Eddie peered at me intently when I stammered out "My mom liked Kennedy too." He obviously hoped I might be someone he could have an intelligent adult discussion with, but he was out of my league. However, we did discuss pop music as equals. It had been a fine year for novelty songs and I knew the lyrics to "Alley Oop," "Sink the Bismarck," "You Talk too Much," and "Itsy Bitsy Teeny Weenie Yellow Polka Dot Bikini." Eddie appreciated all these as well. But though he provided stimulating company, I never felt comfortable with him.

Toward the end of October I met another friend I liked better, even though we probably had less in common. This boy's name escapes me now, but the first time I saw him at school he was in the process of cursing the yard monitor in such a vile yet good-natured way that I admired him immediately. The next time I saw him, on Halloween, he wore a combat uniform with all the accessories: guns, grenade, bayonet, helmet with netting. Except for his youth, he looked like an extra in a movie about D-Day. The foremost neighborhood authority on World War II and anything to do with the army, he could discourse by the hour on gun calibers, tank models, battle outcomes, and Japanese tortures. We roamed around together the next Saturday and he lectured me on Nazi prison camps. I found these topics fascinating and his enthusiasm became contagious. He also knew every swear word I'd ever heard and loved to string them together in long curses: "Goddamn motherfuckin sonnabitchin asswipe!" "Shit ass bastard cornhole mofacky!" and so on, in myriad combinations.

The next Saturday he took me to the army surplus store, farther from home than I'd been since the adventure with Andy. Afterwards we kept daily company. On successive Sundays at the local theatre we saw *The Ten Commandments* (a re-release), *The Time Machine*, and *Thirteen Ghosts*. Each (except *Ten Commandments*) coupled with a companion movie at the reasonable admission charge of twenty-five cents, with popcorn and sodas a dime each.

We took separate ways home from the shows, and I felt apprehensive walking at dusk through the knots of Austrada teenagers, mostly Mexicans in the East L.A. uniform: hair combed straight back, Pendleton wool shirt buttoned up to the neck, new jeans, white socks, and black lace-up pointed-toe shoes.

The night I saw *Thirteen Ghosts*, I kept the disposable ghost-viewing glasses the theatre supplied. The movie wasn't 3-D, but used a process called "Illusion-O" with special lenses in the cardboard frames to make the ghosts either more or less visible at the viewer's discretion. I proceeded to walk the Austrada gauntlet, spinning the glasses casually so as not to show fear. One of the guys, a fourteen- or fifteen-year-old, caught my eye and jerked his head to motion me over. This is it, I thought. Classmate Lopez must have put a contract out on me. But when the mob calls, you have to go.

"Here, lemme see those." The teen took the glasses and put them on. Then he gave them back with a scowl and the comment, "I don' see no ghosts." Then he laughed. He may have wanted to scare me a bit since I looked so obviously terrified, or perhaps his overture was an attempt to dispel the vicious, knife-slashing pachuco image we Wyvernwooders had superimposed over him. I remember contemplating these possibilities all the way home. But I reached no conclusions and saw no more ghosts through the glasses, either.

CHAPTER TWENTY

~ Scrubs ~ Dirt Clods ~ He Used To Be My Daddy ~ A New Addition
~ Dangerous Reunion ~ Hospital Caper ~ Another Parting ~ Finis Luke

I had admired teenagers since I first became aware of them as a five-year-old American Bandstand fan, and by age seven, to become a teen myself was my fondest wish. But while I waited for the long years to unfold, I resolved to emulate them as best I could.

Eddie, the eight-year-old going on seventeen (or thirty), gave me pause—did I want to grow up that fast?—but he didn't retard my ambition for long. My army friend seemed more like a grownup sergeant than a teen, so I had to look elsewhere for a local role model. I settled on Paul Muheler, Carey's big brother. Paul had attained thirteen, and all the elementary school kids feared him, even Carey. Always ready with his fists, he also embodied the fastidious and stylish. He wore a fresh, starched plaid short-sleeve shirt daily, and his carefully-pressed jeans stopped abruptly above his ankles, leaving a good six inches of white sock above his mirror-shined black slip-ons. His flattop with fenders grew longer than Carey's, more like Elvis's on the cover of the current soundtrack album for *G.I. Blues*. He even carried his own soundtrack, the first transistor radio I'd ever seen, which he had acquired from a grandparent. I soon undercuffed and coiffed myself likewise and began to lobby for some black slip-ons. Only the transistor radio seemed unobtainable. I heard they cost twenty dollars or more and my grandparents provided no hope: Daddy lived too far away to expect presents from, and Nanny was only good for shoes, underwear, and an odd dollar now and then.

Paul started seventh grade in the fall, the lowest animal in the high-school pecking order. The first day of school I saw him coming down the street with an apparently bloody face. This checked out with the tales we'd heard of constant violence and race wars at the junior high. But as he drew closer, I saw that he had only been "scrubbed," meaning he'd been tackled by a gang of eighth graders, held down, and smeared forehead to collarbone with lipstick, a rite of passage for seventh-graders, aka "scrubs" in the L.A. area. He grinned good-naturedly while recounting the ordeal. I couldn't wait to be a scrub myself.

Meanwhile, I continued to enjoy my favorite neighborhood sports — sneaking rides on the back of the ice cream truck and throwing dirt clods at girls — with Carey most often, but sometimes alone. One afternoon I became a bit too zealous as I chased a girl and hurled clods. She made it in her front door and slammed it behind her. My last missile made a resounding boom against the door and showered dirt over the porch.

Immediately her irate dad stormed out and accosted me. He marched me to my apartment, where, unfortunately, we found Luke at home, nervously packing for Jane. She had been finally been admitted to the hospital after going back and forth for two days while the doctors first attempted to induce labor, then began to seriously consider a Caesarean section.

Luke stood in the doorway, hand heavy on my shoulder as the irate dad accused me of terrorizing his daughter and vandalizing his house. To my disappointment, Luke nodded respectfully during the tirade. When the dad left, Luke looked at me with the most disapproving expression I'd ever seen him wear. Then he said, in what I took as an implied threat: "I'm your daddy now."

I made no reply. In my experience, stepdads were here today and gone tomorrow, so why bother arguing with them? He didn't press the matter; he had more important things on his mind. The next day, September 24, Jane gave birth to my brother Greg by Caesarian — he supposedly arrived almost two months late. For the next few weeks Jane occupied herself with recuperation and the new baby, but it turns out she had other matters on her mind as well.

One afternoon a month or so after Greg joined the family, I stood with Carey, watching a spider in a huge web on a boxwood bush outside the front of my apartment. The kids playing nearby became a gradation quieter in their chatter, which usually meant an adult approaching. I looked up, then did a double-take. There was Jay! But it couldn't be — I knew enough about the situation to assume he wouldn't be imprudent enough to visit Jane here. But here he was, passing by at a brisk pace, headed for our apartment.

"Jay?" I ventured.

Very casually, he half-turned and gave a preoccupied smile. "Hi, Rick," he said, and kept walking. I stood staring after him.

"Who's that?" asked Carey, as he swept away the web with a stick.

"My uncle." It just popped into my head; somehow I automatically assumed my role in the conspiracy, whatever the conspiracy might be.

As Jane related to me later, my sister Trish demonstrated an even more clever nonchalance when she beheld the surprise visitor. When the doorbell rang, she was busy stacking blocks in the living room with a little friend from next door. The little friend said, "Who's that man?"

Trish looked up at Jay, then back at the friend. "He used to be my daddy," she said, and resumed stacking blocks.

Years later, when Jane laughed over that story, she also provided some background on Jay's clandestine trip to Wyvernwood. The day I saw him entering the apartment wasn't the first time they'd met since their parting in Burbank. He had even dared to visit her at the hospital right after she'd had her Cesarean. Jay also told the story, and though his details are so spectacular as to be of doubtful veracity, Jane confirmed some of the more dramatic elements.

Not many things upset Jay, but a loved one in the hospital topped the short list. He had called my grandmother to find Jane's whereabouts, and Nanny told him of the imminent Caesarian. Thinking the worst, he sped downtown in his old Chrysler, weaving through traffic and running red lights. Unfortunately, a mile or so from his destination, he zoomed around a corner and clipped a motorcycle policeman. He looked back, saw the officer get up, and kept going.

Within a few blocks, two patrol cars forced the Chrysler to the curb. Other squad cars soon arrived, and an officer jerked Jay from the car at gunpoint.

"Pull your license out, Buddy. Real slow."

Jay raised his hands and smiled his widest. "I don't have it with me." He actually did have his license in the secret pocket of his wallet, but it seemed prudent to refrain from revealing his Jay Hill identity since he was currently under investigation for skipping child support payments.

The policeman shoved him roughly against the car, pushing his head down. "Hands behind your back!" The other police moved in threateningly.

"Wait, wait! My wife's in the hospital — going to have a baby — emergency operation!"

"Yeah? What's your name?"

"Luke Langston! She's having an emergency operation right now! I've gotta see her!"

"Why didn't you say so?!" They gave him back his keys and formed a police escort. But when they arrived at the hospital, they continued with him up the elevator so they could check out his story.

He smiled at the nurse guarding the maternity ward, "Tell Mrs. Langston her husband is here," he said, and she preceded their entrance.

Luckily Jane was awake and a quick thinker. Appraising the situation instantly, she identified Jay as her spouse and called him Luke. Thereupon all the policemen shook Jay's hand, wished "Mr. and Mrs. Langston" well, and left.

What would have happened had the real Luke been at Jane's beside is an interesting speculation, and I still wonder why no nurses or roommates exposed Jay when he arrived. People practiced more discretion in those days, perhaps. After witnessing Jay's sometimes phenomenal luck in other situations, I'm willing to give the story some benefit of the doubt.

Jay took another calculated risk the afternoon he came to see Jane and his (presumed) son, and his luck held through several more visits. He said later he'd figured that whatever happened or whoever he met, he'd just handle the situation, that's all. This sort of devil-may-care approach to life was, perhaps, a big part of his attraction for Jane. He may have had some minor faults (pathological lying, sociopathic tendencies), but he was smart, good looking, could make her laugh, and wasn't afraid of anyone.

And he loved her. She knew he did because when he'd first made contact again, she confessed Elvis's recent single "Are You Lonesome Tonight?" had haunted her since they had parted. Jay looked at her and shook his head, as if to clear it. Then he told her solemnly the *same* song had haunted *him*. The interesting thing about Jay was, the story could have been true. You just never knew.

When I returned home after Jay's visit, Jane didn't say a word about him; nonetheless, past experience seemed a clear indication that our days in the current family unit were numbered. And so it turned out. Jane took me into her confidence a couple of weeks later, sometime in mid-November. The eleventh month seemed to be my family's season for evasions; we had moved every November for the last four years. "We're going to be leaving soon," she said. "And you mustn't say *anything* to *anyone* about it. Okay, Honey?"

I nodded solemnly. We were outlaws together, me and my mom.

In subsequent years, sudden moves under cover of night became almost routine, and I never revealed top secret family escape plans, no matter what. But this first time she trusted me, I did break her confidence. Around seven o'clock on the dark evasion eve, I walked over to the apartment of my friend, the military enthusiast. Surprised to see me so late, he nonetheless came outside and began chattering away, telling me all about another Army-Navy surplus store he wanted to reconnoiter.

As he talked I felt guilty for lying by omission. Rationalization came next: since we would be leaving in a few hours, telling my friend wouldn't be dangerous. After all, he had avowed in a recent conversation that, had he been captured by the enemy and interrogated in World War II, he "wouldna told the Japs nothin', not even if the yella bastards cut off my hand with a sword!" Plus, I reasoned, he wouldn't have time to blab before tomorrow morning anyway. So, after swearing him to secrecy, I revealed the evasion plan.

"You're movin'? Tonight?" He stood up and began pacing. "Well, Fuck! God damn shit ass fuckin' shit!" He continued this demonstration of distress for a long minute. I felt I was losing a real friend. I probably was, but now I don't even remember his name.

Around ten p.m. Jay came to pick us up in the Chrysler, now adorned with a Nixon bumper sticker, even though Nixon had just lost. In future presidential races Jay never made his political preferences public, but that election had been the most contested in Jay and Jane's memory, and even he found himself drawn into the general partisanship. We loaded the car with the same basic items we'd been carrying around for the past few years, including my box of keepsakes and treasures. Jane left Luke the TV, the new Dodge Dart, and all the modern furniture—everything they'd bought on the installment plan.

But where was Luke all this time? Afterward I learned further background. He and Jane had sat down for a serious talk the day before. She told him she wanted to leave for good. In his halting manner, Luke implored her to reconsider.

"All right, I'll think it over." she replied. "Just sleep somewhere else tonight so I can think in peace. I need to think!"

Luke agreed to this plan. "Awright, Sugar. I'll come back tomorra right after work." In hindsight this was poor strategy indeed, but it probably never occurred to him that she would desert him without further parlay and that he would never see his presumed first son again.

Five minutes after he departed, Jane began hauling out the boxes. And with that, Luke exits this chronicle as an active participant. I never saw him again and can't remember really missing him, Disneyland notwithstanding. His daughter Trish has no memory of her dad. She has one picture of the two of them, a black and white snapshot taken in front of Nanny's house. Greg, who also bears Luke's name on his birth certificate, knows less about him than Trish does. And Luke, if he's still alive, knows even less about both of them.

But Luke did make a cameo reappearance in Jane's life five years later. She had just returned to her car in a Panorama City shopping center lot, and saw him: a fat man now, but unmistakably Luke, standing beside the now-dilapidated Dodge Dart and searching for his keys. Luckily she saw him first. Ducking into her car, she crouched below dashboard level for ten minutes to be sure he had left. She told me the story with zest; the surprise reappearance renewed the sense of fugitive adventure we'd shared in younger days.

The epilogue on Luke came through his keeping in sporadic touch with Nanny for several years and continuing to list her as a reference for employment and emergencies. In this way she heard he had applied for a job with the railroad; then a couple of years later, that he had been involved in an armed robbery and seriously wounded. Whether Luke was robber or victim remained unclear. In any case, that report marked the last anyone ever heard of him.

CHAPTER TWENTY-ONE

~ Different Dimensions ~ My New Handle ~ A Digression on
the Extended Step-Family ~ An Ironic Career

Leaving Luke to his murky future, the newly-restored (and one child larger) Hill family drove from East L.A. to Glendale, a pleasant suburb near the Burbank neighborhood we'd left only a few months before. Jay had been working steadily all summer on the night shift (a handy schedule for afternoon visits to Jane), and he proudly escorted us to the best-appointed rental we'd lived in so far. The furnished house featured two bedrooms, a paneled garage "rumpus room," back yard with lemon tree, and even a studio granny unit.

We spent the weekend unpacking, and on Monday Jay walked me a couple of blocks to the local school. To my experienced eye, it seemed a promising institution with its large playground and proximity to the new house. While Jay filled out the paperwork, I sat in a plastic chair in the office looking out the window. After a bell rang, I could see students streaming from the classrooms. As had become more frequent, my mind drifted into comic book reveries. The office became a different dimension; in here I somehow floated above the school bells and outside of the normal time-space continuum, somewhere in the interdimensional zone Superman always flew through when he broke the time barrier. And, as I had learned in the Superman "Imaginary Stories" series, further dimensions and alternate universes existed. In a few minutes I would meet my seventh teacher in the twelve months of my educational career so far. I'd be placed in one of the second grade classes where I would meet new kids, probably make friends with some of them. Or if they put me in another classroom, I'd get to know other kids and not meet the first set at all. But somewhere in an alternate universe, would I become friends with the first set?

"Hey, Pal."

I came out of the zone. Jay had walked over from the counter and stooped close to my ear. "I put your last name down as Hill," he said quietly. "Use it from now on."

Jay never officially adopted me. Even if he had been legally free to engage in marriages, adoptions, and other trappings of the state, no one in those days ever asked to see marriage licenses, birth certificates, or the like. So why not proceed with confidence, as if you had indeed secured all the paperwork?

In any case, Ricky Langston no longer existed. This change to Hill made four last names so far, including the "Landry" on my birth certificate. Matching Jay's cool delivery, my only reply was, "How do you spell it?"

Jay looked at me with an "I thought you were smarter than that" expression, and then whispered "H-I-L-L."

Stung by the look, I wanted to explain I had known a Susan Steele and a James Roache in previous schools, and they were living evidence that names which sound like other words aren't necessarily spelled the same. But the secretary seemed to be eavesdropping, and a minute later the vice-principal appeared to escort me to my class.

I never once slipped up and called myself Langston. However, on the first day's assignments, I did print "Ricky hill," with the h in lower case as I'd always written the word "hill" before. When the new teacher gave back the papers the next day I felt chagrin at the h circled in red. She not only classed me as behind in handwriting in general (they had already started cursive in this school), but also thought I didn't know enough to capitalize my last name. I seemed to be off to a rough academic start in Glendale, new identity and palatial home notwithstanding. However, though I never did catch up in cursive writing, I managed well enough otherwise, and I recall no further crises at that school.

The Glendale period lasted only a few months (from late November 1960 until mid-March 1961); but in Jay and Jane's third attempt to keep house, they began to gain traction in the golden decade of the middle-class good life in Southern California. A booming economy and cheap housing could scoop even renegades like them aboard the prosperity train. A month or so after we moved in, they hosted the first in a series of family Christmases, with relatives from both sides journeying to our place. Opening presents on Christmas Eve continued the tradition that Jay started the year before in Van Nuys.

Guests welcomed the innovation: they could bring their kids and dispense family gifts, thereby eliminating the need to wake up with hangovers at dawn on Christmas morning.

At Jay and Jane's house, relatives could also look forward to a fine steak dinner, usually New York cut or better, with baked potato and side salad. This menu emulated the offering at the Sizzler steak house, a new chain that provided a classy night out for aspiring lower-middle class families.

Such innovations, complimented by Jay's charisma and liberality with free drinks, guaranteed him a long reign as Christmas host. As mentioned before, Jay, as with many adult children of alcoholics, never drank to excess, but as a poor kid with aspirations, he understood that the most expensive name-brand liquor characterized the Good Life. Others totems included prime-cut meats, asparagus with hollandaise sauce, sour cream and chives, Cadillacs, Chryslers, starched white-on-white shirts, Italian shoes, tab collars, tightly-knotted thin ties, clean shaves even if a second one were required after five o'clock, expensive watches (or good imitations of such), jaunts to Vegas and Palm Springs, boats, backyard pools, well-calibrated stereo sound systems, and state-of-the-art appliances. But of all these markers of upward mobility, good liquor always topped the most immediately-appreciated list. At parties Jay seemed to be everywhere at once with a bottle of Chivas Regal or Smirnoff, never letting a glass go empty. Over the years, many a light or beginning imbiber experienced his or her first real drunk at our house.

Besides taking care of the social drinkers, Jay saw to it that alcoholics on both sides of the family never needed to worry about tanking up ahead of time as required when attending normal, under-served parties. Jay made an effort to keep them supplied with extra-strong drinks up to and beyond the incapacitation point. And he would even drive them home, leading them by the arm to his car with many semi-good-natured jokes about how drunk they were. But by the next party, any hurt feelings would be forgotten in the glow of Jay's hospitality.

The 1960 Christmas festivities started around eight o'clock, giving time for the guests on Jay's side to get home from their market or butcher shop employment and "clean up." In those days, people dressed up after work rather than dressing down and wore their nicest clothes to visit relatives. Baby Greg, our new addition, also presented well as he gazed from his bassinet upon this, his first Christmas. Prosperously fat (by application of extra-rich milk in his bottle), turned out in a blue velour jumpsuit, and sporting an elaborate curl across the top of his head, he embodied the new decade. Trish and I wore our standard Christmas evening dress: new pajamas and slippers care of Nanny. As the guests arrived we munched on Vienna sausages, crackers, cheese, and See's candy, staring longingly at the piles of presents.

One great dividend in hosting the family Christmas party was that guests all felt obligated to bring gifts for us kids. But now Jay could afford it, and he surpassed them all in largesse to his own children. My presents that year included a basic box camera, a five-transistor radio, and a giant plastic Cape Canaveral jet and rocket set. This latter gift came from Jay's market and probably had been acquired along with the liquor and steaks by unauthorized assistant manager discount—i.e. pulling the car around back of the store and slipping the loot out the delivery entrance.

Though Jay's family paid him the respect of accepting his hospitality, he seemed, even in my limited perception, to be an outsider among them, like a fox brought up by a family of hound dogs. Likewise, while he showed superficial affection for them, he looked upon them with a certain contempt he made no effort to hide when I came within earshot. Thus over time, I learned more of his family history, or at least his version of it.

Jay's Canadian French mother Eileen, and Swedish/French stepfather Ed Depew had transplanted from Minnesota to L.A. in the mid-forties. Ed found work as a butcher and became a wearer of silk socks and jaunty caps, a mumbler of dry asides like, "One more of them Jaybird martoonas and you can take me to my leader."

Ed was much henpecked by his wife; for example, she discouraged him from lounging on their furniture even though it had plastic slipcovers. When we later moved into our first unfurnished house, they sold us a living room set. Ed came over for a beer one day soon after. "First time I ever sat in this thing," he remarked, settling into the de-slipcovered chair. "Made payments on it three years, though."

The beers Ed ingested at our house provided an important supplement, as he labored under orders to turn his paycheck over to his wife Eileen each week. He would steal petty cash from work to enhance his monetarily regulated alcohol consumption, but she often found and confiscated this unauthorized tender. If Ed did manage against all proscriptions to get as drunk as he desired, she had been known to brain him with a frying pan, drag him out to the back porch, and lock the door. He suffered greatly from this treatment in Minnesota, almost freezing to death on at least one occasion. Fortunately, moving to balmy-weather California made his porch sleepovers less life-threatening.

As for Eileen, Jay was her first and favorite son, the role I perceived I had with Jane, but Jay and Eileen had a passive-aggressive, love-hate relationship that seemed altogether foreign to me. For instance, to help insure clarity, I've called my mother "Jane" in this account, but Jay called his mother "Eileen" to her face. I never saw them kiss or otherwise show affection in word or gesture. Where Jane had some embarrassing memories of Nanny's bizarre drinking behavior, Jay's recollections of childhood with Eileen were darker. She had been only fifteen when she bore him, and his earliest reported memory recalled finding his mother on the bathroom floor, drunk and bleeding from a self-induced abortion. At fourteen she had run away with her boyfriend, the Hill fellow whose name Jay (real name Darrell) re-appropriated at age 18 as a protest against being forced to use his stepfather's name in his school years.

Eileen had several other boyfriends after Hill and before Ed. The racier parts of her story came out much later, but from the beginning Jay presented Eileen, when she was out of earshot, as something between Shanghai Lil and Lucretia Borgia.

During much of his early childhood in Minnesota, Jay had been left with his maternal grandfather, a country doctor with nineteenth-century sensibilities. The grandfather's influence remained strong in some respects: Jay became a lifelong self-educator and iconoclast, completely out of the mold of his parents except in his seemingly inherited propensity to mendaciousness. When his grandfather died in 1940, Jay rejoined Eileen, who had settled with Ed. In 1941, Ed, Eileen, Jay, and his infant stepbrothers Edwin ("Eddie") and Fredwin ("Freddie") set forth from Minnesota and settled in East L.A. Stepbrother Barry appeared as an afterthought in 1949.

When Jay finished ninth grade at Hollenbeck High, Ed sponsored him into the butchers' union, bumping his age from fourteen to sixteen in a false affidavit. This seemed a warm stepfatherly gesture, but when Jay began to show better skills than Ed in cutting meat and a real talent for sales, Ed allegedly responded by doing his best to sabotage Jay's career progress, usually by telling tales to the managers.

By the time Jay met Jane, Eileen had become the chain smoking, card-playing, periodic drinker and neatness fanatic I knew her as. But the stories persisted. She had taught her children to be scrupulously clean—or else. According to Jay, she regularly ordered them from the house at seven a.m. and they dared not return until seven p.m. They were strongly encouraged to take showers at school instead of de-sanitizing the bathroom and subject to bodily harm if they made a mess in the house and she discovered it before they could clean up. My own observations of her plastic slipcovers, her practice of scrubbing her floors daily, and the pathological care she lavished on her new 1961 Thunderbird seemed to confirm these stories; however, Jay may have enhanced the more lurid accusations.

In the late 1930s when Eileen delivered twin brothers Eddie and Freddie, her obstetrician declared them among the smallest Minnesota babies to ever survive birth. But the boys resolutely applied themselves to nourishment and were now six-foot-two, big-boned, blunt-featured, and usually over 300 pounds, in marked contrast to Jay's thin elegance. Periodically one of the twins would lose a hundred pounds or so, making it easier to tell them apart, but I still had trouble remembering which one Jay currently addressed as "Hey, Slim."

Whether heavy or light, Eddie distinguished himself as the plodder of the duo, a pleasant, straight-arrow fellow except for stealing everything not nailed down at the market where he worked. Twin Freddie also practiced wholesale thievery on a regular basis, and though barely literate, he mastered the art of keeping a suspicious story within the realm of possibility. The gift of gab trumped all in the frontier society of Southern California, and Freddie employed his in convincing casual acquaintances to join business ventures that didn't actually exist. He also persuaded several women he met in bars that he practiced heart surgery by memorizing a few key terms of the profession, perhaps from the then-popular TV shows *Dr. Kildare* and *Ben Casey*.

Freddie lived in our granny unit for a month while he attempted Community College (then referred to as "Junior College"). In those flush Golden State budget days, any California resident over eighteen could attend tuition-free. But Freddie soon found higher education restrictive. He periodically lived with Eddie, paying no rent and cadging loans. During one of these stays, Freddie seduced Eddie's wife Judy and subsequently ran away with her. After a few years,

Eddie remarried, this time to a personable girl named Dodie. When Freddie contacted Eddie with a tale of homelessness due to bad breaks and Judy's perfidy, Eddie demonstrated the unshatterable bond between twins by opening his home to the wayward brother. Within a few weeks, Freddie had seduced Dodie. Again, Jane and I never heard any of these astounding stories except through Jay, who summed up the family ethos as passive aggression, boundless greed, and all-pervasive backstabbing, though he used different terms.

Eileen and Ed's third child, the afterthought Barry, was four years my senior and technically my step-uncle. However, our relationship over the next few years more resembled cousins of the same age, with me usually acting as leader in our activities together. Like his older brothers, Barry tended to overeat, but he lacked their street shrewdness and garrulity. Decidedly timid, he had no interest in music or fashion, never read a book in his life, and possessed no sense of adventure. He liked nothing better than to stay home, tidy up his room, and build model cars, always Fords. Except for Jay, the whole family remained steadfastly, even fervently loyal to Ford automobiles throughout their lives and never purchased any other brand — or even a replica of another brand.

To remove Barry from the house for her periodic major cleanings, Eileen would drop him at our place one or two weekends a month and for up to a week at a time during summers and vacations. After a couple of years of Barry's perennial guesthood, I no longer felt obligated to entertain him and would wander off on my own, leaving him to sit placidly around the house or mope in my room, homesick for his own much neater abode and solitary pastimes. But even in exile Barry felt a burning loyalty to the Ford Motor Company and nursed a grudge against the General Motors Corporation. He revealed these feelings in notes scrawled around the house on any available scrap paper, cryptic statements like "Chevies are rocks" and "Fords eat Chevies."[20]

Barry also exhibited an irritating practicality. When people asked me what I wanted to be when I grew up, I usually said "doctor" or "lawyer," perceiving these to be high paying as well as high-status careers. I thought Barry's response, "I wanna be a gardener" highly

---

[20] Such partisan sentiments were common in the fifties and sixties among Southern California car enthusiasts, and we can see their current incarnation in truck-window decals of the sneaky-looking little boy urinating on a Chevy or Ford symbol, depending on the preference of the driver.

unimaginative. As he explained, gardeners earned "good coin" and had the good fortune to work outdoors. He demonstrated no love of nature in any of his leisure activities, but perhaps the times Ed had taken him to work at the butcher shop inclined him to a fresh air occupation. In any case, the gardening trade always seemed both menial and unambitious to me in those days, like wanting to be a janitor or a septic tank pumper.

And yet, in a fine example of life's irony, gardening became my first career. After drifting through my teens, disdaining college, and failing to get my big break in songwriting, I became a commercial landscape worker, then a civil service groundskeeper through most of my twenties. Thus I can testify from experience that Barry guessed correctly about the "getting to work outside" part, if not so accurately about earning "good coin."

As for Barry, after high school he found employment in a car accessory factory (a subsidiary of Ford), and after several years on the assembly lines he became a Quality Control Lead. This position entitled him to carry a clipboard, the totem of lower-management refinement in the factory world. He kept the clipboard on the seat of his pristine new Ford Mustang and showed it to me when we both happened to visit Jay and Jane one day in the late 1970s. Barry had grown a moustache and married a woman even larger than he; they kept house in a nice Canoga Park apartment with pool, and he carried himself with the dignity befitting his station in life. He was friendly, but I detected a certain smugness in his appraisal of my decrepit old Chevy truck full of gardening equipment. Yes, I had always acted superior to him in our youth, but time had proved the race is not always to the seemingly swift smart-asses like me.

PART III: 1961–62

Glendale, Sylmar, Manhattan Beach, Redondo Beach

Midget Elvis, Glendale

Bookmobile, Sylmar

Manhattan Beach Home Street 1962

Daddy and Aquarium,
Summer 1962 Redondo

CHAPTER TWENTY-TWO

~ An Upside-Down Year ~ Transistors and Derailleurs
~Between Candyland and Pancho ~ Shots ~ Of Gender and Other Preferences

As *Mad Magazine* pointed out, 1961 was a rare "upside-up" year — i.e., one in which the numerals that form the year look the same when rotated upside down. In the first month of this epoch, the U.S. severed relations with Cuba, President Eisenhower warned against the military industrial complex, John F. Kennedy assumed the presidency, and 19-year-old Bob Dylan hitchhiked to New York from Minnesota to begin his career. Meanwhile, on the verge of eight years old myself, I tracked both behind and ahead of the times. While practicing a hairstyle Dylan would help to make obsolete, I tuned in early to a little invention destined to overshadow almost everything else in the music business.

Soon after we moved to Glendale I began carefully combing my grown-out flattop into an Elvis wave, appropriating generous dollops of Jay's Alberto VO-5 Hairdressing for Men. Photos of me from those days show what appears to be an Elvis impersonator, children's division. From my elaborate hairdo to my lopsided smile/sneer whenever a camera pointed at me, I emulated the King. All I lacked were sideburns and front teeth.

I hadn't yet begun to collect Elvis records, but his image graced the cover of most of the teen and movie magazines I flipped through at liquor store magazine racks. ("Elvis's wild date with Tuesday Weld — Exclusive!!") Engaged in this sophisticated reading, I also became aware of other stars and scandals. The biggest stories of the season revealed and enumerated the production woes of *Cleopatra*, the most expensive film to date. Stars Elizabeth Taylor and Richard Burton rated as many magazine covers as Elvis did in my early reading years.

Like Elvis at Humes High in Memphis ten years before, I adopted a presentation style that didn't necessarily correspond to my behavior. On one hand, the future King of Rock and Roll was a B-average student who pursued an English major. He also played football and spoke politely to authority figures. On the other hand, he wore an outrageous pompadour and dressed like a black Memphis hoodlum. Like my hero, I must have been a sight in the days after Christmas, strolling about the neighborhood in my sharp threads and slicked-back hair with a brownie camera around my neck. Every au courant pop culture follower in 1961 longed for a transistor radio, but thanks to Jay and Jane's conspicuous generosity, I may have been the first second-grader in Glendale to own one, so we can add to the above description a brick-size radio held to my seven-and-a-half-year-old ear. I can imagine the cries of wonder from the porches as I passed by: "Lookathat, Ralph, one a them Hollywood midgets!"

Age-inappropriate dress and accessories are a mixed blessing; they can invite suspicion from peers but can also be a ticket to friendship with older kids. Walking home from school one day, I met a fifth-grader listening to a transistor radio even smaller than mine. Naturally, we stopped to compare equipment. Technologically, my five-transistor had the edge, with a richer sound and sturdier construction. Any grownup would have seen that. But his smaller radio had a plug-in earphone and could pick up police calls, a feature that, in my mind, trumped my unit's overall quality.

The incident presaged a general trend. As previously mentioned, Jay and Jane appreciated the status value of expensive gifts. That such gifts often come with unintended consequences was best illustrated a couple of Christmases later. Then nine years old, I longed for a Schwinn Varsity ten speed, the acme of luxury in the current neighborhood. But Jay and Jane exceeded this wish in order to delight me and dazzle the other Christmas party guests: an imported Royce Union fifteen-speed racing bicycle.

No one had seen or even heard of a fifteen-speed in those days, and riding it in our poor white and Mexican neighborhood compared with driving a Rolls Royce instead of a Cadillac in the ghetto—the local culture encouraged conspicuous consumption, but one could go too far. To complicate matters, the bike featured a genuine, 27-inch adult frame with razor-thin tires, no kickstand, and tiny uncomfortable seat—everything shaved down to the lightest weight possible for racing. The seat could have been eliminated as well, since even at its lowest setting, I couldn't pedal and sit at the same time. I tended to crash almost every time I rode, and the crashes played havoc with the delicate derailleur (aka derailer) gears.

After a year or so of sporadic use I gave up on the Royce Union altogether, as riding it was more vexation than pleasure. I must have seemed ungrateful, and my vague sense of resentment mixed with guilt feelings for not appreciating Jay and Jane's generosity. Many years later, I attempted to describe such mixed emotions in a tongue-in cheek portrait of the modern academic poet, searching desperately through his privileged and homogenized life for something of interest to write about. But inexorably he returns to his own over-pampered self-centeredness:

> *. . . poems of gratitude and praise? Old as the hills*
> *and besides*
> *I'm like a kid who asks for a bike to do his paper route, see?*
> *And his folks give him a 20-speed titanium frame racer*
> *with no brakes and a tiny seat and he's too short to reach the pedals*
> *so he doesn't thank them and he rides it standing up*
> *and crashes into fences a lot*
> *knowing his parents are always watching,*
> *always disappointed ...*
> *Which brings us around to*
>
> *me and my*
> *angst and self-pity.*
>
> *There. Another job well done.*

My new fifth-grade friend with the two-transistor radio belonged to a family poorer than most in the neighborhood (the ten-dollar radio had been his only present that year, and it came from his grandfather). His profoundly retarded sister needed leg braces and speech therapy and had to take a bus to a special school. Presumably her additional care took much of the family budget. He told me these details one day as we chatted in his garage, but I became distracted from his poignant narrative by a pogo stick I saw hanging on the wall. When I interrupted to inquire, he identified the toy from Christmas two years before and added that it didn't work for him so well anymore. After a few attempts, I could bounce all over the driveway and down the sidewalk, away from my friend's tale of family trials. In later encounters with these ingenious vehicles, I've tried to recapture the joy of bouncing a hundred times in a row, but my second grade height and weight just happened to be the perfect size for operating the equipment. We must gather our rosebuds as we may, and never mind the woes of others.

In Glendale I also began to follow more sedentary pursuits. Notwithstanding my initial scorn for Uncle Barry's car model hobby, I became for a time interested in the two most popular models of the day: the Black Widow and the Green Hornet. These hot rod Fords featured garish decals of webs, spiders, hornets, and the like and led the new trend for the sixties, when model cars supplanted model airplanes. The sticking agent continued to be known as "airplane glue" but a few more years would pass before twelve-year-olds stopped bothering with the models and just sniffed the glue.

After I had stared into the hobby shop window for weeks, Nanny made it possible for me to purchase the Black Widow. Our Wednesday dates had ended when I started first grade, but I could be sure of cash or some small present each time she visited. I found her in the living room one Wednesday afternoon when I returned from school.

"Hi, Darlin'!"

"Hi, Nanny. I really need a dollar-fifty!"

"A dollar-fifty? Goodness, what for?"

"I gotta buy the Black Widow!"

She was already handing me the money. "The *Black Widow*—?"

But I was running out the door.

Possession of the latest craze item suffused within me a temporary sense of peace, but when I attempted to put the Black Widow together, I found I lacked Uncle Barry's patience and manual dexterity in such endeavors. So in those early winter months in mild and pleasant Glendale, I concentrated on hair-combing, roaming around with my radio, and photography, at least until I exhausted the supply of film and flashbulbs included with my Christmas camera.

Despite the junior Elvis look designed to attract any aspiring Tuesday Weld in the neighborhood, I had no love interest during this time. However, I did spend a few purely platonic Saturdays with a girl classmate. I happened to be walking past her house one day and we struck up a conversation about the Rocky and Bullwinkle show. I told her about Bullwinkle's Mr. Know It All parody of Wordsworth's

"I Wandered Lonely as a Cloud." The original lines read "And then my heart with pleasure fills / And dances with the daffodils." But as I related to her, "So Bullwinkle goes, 'And then my heart with anger fills — A dollar apiece for daffodils!?'"

"That's funny!" she agreed. Then she smiled invitingly and said, "You wanna play Candyland?" I followed her gesture toward a little card table by the porch, on which the game had been conveniently laid out.

San Diegan Eleanor Abbot designed Candyland for children as yet unable to read, using colored spaces and corresponding cards. I remember playing it as a lowly five-year-old, and so felt no initial interest at the invitation — what would poker shark Eddie at Wyvernwood think if he saw me at that little table? But the little girl's mother, who must have been watching from the door, brought out a plate of chocolate chip cookies, warm from the oven. I decided a game or two wouldn't hurt.

Apparently Candyland was my classmate's one passion in life. For the next few weekends I would stop by in the afternoons for marathon gaming sessions in her front yard. I remember the winter sun filtered through dwarf lemon trees while, with my heightened sense of private fantasy, I jettisoned my worldly scruples and vividly projected myself into a sort of Wizard of Oz quest through the sugary realms (Gumdrop Mountains) and pitfalls (Molasses Swamp) in the journey toward the gingerbread house finish line. Though I've never played Dungeons and Dragons, I imagined a seven-year-old proto-version of it, courtesy of Milton Bradley.

To temper this wholesomeness, I also learned some new and more sophisticated dirty jokes from boys in the class, and one memorable song:

> *My name is Pancho*
> *I work on the rancho*
> *I make five pesos a day*
> *I go to my Susie*
> *And play with her poo-zee*
> *She takes my five pesos away!*
> *Ole!*

Most of the Austrada neighborhood Mexicans I'd dealt with had been dead-serious tough guys, so I sensed a disconnect with this portrait of Latinos as carefree, musical, and irresponsible womanizers. And whether women were perfidious and insincere opportunists, as suggested in many songs and most jokes, remained an open question. Another supposed stereotype I don't remember as set in stone involved the straight male outlook on homosexuals. Certainly when a boy wouldn't take a dare or climb around an apartment construction site, we would all call him a "sissy." But when confronted with the first apparent transsexual we'd ever seen, the attitude of the mid-century kids I knew appeared less judgmental than the retroactive template assumed by modern pop sociologists.

My introduction to the phenomenon came as I stood in line for my smallpox shot. Mass school vaccinations were routine in those days; in addition to smallpox, the medical authorities inoculated us against DPT and Polio, and both seemed to require innumerable boosters. As I inched toward the front of the line, I beheld, among a group of giggling girls, a first- or second-grader who appeared to be a girl in boys' clothes. This odd creature wore a neat white shirt, suit pants, sheer socks, and delicate slip-ons with tassels. He or she looked extremely slender, with hair shorter than any girl's in the school, but longer than any boy's including mine, and styled in dry waves instead of greased down or shaved close. If I looked like a midget Elvis, this kid resembled a dwarf David Bowie.

"Who's that?" I inquired of the boy in line ahead of me.

"Him? That's Dennis. He plays with the girls." The kid resumed staring at the nurses brandishing hypodermic needles, now in action only a few feet away.

As near as I could tell in the few months I matriculated at that school, everyone accepted the extremely effeminate boy for what he obviously was, someone who belonged with the girls. Dennis made no effort to disguise his inclinations, and his parents apparently allowed him great leeway. In order to maintain safety, teachers encouraged the natural divisions between sexes, which usually involved ordering packs of boys to stop annoying girls. But no authority figure ever attempted to pull Dennis from the jump rope and hopscotch areas and drag him to the ball field. Perhaps the latest theories (scientific and otherwise) that some people are born transgender is an idea neither as modern nor as historically resisted as popular media would have us believe.

But back to Glendale. In sum of this period of my life, besides the name change from Langston, the Christmas party, and meeting the interesting relatives, the Hill family's stay in that pleasant city was more of a transition stop, a chance to catch our familial breath and practice passing as normal suburbanites. However, we didn't practice in Glendale for long. In late March, right before my eighth birthday, with the aid of Freddie, Eddie, and a rental truck, the Hill family moved again and shifted to a higher gear on the bent derailleur of our social progress.

CHAPTER TWENTY-THREE

~ My Friend Freddy ~ Spiels on Wheels~ Easter Birthday
~ Rock War ~ Summer Idylls ~The Promoter

The community of Sylmar nestles against the San Gabriel Mountain range at the far northern edge of the San Fernando Valley.[21] By the early sixties this former olive-growing and ranching center had already begun its losing battle against suburbia, but rents remained low by Valley standards. In mid-February 1961, Jay and Jane stepped up the status ladder by renting a newer, unfurnished Sylmar tract home.

Despite Sylmar's growing suburbanization, our new neighborhood bordered horse ranches, pastures, and desert canyons. By contrast, Hubbard Street Elementary School (also within walking distance) featured all asphalt and bungalows, a layout that would be considered stark by today's greenbelt school standards. But in the days when nature predominated, the vast blacktop provided a welcome novelty.

Hubbard became the third school of my second-grade year and my seventh school so far. After the familiar check-in process, an office aid led me to a mixed A2 and B3 class of over forty students. The beleaguered teacher hardly looked at me as she wrote my name at the bottom of her gradebook and waved me to a desk in a rear corner. The seating split down the middle — second grade on her right, third grade on her left as she faced us. When she worked with one side, she expected the other-graders to remain busy, or at least quiet.

At Hubbard I read my first novel and wrote my first poem, both important vocational milestones. I discovered the novel in second grade during one of the teacher's sessions with the older kids.

---

[21] The San Gabriel Valley, which one would think ought to be in closer proximity to those San Gabriel Mountains, is actually thirty miles or so southeast, probably in another shadow of the same range (though they may be called the San Fernando Mountains over there).

Taking a break from in cursive writing exercises to drink from the fountain at the back of the room, I noticed, on a shelf above the tin countertop, a short line of books. Intrigued by a cover illustration of a pig in a frock coat and top hat placing a crown on the head of a decrepit-looking rat, I picked up *Freddy and Simon the Dictator* by Walter R. Brooks.[22]

I began to read even as I slowly returned to my seat. I spent the rest of the afternoon absorbed, all schoolwork forgotten. The plot involves Freddy the Pig's Machiavellian efforts to thwart an *Animal Farm*-like revolution led by Simon the rat. At one point Freddy uses psychological warfare when he captures human villain Herb Garble, Simon's co-conspirator. He shows Garble a "Grand War Dance and Scalping Party" poster announcing that the event will feature Garble burned at the stake by Freddie's Indian friends, with stake and firewood furnished by the local lumber company. Admission is fifty-cents, children half price, and "Supper will be served after the entertainment by the ladies of the First Presbyterian Church." The psychologically devastated Garble agrees to betray Simon, and after many plot twists, Freddy overthrows the revolution. He then becomes a powerbroker in New York state politics and introduces a bill to abolish all schools.

Enthralled, I read every book in the countertop collection, beginning with another Brooks masterpiece *Freddy and the Baseball Team from Mars* and proceeding immediately to the original *Boxcar Children* by Gertrude C. Warner and *The Spaceship Under the Apple Tree* by Louis Slobodkin. And thus began a pattern that worked well for most of my elementary school career: I completed most assignments, earned reasonable grades, and rarely caused trouble. In return, the overworked teachers rarely disturbed my quiet reading. But my handwriting never recovered.

Modern innovation soon joined forces with Freddy to further my new addiction. One day after school, I noticed a large vehicle, about the size of today's deluxe motor homes, parked in the teacher's lot. The Bookmobile, that brainstorm of a Van Nuys library visionary who designed it for weekly visits to "outlying" areas such as Sylmar, had arrived. I stepped up the folding stairs like Aladdin entering the enchanted cave. Before me I beheld a whole trailer full of every

---

[22] *Simon* is still my favorite, but Brooks wrote 24 other Freddy books between 1927 and 1958, and I highly recommend them all. For more on Brooks's body of work, readers are encouraged to look up "Friends of Freddy" on the Internet.

sort of volume, in floor to ceiling shelves tilted upward to hold the contents while driving. Bolted-down tables and a tiny checkout desk completed the furnishings.

The traveling librarian seemed pleased to issue me my first library card, but she informed me that late returns incurred a two-cents-per-day fine and that I would be assessed a twenty-five cent charge if I lost the card. Looking back, she seemed to sense my chronic inability to keep track of library material, a character flaw that has plagued me from that day to this. But I barely noticed her warnings and admonitions, so fascinated was I at the 1964 expiration date stamped on my ticket to seemingly unlimited reading. That year seemed so far forward in the mists of time! By 1964 citizens would enjoy rocket travel, monorails, and all the comforts of the Disneyland House of the Future. Families would have jet cars, robot servants, and wardrobes like those in comic book depictions of Krypton, Superman's home planet. Back at Wyvernwood I had seen conclusive evidence for most of the above in the 1960 movie *The Time Machine*, wherein the time traveler lands briefly in 1964, right on time for a nuclear bomb attack.

I had already become a steady customer at the library by the time of my eighth birthday on Easter Sunday, April 2, 1961. In historical context, that date fell a few weeks before the Bay of Pigs invasion and only days before the first rocket belt flight by American inventor Harold Graham. But the historic value for me involved its combined birthday and holiday gifts: a new watch and five dollars cash, plus an Easter basket filled with green plastic grass and plenty of candy. Trish and I opened our baskets at daybreak; they had been thoughtfully left out in the living room the night before by late holiday sleepers Jay and Jane. In those early years, my mother and grandmother sometimes spoke vaguely about the family attending church for Easter, but the services always commenced a bit too early to actually get up and go. We did, however, receive new Easter outfits and shoes, the element of the holiday that Jane and Nanny remembered most fondly from their childhoods.

Around noon of that memorable day, after filling my pants pockets with the few candy eggs I hadn't already consumed, I proceeded to explore the new neighborhood. Strolling along and enjoying the warm sun on the back of my neck, I took frequent downward glances to admire my shiny slip-ons. I remember a pleasant sugar buzz and a vivid sense of well-being at having attained the dignified age of eight.

Turning a corner, I came upon a vacant lot where twenty or so kids engaged in a neighborhood rock fight. Actually, they were mostly throwing dirt clods, plentiful on that field of battle. The teams seemed evenly divided, so I fell into the ranks closest to me. As I moved among the troops, a few them of gave me the businesslike but appreciative nods that reinforcements always receive when they join a battle in progress.

Missiles began falling to my right and left; probably forty-eight of fifty throws went wide, about average for rock fights. My first scrabble for ammunition turned up a beauty of a hard, smooth stone with perfect throwing dimensions. Taking general aim at the group across the lot, I let fly.

A few years later I became a fairly accurate softball pitcher and developed a decent aim in bowling, darts, pocket billiards, and other target games. But what happened next must be credited to beginner's luck. My missile arched in a perfect trajectory and, with a sound like a bat hitting a watermelon, struck one of the opponents dead center on the forehead. With a cry of shock and pain, the boy put his hands to his head and brought them away bloody. All movement on our side abruptly ceased. His teammates rushed over to surround him. Then everyone's eyes turned on me.

"Hey! That wasn't no dirt clod!"

"Who's he?"

"No fair!"

More voices rose—loud and angry voices. I looked around stunned, my sugar rush gone. I heard a commotion on the other side of the field and saw a grownup lady approaching rapidly. At the sight of her, my teammates backed away from me with the unanimity of synchronized swimmers, effectively fingering me as the perpetrator.

"Go away from here!" the woman yelled, a touch of hysteria in her voice. The victim's mom, it had to be. "You're not from this neighborhood! Go away and don't come back!"

The expressions of the kids who remained on the field would remind me later of the outside-the-courtroom faces on TV news clips, the scenes where murderers are escorted to court through a cordon of victim's relatives. I turned and hastened from the accusing faces, a pariah among decent people. I remember no great concern on my part for the bleeding kid; it seemed to me that a few painless stitches, as I'd gotten from the doctor in Alabama after I ran into the parked car, would fix him good as new. If anything, I felt a dull resentment against him for getting in the way of the rock and spoiling my perfect day.

Life in Sylmar offered more than reading and armed conflict: I entered smart society as well. One day toward the end of the school year, teacher sent me to the B3 side for an advanced reading group. A couple of older girls there gave my slick hair and cultivated Elvis smile an appraising eye, and I remember one young lady in particular whose relatively tight skirt and upswept hairdo marked her as a fellow midget teenager. The next week on the way to the La Brea Tar Pits, a field trip destination visited eventually by every student in the L.A. Unified School district, I sat with this sophisticate in the rear bench of the bus, the only seat unsegregated by gender. On the long rides to and from the tar pits, we discussed literature (mainly Archie comics and movie magazines), culture (the museum was dumb, but the sabertooth tiger skeleton made the trip worthwhile), and music (we both loved the calliope accompaniment in the current hit, "Goodbye Cruel World: I'm Off to Join the Circus").

When school let out for summer vacation I lost track of this almost-girlfriend and reverted to more manly pursuits. Like Robbie before me, I sold flower and vegetable seeds door to door, supplied by mail from a Midwest company that advertised their business opportunities in comic books. In June I made a few forays to the nearby desert, which, though within walking distance, had it all: lizards, Joshua trees, and nerdy teen rockhounds in khaki shirts tapping away with little hammers in search of quartz. The scenic route to the nearest shopping center (where I spent my seed earnings on more comic books) took me down a long dirt road unchanged since the olive grove and ranch days. I could stand on the bottom rail of a corral along the way and pat actual horses on the nose, pretending I had gone back in time to the cowboy era.

In another historical fantasy excursion, I spent a few summer days emulating the Laurel and Hardy portrayal of hoboes I'd seen on early Saturday morning TV. To get in character, I cut an old pair of jeans ragged at the bottom, put on a cast-off shirt of Jay's, and fixed a bindle on the end of a stick. I paraded around the neighborhood faux-puffing on a candy cigarette and sloshing through gutters in celebration of the hobo's total freedom from social convention. I eventually sat right down in an irrigation runoff to enjoy the cool water. Today, neighbors observing a child thus occupied might raise an alarm, but their forbearers left me to languid contemplation of the stream as it detoured around me.

Though we lived in Sylmar for a full year—practically a lifelong homestead for our family—I made no close friends. Over the last several moves I had grown used to entertaining myself, though I remained willing to team with other kids on an ad hoc basis when plans and inspiration meshed. One day in July I saw one of my former classmates outfitted in long pants and shoes, and I inquired as to why he had submitted to such vestments in the summertime.

"Vacation Bible school," he replied. He showed me three or four mimeographed illustrations of Bible scenes with added stickers and coloring. "Wanna go with me tomorrow? They got snacks and stuff."

The "vacation" part of Vacation Bible School sounded festive, so I accompanied him the next day, wearing my school clothes and carrying a dime from Jane for the collection. She was always mildly encouraging when I showed an interest in religion. But though the Bible stories seemed interesting, I only stayed for one session—the class seemed too old-fashioned, somehow: the sort of old-fashioned that didn't excite me the way dirt roads, cowboys, and hoboes did. Plus, I just didn't feel right wearing shoes in July.

Later in the summer, I worked all day with the same kid to stage an elaborate performance inspired by KTTV Channel 5's Wednesday night wrestling matches. Announcer Dick Lane would holler his trademark "Whoa Nelly!" at the antics of fearsome Freddie Blassie (who coined the phrase "pencil neck geek"), the mysteriously masked Destroyer, the hugely fat Zebra Man, and other perfidious villains.

Inspired, we put together our own neighborhood show. My friend acted as both wrestler and crew supervisor; I cast myself as announcer, wrestler, and snackbar manager. One morning before eight a.m., using garden hoses, lawn rakes, and two old mattresses, we began building a fight ring in his garage. After more than four hours of intense labor, rehearsal, and organization, we marched, town crier style, throughout the neighborhood. "Come one! Come All! Big wrassling extravaganza!" Word spread and young customers turned out by the dozens to pay the ten cents admission. We also offered bags of popcorn and paper cups of Kool Aid, prepared by our assistants, the mother and sisters of my partner, at an additional five cents per.

"Lay-deez and Gentlemen!" I bawled to the capacity crowd in the garage. "Our first match is Bluto against the Alien from the Future!" I hastened behind the bedsheet hung at stage left, which hid the backstage area and passage to the kitchen. "Bluto," my business partner, had already donned his fake beard and sailor hat. As I put on my rain boots and a space helmet similar to the one I'd had in San Pedro years before, he slipped through the sheet and strutted on stage. After waiting a strategic moment for his applause and boos to rise and fall, I joined him in the ring, holding my clasped hands above my head.

Both of us portrayed bad guys, a strategy that, in my professional opinion, demonstrated better showmanship than KTTV's practice of matching villains with insipid good guys and having the good guys win more often than not. We presented an exciting match, with plenty of dirty fighting on both sides—we knew the drill. For the other bouts we had provided a forum for several neighborhood actors, including one fourth grade Amazon who dominated her match against a spindly third-grader in a ski mask. Overall, our show was a great success. Besides the most fun I'd had in years, my partner and I cleared two or three dollars to split between us after covering supplies and small honorariums for kids who served as actors, roustabouts, and snackbar attendants.

Looking back, I think the managerial aspect of the enterprise— giving orders, collecting money, and counting the house—provided the most fun. When my wife and I went on a Busby Berkeley movie jag a few years ago, I empathized with the stage manager characters in those films— Backstage Drama! Last-minute decisions! Artistic Angst! And a couple of years ago my promoter days came back to me when I thumbed through *My Life Inside Rock and Out*, an autobiography by Bill Graham, the famous rock music impresario. The book chronicled Graham's trials and triumphs in putting together shows and tours in the 1960s and 70s—how he worked from behind the scenes, simultaneously handling (and sometimes mishandling) finances, accounting, and the psychodynamics of crowd control and artistic temperaments. As I read the book, I could relate. I've been there, too, Bill.

CHAPTER TWENTY-FOUR

~ Merchandise on Approval ~ Flaming Star ~ High Society in the Short Term
~ The Iron Lady ~Last Stand of Ereeky Longston ~ A Pass on Scouting
~ Public Service and Contemplation of Fleeting Time

As any eight-year-old will tell you, that year of growth provides opportunity for much expansion beyond young childhood. In Sylmar I stretched my boundaries in reading, getting around on my own, pursuing many hobbies, running a business, and learning the joys of consumer culture.

Nanny had previously seeded my coin collecting hobby with some Indian head pennies, and my interest quickened when the lady next door bestowed a handful of old and/or rare Lincoln cents in exchange for putting her vast penny collection into bankable form. Hour by hour I stuffed coppers into those slightly-too-tight paper rolls, but the 1912D I found made the toil worthwhile. Nanny then went one better with an 1865 three-cent piece and several silver dollars I kept until junior high.[23]

I would introduce my forays into commerce by noting that the business model of the twenty-first century assumes people are basically dishonest and untrustworthy. Risk nothing; cash or debit card up front. But until the early sixties, a vestige of the old American idea of inviolable personal integrity made it possible to start my flower seed business with no investment. Furthermore, companies with advertising in the back of comic books would send any kid a box of toy soldiers or a chemistry set COD. You could also send for free or cheap coins and stamps, and those companies would include in your package merchandise sent "on approval," with confidence you would pay or send the item(s) back. On reflection, I may be at

---

[23] In summer 1966 I sold most of them to an old robber at a coin store to finance purchases of Bob Dylan, Beatles, and Rolling Stones records.

least partially responsible for the trend away from consumer trust. Presumably most kids — or their parents — strove to be conscientious about these transactions, but I'm afraid I still owe for some buffalo nickels and genuine Caribbean-country-you-never-heard-of stamps lost in my room or missing in a move.

Another area of trust seemingly unthinkable half a century later involves, as I have alluded to previously, the presumed safety of children in situations that would horrify parents today. On their weekend driving jaunts, Jay and Jane thought nothing of leaving their three youngsters in an unlocked car for hours while they shopped. They also felt comfortable trusting their toddler to the supervision of a flighty eight-year-old. Jay worked six days a week, so I usually spent Saturday mornings at home, babysitting Trish while Jane shuttled back and forth to the Laundromat with Greg. Though I did remain in the house as instructed, I generally ignored Trish. Like me she had learned to entertain herself, and she usually played on the living room floor with her imaginary friend "Ballerina."

Meanwhile, having learned to operate the hi-fi console recently purchased from Goodwill, I played and studied the three records Jane and Jay had thus far collected. The first spin was always Elvis's "Flaming Star," the title track from his latest movie wherein he plays a half-breed caught between settlers and Indians in the Oklahoma territory.[24] The lyrics to "Flaming Star" seemed to me the epitome of manly poetry, as deep and noble as boys of a previous generation might have found Homer or Tennyson. The invisible flaming star that foretold death always loomed over a warrior making his way in the world; when the star became visible to the warrior, his demise would soon follow. Elvis intoned this legend with all possible seriousness, accompanied by a synthetic Indian tom-tom beat and electric guitar licks to set the mood.

I also played over and over one of the two complete LPs in the family collection: *Something For Everybody* by Elvis, a foray into more polished "rhythms" (fast songs) and ballads, as befitted the King turning a mature 26. The other album, a live nightclub recording by Red Foxx, featured such shockingly risqué humor as this paraphrase: "Some fella tryin' to teach me to play golf. He say we got to tee-off

---

[24] The song came on a special edition 33⅓ platter the size of a 45, a promotional record sponsored by the Singer Sewing Machine company, who also bankrolled Elvis's comeback special six years later.

first. I say, 'Look here, man, if I tee-off, I'm gon' do it behind the barn!'"

I first heard this adult entertainment when several grownups came over for cocktails. At that soirée, Jay and Jane served refreshments from new five-bottle stock of liquor displayed on a rolling glass table. The starter bar focused Jay and Jane's aspirations to gentility, but overall the house had a sort of conservative beatnik ambiance with its spray-paint black Styrofoam tikis, gigantic Mexican pottery ashtrays with holders for up to sixteen cigarettes, and a faux-Incan sun goddess plaster wall plaque. Most of our basic furnishings came from Goodwill or the Salvation Army store. (Jay called them "Good Willie" and "The Sally.")

To personalize the low-budget items, Jay also began to teach himself home improvement crafts. A quick study, he would in future houses install paneling, tile, and landscaping; turn garages into rumpus rooms; wire and plumb; pour concrete, build block walls, and install sprinkler systems. But it all began in Sylmar. For bookshelves he gilded cinder blocks and stained plank shelves walnut; he painted an ancient desk and metal reading lamp in matching brown. His first construction effort produced a vanity table from wooden orange crates (with a Jane-sewn curtain over the crates) and a hand-sawed Formica top.

Funding for further ventures came with Jay's promotion to manager at King Cole Market in Burbank, where he grossed a hundred dollars ("a bill" in his parlance) per week. He also jumped on the fast track to supervisor of the four-store chain, a goal he achieved a few months later at the princely sum of two bills a week. Another family legend: when the King Cole owners chose Jay as a candidate for the supervisor position, they invited him to dinner at one of the finest restaurants in Burbank. He discovered at the last minute that his only suit had been lost or damaged in our move from Glendale. Such a setback might have daunted other men, but he swept into the restaurant "like I owned the place!" wearing slacks, a silk tie with a sapphire pin (his most valuable treasure), and a button-up sweater. "And at the next dinner," Jay reported, "they all wore sweaters!"

While still a one-store manager, Jay conceived another funds-stretching scheme. Jane would shop at his store during the pre-dinner rush when all personnel available manned the cash registers. She pretended not to know Jay as she proceeded through his checkstand, where, fingers flying, he would either miss or mis-price items, lowering her grand total by at least fifty per cent. This discount served them well for years and its success paved the way for more innovations like the blue chip stamp scheme, to be described in detail later. In sum, all but the last few weeks of Sylmar were a winning streak for Jay, and we passed for middle class right through the end of my second grade year and on into summer.

More evidence of normality came when I took the unprecedented step of entering a new grade *at the same school.* But I enjoyed minimal social continuity when I returned in the fall. My previous B3 classmates had become A3s in another building, and most of my former fellow A2 classmates (now newly minted B3s) were also thus assigned. So of my class only I and one other late transfer from the year before were put in the charge of infamous Mrs. Yamamoto.

This venerable educator, a stiff, grey-haired Japanese matron no more than five feet tall, provided the best illustration I have encountered in person or in print of the term "Iron Lady," not excluding Margaret Thatcher herself. Mrs. Y organized her classroom as a milder version of the Japanese military school model. We had to line up in strict formation after recess before we could march back into the classroom. In class we were admonished to sit up straight in our chairs. We did our work (or free reading, if we were unobtrusive about it), with no talking among ourselves except when permitted to do so during arts and crafts period. Those among us who dared break a rule were held up to ridicule. "You don' know class rule? Ha! Ha! Yes, you know! You KNOW class rule. You sit in punish room foa quawta howa!"

By "punish room" she meant our classroom's walk-in closet—not exactly an isolation chamber since it had no door to shut out sound and light, but even so, one felt lonesome back there. We needed a coat closet: high-desert Sylmar suffered colder temperatures in the winter than most of Southern California. Once in December when classmate Steve and I made an attempt to reach the nearby mountains (they were further away than they looked), hailstones pelted us for a few minutes.

But speaking of the coat closet, I returned from lunch one afternoon to find Mrs. Yamamoto holding a familiar yellow raincoat. Heavy rain had fallen one morning the week before, and when the sun came out in the afternoon, I'd forgotten all about the coat and neglected to take it home.

"Who slicka?! Who rain slicka dis?!"

"It's mine," I mumbled, and shuffled up to claim it.

But she held it tightly, looking severely first at me, then at the inside collar of the coat. "You Areechar Heel! Why dis laybo say Areeky Longston!"

Longston? But then I remembered: Jane had written "Ricky Langston" on the label two years before. (The coat fit a bit tightly on me now, but remained serviceable.)

"Uh, that's another name, mumble mumble..."

"Yes! What you say? Why two name you?"

As Mrs. Y waited for a clearer answer, I wondered how to best evade the question. Despite the Hills' relative stability at this point, I had fully internalized that I belonged to a family that lived beyond normal rules and sensibilities. And when in doubt, reveal nothing about anything. So I kept on mumbling until she handed over the coat with a suspicious glare. We both knew there was more to me than met the eye.

Mrs. Yamamoto wasn't the only tough female I had to deal with in the classroom. A chubby girl named Rose sat across from me at the table configuration Mrs. Y preferred over individual desks. Rose and I were always paired during arts and crafts, and she enumerated my artistic shortcomings in the bluntest terms.

"Your turkey looks stupid and your pilgrim is a mess! Can't you cut right?"

"This is the way it's supposed to look. Yours is stupid."

"Is not!"

"Is so!"

The above exchange took place in mid-November, the month for drawing Thanksgiving icons. Despite my vigorous defense, I knew my turkey and pilgrim appeared woefully primitive when displayed next to Rose's. In eight different classes in seven schools so far, I'd found myself sometimes ahead of others in academic pursuits and sometimes behind, depending on the teaching pace of the current institution. But apparently I had some chronic shortcomings. I remained particularly untalented in cutting and pasting neatly, and having to use right-handed scissors didn't help matters. I now suspect that I suffered from mild dyslexia, not uncommon among left-handers in the right-handed world. But Sylmar marked the first realization that, in some areas at least, I couldn't overcome my limitations.

However, all self-doubt swept away (at least temporarily) when, during a "Language" unit, Teacher assigned us to write our own poems. Most of my classmates were as incompetent at this task as I had been at cutting out turkeys, but I demonstrated a flair for rhyme and became immediately consumed with versification. I let my latest Freddy book lie as I worked feverishly—revising for rhythm, scribbling, erasing, moving lines, changing line breaks, revising again. I even took my poem home and worked on it over the weekend.

When I brought my creation back Monday and showed it to Mrs. Yamamoto, she nodded approvingly. "You read foa sheh time!"

During share time, students read short paragraphs on inspiring topics, like rockets or dinosaurs, or gave talks on their dads or their pets. Some kids lived on small ranches and shared about their farm animals; girls showed their model horses and sewing projects. In my first public performance since the wrestling match, I presented the following original composition, entitled "Rain." Those familiar with my current poetry will detect in this seminal effort much of the sensibility of my later work. I have added end punctuation, ellipses and capital letters, to help capture the original pace and emphasis of the reading; otherwise it is presented here exactly as I recited it in late 1961:

> *The rain…is water.*
> *The water…is rain.*
> *It rains on the plains*
> *and here, too —*
> *But when it rains here,*
> *there's nothing to do!*
> *So…I sit and sit…*
> *And wait and wait…*
> *but when it stops,*
> *It's TOO LATE —*
> *Too late to play*
> *Too late to say*
> *Hooray!*

Yet another mark of my burgeoning maturity at Sylmar came with election to the school Service Patrol. In exchange for an official green sash and certain privileges, boys from third grade on up could volunteer to serve the school during one recess per day. According to school authorities, we represented the local equivalent to a nation's military or civil service, though a more cynical view might place us in closer relation to prison trustees. In any case, both the Safety Patrol and Service squads had the freedom of going into class five minutes late after recess duty. When the bell rang, we'd leave our posts and all crowd around the drinking fountain like enlisted men on leave at a downtown bar ("Hey! Save some for the fish!"). Then we'd swagger into the restroom and see who could pee the highest on the old-fashioned urinal.

Older boys worked their way up in the Safety Patrol section: they guarded drinking fountains, halls, and gates, maintaining order by the authority of their sashes. All new third-grade recruits reported to the Service sector where we drew various assignments. My first job was running the bowling game for kindergarteners. I set up the small plastic pins, making sure everyone had a turn with the plastic balls, and kept an eye out for little bowlers who tended to wander off-site.

As I ran after wild shots and picked up kindergarteners who'd fallen on the asphalt, I contemplated the inexorable passage of time. These miniscule beings knew nothing of real games. They'd never sold flower seeds, nor organized a neighborhood show, nor checked out a book from a library. Ignorant of literature or literary composition, they had never pulled a knife on anyone nor rode a city bus by themselves. They looked so innocent and small—I had to bend over to make eye contact with them.

And yet it seemed only yesterday when I too had been a carefree child, wandering around Bert's alley in my first space helmet, singing the Popeye song. And during one recess when I actually heard one of my charges lisping "I'm Popeye the sailor maaan ..." the performance struck me in the depths of my eight-year-old soul with a deep, nostalgic pang for the lost days of youth.

CHAPTER TWENTY-FIVE

~ April Fool ~ Truth, Beauty, Fortitude, and Service, More or Less
~ Jay's Sensitive Side ~ A Prince in the Market

On April Fool's day 1961, I wore my favorite footwear. This obscure fact lodges in my mind because, when I emerged from my room at breakfast, Jane smiled and then, pointing at my left foot with an air of concern, said "Your shoe's untied."

When I looked down at my new black slip-ons, she laughed like a schoolgirl. She had always been cheerful, even under duress, but during the 1961–62 Sylmar period she seemed genuinely happy. Jay had become the longest love of her life, and he seemed to have gotten over his general instability and block against keeping a job. They fell comfortably into suburban life and spent whole weekends decorating the new house. They even bought some lounge chairs for the back yard and a two-foot-deep wading pool. I still bear a scar from a shallow dive into that pool during an August rainstorm while wearing the now definitely too-small Ricky Langston raincoat over my bathing suit. As I scraped the bottom of pool, the metal clasp on the garment dug a furrow in my chest. I never repeated that impulsive experiment, but I did henceforth feel more empathy with Jay's childhood story of wearing a Superman cape and jumping off the garage roof.

Except for an occasional drive-in movie, neither Jay nor Jane cared for excursions or family outings. I had begun to like sitting around in the evenings reading novels as much as they did, but several of my Safety Patrol colleagues belonged to the Cub Scouts, and one of them invited me to the yearly new-member orientation. The proceedings seemed confusing, and according to the mimeographed sheet I picked up, the charges for uniform, registration fee, and first dues came to a vast sum, around fifty dollars.

I presented the sheet to Jay and Jane, neither of whom showed much enthusiasm. Jay said, "That's a lot of money, pal. You ready to wear a cap over your fancy hairdo?" Jane postponed a verdict with, "I don't know, honey. We'll think about it."

They probably would have financed the endeavor if I had shown real enthusiasm, but I had an inkling of the Scouts as an impenetrable in-group where I would never feel comfortable, much less shine. So I didn't press the issue, and some years later I would come to the same conclusion about the United States Armed Forces. In retrospect, I think I saved myself and both organizations some headaches.

Fortunately for my social growth, my wrestling show partner introduced me to the Woodcraft Rangers, a sort of poor kids' Cub Scouts, only co-ed. The Rangers were conceived by Earnest Thomas Seaton, a Scotsman born in the mid-nineteenth century. He had helped organize the Boy Scouts before he broke away to start his own group. According to the Ranger website, "Seaton ('The Chief,' AKA 'Black Wolf') was an award winning wildlife illustrator and naturalist as well as a spell-binding storyteller and lecturer, a bestselling author of animal stories, an expert with Native American sign language and early supporter of the political, cultural and spiritual rights of First Peoples." The Rangers evolved over the next forty years and are still active today, though mostly as a vehicle to give inner city kids a little time off the streets.

I could join this tribe for two dollars, plus twenty-five cents dues per week. Jay and Jane had no objections this time, and this more laid-back organization seemed more my style anyway. Though Rangers had no official uniforms, we did wear our "coup sashes" to the weekly meetings. Each feather-shaped coup sewn on the sashes stood for a noble attribute: Truth (green) Beauty (blue) Fortitude (brown) and Service (yellow). Members earned coups by helping others, learning woodcraft skills such as building fires and tracking, and constructing useful items along the science project line.

New Rangers strived for eight coups of each color. Success would advance the achiever from tenderfoot to "Sachem" level. In my zeal for tribal status I jumped on the fast track. The neighborhood chapter had been seeking a tribal name, and they unanimously approved my inspired-by-Elvis suggestion of "The Flaming Stars." That earned me a Service coup, and I parlayed the idea into a second coup by constructing a treasury container from a cigar box covered in construction paper with a flaming star drawn on the lid. That I would do all the work myself to get the coup went without saying, but I saw nothing unethical in concentrating on the drawing and having Jane help me with the cutting and pasting part.

In the ensuing months I didn't shrink from cutting further corners for fast coups—Fortitude, Truth, or otherwise. If the task called for, say, observing tracks in the woods for a mile, I would follow horseshoe prints down the dirt road for a block or two and call it good. I don't know if or how much Jay's Modus Vivendi influenced me in this area, but I was learning the ways of the world, or at least a popular view of them.

Meetings took place at members' homes on a rotating basis. May, a hefty, brown-complexioned older Sylmar native, had been our tribe's permanent adult supervisor for several years. She had a Spanish surname, but wore grey braids wound on her head and looked authentically Indian. Rides in May's old station wagon provided the warmest group times I'd had since San Pedro. Despite a range of ages from eight to twelve, all the boys and girls strove to be companionable. May led us in singing "Sippin' Cider Through a Straw" ("cheek to cheek, and jaw to jaw—just sippin' Ci...der through a straw"), "Amsterdam" (which featured an opportunity to yell the swear word "damn" in the chorus—"Amster, Amster, dam! dam! dam!"), and other summer camp songs from the 1920s and 30s.

We attended regular Wednesday night presentations at the Griffith Park planetarium, and once we took an all-day trip to the official Woodcraft Ranger camp at the Stanley Ranch in Saugus, then the rural outskirts of the county. Rangers in good standing could pay the discount five-dollar rate for a weekend at the Ranch, including two nights sleeping under the stars, five meals, horseback riding, and swimming. Everyone in my tribe expressed avowed interest in the weekend excursion, but to my surprise, only I actually signed up. Even the bigger kids felt apprehensive about spending the night in new surroundings, but I was an old hand at new surroundings.

On the plus side, I did enjoy the swimming and horseback riding, but the camp seemed too regimented for my taste—even more lining up and marching around than at school. Most of the kids weren't Rangers, and the ones picked to lead the evening Great Spirit prayer ceremony had to read the proceedings from a sheet. I knew the ersatz Noble Red Man ceremony by heart from our weekly meetings but found no opportunity to share my expertise. I did make a few critical remarks to a fourth grade bunkmate, dropping in Ranger lore and technical terms as often as possible, but he didn't seem much impressed.

When May brought me home Sunday afternoon, I found out I'd missed a near-tragedy. Jane had felt unwell when I left on Friday, and on Saturday she had coughing spells so severe that she could hardly breathe. When Jay rushed her to the hospital, the doctor on duty diagnosed pneumonia, still a serious disease now but much more so in those days.

Jay could handle great pain himself, as I saw when he broke his leg a few years later. He always had a steady hand in fixing wounds and he never showed any fear of dangerous people or situations. But from his youngest days, perhaps from the time he found his mom bleeding on the floor, he had had a phobia of hospitals, a terror of loved ones hurt, and an aversion to copious blood.

These feelings reared up when he waited in the emergency room. Finally, the doctor on duty came out to tell him Jane was out of danger. "But," he added, "we almost lost her. She's allergic to penicillin and we had trouble stabilizing her. If she had arrived ten minutes later, she'd be gone now." At this pronouncement, Jay fainted, fell backwards, and hit the floor. The doctor stitched up a gash in his head, then ordered him to leave the hospital for his and everyone else's safety.

Jane lay in bed at home when I returned from camp on Sunday, and Jay told me the whole story. Looking back, I find two interesting aspects of his narrative: (a) that he related the details to me at all, since telling an eight-year-old his mother almost died seems unnecessary at best, and (b) that he revealed his fainting incident with such candor. Though probably the most private person I've ever known, he had the charismatic gift of being able to tell potentially humiliating stories about himself with humor rather than bluster or excuses. Over the years I saw how this rare trait tended to disarm listeners, even those put on guard by previous incidents of his shading the truth.

I had the opportunity to view Jay in full charismatic mode a few days later when, prompted by Jane, he took me to his King Cole Market worksite. This event marked one of two instances in my childhood years (both instigated by Jane) in which we spent formal Father and Son Time together. Neither of us desired this matchmaking; our relations stayed amiable but distant for the most part (until I became a teenager), and amiable but distant perfectly described the way we both felt most comfortable. However, neither of us openly opposed Father and Son Time, so the outing went forth.

In keeping with Jay's executive status, we arrived at the Burbank King Cole store about nine. He seemed to gear up when we walked in the front door, assuming a focused but relaxed manner. He introduced me to a manager and assistant manager who looked upon me with benevolent interest. Jay rushed off to address some logistics problem, and I drifted to the magazine area. King Cole occupied a niche known today as a "premium" market, meaning they stocked a larger selection of luxury foods and Grade A produce than most stores. Most impressive of all, a separate liquor department featured a huge magazine stand, well-stocked with my kind of reading matter. In preparation for study, I chose some candy and attempted to pay for it at the liquor counter, but the clerk waved away my nickel. "No charge," he said, giving me the same benevolent look I'd seen from the managers a few minutes before.

I sat on the floor with Superman Annual #3, a very special issue I'd seen advertised and had longed for, but despaired of finding. The Sylmar liquor stores probably caboosed a long distribution train and rarely stocked a full range of comics. The only annual carried by my neighborhood source was the Lois Lane special, full of imaginary marriages for the Man of Steel, all of which seemed to follow the lead of TV sitcoms.

But here I beheld the magnificent Giant 1961 Superman Annual # 3: eighty full color pages. Novelist Somerset Maugham, who, as related in a memoir, burst into tears when he held an original Keats manuscript, couldn't have known more happiness than I felt when I held that annual. The lurid cover depicted the Man of Steel in all sorts of incarnations: an old man, a prisoner in Kryptonite chains, an evolved futuroid with a high forehead, etc. While I didn't possess the twenty-five cents to actually purchase the book, I did have plenty of time to peruse it, for I reasoned correctly that the clerk wouldn't pull the "Whadaya think this is, the public liberry?!" on Jay's son.

I had just finished "The Ancient Superman," an imaginary story set in the far distant future of 2015 or so, when Jay hurried by, trailed by one of the assistant managers. He noticed me and stopped. "You want to make some money?" he said.

"Sure!" As a matter of fact, I had an immediate need for twenty-five cents.

Jay said he'd pay a penny apiece for each shopping cart I retrieved from the lot and brought to the rack in front of the store, with the understanding that they had to be King Cole carts. "I was paying another kid to bring 'em in," he explained. "But he stole from every store within two miles. The Vons manager gave me hell."

I worked with alacrity for the next hour or so, clearing the lot and adjacent walks and alleys, pushing cart after cart into the store, sometimes waiting impatiently for customers to finish loading their cars. As I pushed three carts together past a bus bench, a black kid about a year older than I gave me a sullen look. "Mr. Jay tell you to bring in them carts?" he demanded.

"He's my dad."

The kid changed his expression to inscrutable and sauntered away. On the same trip I passed a white teenage boxboy by the door. He had pimples and a pompadour, and he too gave me the kind of stare Hawaiians call "the stinkeye."

Jay stopped me before I could go out again. "Wait for me a few minutes, and we'll go to lunch," he said.

I resumed the Superman annual. When Jay returned, I closed the book to put it back. "Keep it," he said. He grabbed another handful of comic books and gave me those, too. A few of the management team gathered around him. Without looking at them, Jay walked out, and we all followed. In the car he gave me a dollar, probably twice what I'd earned at a cent a cart. "You're running rings around the box boy," he grinned. "He's scared to death I'll fire him."

At a coffee shop down the street, I had a hamburger and malt while Jay's entourage followed his lead in ordering steak sandwiches and coffee. I listened as they exchanged stories of celebrities coming to the Toluca Lake store: comics Phyllis Diller and Jonathan Winters seemed to be regular shoppers, and both stars, in the retail clerks' judgment, showed evidence of certifiable insanity.

Everyone deferred to Jay, looking at him surreptitiously to gage his enjoyment of their stories. Store manager Dan told of his encounter the year before with a stickup artist called the "Man from Mars," so named because of the alien mask he wore during robberies. "It was right after closing," said Dan. "This guy comes out of nowhere with a gun and the mask and all—he must have snuck in earlier and hid in the back. He shut everybody but me in the dairy case—told 'em if they came out he'd kill 'em."

I had been glancing through the comic book, but now I gave

Dan my full attention. "One of the butchers came out anyhow," he continued. "He made it downstairs and called the police from the liquor phone. Meanwhile the guy marches me upstairs to open the office safe."

"How'd you get the combination?" asked Jay. "Only the supervisor is supposed to know it."

"The supervisor wrote it down on a piece of paper so he wouldn't forget, and I knew where he taped the paper under the desk." Dan grinned and shook his head. "I really thought the guy was gonna shoot me. So I opened the safe — and I almost got killed anyway."

"What happened?"

"After the butcher called, a couple Burbank cops snuck up the stairs. When the guy came out of the office, he had me in front of him, holding the money, with the gun poking in my back. A cop pops up and shoots him right between the eyes. I could feel the bullet go past my face and the guy fell on me, bleeding like a stuck pig. He never pulled the trigger."

"Man," said one of the spellbound listeners, "I wanna take you to Vegas!"

"Yeah," Jay said. "Except he shit his pants when the cops started shooting."

Dan smiled a little while everyone else laughed uproariously. Jay finished his sandwich quickly and the rest followed suit.

When we returned to the market, Jay rushed up to the office. Emboldened by the employee status I'd earned by returning carts, I wandered to the cavernous backroom, strictly off limits to civilians. Climbing the wooden stairs to the offices, I imagined The Man from Mars coming down the hall, gun drawn and desperate and me, a private detective, shooting him right between the eyes.

Back downstairs I wandered through mazes of stacked boxes and checked out the employee break room, where I read an instruction pamphlet for boxboys. The comic book format featured a cartoon devil, the sophisticated gentleman version in a suit and van dyke beard, who gives a new hire a tour of boxboy Hell. Careless young employees sent to this perdition found themselves punished for such sins as forgetting to pack the cans around the outside of the grocery bag or for putting bread at the bottom of the bag where it would get squashed. It must have been a good instruction manual, for I follow its admonitions to this day whenever I bag my own groceries.

As I roamed through the produce bins by the freezer section, the wooden crates launched me into a fantasy about a ship bound for Skull Island. Channel 11 had recently shown a ruthlessly edited version of King Kong, and I'd been profoundly impressed. In the fantasy, I led a mutiny against the movie producer, exhorting the ragged Asian crew to lock up the swells in the fo'c'sle, whatever that meant.

"What you do here?" An actual Asian voice startled me from my reverie—it belonged to the produce manager. "You go!" he said sharply. "You go, I call po-reese!" The accent sounded similar to Mrs. Yamamoto's, so I had no trouble understanding him. But I felt not at all intimidated—this guy didn't look nearly as fierce as my teacher did.

"My dad is Jay Hill," I explained.

An immediate transformation ensued. "Ha? You Jay Heeah boy? A beneficent smile lit his face. "Ha! Ha! Jay Heeah boy!" Giggling convulsively, he produced a pocket comb and actually began combing my hair, clucking and smiling as he did so. A peasant in nineteenth century Japan confronted with the emperor's son couldn't have been more obsequious.

He pressed a tangerine on me. "Good, sweet! Ha ha!"

I edged away, embarrassed, mostly for him. I hurried to escape, crossing the threshold back into the civilian sector. He followed me halfway down the detergent aisle, still proffering the fruit. Finally he retreated to his domain with many over-the-shoulder nods and smiles.

Relieved, I wandered back to the front of the store. I found Jay and watched him lay off a clerk, giving the younger man a generous severance check and a promise to hire him back when they needed more help at Christmas. The guy took it well. In those days you could be fired for any reason at no notice. On the other hand, you could walk across the street and get another job under any name you liked, as Jay often demonstrated.

I finished the afternoon reading comic books and we drove home, all done with father/son bonding for the next few years. If questioned, both Jay and I would have concluded that all went well on the work visit. But I never asked to go again and he never invited me back. We'd been there and done that, as they say these days.

CHAPTER TWENTY-SIX

~ Board and Care ~ Sold American! ~ Disorientation and the Xmas Tree
~ An Amazing Adult Fantasy

"AND— they have HORSES!" Jane beamed at me from the front seat. We were all in the car somewhere on the rural side of Sylmar: Jay driving, Jane with Greg on her lap in the front seat, Trish and I in the back. "I bet you'll be riding like the Lone Ranger by the time we get back," she continued. "Remember you used to ride Silver till you fell asleep, then I'd take you to bed in my arms?"

I winced at the embarrassing early-childhood reference. "Uh, how long are we going to be at this place?"

"Just a week or so, Honey."

Or so? Did she mean *more* than a week? This plan seemed suspiciously vague to me. I lapsed into a disapproving silence.

Jay pulled into the dirt driveway of an old wooden house. It seemed spooky with its attic window and smoking chimney. But vague foreboding could not distract me from a more important issue: "So, do I still have go to school while you're gone?"

"Uh-huh," said Jane. "You can walk with Charlie, the older boy. The Sudduths have three kids. I think Charlie's in third grade, too, and he's excited about meeting you."

Jay turned off the ignition. The screen door of the house banged and some people moved toward the car, picking their way over the lumpy driveway. One of them, a chubby kid, definitely looked younger than me—first grade, maybe second at the oldest. And he didn't appear to be all that excited.

This latest of Jay's brainstorms seeded when Jane contracted pneumonia. She recovered fairly quickly and soon resumed smoking two packs of Tareytons a day. A happy ending, but it set Jay to contemplation of the swiftness of time, and how, to paraphrase Frank Sinatra, "We gotta live, live, live until we die!" The upshot was a second honeymoon getaway a couple of weeks before Christmas — actually their first, not counting the few days they spent alone in the Van Nuys apartment when they initially moved in together.

I have no memory of discussion or warning before the plan commenced, but suddenly Trish, age four, Greg, fourteen months old, and I, eight-and-a-half, found ourselves living with a family across town for what seemed like an interminable time.

We weren't exactly abandoned. For Jay and Jane, the interval undoubtedly zoomed by, but for me, and presumably for Trish and Greg, it was an upheaval totally unexpected, its slow passage aggravated by not knowing how long it would last. One day I inhabited my own room in the familiar if bohemian surroundings of our house. I had my morning and evening routines, Jane's comfortably bland home cooking, my chemistry set in the garage (from which I concocted many test tubes full of ink, but little else), comic books, library books, coin collection, and the family Elvis records, plus numerous independent pastimes around the neighborhood. Then suddenly, financed by Jay's executive Christmas bonus check, I found myself at the mercy of complete strangers who took in babysitting for extra income.

About the same ages as Jay and Jane, our hosts were old-fashioned folk from Northwest Colorado who made my old babysitter Bert and her family seem cosmopolitan by comparison. The husband, an acquaintance of Jay's from one of the stores they had both clerked, now worked at the White Front in Canoga Park (an extra-long commute in those days). With their ancient house, horses, chickens, and garden, they kept the tradition of the old San Fernando Valley. As a Woodcraft Ranger seeking tracking coups, I had enjoyed the retro-cowboy ambiance of their area across town, but the scene became less romantic in longer doses.

The introductions in the driveway passed in a blur; Jay and Jane made their exit. Mrs. Sudduth gave me a tour of the house. They actually used their fireplace instead of central heating and sat around on furniture Nanny's mom would have shunned as old-fashioned — nary a tiki or gigantic ceramic ashtray anywhere.

"You'll sleep in the boys' room." She meant I would be sharing a bunk bed set with *first*-grader Charlie, who hung back shyly, casting furtive glances at my slicked-back hair and slip-ons. He wore a grown-out butch and scuffed brown brogans caked with mud and worse.

"Charlie, you show Ricky round, and then come back for chores."

Chores. I had last heard the word on *The Real McCoys* TV show, the one where a bunch of West Virginia hicks move to the San Fernando Valley. With theatrical listlessness I followed Charlie on his tour of the property. He proudly pointed out two horses, a goat, and numerous chickens.

"What do you do for fun?" I inquired after seeing all these wonders.

Charlie launched into an account of 4-H activities. I yawned. The conversation lagged until we returned to the house. In the living room Greg slept in his playpen and Trish chatted quietly with her imaginary friend Ballerina. Mrs. Sudduth bustled about in the kitchen. "Charlie? Time to set the table, son."

I watched with little interest as Charlie performed this task, then sat silently through the family prayer intoned by Mr. White Front. He still had on his company shirt. After a passable dinner of franks and beans and white milk, everyone went to bed. As near as I could figure (I'd lost my watch last summer) it couldn't be later than 7:30. At home I had lobbied vigorously for my official 9:30 bedtime. Charlie seemed impressed when I told him this, but not impressed enough to say something to his mom about staying up a little later. He did announce as we put on our pajamas that he burned with ambition to own his own sheep, "An' my dad's spozed to take me to the auction this Saturday to get one! You can go with us!"

How nice. I had barely donned my pajamas when Charlie's mom barged in to say the "Now I lay me down to sleep" prayer and kiss him goodnight. Charlie climbed into the top bunk, where he mumbled all night in his sleep. I lay awake for what seemed like hours afterward, listening to his periodic outbursts and contemplating the "if I should die before I wake" business.

The family rose up and bustled at 5:30 a.m. instead of the civilized 7:00 I had grown used to. Breakfast consisted of oatmeal, a concoction I'd always detested, or soft-boiled eggs, the only kind of eggs I didn't like. After the first night's tolerable franks and beans, dinner became a cavalcade of unfamiliar repugnancies: liver, mealy meatloaf, something with turnips. I had always shunned liver; now turnips joined the short list of vegetables I didn't like, and the meatloaf smelled like nothing in my experience. The fourth night's entrée featured fish with bones. I had never eaten any seafood except cafeteria fishsticks, and the bones seemed both unsanitary and dangerous.

Concerned that Charlie might emulate my tendency to ignore items I didn't like, Mrs. Sudduth said, "Now, Ricky, in this family, we clean our plates before we leave the table, and while you're with us, you're like part of the family."

Not a chance. This scene smelled like the old Northridge lady babysitter and the tomatoes all over again, and human dignity was once again at stake. So I sat defiantly, staring down at the bony fish for over an hour before they relented and ordered me to my bunk.

The next Saturday, on a crisp, school-free morning when I longed to be concocting chemical ink in my garage laboratory or laying around my living room reading comic books and listening to Elvis, I instead accompanied Charlie and his dad to the livestock auction in Sun Valley. The mission: to purchase Charlie his very own sheep. As we bumped along San Fernando Road in the family pickup truck, the lucky lad practically vibrated in his excitement.

Except for the late-model trucks at the auction grounds the ensuing scene could have taken place in 1910: Cowboy hats everywhere, dirt pathways, crowing chickens, manure in the air and underfoot. Sales took place in a large open area, and the auctioneer sounded as nasal and rapid-fire as the one on the Lucky Strike commercials. Sheep weren't on the block until late afternoon, so we spent all day wandering around dusty pens and corrals watching every kind of livestock transaction—goats, turkeys, bulls, even peacocks. One cowboy persevered in selling what seemed to be a good-looking horse except for one red, weeping eye. The bystanders joined in a heated discussion as to the seriousness of the defect.

"Who'll give me seventy-five?" The owner had the bridle wrapped around his fist and held the horse's head rigid by a short halter.

Voice from the crowd: "Give you ten dollars."

Another voice: "Ain't worth that much if his eye's bad."

The owner sounded indignant. "He's a two-hundred dollar horse, but I got to buy a filly for my wife. He just got something in his eye, is all."

Someone offered twenty dollars; someone else twenty-five.

"If you fellas ain't serious, I'll have to—"

"Thirty!"

"Forty!"

Mr. Sudduth, caught up in the excitement, bid forty-five, while Charlie looked on yearningly. Someone else bid sixty and no one ventured higher. The seller seemed relieved as he took the money, and so did Charlie's dad. We made our way slowly to the sheep auction, where, after interminable prospects, our team bid successfully on an ugly one. Charlie waxed ecstatic, and in spite of my general irritation and cynicism I recognized a touching father and son moment, like on *Leave it to Beaver*. But the glow only made me homesick for my own world, unsteady as it was.

We loaded the sheep into the horse trailer brought for the purpose and added three or four red chickens in wire cages. Charlie glowed all the way home, and he set immediately to work washing the new acquisition, since the sheep came with legs and rear end encrusted with manure and urine. I declined to help and muttered some dry brilliance like "Don't forget to scrub his butt!"

Charlie's father overheard this arguably insensitive remark, and he, an otherwise mild-mannered fellow, was moved to give me a heated, inarticulate lecture on manners, attitude, and respect. Apparently he had been enduring my smart-aleck-kid presence with as much teeth-gritting as I'd been enduring his rules and regulations. I felt more surprised than cowed by the outburst, but the scene brought on a deeper homesickness than I had heretofore suffered.

The remainder of the two weeks in exile remains a blur of cold mornings, unpalatable food, and general disorientation. The walk to school started from the wrong direction, and all the kids from this side of town were strangers. I had a yen to keep walking to my real house, but getting caught in the free world during official hours would, I imagined, probably land me in reform school for longer than my current sentence at the Sudduths.

Meanwhile, second-honeymooners Jay and Jane enjoyed their last extended alone time together for many years. First they drove to Palm Springs, the desert spa and winter getaway of the stars. The town had crept past its glory days of the forties and early fifties, but the weather seemed pleasantly summerlike after the December morning frosts of Sylmar. They stayed at a motel with a pool, evidenced later in Polaroid camera shots of Jane demonstrating a jackknife dive and of Jay in a bathing suit. This artifact is the sole image ever taken of his bare torso, and I don't remember seeing him without a shirt in the next forty-plus years.

Next stop, Las Vegas: the town we'd fled in abject poverty two years before. This time they had money to play with and no kids to worry about. After their return California, the next week or so, became a working honeymoon. Jay installed Jane as the chief cashier of the Christmas tree concession in the parking lot, one of the business innovations that earned his bonus check. They slept in a little travel trailer on site, had all their meals together, and enjoyed the Burbank nightlife like carefree young marrieds.

They hadn't altogether forgotten us kids, though. One morning of the second week Mrs. Yamamoto announced to the class, "Areechar Heel's mahda and fahda" had donated "dis veh nice" Christmas tree. Sure enough, there in the corner sat a beautiful, top-of-the-line blue spruce.

This was all news to me. Jay and Jane had apparently come home for fresh clothes and brought along a tree appropriated from Jay's supermarket lot, arriving in the afternoon after I'd gone home but before Mrs. Yamamoto had departed. As we all made construction paper decorations, the whole business struck me as something out of *The Twilight Zone* or *One Step Beyond* TV shows. Mrs. Yamamoto had seen my parents and I hadn't, and she thought of shiftless Jay and Jane as upper-crust philanthropists. But why hadn't the philanthropists made contact with me while they touched down in the neighborhood? Would they ever come back, I wondered, or would they merely continue to make mysterious visitations?

Again, it's easier to understand Jay's view from a distance. He and Jane had been through much turmoil since they met. For the sake of true love, they had left their spouses and suffered the numerous consequences that came with their bold act. They had plunged into poverty, and the strain had torn them apart twice. But against all odds they had reunited and risen up from destitution, only to almost lose one another with Jane's pneumonia scare. A couple of weeks together should not be so much to ask of the kids — they had paid to have us stay with a nice family who had horses and had even raised my classroom status by delivering a high-class tree on their vacation time. Yes, all so reasonable in hindsight, but so baffling to me at the time.

Jay and Jane finally appeared at the Sudduths a couple of days before Christmas. As we bade our hosts goodbye in their front yard, my studied reserve melted when Jay handed me a dozen comic books. I recall only one by name and issue: *Amazing Adult Fantasy* # 8, subtitled "THE MAGAZINE THAT RESPECTS YOUR INTELLIGENCE." I allowed Charlie to join me in perusing the intelligent literature while the grownups continued their interminable jawing. Having been sprung, I felt sympathy for the poor fool who had a life sentence at this prison farm.

Postscript: After seeing a certain internet article a few years ago, the memory of that last afternoon at the Sudduths' has fueled my own personal amazing adult fantasy, as follows: The second honeymoon and family reunion take place a few months later, so that instead of handing me *Amazing Adult Fantasy* number 8, Jay gives me number 15, the famous one featuring the debut of Spiderman. In my fantasy, I don't even read the issue; instead, exhibiting unusual prescience in such matters, I put #15 in a safe, dry place for the next fifty years without opening it, thereby maintaining its mint condition. Then, as a result of all those improbabilities, *I* am the mystery seller I read about on the internet, the fellow who, at a 2011 online auction, sold that comic book for *1.1 million dollars*.

Yes, the auction actually happened, and it makes for a nice dream of easy wealth. The reality, however, is probably more like this unconfirmed speculation: Charlie, inspired by seeing my comic books that day, bought *Amazing Adult Fantasy* #15 a few months later and hid it from his parents in the attic. In late 2010, he returned home to settle deceased Mr. and Mrs. Sudduth's affairs. He found the comic book, auctioned it off for 1.1 million, and bought a sheep ranch in Northern Colorado, where he is even now writing disparaging things about me in his childhood memoir.

CHAPTER TWENTY-SEVEN

~ The Robot Commando Hoax ~ The Last Good Year?
~ High Cotton and Sand Dunes ~ Grade Inflation and Great Literature

Christmas arrived only a few days after the Sudduth imprisonment, and the year's holiday celebration (funded by Jay's bonus) brought the most presents we'd had so far, an outcome which left our recent abandonment and its trauma forgiven, pretty much.

My favorite toy was Robot Commando, who, enlarged by trick photography, would have made a much better movie villain than the actor in the tin suit who inspired my Robbie the Robot project in San Pedro. The toy robot stood only eighteen inches high and required something like twelve D batteries, but he featured an impressive arsenal. After dialing one of several specific functions on the plastic handle of the attached microphone unit, the young operator could shout commands like, "Forward!" and "Fire!" into the mic. Robot Commando would then wheel forward, or launch missiles from its head, or pitch cannonballs in stiff, overhand ambidextrousness.

Commanding such a monster was exciting at first, but I quickly discovered that the same robo-actions could be achieved by setting the dial and simply blowing into the microphone. I showed Jay, and he explained the mechanics: the force of breath expressed in yelling commands moved a sliver of metal in the mic, which closed a circuit to activate whatever command the operator had dialed. In short, RC had no capacity whatsoever for actual voice recognition.

Though toy science had made only a faux first step toward artificial intelligence, the space age continued to ramp up in 1962. John Glenn would soon orbit the earth, and by year's end we'd face nuclear annihilation with the Cuban Missile Crisis, not to mention a future plague of digital beeps and numbers from that year's invention of the now ubiquitous liquid crystal display (LCD).

All signs thus far had pointed to our experiencing these innovations in Sylmar. But soon after Christmas, Jay became restless and took out his irritation on our landlord, who had the bad timing to stop by in January to inquire about our intentions for the house. When we rented the place, Jay and Jane had led the man to believe they were seriously interested in a lease-to-own arrangement. Had they come up with five hundred dollars, the house could have been theirs on a twenty-year note at ninety dollars a month. Instead Jay practically shut the door in the landlord's face, and afterward he fumed to Jane about how pushy the "ying-yang" had acted. Having witnessed this scene, I felt not much surprised when, a few weeks later (February 1962, in the middle of the school semester), we shook off the desert dust of Sylmar. With the assistance of Freddie, Eddie, and a rented truck, we migrated to Manhattan Beach.

In retrospect, the beginning of 1962 seems a sort of high water mark (or perhaps a demarcation line) for American culture. The subjective feeling of national confidence overflowed for the first time since the 1920s. Kennedy was our vigorous young leader, and "vigor" seemed to be his favorite word. Science featured all progress and heroes; pop music remained all-American, with a little "Volaré," and suchlike Italian imports for spice; the Beatles and their wake of British bands remained as yet a strictly overseas phenomenon.

Other amateur sociologists have waxed eloquently on '62 as a cultural watershed. The following is from a chapter titled "The Last Good Year" in the erudite *Catalogue of Cool*, first published in the 1980s:

> Sixty-two seems, in retrospect, a year when the singular naiveté of the spanking new decade was at its guileless height, with only the vaguest, most indistinct hints of the agonies and ecstasies to come marring the fresh-scrubbed, if slightly sallow complexion of the times. On the first day of that year, the Federal Reserve raised the maximum interest on savings accounts to 4 percent while "The Twist" was sweeping the nation. A month later "Duke of Earl" was topping the charts, and John Glenn was orbiting the good, green globe [...]The Seattle World's Fair opened, followed five weeks later by the deployment of five thousand U.S. troops in Thailand [...] By the time the grass of '62 had withered and died, the discovery of DNA's double helix had garnered the Nobel Prize, Kennedy had ordered the blockade of Cuba, "He's A Rebel" topped playlists and eleven thousand military advisers were in South Vietnam.

Against this culturally ominous background, the Hill family went upscale for a while. An L.A. bright spot since the turn of the century, Manhattan Beach featured, besides its spacious shoreline, a region of gigantic sand dunes a mile or so from the coast, where neighborhood kids played among the bulldozers. From this grainy cornucopia, much cement was concocted and many rocky shores replenished. In the thirties, even Waikiki Beach had been supplied with sand via barges from those massive dunes.

Many celebrities called Manhattan Beach home in those days. Legendary surfer and board shaper Dewy Webber ran a shop near the pier, and Thomas Pynchon lived off 33rd Street. The famously reclusive writer hung out at the Fractured Cow, a local coffee shop, while he worked on his novels *The Crying of Lot 49* and *Gravity's Rainbow*.

Amid all of these attractions, Jay and Jane found a corner-lot house six or eight blocks from the ocean, with rent probably $125 a month (as opposed to $90 for the Sylmar house). The place, given its layout and location, is likely worth around a million dollars in the second decade of the twentieth century — a median home price by current Manhattan Beach standards. But $125 per month seemed pricey then, especially since, along with giving Sylmar the air, Jay had shook off the dust of his supervisor job. But having started at a clerk's wages at a South Bay market, he had been promoted to night manager, aka "third-man," within a couple of weeks.

Grand View Elementary school, where I entered my second third-grade class, seemed mighty ritzy (to use a term Nanny liked) after Hubbard Street's drab bungalows and blacktop. Built on a hillside with classroom rows terraced a la Italian Riviera, each classroom had its own sliding glass door and patio. No Wyvernwood-style treks to the dairy for field trips; instead we took a school bus to the opera (student price, fifteen cents), had our choice of twelve- or eight-ounce milks in the cafeteria, and received on our report cards E's (Excellent), S's (Satisfactory) and U's (unsatisfactory) instead of the bourgeois A's, B's, C's, D's, and F's used by most L.A. schools.

To skip ahead a bit (and only a bit, as we didn't stay long) I gained much by those innovations in the local report card. In an expansive moment, Jay had promised me a dollar for every A grade I earned at the new school. Given my previous marks in Handwriting and Art, he must have figured on a maximum payout of three dollars for Reading, Arithmetic, and Social Studies, with Arithmetic a longshot.

On grade day teachers instructed us to deliver the cards in their sealed envelopes to our parents, but little knots of kids all down the street had stopped to take early peeks. I tore open my envelope, reasonably confident I had done well. Of course I knew from my ten schools so far that such matters could be highly subjective. All I could really count on was an A in reading. But as I scanned the oversized report card, I saw to my amazement and delight that the format included separate grades for subcategories within each subject. I earn not only an E (equivalent to A) in reading, but also an E in Reading Comprehension, another E in Vocabulary, a third in Oral Expression, and so forth. In Arithmetic I had an overall E, with more E's in "Understands concepts," "Applies concepts" etc. With all the categories and subcategories, I ended up with 23 E's altogether!

When I burst into the kitchen waving my report card, Jay and Jane were sitting at the Formica table, drinking instant coffee with half-and-half. Jay had dressed for the four-to-midnight shift in white on white shirt and thin black tie, his black shoes shining like mirrors. He would be looking sharp on the job that night, even after the store closed and he supervised the produce restocking and liquor deliveries.

"I got twenty-three A's!" I shouted. "Twenty-three dollars!"

Jane took the card. "Oh, that's so wonderful, darling! Look, Jay!"

Jay studied the document, then looked up with no expression. "These aren't twenty-three A's."

My face grew hot. "Yes they are! E's are the same thing as A's!"

"Sure, but all these grades under the grades don't count separate — they just add up to the main grade for the subject."

"Yes they do! They do!"

A discussion ensued, in which he pointed out the subgrades were indented on the card and in smaller type. I held my ground: he had promised a dollar for every A, and here were 23 of the local equivalent, no matter how formatted. Throughout my impassioned argument, Jane looked grave, but seemed to be on the verge of smiling.

"They're same as A's! Aren't they, Mom?!" I demanded.

Now both of them wore irritating smiles. "Don't get hot, Charlie," said Jay, reaching in his front pocket for his bankroll. "I'll pay off." Twenty-three dollars meant real money in those days, at least a day's take-home pay. But Jay peeled his lone twenty-dollar bill from the outside of the roll and three bills from the ten or fifteen singles constituting the remainder.

Jane put her hand on the back of his neck; then she reached out to hug me. Jay took a last gulp of coffee and stood up to leave for work. I felt triumphant. He had tried to wriggle out of it, but logic and justice had won out.

I had been a sort of incipient teenager even before we moved to Manhattan Beach, but there I began to rise (or descend) to another level of that peculiar state of mind. In previous schools I had, despite my Junior Elvis look, kept a fairly low social and academic profile. But at Grand View I combed my hair even more flamboyantly, drew tattoos on my hands, and at the local Woolworth's I bought a huge fake gold and diamond ring for twenty-nine cents, a knockoff of the manly jewelry also favored by the stars of the era. I became a seeming extrovert in school, quick to answer questions, give my opinion, and generally show off in class. To demonstrate my sophistication, I affected even tinier handwriting than usual, making my low-grade penmanship even harder to decipher.

Increasingly outspoken, I once offered the argument that the technique of borrowing in subtraction as demonstrated by our teacher Mrs. Brach, was all smoke and mirrors. "Try it on a number with more than one zero," I demanded. "You can't borrow when there's nothing to borrow from in the next zero."

Mrs. Brach stood at the board as if in deep thought. She chalked "10,000 –1". Then, slowly, as if figuring it out for the first time, she demonstrated how to keep borrowing, replacing zero after zero with nines until you reached an actual number you could borrow from. Thus she included me in on the discovery, and for the first and probably only time in my life, I glimpsed the glorious symmetry that mathematicians wax over so ineloquently.

At twenty-three Mrs. Brach (who used her maiden name when I first met her, but got married during the semester) was by far the youngest teacher I had ever known. In the grainy photo of her I took with my Christmas camera, she looks about seventeen. She topped all other teachers in approachability and forbearance, and she had the gift of making each student feel like she took a personal interest — an unusual approach for those crowded classroom times.

I basked in the attention and showed off even more. Never one to shy from recycling my writing, I copied out my "Rain" poem and presented it to her. Every day I showed her something — books I'd checked out, a multiplication table I did on graph paper up to 20 X 20, and short creative writings. Her enthusiasm tempted me to copy from memory some poems I'd read in the children's poetry books and pass them off as my own. My plagiarism must have been obvious, but Mrs. Brach let it go. Occasionally she'd say something oblique like, "Ricky, you're going to have to learn there's other people in the world," but she said it with a smile, and all such talk skimmed over my head anyway.

One afternoon soon after my arrival, Mrs. Brach set me firmly on my future career path. The memory is vivid even now: I enter the classroom from a sweaty playground session to find the lights off and students sitting quietly at their desks, some with their heads down. The room is deliciously cool and dim. I take my seat and Teacher begins to read. She gently imitates the accent and intonation of the young boy narrator as he relates his adventures. Somehow he has found himself among an old-time Southern family, all of whom work hard at their dignity. The family members are also kindly to the boy, but they are in a blood feud with another noble clan.

At the request of a beautiful young woman, the narrator retrieves a Bible from the frontier church. When he arrives, the church is full of pigs. He reflects that since church floors are so nice and cool in the summer, pigs like churches even more than people do. "If you notice, most folks don't go to church only when they've got to, but a hog is different." He shakes the book and a mysterious note falls from it. He knows it is from the girl's suitor — who is one of the Enemy. She elopes that night and much violent tragedy ensues.

As I found out afterward, the passage came from *Adventures of Huckleberry Finn*. Eddie back in Wyvernwood had mentioned the book, and I had by now heard of Huck Finn in cartoon knockoffs. My first impression was of a dumb hick in rags. But this Huck could read, think, and talk, and he had a sense of humor. The passage about hogs liking the cool floor of the church is ever associated with the first time I heard it as I felt the cool desk on my cheek and entered a sort of trance state, exquisitely relaxed, yet perfectly aware.

Mrs. Brach graced us with an afternoon reading session only a couple more times during my Grand View tenure, but I checked the book out from the school library and finished it. For many years after, I built rafts from popsicle sticks (I would bring home fistfuls from the drive-in movie snack bars, where they served as coffee stirrers) and dreamed of floating down the Mississippi. The Grand View library also had a large "biographies for young people" section, and I checked out all three books on Abraham Lincoln, whose adolescent adventures on trading scows down the Mississippi made him seem like a real life Huck Finn. From the paperback rack at the liquor store, I even bought Volume I of the Carl Sandburg Lincoln bio.

I made the essential bookworm breakthrough around then—the reader is no longer conscious of words as such on the page; content flows into the brain like a multi-dimensional movie. Starting one rainy Saturday that spring, I spent many hours on the couch with the *Journeys Through Bookland* partial set Nanny had given me a few years before. I read excerpts from Robinson Crusoe, Aladdin, The Swiss Family Robinson, Norse Myths, Sinbad, Alice in Wonderland, Pilgrim's Progress, The Odyssey, and more, plus poems by Poe, Wordsworth, Longfellow, Tennyson, Pope, et. al., absorbing language cadence, antique ideas, and obsolete sensibilities.

It's an odd picture, looking back: the nine-year-old with teen gangster hair, flashy clothes, garish rings and ersatz tattooed hands who, while entranced and uplifted by the classics, seemingly makes no particular cultural distinction between Great Literature and Bullwinkle cartoons.

I haven't changed much, come to think of it.

CHAPTER TWENTY-EIGHT

~ Ripening Teen Infection ~ Horse Girls and Pool Girls
~ Heartbreak #1~ Grandma Glasses ~ Hawthorne's Finest
~ Stars Like Grains of Sand ~ Dirty Fishing

That spring of 1962 I spent many hours reading at home in Manhattan Beach, but when not so quietly occupied, my precocious teen sensibility tried everyone's patience. Daily I became even more a junior James Dean—flamboyant but moody and prone to smart-aleck comments. Jay first said around this time, "Pal, you can think anything you want; just don't say it out loud." But I didn't understand the distinction and continued to be a sardonic little wiseacre.

Naturally, a couple of little girls at school were attracted by such savoir faire. One day I strolled through the city park behind Grand View Elementary with a talkative classmate. I don't remember her name, but she had honey-colored hair and was going through the stage where almost-adolescent girls (like Elizabeth Taylor in *National Velvet*) "would give up heaven to have a horse." This would-be Velvet carried with her at all times a horse-decorated notebook, a horse novel for young readers, and a plastic horse with combable mane. As we walked she described a room completely given over to equine worship: bedspreads, curtains, more books and more plastic horses. At one point she actually stopped on the sidewalk and passionately but redundantly exclaimed, "I LOVE horses."

Perhaps I remembered my Sylmar ranch exile too vividly to humor such feelings; in any case, I didn't pursue the relationship. I took things a little further with Denise, who shadowed me on the playground and sat unbidden beside me at lunch. One day at recess she blurted, "Wanna come swim in my pool?"

In my mostly apartment-kid history, a private home pool seemed the height of Aladdinic luxury. I appeared at her house at eleven a.m. the next Saturday wearing my bathing suit under my shorts and carrying a rolled-up towel under my arm.

Her mother greeted me at the front door. "You must be the famous Ricky," she said with a mocking smile. "Well, Denise is breathlessly expecting you. Let's go give her the good news."

Puffing on a cigarette, she ushered me through a living room and a sliding glass door to the patio. It was true; they actually had a pool, a kidney-shaped wonder surrounded by philodendrons, azaleas, cushioned wrought-iron lawn chairs, even a gazebo: a vision of California heaven right out of *Sunset* magazine.

I couldn't swim—had rarely been in a pool—but I jumped off the diving board and flailed my way to the side several times in succession. Denise mostly bobbed in the shallow end and watched me, but at her mother's urging she demonstrated the backstroke and Australian crawl. Her expertise gave me a sense of, for lack of a better term, class difference. While I'd been picking trash in San Pedro and sloshing through gutters in Sylmar, she'd been taking swimming and dancing lessons.

After a break for sandwiches and iced lemonade, we took the obligatory break to forestall cramps and drowning before returning to the pool. In this refined strata, decadence was creeping in: the break was only a half-hour instead of the one-hour mandate practiced in lower class gatherings. Denise's mom had been in and out of the house during the first swim session, but now she lingered on the patio, observing my flailings in the deep end. "Sweetheart, can't you swim?" she asked with what I perceived as yet another mocking smile.

Denise's adoring stare didn't cease for a minute, but I left the pool immediately in acute embarrassment. "Gotta go home," I mumbled, drying myself. "Gotta do some stuff." I strode with dignity out the side gate, my soggy towel tucked under my arm, neither saying goodbye to my hostess nor her mother.

I received comeuppance for this boorish behavior soon enough, for I fell in love with Rebecca McCain, the most beautiful girl in the third grade. Rebecca reminded me of Tuesday Weld, the ubiquitous movie magazine cover girl, except that she improved on Tuesday's coiffure with two long twin braids, Indian style—the perfect pale princess of the Hopi Indians, the tribe we examined in depth in our social studies unit.

Unfortunately, Rebecca gave me no encouragement at all. When I turned up my manly charm (consisting of even more carefully combed hair than usual, smoldering looks, and offhand references to pop songs and Norse mythology) she reacted politely, but barely.

She lived some distance from school in the opposite direction from my house, but I proposed to walk her home. Taking a cue from old movies and songs, I said, "Uh, you want me to carry your book?"

"No, that's all right." She tightened her grip on the social studies text. As she explained briefly during the walk, her parents required her to bring home at least one book every day, even though Mrs. Brach never assigned homework. When we arrived at her door after not much more conversation, her dad took one look at me and, likely foreseeing an irritating future of greasy-haired suitors, proceeded with grunts and head shaking to express disapproval. His abhorrence should have endeared Rebecca to me, as it does in all the standard Hollywood reverse-psychology scenarios. Instead, after mumbling something about doing her chores, she practically pushed me out of the house.

I made the long trek home in a dark mood, but the next Saturday afternoon I again walked the mile or so to her abode while fantasizing a vaguely glorious future. In sync with my transistor, I sang Elvis's "Good Luck Charm," imagining myself strolling along a crowded avenue in a movie musical, singing to Rebecca who held my arm and looked up at me adoringly as we made our way to the church to get married. The lyrics to "Good Luck Charm" are less than inspired and Elvis's delivery is relatively perfunctory, but at the time the song seemed the soundtrack to a profound love.

When I arrived, Rebecca's mother declared her daughter not home. From the woman's furtive look I doubted the claim. As I departed, a curtain moved. In what seemed like eons later (though actually only two years), I first heard the Beatles' "No Reply." The song's scenario, in which a young man goes to his girlfriend's house and sees her peeping through her window without answering the door, instantly brought back the pang of rejection and longing I felt as I trudged back home that long ago day in bleak Manhattan Beach.

I discontinued my active pursuit of Rebecca, but for weeks afterward the lovesickness ached with no less severity than the love-gone-wrong discomforts of my teens and early twenties. Rebecca was no soulmate; I hardly knew her. I felt no physical lust or even tactile longing, yet the seemingly unbearable pain, fabricated largely from hurt pride, apparently knows no minimum age.

Another such blow to my self-esteem struck soon afterward. Mrs. Brach (I've called her that right along because I don't remember her maiden name) had married three weeks before summer vacation and invited the whole class to the wedding. We never met Mr. Brach, except to see him sweeping her down the aisle, but we understood that he must be quite a guy. I wondered why they didn't wait until the school year ended, but they both demonstrated their affection for us when, on their honeymoon in Hawaii, they bought us all giant pencils with hula girls where the eraser should be.

The day before Mrs. Brach departed, she noticed me squinting at the chalk board and sent a note home, recommending a vision checkup. Jane complied, and a week after the official exam, the ophthalmologist's secretary presented me with an elegant case inscribed "Manhattan Optical" containing a pair of grey, fade to-clear plastic rimmed spectacles.

I dutifully carried the glasses to school. A substitute teacher presided over us during Mrs. Brach's honeymoon, and we took advantage by moving about the classroom during work periods. I stepped to the back of the room and tried on the glasses. Looking up at the chalkboard, the clarity of the letters and numbers astounded me — I felt as if I had telescopic vision, like Superman.

I knew that no movie stars wore glasses, but the grave extent to which my new eyewear could affect my conscientiously hip '62 image hadn't occurred to me yet. Vision correction is fairly common in the lower grades now, but almost no nine-year-olds wore glasses then. Nevertheless, one of my classmates standing next to me in the rear of the classroom knew exactly how to react.

"Grandma Glasses! Grandma Glasses!"

I turned quickly. A chubby, bucktoothed little nobody stood a few feet away, pointing at my face and jeering. Reflexively, I clawed off the specs, but he kept it up. "Grandma Glasses! Grandma Glasses!"

Immediate action seemed indicated. I closed the distance between us in a few strides and pushed him with light-to-moderate force. To my surprise he doubled over and staggered backwards in a performance worthy of a professional basketball player "flopping" to draw a foul call from the referee. The substitute teacher, an old lady who had eyed my hairdo with distaste when she took attendance, hurried from the front of the room. "Stop it! Get back to your seat! Do you behave like this when your teacher is here?"

A friend of the chubby kid, another nobody who'd apparently been chafing at my class antics, saw his chance. "Mrs. Brach is always yelling at him," he testified.

The substitute teacher ordered me to stay in the room while everyone else filed out on the patio to practice our Hopi Snake dance for parent visitation day. The two who betrayed me smirked as they went. Rebecca McCain walked just ahead of them, seemingly oblivious. Though she had seen me insulted and unfairly punished, she sent no loyal movie girlfriend look of encouragement back over her shoulder.

I stared at my spelling book while the sacred Snake dance proceeded without me. With expansive tales of my Woodcraft Ranger background, I had talked Mrs. Brach into appointing me one of the dance leaders. But now, from the empty classroom, I heard my understudy intoning my line, "Hi-oh-wa—hoy!" the signal to begin.

I hated them all. The chubby kid and his rat friend were subject to my murderous stares for the remaining weeks of the semester, and they took care to avoid me outside of class. I never started a conversation with Rebecca again, and despite suggestions, urgings, cajoling, and threats by parents and teachers, I refused to wear glasses for several more years.

But all was not existential angst at Grand View. Despite becoming ever more the brooding junior James Dean (I learned later that he had been nearsighted, too), I did make one good friend. Steve, a short kid with a butch and a wry outlook on life, reminded me a little of Wyvernwood Eddie, but without Eddie's menacing edge. Steve had an engagingly rapid-fire delivery of dirty jokes I hadn't heard yet, and he loved *Mad Magazine*. I had read a few *Mads* before, but Steve's explications primed a deeper appreciation of Alfred E. Neuman and Co. For years afterward I bought the magazine every month ("Our Price 25¢ Cheap"), and when I had a fresh issue I took a break from Abe Lincoln and Stephen Douglas, Huck Finn and Jim, Loki and Thor, and Crusoe and Friday to read Dave Berg and Don Martin, Mad's premier writer-illustrators.

As I perused *Mad* back issues at Steve's house, he played his 45 rpm record collection. One rockabilly novelty number I'd never heard has now been identified, in my exhaustive research for this book, as "Haunted House" by Jumpin' Gene Simmons (not to be confused with the younger Gene Simmons in the theatrical band "Kiss"). I have a sometimes maddening knack for remembering lyrics, and without benefit of hearing the ditty again, the line about drinking hot grease from a frying pan lodged in my head for over fifty years.

Steve also introduced me to another memorable record more familiar to the public at large. The A side had debuted around Christmas of '61 on Candix, an obscure local label. "They're all high school guys from over in Hawthorne," Steve told me. Hawthorne shared a border with Manhattan Beach, so this group was truly local, and the early morning radio show kept it on the playlist.

The song, "Surfin" by a band called The Beach Boys sounded like nothing I'd ever heard, a combination of primitive guitar, drums, and lead vocal with more sophisticated background harmonies. The infectious doo-wop background "bom, bom, dit th ditha da, bom, bom, dit th dithada" blended with the story about getting some girls, skipping school, and going surfin', and the whole thing sounded more authentically teenage than anything on the radio. The only odd element of the song was the singer's insistence on waking up early to go surfing. All the cool people I'd seen in movies and read about in books always woke up late. But, as Steve explained, "You gotta get out there before the wind blows out the waves." While we listened to "Surfin'" over and over, Steve told me everything he'd gleaned about the sport from his big brother Neil, who actually surfed. We had moved to Redondo Beach, even closer to Hawthorne, by the time the Boys' first big hit "Surfin' Safari" came out. And when the band made it huge a year later with "Surfin' USA," I felt like one of their extended family.

The Beach Boys probably provided the catalyst for my actually going to the beach for the first time since San Pedro. On a beautiful Saturday afternoon in April 1962, equipped with towel, transistor radio, and a peanut butter sandwich, I set off for the half mile walk to the shore.

The wide beach stretched forth practically deserted by 21st century crowd standards, but lifeguards sat stolidly in their duty towers and snack stands were open.

After splashing in the water a bit and imagining myself surfing, I lay on my stomach in the sun, head hanging over my towel as I took a close look at the sand. A science-minded classmate had recently announced that all the grains of sand on all the beaches of the world numbered fewer than the stars spread across the universe. I pondered this idea as I counted sand grains, but after I reached a hundred and observed how little space they took, I sat up. Noting the wide expanse of sand stretching past the pier as far as I could see, and recalling all the coasts on the school maps of North and South America, Europe, Africa, and elsewhere, I concluded that, even though the scientific kid owned the entire oversize paperback How, Why Wonder Books series, with volumes on dinosaurs, rockets, electricity, atomic energy, stars, etc. etc., he must have been exaggerating what his sources said about the plentitude of stars. Now I realize that he deserved more research credibility, for recent views of the universe, with estimates of stars numbering in the multi-trillions, would seem to have proved him right.

Healthy sea air and scientific inquiry are good for a growing lad, but the innocent beach trip had unintended consequences — it provided the first turning onto an inexorable path to crime. I took the next fateful step the following weekend. I had determined to explore the Manhattan pier and had put the word out on my intentions. Most of the boys in my neighborhood were reticent about leaving their home block even if their parents would have let them, but one of the more adventurous guys agreed to accompany me. We arrived during a "run," when small fish come in large numbers to spawn. People of all ages were snag fishing — instead of a baited hook, the angler employs a line of eight or ten hooks in a dipping motion a couple of feet below the water's surface until a passing fish snags on one of the hooks.

The bait shop on the pier sold strips of snag hooks and lengths of fishing line for a quarter each, with lead sinkers an extra five cents. So for a sixty-cent investment my companion and I joined the action. Taking turns, we quickly pulled in twenty or thirty of the small fish, collecting them in an old shoebox we'd found by the trash can. We could have thrown the wounded fish back into the sea, but neither that notion, nor the thought of our sport being unsporting for the fish, occurred to either of us. After all, everyone was doing it.

My partner didn't want his mom to know where he'd been, so I brought the shoebox home. Jane expressed no interest in cooking the dead fish, and Jay strongly recommended that I "get rid of them before they stink up the house."

Our Indian unit at school had recently covered Hopi farming methods, including planting a fish with each corn seeding. Until now I had wished we could study the Navajos, the region's more warlike group who treated the Hopis like junior-high scrubs. But now, taking a tip from the gentler tribe, I took the dead fish to the back yard and buried them under a boxwood bush that looked like it could use some nourishment.

That ritual concluded my interest in fishing, but my excited account of the afternoon's adventure must have rung a childhood bell for Jay—perhaps early memories of lake fishing with his grandfather in Minnesota, or some rare ocean escapes from his citified boyhood in East L.A. In any case, my adventure galvanized him into the first of a series of obsessive hobbies, and my descent into crime began right after my ninth birthday—a tale I will relate in the next chapter.

CHAPTER TWENTY-NINE

~ The Stamp Syndicate ~ Family Sparkplug ~ Morals and the Lack Thereof ~ Chess and Fish ~ Criminal Revision ~ Waiving Revenge

I ask the reader to please bear with me, for the story of my criminal career must be prefaced by a short lecture on trading stamps. To understand the popularity of these items, one must think of them as a primitive version of the elaborate "miles" schemes touted today by airlines and credit card companies to entice consumers into buying more product while remaining loyal to the company and reaping "free" merchandise and travel. Virtually all markets and gas stations during the nineteen-fifties and sixties gave variously colored stamps at the rate of one regular unit for every ten cents of goods purchased; shoppers could thereby accumulate one 24-page book of stamps for every $120 spent and trade the filled books for everything from towels to TV sets. At the high point of the stamps' popularity, some gas stations even offered double stamps and free glassware to help sell their 25-cent per gallon gas. Warren Buffet, a heavy investor in at least one stamp company, is reported to have said, "When I was told that even certain brothels and mortuaries gave stamps to their patrons, I felt I had finally found a sure thing."

According to Greenpoints.com, S & H Green Stamps pioneered this consumer phenomenon:

> Sperry & Hutchinson began offering stamps to retailers back in 1896 ... [W]hen the program reached its zenith in the mid 60's, they were printing three times as many stamps as the US Postal Service and [the S&H] catalog was possibly the largest single publication in the country. It was estimated that 80% of US households collected stamps of one sort or another, creating an annual market for S&H alone of about $825 million.

Eight hundred and twenty-five million dollars for stamps each year seems as unbelievable as trillions of stars in the universe, but that figure included only one distributor. Also available across the country were Blue Chip Stamps, K&S Red stamps, Yellow, Pinky, and Plaid stamps; Top Value, Mor-Valu, Shur-Valu, Big Bonus and Double Thrift stamps; not to mention Buckeye, Buccaneer, Two Guys, King Korn, Eagle, and Regal brands. After a fierce commercial war, The Blue Chip Stamp Company eventually captured the Southern California market from S&H, and a dozen Blue Chip redemption centers full of merchandise sprung up over the Los Angeles area.

Enter the Hill mob. From unscrupulous stamp reps who supplied the store where he worked, Jay began to acquire, for a few surreptitious dollars per giant roll, enormous quantities of this alternate currency. He supplemented the illicit supply by straight pilferage on his own, so lax security apparently prevailed at all stages of distribution.

The process of turning ill-gotten stamps to profit began immediately. On Tuesday night, two days after my snag fishing trip, I retired at my 9:30 bedtime after drinking my usual large glass of chocolate milk. When I awoke around midnight to use the bathroom, I saw Jay and Jane bent over what looked like a pile of paperback books at the kitchen table. Both had odd expressions, as if they had eaten something unpleasant.

After school Wednesday, four sealed rolls of Blue Chip stamps and a stack of blank books sat on the kitchen counter. I found Jay in the living room assembling two new fishing rods and reels. He took the next day off work and escorted Jane to the pier, where they caught several fish and seemed even more excited about the sport than my friend and I had been. Apparently more stamp licking ensued; on Friday Jay brought home two additional rods and reels, plus a tackle box and other gear.

When Jay became interested in something, it absorbed 100% of his attention. He read a fishing magazine at dinner and lay in bed before work the next day studying a paperback boating guide. The next Sunday we rented a small motor skiff and tried the new equipment and knowledge out by the breakwater. The smell of diesel fuel and incessant rocking provided me with my first case of seasickness, and we didn't catch any fish. Nonetheless, Jay and Jane were dedicated anglers for several more weeks before they dropped the whole business abruptly, as they had enthused over and then dropped tiki painting and cameras the year before.

Nonetheless, Jay's interest in amassing stamps continued for many years. The loot supplied both hobby items and consumer staples: dishes, bedspreads, pillows, toasters, rugs, radios, silverware, cameras, space heaters, ashtrays, and much more. The household cash saved from these items could then be applied to more esoteric family budget items such as liquor, cigarettes, restaurant meals, and other items unavailable at the Blue Chip store.

But as Jay always said, "Nothing is free." Before the stamps could be redeemed, someone had to paste them into the aforementioned blank books. If the Blue Chip company had fielded investigators (as perhaps they should have, considering the leakage at all points in their supply line), and if one of their agents had put our kitchen under surveillance during evenings or weekends, he would have observed a slick operation indeed. Jay sat at one end of the table, cutting and stacking page fillers consisting of either blocks of fifty small stamps or strips of five large ones, a later innovation. Jane, Trish and I (and sometimes Jay when we had a large order) pasted in the goods. Only Greg was excused from duty in the family racket.

Legitimate stamp savers licked their stamps, but the human tongue is inadequate for the quantities we were handling. After some experiments, we settled on washcloths dipped in water. The cloths must be not too wet, but not too dry either—Jane and I became adept at judging how much moisture was just right. Touch a pre-cut sheet of stamps to the cloth, place it with practiced motion into the book, and the filled units came off the line like World War II battleships at the Kaiser shipyard.

At not quite five years old, Trish was an indifferent worker (probably because she had no idea what we were doing and money had yet to become an incentive to her), but I waded right in to the scheme—at the Jay-authorized, five-cent per book payment, I could earn twenty or thirty cents an hour during hot stamp runs, a princely wage for a nine-year old whose legitimate allowance had been that amount per week.

Once the Hill gang had a stack of filled books, we'd drive to one of the Blue Chip redemption centers in the area. Clerks gave only cursory attention when they checked to see if all book pages had been filled; nonetheless, a caper is never a sure thing until you make a clean getaway with the loot. I usually stood by, feigning boredom, as the clerks fanned through the books. Tension mounted as I imagined suspicion, accusing looks, alarm bells, and undercover guards moving in to block our escape.

Of course we took precautions. The stamps from each roll had the same serial numbers, and on Jay's orders Jane cut stacks from several different rolls so we could alternate numbers on successive book pages. Jay was always clever, but on reflection, the scheme of repeating a recurring pattern every 3-5 pages could only be effective if the pusher were redeeming a single book. Presented with ten or twenty books filled by this method, any conscientious clerk should have figured out we were up to something. It would have been more logical to paste a book-and-a half of one number, then fifteen pages of another, twelve of yet another, and so on. Such a pattern would suggest we had legitimately acquired blocks of stamps from expensive purchases and entered them as they came. Any large family, little league team, or other big-spending stamp-saver would have done it just so.

Such musing leads me to conclude that, while Jay definitely demonstrated sharpness in his young manhood, he by no means achieved criminal genius. His many schemes, including Accomplice Through the Checkout Line, Blue Chip Stamps, Cash Coupon Laundering, etc. — each had a fatal flaw that authorities could have discovered had they been more observant. But people seemed less suspicious in those days. And to give Jay his due, he also practiced the maxim he preached to all who followed in his petty-crime footsteps, namely: "Don't get too greedy." We alternated stores, never took in more than twenty books at a time, and made no purchases requiring special order. Jay must have had good intuition as to where the safe side of the greed line terminated, for he never got caught at this or any of his other schemes. In the Jay Hill world view, crime paid small, but it paid, and the lesson wasn't lost on me in my formative years.

This family story raises questions about individual and corporate morals. Had the aforementioned imaginary Blue Chip G-Men busted up the racket and hauled us before a judge, and had His Honor asked me if I knew I had had done wrong, I would have had to admit to perfect awareness that my five-cent payment for each book amounted to ill-gotten gains. But under money's spell, I developed a fine sense of rationalization, probably along the same lines as Jane and Jay's ("What did a few books matter to a company making millions?" etc. etc.)

I sometimes wonder what would have happened had I been one of those lads born with unimpeachable moral fiber — if I had refused to participate and exhorted Jane to denounce the whole operation as an abomination? Would she — and Jay — have heeded? Perhaps not. But I'm sure they would not have forced me to participate, and with a dissenter in the house, the racket might have been dropped much sooner. In any case, I was apparently born with impeachable moral fiber and gladly lined my pockets without troubling overmuch with ethics.

Another interesting development in our family dynamic also began with the fishing craze I initiated. In subsequent years I would discover a new pastime, and, usually right before I lost interest, Jay would become obsessively focused on mastering the activity, spending many stamps and/or much money in the process. Examples abound: a couple of years later on a lazy summer day, my Norwegian immigrant friend Harald and I wrote the names of chess pieces on scraps of paper, taped them to a plastic checker set, and attempted to learn the game by comparing notes on chess matches we'd observed at school. Jay saw us at it and came to investigate.

"How do you win this game?"

"You get the King," I replied. "But you don't jump him; you just go straight to him."

Harald demonstrated how a knight moves, and Jay watched the game a while longer. The next day he brought home a small plastic chess set and a book on strategy. Within a month or so we had four more sets, including the Blue Chip Stamp consumer standard, the giant size Tijuana Modern version in wood, the classic Henry VIII plastic figurines on a faux marble board, and the traveling model featuring compact plastic pieces, each with a magnetic base.

After a few days Harald and I drifted on to backyard swimming and building model cars, but Jay worked for hours on chess problems he found in books and newspaper columns. Jane soon drifted into the game and proved to be a natural, able to beat Jay more often than not. He redoubled his efforts and eventually outclassed her, but in the meantime he good-naturedly declared her the family champ. Soon after the chess fad struck, our gold Zenith 21-inch TV set stopped functioning, and they didn't bother to take suspected faulty tubes to the self-service testing machine at Thrifty Drug Store. I would come home from my paper route (more on this later) wishing they had gotten the TV fixed so I could watch a little *Andy Griffith* or *Beverly*

Hillbillies. But the house would be silent except for an occasional murmured "Check" from the kitchen or bedroom.

Jay's most grandiose obsession involved tropical fish. The aquarium craze began later in '62 after we'd moved from Manhattan Beach to Redondo Beach. One Saturday, I took a break from shopping center wanderings to enjoy a twenty-five cent hot dog at the Woolworth's lunch counter. Afterward, with my recent Blue Chip Stamp earnings burning a hole in my pocket, I strolled through the pet section's bird cages, guinea pig boxes, and aquariums. Suddenly I yearned for an animal companion. In Sylmar I'd kept a small turtle in a container that featured a plastic island and palm tree in the middle, but the little fellow hadn't lasted long as a lonesome castaway. Birds seemed more interesting to me now, and I would have liked to buy a parakeet. But I saw that they cost two dollars each, plus five dollars for the smallest cage.

I moved to the next aisle. "How much are the fish?" I inquired of the pet department clerk, who looked a little like a parakeet.

She must have been paid on commission. "Ten cents each," she chirped, "and the bowl is nineteen cents. We have a sale on colored gravel and ornaments, and the large box of guppy food is much more economical ..."

By the end of her spiel, I had spent over two dollars on two guppies and all necessary equipment to accommodate them: small glass bowl, bag of gravel, fish net ("to catch them and put them in a glass while you clean their bowl"), a ceramic deep sea diver decoration, and a cylindrical container of food flakes.

At home Jay and Jane greeted me with more parental admonitions to avoid spilling water or food in my room than interest in my new acquisitions. But a few days later I awoke to excited voices in the middle of the night.

"Jay! Get him! There! Quick!"

"Damn! The bitch ate another one!'

My ceiling light shone on my parents as they hovered around my fish bowl. I sat up to investigate. Jane turned, her eyes glittering with excitement. "The momma fish is having babies! We've gotten three out of there, but they're both eating the babies if they catch them!"

Jay and Jane stayed up most of the night collecting the surviving spawn in a water glass. I watched for a while, then went back to sleep. The next day Jay came home with a ten gallon aquarium, a vibration filter system with yards of plastic tubing, and several paper cartons, like the containers for take-out Chinese food. Each carton held a tropical fish pair: swordtails, black mollies, angel fish, neon tetras, and catfish. Jay and Jane gave names to this first group and watched them for hours. Soon I too developed an interest in "Sneaky Pete," "Gramps," "Angel," and the rest.

Within a few weeks we had several more aquariums in the house: four or five ten-gallon standards, a couple of deluxe twenties, and a few intermediate sizes. Jay continued to bring home new tanks, pumps, and such almost daily, and the small house began to resemble the local tropical fish store. Eventually he removed the linen closet doors and emptied the shelves to make room for two twelve-gallon tanks. The master bedroom housed ten tanks stacked on dressers and in chromed sheet metal racks. Soon four tanks appeared in the living room and two in the kitchen. When Nanny visited one day, she discovered to her horror our kitchen freezer full of frozen brine shrimp, a delicacy for the thoroughbred guppies Jay now bred in various tanks. Eventually a fifty-gallon industrial unit dominated the garage work bench, where, from pepper-grain-size eggs, Jay hatched his own shrimp. The bubble of filters and hum of air pumps were omnipresent on the property. One night the electricity shut off briefly, and we all sat up straight in bed, alarmed by the sudden quiet.

Like humans, guppies tend to have their young after midnight, and during those fervent fish collection months I'd hear Jay and Jane up until the early morning hours, hovering over a tank like a team of OB-GYNs working hard to save as many babies as possible from omnivorous parents. The new shrimp-fed guppies no longer had individual names, but the males evolved into lean thoroughbreds with gigantic and colorful fan tails, and the oversize females produced large litters. Within a couple of months Jay had become a walking encyclopedia of aquatic breeding expertise, and no doubt he could have gotten a job as manager in any tropical fish store in the nation. Reflecting on his monomaniacal zeal and the problems it sometimes caused, I also note in retrospect that his curiosity and energetic pursuit of hobbies compare well with the sedentary ball game watching and drinking which encompassed the leisure time of many of my friends' dads. Of course those dads also tended to keep their jobs, pay their bills, and steer clear of shady deals, but no man is perfect.

Backing up a bit to fill in the chronology, we moved to Redondo Beach in late May 1962 as an economy measure—even with the added buying power from Blue Chip Stamps, we couldn't afford Manhattan Beach rent. Since our new house was only a few miles distant, Jane drove me to Grand View for a few weeks so I could finish the semester. This arrangement gave me a more comfortable sense of connection than I'd had with other moves, but somehow it didn't occur to me until the last day of school that I would never again see Mrs. Brach, or Steve, or the girl who loved horses, or Denise with the pool. Or Rebecca McCain. Children are wonderfully adaptable, but the pang of unrequited love Rebecca provided continued to haunt me for the next several months.

More than fifty years have passed, and it's odd to reflect that the object of my first heartache is or at least looks like a grandma now. As a grandpa, I wish her well, wherever she may be. But when I remember the kid who jeered "Grandma Glasses" at me... and his friend who ratted me out to the substitute teacher... Oh, well. Let it go, let it go. Stronger doses of unrequited love and betrayal are yet to be chronicled in my adventures beyond third grade, so why waste time now with snagging at small fish?

CHAPTER THIRTY

~ Memory After All ~ Smoking Hideouts and Construction Sites ~ Language and Bongos ~ Young Sleuths ~ A Flexible Nightmare

In my early notes, the Redondo Beach period (mid-June 1962 to mid-January 1963) seemed a mere prelude to the more noteworthy Huntington Beach years. But further reflection recalls several significant events of the period. I braved the wilderness and made my mark as a modern artist. The major illness of my life sidelined me, but I rose from my sickbed to become a fighter, first of renown and then of infamy. I saw my grandfather for the last time and experienced the worst physical pain I'd suffered so far (except perhaps for my circumcision at birth, a memory I seem to have blocked). In Redondo I also took up smoking, defeated and then joined forces with an outlaw, and learned to walk on stilts—all the while residing in a house which, as related in the last chapter, resembled a home version of Sea World. So the record shows a fairly interesting half-year after all.

The Redondo neighborhood we moved to is an upscale area now, with a median home price of $825,000 when I last checked in 2012. But when we took up residence fifty years previously on a no-sidewalk street of modest stucco homes built in the late forties, each would sell for ten thousand or so. In those days, Redondo played the ugly sister to Manhattan Beach. Where the latter provided sand for Waikiki and a retreat for renowned literary icons, the former blotted its coastline with oil wells and a shabby pier, and its most famous denizen, according to its Wikipedia entry, is a former *Playboy* cover girl who started her own porn distribution company.

My last commute from Grandview Elementary left me the whole summer to acquaint myself with the new town. I began this task slowly, usually with an exploration of morning TV reruns. From Our

Gang episodes, I absorbed ancient 1940s slang ("Say, is this mug on the level?") and became a shadow-boxing enthusiast after watching the "Glove Taps" episode where Alfalfa boxes with Butch. And still smarting from the one-sided romance with Rebecca McCain, I joined Spanky and Alfalfa's He-man Woman Hater's Club, at least in spirit. Once burned, twice shy: during the whole time at Redondo, I had no girlfriends and don't remember talking to girls at all. None of my friends even had sisters.

After several afternoons of solitary wandering among the hilly streets and vacant lots or on excursions to the local shopping center (where I made the purchase that kicked off the family fish mania), I began to meet the neighborhood guys. Two brothers lived next door, one a sixth-grader and one in seventh. Their mom, a dark brown lady, always seemed to be hanging laundry in the back yard, but she never said a word. Their dad, a blonde plumber, owned the first TV set I'd ever seen with VHF and UHF receiving capability. Only two UHF channels broadcast locally at the time: Channel 36 (which specialized in bullfights) and Channel 28, a dry, pre-PBS educational entity featuring a cavalcade of talking heads. As Jay explained when I reported the new phenomenon, the VHF/UHF combination could pull in eighty-three channels. According to *Popular Mechanics*, a wide variety of stations would soon proliferate on the airwaves. Such speculations seemed sheer hyperbole to me at the time, but Jay called it right: the modern TV age had dawned. Telstar, the first worldwide communications satellite, launched in July to great fanfare, and a number one pop hit "Telstar" by an English group called The Tornados sold five million copies.[25]

Jimmy, a tough fifth grader, became my first best friend in the neighborhood. Like my Wyvernwood pal Carey, Jimmy could spit expertly through his teeth and did so every few minutes. He wore a Careyesque flat top with fenders, and like my army-expert friend he cursed artistically and often. Jimmy adorned his blue canvas school binder with spider webs on all corners, and he also drew spider webs on his hand between the thumb and forefinger. But his prime claim to glamour and sophistication came with owning the first set of bongo drums I'd seen up close. Of course I was familiar

---

[25] The worldwide interest in Telstar, along with the best-selling song dedicated to it, provides a perfect illustration of how our sense of technological wonder has diminished in the modern era. Offhand, I don't recall a single number-one hit named after a cell phone tower.

with Preston Epps's great hit single "Bongo Rock," and Maynard G. Krebs, the lovable beatnik on *The Many Loves of Dobie Gillis* TV show, also did much to popularize bongos in that era. Jimmy let me try my hand(s) at the skins and even showed me how to tune the drums by waving a lit match at a particular point to tighten the drumheads and produce a higher tone. "But not too close, dipshit, or you'll burn a fuckin' hole in 'em!"

In addition to his conscientious record of never leaving a neighborhood construction site without destroying, defacing, or stealing something, Jimmy made his mark by organizing the neighborhood smoking parties. One or more of us would steal cigarettes from our parents (everyone's parents smoked in those days), and in a garage or other hideout we would light up one at a time and pass the cigarette around, peace pipe style. Looking back, we probably acted with more secrecy about our smoking than we needed to since our parents had all gone through the same furtive rites of passage themselves. Still, one never knew what a dad or mom would do at any given time. One father (a smoker himself) forced his son, a boy I knew, to eat a cigarette. But most parents saw nicotine addiction as inevitable, and most kids became confirmed smokers by age sixteen, when they could then buy them legally.

During those parties I first heard the communal smokers' slang known to all junior high and high school bathroom practitioners. To "hot box" meant to inhale so deeply that the cigarette became overheated and the smoke harsh. To "nigger lip" meant to unduly wet the end of the cigarette when it came your turn. Even in those days we understood the taboo against speaking "the N word" in mixed company. We also agreed with our TV shows, teachers, and social studies books that prejudice was un-American and downright sinful. But my peer group, in keeping with our junior desperado aspirations, followed a double standard when it came to language, and we reserved the right to democratically disparage every racial, ethnic, and social group of anyone not in our immediate presence.

Besides the use of "nigger lip," I first heard in Redondo a number of jokes involving stereotypical black characters, usually pornographic Steppin' Fetchits, who said things like "Fo' a nickel ah will" when a nymphomaniac demanded their services. Also during these smoking sessions, I first heard parents referred to as "my old man," as in "My old man brought back some twitchin' Nazi knifes and stuff from the war" and "my old lady," as in (from one of the brothers next door) "My old lady ain't a beaner; she's a pure-blood Indian." One kid brought great ridicule upon himself by saying something like, "My old *woman* was born in Ohio," instead of "My old *lady* was born in Ohio." Led by Jimmy, the guys reacted like self-righteous English professors to this irregular usage, throwing up their hands and howling "My old woman!" with exaggerated mirth.

Jimmy's family included his brother Timmy, a shy kid my age, and their single mom, who, according to neighborhood gossip, often entertained drunken men late at night. This seemed normal enough to me, but from time to time Jimmy and Timmy's family did distinguish itself by becoming destitute to the point where those perceptive neighbors donated clothing to the kids. They administered the charity discreetly; Jane only told me about it after I remarked to her one day that I'd seen Timmy wearing a pair of my old tennis shoes.

But I knew that Timmy and Jimmy's mom could by no means be considered entirely destitute, for she owned *Elvis's Greatest Hits Volume One*. I'd go over to their place (a delightfully parent-free zone) after school or sometimes after dinner and talk Jimmy into playing Elvis while he did his homework, which, after a few minutes, usually segued into his decorating the corners of his mimeographed homework pages with spider webs.

I had heard "Hound Dog" and "Blue Suede Shoes" on Luanne's record player back in San Pedro, but was more familiar with Elvis's Contemporary Adult Sound of 1961-62. "Heartbreak Hotel" and "Jailhouse Rock" seemed archaic at first, but the older songs grew on me quickly. In the younger photo on the album cover, Elvis actually sported those sideburns people still joked about in 1962, though he hadn't grown them back since he left the army in 1960. In my opinion, The King had erred in bowing to politer fashion, and I resolved to grow sideburns myself as soon as I possibly could.

The brothers next door introduced me to a near-teenager down the street: a huge seventh-grader, though not dangerous once you got to know him. One weekend he invited me along with Jimmy and the brothers for a sleepover in his garage loft. The announced goal was to stay up all night, an exciting proposition in those days of universally strict bedtimes. His parents kept a polite distance, and we made the most of the amnesty, eating burnt Jiffy Pop, drinking innumerable Shasta sodas, and laughing uncontrollably at jokes like "'Fo' a nickel ah will."

At some point toward morning when we were all winding down but reluctant to give in to sleep, I discovered a collection of Hardy Boys books stored in the loft. This series, first introduced in the nineteen-twenties, featured Frank and Joe Hardy, idealized boy "sleuths" in the days when detectives reigned as the ultimate in cool. The boys often assisted their father, Fenton Hardy, a private eye and former policeman. In addition, they managed to fall into many exciting capers of their own. Frank and Joe owned their own cars, plus airplanes, iceboats, and detective gear (paid for with treasure collected during their adventures), and a crew of loveable sidekicks attended them. These supporting players included ethnics Tony Printo (Italian) and Phil Cohen (Jewish), plus portly Chet Morton and his lovely sister Iola, who was sweet on Joe, the younger, more impetuous Hardy brother.

All the Hardy Boys books carried the "Franklin W. Dixon" byline, but years later I discovered the series employed a succession of ghost writers. The publishers are even yet cranking out fresh product, from pre-teen Hardys at the third-grade reading level to a recent young adult series featuring Frank and Joe as nineteen- and twenty-year-olds. In the first of these edgier stories, Iola is killed by a terrorist bomb and both brothers pack guns.

The original volumes, each with delightful gadgets and a cliffhanger in every chapter, seemed exciting enough for me. After reading half a book in the early morning of the sleepover, I took home ten titles, raced through them all within two weeks, and returned to borrow more. Eventually I read all of the first 27 books while continuing my classic studies in *Journeys into Bookland* and my more sophisticated modern fare.[26]

I could have read all summer, but I saw myself as a man of action as well as a scholar. Nowadays construction sites are fenced off and even patrolled by security guards, but then workers kindly left everything wide open, thereby providing fresh-air recreational activities for neighborhood kids. One day we found a load of sand placed conveniently at the bottom of a two-story building in progress. Someone's dad had told him about WWII parachute school training, and we brought the story to life by jumping off the second story into the pile. We also enjoyed walking tightrope style

---

[26] Walter Brooks, author of the Freddy the Pig series, wrote for *The New Yorker* in his younger days. Once such sophistication is attained, it of course attaches itself to the author's entire body of work.

across two-by-fours laid between buildings and played tag among the roof studs of half-finished, two-story apartments.

As for ground-level activities, everyone had stilts fashioned from six-foot lengths of two-by-fours we found around the sites with almost any short pieces of lumber attached for footholds. In our view, stilt-walkers had the perpetual right of way in all traffic situations, and we proved it often by stilting into the street with no apparent concern for oncoming cars. On a related note, I didn't walk on stilts again for almost forty years, when I had occasion to try a pair at the interactive Greenfield Village section of the Henry Ford Museum in Detroit. But I can report from experience that, like riding a bicycle, the skill of stilt-walking comes back quickly, as does the tendency to run down nearby pedestrians and lurch into traffic.

As summer progressed, we stole enough lumber to build go-carts, cannibalizing wheels and axles from any wagon or other rolling toy left on the street. Our homemade vehicles featured poor steering and no brakes, and they provided much in the way of stimulation for automobile drivers who encountered us on the neighborhood hill, racing three or four abreast.

I envisioned my first drivable dream car as a custom go-cart. It would be a Black Widow or Green Hornet in a neighborhood full of generic wooden jalopies. I'd already built the jalopy; now I planned to upholster it with black sheet rubber and rig ropes to an old steering wheel (on reflection, this would have worked even less well than unencumbered ropes). I would also build a box in front, where an old battery would represent the hot rod engine. Step-granddad John had vaguely promised an old steering wheel and battery and I had begun to investigate sheet rubber availability.

But my grandiose engineering plans were superseded by summer camp, namely good old Stanley Ranch, cultural holdover from the summer before. In the interim I'd attended a couple of Manhattan Beach Woodcraft Ranger meetings and found them less engaging than those of the Sylmar tribe. The only Manhattan group trip took us to the local jail, where the officer in charge took us into a solitary confinement cell and demonstrated how dark it was when the lights were turned out. Nonetheless my desire for the full-week Ranger camp experience had been rekindled, so in the glow of my academic triumphs and Blue Chip Stamp-pasting diligence, Jane and Jay had promised to finance my wilderness experience. The intervening several weeks and move to Redondo hadn't dimmed my ardor as they might have hoped, so they scraped up the $35 fee. All set to go—but not before I did some painful scraping of my own.

In addition to stilts and go-carts, neighborhood vehicles included bikes of all sizes, scooters, and occasional Flexible Flyer sleds. These last embodied a misguided attempt to provide California kids with the thrill of snow sledding. In design, the Flexible Flyer appeared identical to a regular sled except for tiny wheels instead of runners. The rider lay down on the wooden deck and held onto stationary metal handles in the front, onto which hand brakes similar to those on a bicycle had been attached.

A few days before my scheduled camp departure, I found an upside-down Flexible Flyer in the gutter about halfway up the hill at the end of our street. I didn't stop to wonder *why* the sled lay upside down in the gutter; instead I dragged it to the top and mounted the deck for my first-ever experience with the demonic device.

With a slight sense of unease, I noted the proximity of my face to the street. But I took a deep breath and resolutely pushed off with my foot. Almost immediately I found myself going faster than I'd ever traveled on a bike. Three-quarters down the hill, with velocity increasing each second, I squeezed the brakes lightly, hoping to slow the thing down a bit. Instantly the front wheels locked. The rear of the sled upended, and for a second—it seemed much longer—I performed a traveling handstand, gripping the front of the sled with my body perpendicular to the ground, while the locked front wheels continued to slide down the hill. Then the forward momentum flipped me on my back and I slid another several yards on the asphalt, twisting and turning with the sled on top of me.

Finally I came to a stop in the middle of the street. Slowly, painfully, I untangled myself from the sled and left it in the gutter. Patches of both arms had been scraped raw as were areas of my legs, stomach and back. Limping stiffly, I made for home, in such pain I could barely get enough breath to cry. When I stumbled through the front door, Jay and Jane looked up from cleaning one of the living room fish tanks. Trish was directing a musical comedy with her dolls and Greg reclined in his playpen, burbling to himself. All conversation stopped as I entered, bloody and hyperventilating.

Jane hurried to meet me. "Oh God, Honey, what happened?"

Jay looked more concerned than I'd ever seen him. "Here, Pal, let's get the shirt and pants off."

They led me to a chair and I fumbled with my belt and buttons.

My pants hurt coming off, the shirt even more. Every part of me burned and throbbed. Jay and Jane working together took most of an hour to clean the dirt and gravel from the wounds and apply ointments and dressings.

When my wife heard this story a few years ago, she asked, "Why didn't they take you to the hospital?" As we'll see later, certain episodes of ill-health did call for hospitalization, but parents usually took care of first aid in those days. Jay hadn't been in combat like many dads in the neighborhood, but he could sterilize a wound and fashion a butterfly suture if necessary, lance a boil, splint a finger, and improvise a sling for a sprained arm. His country doctor grandfather had been his idol, and he might indeed have followed in the old man's footsteps except for his tendency to faint in hospitals.

With the wound dressing completed, they propped me in front of the TV, with a Seven-Up to wash down two aspirins. I had trouble sleeping the next couple of nights, for any way I turned felt uncomfortable. But 72 hours later found me tossing in my camp bunk.

CHAPTER THIRTY-ONE

~ Prefab Wilderness ~ Race Relations ~ The Modern Artist
~ Surfer # 1 ~ Briefly Good to Be Home

In *Manufactured Wilderness: Summer Camps and the Shaping of America's Youth,* author Abigail Van Slyck notes that parents have been packing city kids off to organized country settings since the 1880s, and, according to her theories, doing so for complex social reasons. A reviewer summed up Van Slyck's thesis:

> She argues that summer camps delivered much more than a simple encounter with the natural world ... camps provided a man-made version of wilderness, shaped by middle-class anxieties about gender roles, class tensions, race relations, and Modernity and its impact on the lives of children.

In my camp experience I did encounter most of the learned sociologist's list of middle-class anxieties. While I can't dispute her points, I would note that, for me, the negatives of camp at least seemed to have more to do with homesickness than class tensions, race relations, or the impact of modernity. I would argue that, under any conditions, a week away from home and family is a long, long time to a little boy.

As an (almost) fourth-grader, I would have felt insulted had anyone called me a "little boy," and on balance my time at camp passed as a reasonably pleasant experience. True, that region of North San Fernando is brutally hot in the daytime; activities were low-budget, and food adequate at best. Regimentation was definitely excessive, and yes, the staff had minimal training. But for all the drawbacks, we did get to ride real horses, swim in a pool, shoot BB guns, and sleep under the stars for a whole week.

To start at the beginning: Jane drove me to the camp drop-off location in downtown LA, a scene reminiscent of an army induction station, with counselors acting sergeant-like as they herded everyone into "squads" for the busses. Boys and girls between eight and fifteen had been organized by age and seemingly coincidentally by race, with whites, Mexicans, and African-Americans about equally represented. Most of the ethnic campers came on "scholarship." A priority of the Stanley Ranch was to give inner city kids a chance to breathe some country (or in this case, desert) air, and the Woodcraft Rangers made a real effort to recruit wilderness-starved children whether their parents could afford the fee or not. Nowadays in this supposedly integrated age, Stanley Ranch remains in business, but operates strictly for inner-city campers. Suburban kids go to computer camp, or band camp, or somewhere a little more glamorous than the Saugus hills.

When we lined up for the bus I carried my new Blue Chip Stamps sleeping bag, plus a knapsack containing the rest of the gear specified in the camp flier: flashlight, second pair of jeans, two short-sleeve shirts, two changes of underpants, bathing suit, towel, soap, toothbrush, and toothpaste. Jane also packed a large box of Band-Aids for my Flexible Flyer wounds. This load seemed substantial at the time, but my equipment compared to today's camp gear was as primitive as a Confederate army private's outfit would be next to a modern U.S. Army infantryman's. According to Nikki, a camp counselor who blogs about his or her experience at 21st Century sites:

My campers came ... with their portable DVD players, iPods, personal fans, brand new, monogrammed wardrobe, laptop computers, cell phones, feather mattresses and oh yes, even air purifiers. (Imagine trying to fit 10 of those things into one cabin!) If that wasn't enough, many parents insisted upon lavishing their children with huge gift packages each day of camp, chock full of delightful trinkets that would most likely never end up coming home. By the end of the week, my cabins looked like small toy stores.

In the medical clearance line at the processing station, a camp employee dressed in a white coat seemed concerned about all my Band-Aids, but after consulting with Jane, he stamped my registration card. I then crowded onto the bus with my squad and three or four other groups for a hot and noisy ride to the Stanley Ranch.

When we arrived, last week's sunburned and self-assured campers took our places on the busses headed back to the city. Jerry, our squad's counselor, couldn't, by camp custom, have been older than eighteen or nineteen, but from his height, girth, and easy authority, he seemed more like thirty-five or forty. "Follow me, shrimps," he growled, and marched us to our sleeping area, a sort of open-air bunkhouse where iron-frame single beds with thin mattresses had been arranged among the oaks. The effect was reminiscent of tract homes in an upscale suburb built around existing trees. As noted earlier, Van Slyck may have been onto something with the "manufactured middle-class wilderness" business.

But we had no inclination for sociological reflections as we marched to dinner in the mess hall. The meal featured diced beef over rice with chocolate pudding for dessert, all agreeably evocative of school cafeteria food. In table conversation I found out that, as with my weekend stay the year before, most of my bunkmates at this Woodcraft Ranger camp had never heard of the Rangers; they chose the Stanley Ranch because this camp charged less per week than any other in the greater Los Angeles area. Several came from single-mother households; a couple had parents off somewhere else on vacation. A tall kid, who announced as we sat down that he was Jewish and didn't eat bacon, had what later seemed like a life sentence of three weeks, which meant three repeated cycles of the usual one-week program.

After dinner we marched back to our bunk area and gathered around Jerry as he told "Man with the Golden Arm," a classic ghost story I heard that evening for the first time. Jerry seemed like a nice guy, even if he called us shrimps. He possessed great social sensitivity as well, which he demonstrated a couple of days later when a fat boy in my section called a black girl "nigger" when she beat him in tetherball. Jerry gave the perpetrator a righteous dressing-down. "You better say you're sorry or your ass is grass! How do you like it when somebody calls you Fatso? Huh, Fatso? Come on, how do YOU like it, Fatso?!"

Each evening at nine p.m., a scratchy record played Taps over a loudspeaker, the signal for retiring to our bunks, tired or not. With my nearsightedness, I couldn't make much of the bright stars everyone commented upon. But having never seen stars outside of *How And Why Wonder Books*, I didn't miss them. I hadn't worn my glasses since the day of the "Grandma Glasses!" taunt, and I would have bombarded Jane with outrage had she even suggested bringing them to summer camp.

I liked the smell of the oaks and sage, and after the sweltering day, the night seemed agreeably cool. As usual I had some trouble finding a position that didn't press on several of my scabs, but finally I drifted off. When I awoke around six the next morning the rest of the guys still slept peacefully, so I climbed quietly from bed with plans to go exploring.

"Hey, you!" Jerry stage-whispered. "Back in your bunk till reveille!

Reveille sounded at seven o'clock, and time passed slowly until then. I spent the interval wishing I'd packed something to read, picturing all the books in my private room back home. I thought fondly of Jay and Jane, made a vague resolution to be a more attentive brother to Trish and Greg, and even missed the tropical fish whose names I knew. I then pursued some superhero/science fiction fantasies I usually saved for long showers — I had an Isaac Asimovian serial going that featured a race of seven-foot-tall super-geniuses who patrolled the universe fighting bad aliens. With all reveries exhausted, I tried counting to sixty over and over (using the one-elephant, two-elephant method) to get a sense of how many minutes had passed, but I kept losing count. This enforced meditation took place each camp morning; no matter how tired the day's activities left me, I couldn't sleep past the bright morning light of six o'clock.

Following reveille, we rolled up our sleeping bags and marched to the mess hall for breakfast, where we roughed it by eating frosted flakes right out of the individual-serving cardboard boxes. The sides of the boxes came perforated, and the wax paper inner wrap didn't leak milk if you ate fast enough. We then marched back to the huge, school-style bathrooms for monitored teeth brushing. The general routine was similar to my weekend stay the year before, but the next phase came as a real surprise: weeklong campers had to perform an hour of work — usually raking and picking up trash — every morning before we did anything fun. The counselors called it "policing the area," and from their diminished patience with our pre-teen goofiness, I don't think they liked having to do work at summer camp any better than we did.

"You guys want to swim? You want to ride horses?

"Yeah, but—"

"Then get rakin'! Let's see some hustle!"

Already the day had grown too hot for hustling, and no one wanted to appear eager, so we mostly leaned on the rakes. One kid found a cigarette butt, and everyone else reacted to the discovery with what seemed to me inordinate excitement. I had been hanging out with older guys at home, so my own age group as gathered here seemed, in my mature judgment, a bit childish. Perceiving my indifference, one of my bunkmates began to question me. Had I ever smoked? Certainly. I recited a volley of smoker's slang to prove it. Well, did I know the "Winston tastes bad" jingle? Of course. I sang the entire verse with blasé delivery.

Around 10 a.m. the counselors finally organized the advertised activities: swimming, horseback riding, crafts, and playground games. The Ranch proper consisted of a few acres of scrub brush and cleared parade areas with a few buildings, including the camp office, the mess hall, and a larger "lodge," used for indoor activities, in the center of the complex. The rest of the grounds featured a medium-sized pool with separate boys' and girls' locker rooms; four bathroom buildings with community showers in each and outside sinks around the perimeter; and a blacktop area with the full range of school games: tetherball, foursquare, and basketball. The corral, home of ten or so horses past their prime, could be found a quarter mile away down a graded dirt road.

But something important seemed to be missing. Unlike all the camps I read about before and after, Stanley Ranch had no adjacent lake. This state of affairs seemed quite unorthodox—even the horrific camp in Allen Sherman's comic song "Hello Muddah, Hello Faddah, Here I am at Camp Granada" (which came out a year later) had a lake, albeit one with alligators. We were also bereft of bungee jumps, waterslides, computers, acting coaches, or other staples of 21st-Century camps where, according to Nikki, the modern counselor:

> [...] there are classes like trampoline, circus, modeling and manners, mountain biking, jet skiing, ropes courses, waterslides, sailing, kayaking, etc. Each activity has the best and newest equipment on the line, with enough so that each child can participate at the same time.

We did get to go swimming in the heavily-chlorinated pool three days of the seven, adhering to a complicated alternating-squad schedule. But to my great frustration and shame I didn't pass the swim test on the first day, and consequently found myself barred from the deep end of the pool where all the action was. Almost every other boy and girl my age had attended YMCA or Red Cross swimming lessons; the mandatory test was a fun race to them. The tall kid who didn't eat bacon couldn't swim either, but, using a determined dogpaddle, he made it across. I hoped to do the same, but my non-standard water locomotion proceeded more erratically — sometimes I could navigate deep water across a pool; sometimes I couldn't. This time I floundered in the middle and lunged off course to grab for the side.

"Don't sweat it," the pool counselor said. "You can come back after supper for lessons and a retest."

After a spaghetti and meatball repast, my squad drifted off to play basketball and tetherball in the long summer evening. I returned to the pool. The only other non-swimmers who showed up were two black kids about my age, brothers as it turns out, from the squads on the other side of the camp. The "lessons" consisted of the pool counselor repeating the test rules: "Get across the pool any way you can without touching the sides, and you can swim in the deep end from now on."

The brothers tried first and both of them made it, splashing across the pool with no skill but lots of movement and sufficient aim.

"Okay, Mr. Band-Aids, you're up."

I started across resolutely, but about three-quarters across I made an unplanned, gradual detour that bumped me into the side. The counselor's whistle blew at the instant my hand touched the cement. As I climbed out, he shook his head. "No go. Try again tomorrow night."

The brothers had already dressed. I sat on the bench and stared into space.

"That's all right, boy," the bigger kid said. "You'll make it tomorra."

I scrutinized him carefully for any hint of the superiority or sarcasm I had come to expect from the kids back in Redondo. But my fine-tuned defensiveness could detect only something uncomfortably close to pity. I stood there dripping, band aids hanging half-off every shank, feeling profoundly homesick.

We talked a few minutes while we dressed; or rather they talked to me. The older brother was ten, the younger eight or nine. In a movie version of this chronicle ("based on a true story"), the brothers would turn out to be the same duo I'd met at Nanny's back in 1957, but no such luck in real life. These brothers weren't sure how to feel about this camp business either, having never ventured beyond their Central L.A. neighborhood. They had also never been in a pool before today, which made me feel even worse about failing the test.

The next night I failed again. A year later, without teachers to distract me or peers to make me nervous, I taught myself to swim in a three-feet-deep backyard pool, mastering the skill in one focused afternoon. Subsequently I became a good and relatively fast swimmer, but I never managed to perform under pressure at camp. I spent the remainder of the week in the shallow end with the few second- and third-graders who couldn't swim either.

You lose a few; you win a few. The day after my final swim test attempt, my squad rotated to afternoon arts and crafts. Former U.S. Poet Laureate Billy Collins wrote a funny and poignant poem called "The Lanyard," about making his mom a gift at his summer camp. He presents her with the plastic lanyard, taking the attitude that the gift equaled the sacrifices mothers make for their children. The memory provides a bittersweet epiphany for the grown-up son, but at least Billy managed to braid his mom a decent lanyard. I showed myself as much a failure at that craft as I'd been at swimming: my lanyard ended up crooked and loose, with skipped stitches. Rose, my nemesis back in Mrs. Yamamoto's class, would have laughed witheringly at the sight of it.

I wandered off to sit under a tree. Too soon afterward, the counselor in charge called me back for the next craft, which involved carving faces into fist-size chalk cylinders. Some of my squadmates demonstrated a fine hand with the knife — one quiet boy proceeded to carve a beautiful face, complete with raised pupils and eyebrows. Meanwhile, my chalk visage turned into something a clumsy five-year-old might produce. But then I had an inspiration. I carved a deep indentation in the forehead and made the eyes even more lopsided on purpose. I scraped lightning bolt patterns in the cheeks, then carved one stumpy horn on top, a la the "flying purple people eater" song. This feature gave the face a decidedly low forehead, and when I finished, the thing looked like something that might sit atop an extraterrestrial totem pole.

I expected the crafts counselor, a shorter and thinner young man than our squad's Jerry, to accuse me of wasting my chalk, but you never know with adults. He picked up my carving and gave it a look Mozart's piano teacher might have given little Wolfgang when he first saw what the lad was scribbling at the piano. "Wow!" he exclaimed. "This is really, really creative!"

He called over another crafts counselor who seemed equally impressed. These two must have had the same beatnik art teacher at the same junior college. Where'd you learn to do this?" the second one queried. "Do you paint and stuff, too?"

I shrugged modestly, as befit a Modern Artist who has finally achieved Recognition. We all contemplated the fruit of my genius for a few seconds, then somehow the glances of all three of us settled on the gifted kid's beautiful carving. The boy didn't look up; he kept working, delicately smoothing the chalk cheekbones with his knife.

The first counselor smiled at the kid and took the carving from his hands. "This one is really good ... technically" he said "But *this*" — holding up mine — "well, *this* is really original! It's — " his eyes glazed over as the other arts counselor nodded sagely — "like you're ... exploring a whole new way of looking at things!"

If I could go back in time, retaining my current consciousness in my then nine-year old body, I might ask those aspiring art critics what I've always wanted to ask established practitioners: "How can you tell if the abstract artist has made a wrong turn in his 'explorations'? And how can you be sure of the difference between a visionary and a joker who has read *Mad Magazine* parodies of modern-art pretentiousness?" But at the time, I felt happy enough to have received any notice for anything.

The remainder of the last camp afternoon featured contests and activities. To my surprise, I won further recognition: a second place ribbon in BB gun shooting, an especially notable accomplishment considering I could barely see the bull's-eye on the target. I hadn't fired anything but dart guns since Daddy had taken me out to blast at cans with a .22 rifle in 1957, but perhaps heredity was at work. Jane was always crack shot, too.

Later, still damp from a truncated pool session, we rode the horses our second and last time. The evening's chuckwagon barbecue included blackened hot dogs, canned beans, and roasted marshmallows. Afterwards, an entertaining comic wrestling show commenced in the lodge where the wrestling counselors, obvious Red Skelton fans, hammed it up in tribute to Clem Kadiddlehopper, Freddie the Freeloader, and the rest of Red's gallery of characters.

After breakfast the next morning, the authorities excused us from policing the area. Instead we packed, said goodbye to our squad counselors, and joined the lineup for the busses back home. The de facto segregation seemed to have broken down as we departed: my bus had plenty of Mexican and black kids I hadn't seen much of the whole week. Last on board came the seniormost camper of all, a Mexican about fifteen wearing shades, a ten-hair goatee and a pork pie hat. The Beach Boys "Surfin' Safari" dominated all pop radio playlists, and the surfing mystique had apparently crossed all racial and social strata, at least for the moment. By way of honoring their chieftain with the latest status badge, the Mexican kids called him "Surfer."

"Hey, Surfer!"

"Yo, Surfer, sit over here, man!"

As we departed the manufactured wilderness and rolled down the highway to our natural domains, I strained my ears toward the bus driver's big transistor radio. I hadn't heard a radio or seen a TV screen in seven days, and the Rivingtons's "Papa Oom-Mow-Mow" sounded sublime. Surfer seemed to be enjoying it, too—he slouched back with his eyes half-closed, bobbing his head to the music.

When we arrived at the lot downtown, I saw Jane waving and smiling like I'd been gone for years. It seemed so to me, too. She admired my tan, and as we drove home, she told all the latest fish anecdotes and enumerated the new aquariums Jay had acquired. She said he was home from work and decorating their back panels right now with special lacquer paint for a stained-glass look.

I sighed luxuriously as we pulled into our driveway, imagining the long, unstructured summer ahead. Jane said that Daddy would be visiting in a few weeks, and, when I told him about my BB expertise, we might go target shooting with whatever gun he brought. Meanwhile I could finish my go-cart, play on the construction sites, check in with my neighborhood pals, and roam around town—a new shopping center would be opening soon, and maybe I'd even find my way to the Redondo pier. It felt good to be home.

Two days later, I came down with infectious hepatitis.

CHAPTER THIRTY-TWO

~ Where the Yellow Went ~ Defying Medical Authority ~ Enforced Leisure
~ Nikita and Locky ~ The Architect of the Future
~ Fellows with Time to Spare

Hepatitis A, the ailment that sidelined me for much of the summer of 1962, is an infectious liver disease spread by first-, second- or even third-hand contact with infected fecal matter.[27] The disease is still common in children around the world; a recent outbreak in California was spread via infected pomegranate seeds from Turkey. But since the A strain does not cause permanent liver damage, it is taken less seriously today than the potentially deadly hepatitis B and C types. Nonetheless, hepatitis A is painful and debilitating in its acute stage. The victim must be quarantined for several weeks initially and is forever prohibited from selling or donating blood.

The onset came two nights after I'd gotten back from summer camp. I reclined in bed reading *The Mystery of Cabin Island*, the first in a new stack of Hardy Boys books I'd borrowed from the seventh-grader who lived up the street. I rose to relieve myself, and as I walked down the hall I felt increasingly light-headed and nauseous. My urine looked remarkably yellow, but as I always showed great reticence about discussing bodily functions, I did not inform my parents. I navigated woozily to my bed and book, but I couldn't seem to focus on the words. A few minutes later I stumbled back down the hall to throw up, but made it only halfway to the bathroom.

Jane had also been reading in bed and came running when she heard me. After cleaning up and settling me back under covers,

---

[27] The rapid proliferation in epidemics should raise questions of how much uninfected (and thus undetected) fecal matter one comes in contact with when the disease isn't around to call attention to the contact. But it's probably best to leave such inquiries to professionals.

she fetched Jay from the garage, where she'd found him harvesting brine shrimp.

"Jay, look. His eyes—they're all yellow!"

Jay looked concerned, but he smiled. "When they say, 'Wonder where the yellow went,' we can tell them Ricky got it all!"[28] He stayed calm and cheering until they took my temperature, but then he became more agitated than I'd ever seen him. "Hundred and four and a half! Wrap his face and chest in wet towels—cold ones! I'll start the car!"

Jay told me later his grandfather had been through the flu epidemic of 1918 and subscribed to the view that brain damage would inevitably occur when a fever reached 105 degrees. As I learned in adulthood, this is actually true only in cases of hyperthermia (heat stroke), but Jay believed his grandfather above all medical authorities. He roared to County General Hospital, running lights and swerving around corners.

I would have enjoyed the ride if I weren't so sick. I stretched out in the back seat with my head on Jane's lap, and she held a cold towel to my brow. When we arrived, the doctors and nurses showed almost as much anxiety as Jay about bringing the fever down. Unfortunately their method consisted of stripping me naked, laying me on a gurney, and covering me with ice-cold wet sheets—with my nudity visible to parents AND the doctor AND several nurses each time they changed the sheets. I felt too weak to protest, but in my view, the procedure seemed too low-tech for the modern age. John Glenn had orbited the Earth a few months ago, so why should the entire hospital staff stand around watching me freeze to death naked instead of doing something in keeping with the space age?

"Can I take a pill or something?" I inquired weakly.

"No, son," intoned the doctor. "We'd better not give you any antibiotics or aspirin until we can rule out your liver."

I knew nothing of livers and antibiotics; nonetheless, his answer filled me with indignation. If I couldn't have a wonder drug or even an aspirin, we might as well be in Abe Lincoln's day, when, as I'd read in three biographies, multitudes died of the milk fever, whatever that was. It couldn't have felt worse than this. If my Flaming Star had drawn near and they couldn't do anything to help

---

[28] Jay referred of course to the uncannily catchy toothpaste jingle "You'll wonder where the yellow went / When you brush your teeth with Pepsodent!"

me, why couldn't I go home and soak in a bathtub full of cold water until the end came?

After a couple of hours of cold, wet sheets, the doctor prescribed that very plan: "Give cool baths as fever indicates." But they also instructed Jay and Jane to bring me back tomorrow when the lab opened for blood tests.

We dutifully returned the next morning. The non-emergency wing of the hospital was a foreboding place of highly polished linoleum floors, whitewashed walls, iron beds, and a strong stench of disinfectant that reminded me of polio shots at school. Sure enough, after the assistant placed me in a small room, a nurse entered and jabbed me with a large needle. As I watched my blood gush into various vials, my head began to spin.

"Dizzy," I muttered, as she removed the needle. "Gotta lay down."

Jane put her hand under my shoulder to ease me to a horizontal position on the gurney, but the nurse firmly set me back upright. "Sit up!" she commanded. "Put your head between your knees until the dizziness passes." Her starched white dress, white stockings, white hat, and spotless white shoes bolstered her unquestionable authority.

"Jus' needa lay down … I half-whispered, staring down at her shoes. Dark fuzz spread all around them, all around the room. And sparkly bits between the fuzz …

"Put your head between your knees!"

With her helpful push at my neck, I complied. But I felt worse than ever. Suddenly outrage welled up. First they freeze me to death with the whole hospital staff looking on; then they jab me; then they bend me like a pretzel and make me even sicker. With woozy determination, I jerked my head up and shrugged her hand away. "Gotta lay down!" I insisted, and proceeded to stretch out on the gurney.

Jane didn't know who was right, but she followed her heart and planted herself so the nurse couldn't get at me. Once prone, I felt better and from that moment on, my attitude toward the medical profession could be summed-up politely as "One should consider professional advice, but ultimately the patient must take responsibility for personal health decisions."

A couple of days after the blood tests, the doctor diagnosed what he'd predicted: the infectious type-A hepatitis, lately on the rise in Los Angeles County. As I found out later, Jane and Jay initially attributed my case to sending me, with all my still-healing scrapes, to close association with inner-city campers of dubious hygiene. But a few days later, a mom from up the street came to our house and asked if I could play with her little boy, who also had hepatitis. The five-year-old kid had never been out of the neighborhood. The mini-epidemic also struck the next block, infecting a couple of other kids who had never seen me or gone to summer camp.

So much for circumstantial evidence, not to mention my vacation plans. The doctor placed me under house quarantine for next four weeks except for hospital blood tests. No treatment existed then (and none now) for Hepatitis A except rest. Fortunately, I felt the acute nausea for the first few days only; afterwards I had no symptoms except general weakness and fatigue.

I adapted well to solitary confinement and inactivity. Upon arising I turned on the ancient console TV set Jay and Jane had bought for twenty dollars at a pawn shop. They had first installed the set in their room—a second bedroom TV meant luxury in that neighborhood. But when I fell ill, they demonstrated their love and concern by bringing it to my room, complete with a five-gallon fish tank to place atop it. By now we had tanks on every available surface in the house.

Morning TV featured Our Gang and the Three Stooges, plus an occasional Bob Steele western from the 1930s. Frequent commercials and interesting public service messages punctuated the on-screen entertainment. One message from Radio Free Europe presented Khrushchev pounding on the U.N. lectern with his shoe, shouting, "We will bury you." A DPT immunization alert featured cartoon characters "Dippy" Diphtheria and "Locky" Lockjaw, the latter a flabby, slouching character out of a nightmare who trembled and made plaintive noises through clenched teeth.[29]

About nine a.m. I'd have breakfast: always Cocoa Puffs or some other heavily sweetened cereal, plus an egg and toast to keep up my protein level, as prescribed by Jay the self-taught nutritionist. I'd read or watch more TV until lunch, usually a tuna sandwich on white with Campbell's tomato soup and a 7-Up soda, the Protestant chicken soup of the era. We kids switched from Coca-Cola or Dr.

---

[29] A recent web search revealed that Locky has morphed into "Tuffy Tetnus," but Dippy and his friends "Whoopy Whooping Cough" and "Ruby Rubella" are still frightening children in a coloring book distributed by the Texas Department of State Health Services.

Pepper to 7-up when we got sick, as most adults switched to Kool or Salem mentholated cigarettes when they contracted a cold or flu.

One afternoon when I felt a little better, Jane taxied me down the street to play with the younger hepatitis sufferer in the neighborhood. We both felt too listless to bridge the age gap, so I only visited once. But almost every day after lunch I worked on the grand architectural project I began early in my illness. Using a dozen packages of clay, each with four thick bars of varying colors, I built a miniature city of the future, including the ubiquitous monorail system common to all advanced civilizations in science fiction. I modeled my structures on the covers of Jane's Ace Double science fiction novels, and a half-century or so later, one could surmise that architects who designed "modern" skyscrapers like the Gherkin Building in London and the Burj Khalifa in Dubai were likewise influenced by Ace Doubles when they were youngsters.[30]

The bottled city of Kandor, capitol of Superman's home planet Krypton, also provided a model for my civic plan. As all Superman aficionados are aware, Kandor had been shrunk and placed in its bottle by Brainiac, a space android who, directed by an advanced civilization, flew around to various planets in the universe collecting cities for later scientific study. Over the summer my project spread over three levels of plank-and-block shelves (the same ones we'd had in our living room back at Sylmar), and featured more than twenty structures. Gazing from above at my diminutive metropolis, I felt like Brainiac himself.

Jane read science fiction as avidly as I read the Hardy Boys, so I enlisted this local authority on all aspects of space travel to assist me in naming my buildings. On slips of paper she wrote "Intergalactic Spaceport," "Venetian Embassy," and the like, and I placed a tag by each edifice, as in a museum display.

This tactile approach to other-worldliness inspired me to read some of the Ace Double novelettes and other science fiction Jane liked. Most of the tales had stock Hollywood Western plots set in exotic interplanetary locales, but some featured time travel in all its convolutions. I found the latter most intriguing and still do—my daydreams have featured time travel ever since, and I have actually succeeded in traveling more than a half-century into the future,

---

[30] Each Ace Double volume featured two lurid covers (often depicting a city of the future in backdrop) and two novelettes; the stories were placed back to back and the reader turned the book over and upside down to commence the second story.

though the process has been significantly slower for me than for those with super powers or time machines.

Unfortunately, most of the future wonders so confidently predicted by early-twentieth-century science fiction writers have failed to materialize by now, the much-heralded twenty-first century. We do seem to be going through the "crazy years" described in Robert A. Heinlein's future history series, and we do have a few appliances and fashions dreamed up by mid-century writers. Heinlein first described the water bed and cellular phone, and various free phone-aps fulfill the promise of translator helmets in many stories. Men with shaved heads, an extreme rarity at midcentury (only Yul Brenner and Mr. Clean come to mind), are now as ubiquitous as flat screen TVs. But the years 2001 and 2010 passed without a space odyssey or its sequel. Where are the flying cars and rocket belts and luxury cruise ships to Venus? Where at least is the moon station? We have GPS devices to help us around town and talking computers to irritate us when we call our HMO plans, but where are the *real* robots — the ones capable of holding an intelligent conversation, mixing martinis, and moving furniture? Yes, all these wonders may yet transpire, but the grand upward curve of scientific advancement is so much more gradual than our sci-fi sages led us to believe.

In a poem I wrote right before the millennium dawned, I touched on the poignant disappointment experienced by early science fiction fans, especially those, like me, who long for time travel as well as future innovations. The regret comes, as disappointments usually do, because of unreasonable expectations. Humans predict *what* will happen more accurately than they are able to predict *when*. Humanists like Heinlein seem to be as prone to this sort of wishful thinking as Christians obsessed with End Times.

Instead of recounting the dull evenings of my quarantine, I will end this discursive chapter with that composition:

FELLOWS WITH TIME TO SPARE

When heartaches cease to burn and shadows give,
we can still work up a certain sorrow —
a damp sigh for our inability
to escape this present moment.

Physicists fix space-time continuums,
so why can't we grab some dames and take in
the series where Babe Ruth called his homer,
or homestead some southern Cal beachfront
before it got so high-priced and crowded?

No chance. And no fast-forwarding either.
Though we sigh for rocket belts and robots,
anti-grav shoes and galactic vacations
with lovesick, six-armed Martian princesses —
we won't live long enough to enjoy them.

Oh, the pity, boys, the timeless shame of it,
this life on track, this shelf-awareness.
We can't wait for something bad to happen —
something to take our mind off our troubles.

CHAPTER THIRTY-THREE

~ Late News with Daddy ~ The Scandal of Adult Reading ~Change Your Filter, Buddy ~An Unpleasant Milieu ~ Tough Guy Commencement

In mid-August 1962, my grandfather flew from Alabama to visit us in Redondo Beach. Daddy never left his house unarmed, so, in similar preparation for his last flight in 1958, he wrapped his .38 pistol in a paper bag and carried it in his suit pocket. The airlines had strictures against traveling with loaded guns even then, but as long as the passenger didn't bring a rifle or wear a visible shoulder holster, the authorities weren't overly inquisitive.

During his stay, Daddy took up residence in my room amid the Venetian Embassy and Intergalactic Headquarters. Still confined to the house by hepatitis, I slept on the living room couch but continued to expand my future city project most days while Daddy and Jane drank coffee, smoked cigarettes, and chatted in the kitchen. He would return to my room for a midday nap, and afterward I would attempt to interest him in my favorite shows. I could understand why the Our Gang comedies with Spanky and Alfalfa wouldn't appeal; the gang had been Jane's age when Daddy was already grown-up. But another series, starring actors who were roughly his contemporaries, might be more in his line.

"Do you like the Three Stooges, Daddy? They're from the old days."

"Naw, Buddy, I'll just watch the news."

So I'd sit with him viewing Walter Cronkite, who had begun as CBS anchor in April of that year. Daddy had been my age in 1899, before cars, planes, and radio, so the goings-on Walter reported must have seemed bizarre indeed—Marilyn Monroe found dead, Berlin wall tightening, NASA working on the next Mercury mission. But Daddy took it all in without comment as he prepared his cigarettes for the next day. I found out later he had experienced some heart trouble in the last year, so, at the recommendation of his doctor, he had begun to employ a cigarette holder of the sort President Roosevelt had made famous. To operate the holder, the smoker inserted a white fiber filter into the shaft and stuck the cigarette in the end. Daddy would install his filter; then, using his whittling knife (sharpened often with an oiled whetstone he'd brought with him), he carefully cut a fresh pack of his Pall Mall straights in half, one cigarette at a time. Employing this strategy, he could light up 40 times during the day and yet only smoke one pack—and the filter took care of all the poisons. He explained one afternoon: "See, Buddy? See how yella that filter is? You got to change your filter every day."[31]

Though Daddy rarely left the house during his short visit, he always wore a white shirt and tie. He chuckled politely at Jay's jokes and looked politely at the fish. He whittled on the front steps, took his naps, and retreated to the TV news. I think we both felt an inchoate longing for our old closeness, but it had been three years since I'd seen or even spoken with him, and almost five years—half my life—since we'd lived together.

By now I had heard many stories of Daddy's itchy trigger finger, so the day he visited Nanny and her husband John, I figured John would be in trouble. To my mixed relief and disappointment, no mayhem resulted. I had nothing against John, but it would have been neat to see Daddy in action after all the stories. More realistically, it would have been a much more interesting visit for Daddy if we could have taken him to Disneyland, or sightseeing, or target shooting. But my quarantine stymied all such plans. After a week or so Daddy packed his gun, filters, white shirts, and whetstone and flew back to Alabama. Our last picture together, taken before he left for the airport, shows us standing in the living room, six feet apart, flanking a low shelf unit full of science fiction and western paperbacks with an aquarium on top.

August slipped by in the seeming endlessness of my confinement. By Labor Day my future city sculpture looked as bulbously art deco as any interstellar metropolis on the science-fiction covers. Shuttling between centuries, I began *The Adventures of Tom Sawyer*, with all

---

[31] In my early adulthood I began to exhibit signs of incipient health-consciousness, trying various diet and exercise regimens. Looking back now at Daddy and his filters, it occurs to me that he might have passed on this inclination to clean living.

its odd and mysterious depths beyond the iconic scenes. Despite winning and losing a girlfriend, testifying against a murderer, and finding buried treasure, Tom, too, felt the ennui of summer.

In my own ennui, I had attempted a few of Jay's Louis L'Amour and Max Brand western novels, but I discovered another, even more interesting branch of reading beyond my age range when I found Jay's cache of Men's and Nudist magazines in the hall closet (probably moved from the bedroom to make room for a fish tank). As I'd first discovered with Eddie back in Wyvernwood, *Stag, True, Swank*, etc., featuring exposes of Las Vegas call girl rings, tales of sadistic Nazis and Japs in WW2, and the like, served as the blue collar versions of *Playboy*. These grittier publications also featured black and white photos of models who lacked the girl next door wholesomeness of *Playboy* playmates.

The nudist genre took an entirely different approach in its presentation of naked women. None of the tableaus by pools or with desert backgrounds even approached erotic; the photos, taken at "sun worshiper" colonies, depicted families in their birthday suits with all ages represented. In 1962, if a fellow wanted to buy a legal publication exhibiting a woman's pubic hair, he would also have to view the woman's husband, children, and even parents in poses straight from a church picnic pictorial, only sans clothing. Several recent court cases had declared such publications non-obscene, and I found them interesting and informative. To my mind, the scandal was all about their cover prices. Bad enough that comic books had risen that year from ten to twelve cents each, but men's magazines sold for fifty cents, and the nudist books, illustrating the law of supply and demand as well as the human form, sold for two or even three dollars each! Except for occasional lapses, grownups seemed to have inexhaustible supplies of money, but such outlays still seemed extraordinary extravagant.

In other pastimes, I still watched TV daily, but had not yet become an addict. I could take or leave the Three Stooges, Our Gang, Nikita Khrushchev, Locky Lockjaw, and prime time programming. Neither had I yet become obsessed with pop music radio; that would begin next year. The Rolling Stones played their first London show in July and Parlaphone Records signed the Beatles in September, but no one foresaw that English bands would soon dominate the airwaves.

The current American pop songs certainly seemed tired. Connie Francis belting out "V-A-C-A-T-I-O-N" comes to mind—it had by

August lost any excitement it aroused back in June. Little Eva's "Do the Locomotion" provided one bright spot in the hit parade and climbed to number one on August 25. Eva, a teenage babysitter for songwriter Carole King, had a perfect tough kid phrasing on the song that reminded me of the black girls I'd overheard at camp. Her voice and delivery brought on vague stirrings — perhaps even more so than the stirrings conveyed by the *Stag* pinup girls.

I began stirring all around as the hepatitis loosened its lassitudinous grip on me. The doctor suspended my quarantine a week before school started, and I went forth to roam the neighborhood. Stilts and go-carts had become passé, and the smoking club apparently disbanded. In the bittersweet transition between summer and fall, the year seemed poised like a wave about to break. Kids had already gone with parents to Sears and the new Zody's discount store to purchase school clothes and new notebooks. Even though we would never admit it, we were anxious for school to take up.

Jefferson Elementary became my ninth school so far. On its current website, it declares itself a well-organized institution, dedicated to quality education and good community values. In my day it seemed a bit less organized, with young scholars spilling out the doors of the classrooms. Rather than instituting split sessions when they ran out of bungalows, the local board of education transferred all fifth and sixth graders to a former adult school site and invented a proto version of the modern middle school. This rearrangement meant Jefferson's fourth graders suddenly found themselves promoted to playground elders. Looking to the world history of that era, one can see certain parallels between nine- and ten-year-olds elders at my school and the leaders of various developing nations who also didn't seem quite ready for regional power.

My new teacher's dumpy figure, tortoise shell glasses, and timid manner contrasted unfavorably with the vivacious Mrs. Brach of third grade. This one had come straight from her credential program and her name now escapes me, but I remember she seemed to fear her boy students more than we boys feared Mr. Grapis, the school principal. Grapis, a stocky, fortyish former military man wore a dark crew cut, blue suit, and permanent frown. In the next few years, I would meet several principals who could have come from the same casting call.

I sensed immediately that this new school would be a different experience than I'd enjoyed at Grand View. The gender ratio in the 36-student classroom stood at approximately 70 percent boys to 30 percent girls, an overabundance of male energy even for an experienced teacher. Most boys affected the autopilot aggressiveness I wouldn't see again until junior high, as manifested in more-or-less constant pushing, shoving, and general rudeness. Daily fights broke out both in and out of school. The girls coped as best they could: at recess they huddled in the jump rope area of the blacktop; in class they kept their eyes on their superior penmanship until they could hurry home after school.

A handful of Mexican boys from different classrooms stuck together on the playground. All white kids understood that their Hispanic heritage provided vast experience in fighting and access to switchblade knives. Rudy and Jesse, our representatives to this group, were older, though no larger than their classmates—I don't know if a nutrition issue accounted for their smaller stature or if kids from Mexico had been placed in classes according to size rather than age. Either way, in those days school officials dropped new immigrants directly into school with no language instruction at all.

After two years of immersion, Rudy and Jesse spoke English well and, by proving themselves the best fighters on campus, had risen above the unorganized scrabbling on the playground. The rest of us had to account for ourselves, and I began inauspiciously. Though of average height, I remained thin and pale from my illness and months indoors. The weekend before school started I'd suffered a haircut so short that I couldn't manage a pompadour, and I left off my flashy rings until I could get the lay of the land. Jane and Jay initially insisted I wear my glasses, but I pocketed them before I'd walked fifteen yards.

The campus had no grass at all except on the off-limits front lawns. Some boys played kickball on the blacktop; others strutted around, intimidating those they could and making arrangements for after-school fights with those they couldn't. Though scuffles broke out on a regular basis, official edict prohibited violence of any kind on campus. Offenders were subject to a paddling with a large tool constructed for the purpose: an oak slab with a handle and holes bored in the business end to hasten its speed. As a result, fights among the older kids rarely occurred spontaneously; instead, friends acted as seconds to arrange later engagements, as had been the custom among adult gentlemen in the eighteenth and nineteenth centuries.

The first week passed slowly in this unpleasant milieu. New

stiff jeans bought large for growth and thick plaid shirts worn over itchy new underwear made the usual Southern California early-September heat wave even more unpleasant. The long school year seemed to stretch interminably forward. On the second of many Thursdays to come I had made my afternoon recess solitary walk around the playground and took my place in the classroom return line. Behind me a couple of girls chatted with Brent, who sat beside me in class. My mind drifted far away, possibly on the latest-read chapter of *Tom Sawyer,* and I didn't acknowledge them. Probably to show off for the girls, Brent interrupted my reverie by shoving me vigorously. Caught by surprise, I stumbled and almost fell. Brent laughed at my obvious confusion and the girls tittered.

I cared nothing for pecking order status at that point—though I soon would care overmuch—but Brent's assumption that I would submit irked me. I lunged forward and shoved him back. After this mutual challenge we should have made terse arrangements to fight after school, but we were as yet inexperienced in the niceties of Jefferson social combat. Instead Brent snarled, "You punk!" and moved forward to grapple with me.

In those days, fights among boys under age ten could be most accurately described as wrestling matches. If anyone struck an actual blow, it came as the result of unorganized flailing secondary to the main aim: to pin the opponent under you and demand his surrender. But as Brent reached for a wrestling hold, I did something he hadn't expected: I raised my hands and crouched in the Hollywood boxer style I'd seen in the Our Gang bout between Butch and Alfalfa and practiced on my own in front of the bedroom door mirror.

Brent looked puzzled, then again tried to grab me; as he moved in I punched him in the face. He reeled back in surprise, and I pressed forward. In a few seconds I landed two more blows to his face and a straight shot to his stomach. The last punch took the fight out of him; he lowered his hands and stepped backwards, silently conceding the match.

As decreed by the unspoken rules I later came to understand well, Brent was heretofore obligated to defer to me, much as a wild dog bested by another in the pack deferred to his conqueror. I could cut in front of him at the drinking fountain and he must step aside on a sidewalk when we encountered one another. Custom also obliged him to feign friendliness, lest I target him for rough teasing and further challenges.

I had further to go up the social ladder that day. News of my victory over Brent spread quickly and my second fight took place immediately after school. Bill, a classmate hungry to raise his ranking, confronted me as we stepped off school grounds.

"I choose you off!"

I handed my notebook to Brent. Boys made a circle around us, and the battle began. Again my rudimentary boxing trumped wrestling: a few quick, well-aimed blows to Bill's face and midsection forced his surrender. It seemed so easy. I hadn't been hurt in the slightest in either fight. As Bill slunk off, now-friendly onlookers surrounded me.

"Awright, Ricky!"

"I knew you could take him!"

I knew it, too. With scientific Our-Gang-style boxing I could take them all. My afternoon stride home featured much more swagger than the diffident morning walk I'd exhibited when I left for school.

CHAPTER THIRTY-FOUR

~ The Giant Killer ~ Hubris ~ The Administrator Who Created a Monster
~ Pride Comes Before

My great leap to top fourth-grade status occurred a few weeks after the fights with Brent and Bill. I had come out of my shell at school, impressing the teacher with my reading skills and demonstrating a solid grasp of the multiplication table up to elevens. My handwriting still rated sub-standard, but I deflected attention to this fact by proposing, during a cursive practice session, that I write and direct a play instead. Teacher granted permission and I skipped handwriting period for a week as I plagiarized heavily from an Our Gang episode wherein the gang stages the Aladdin story in forties slang ("Say, is this guy on the level?").

The performance was a resounding success among fellow students permitted to view it when normally we would be improving our penmanship by copying dictionary definitions. I had yet to hear of Ernest Hemingway, but I suddenly became a sort of Ernest in miniature: a well-traveled, self-aggrandizing tough guy who could write. Boys in class deferred to me and girls seemed to inspect me with some interest, though I had no time for romance at this stage of my career.

But then a Tom Sawyerish chance to be a girl's hero came my way. As if the class weren't stressful enough for the teacher, she also had to deal with a major problem child: a huge, emotionally disturbed kid named Mike who caused trouble at any opportunity. Nowadays when I see a certain kind of boy in the company of a harried mother, Mike comes to mind. These sons wear a chronically petulant look and are never far from a screaming tantrum, usually timed for when the mother is interacting with other grownups. If school nurses had dispensed Ritalin and other drugs for hyperactive children in 1962, they would have stuffed Mike with them like a Thanksgiving turkey. Unmedicated, he threw cyclonic tantrums, disrupted class sessions, and bullied everyone except Rudy and Jesse, the Mexican kids.

Mike had stepped on my foot once on purpose, but taking due note of his size and craziness, I followed everyone's lead and let him get away with it. Then one afternoon recess, he snatched a jump rope and lassoed a girl, pulling the rope tight against her bare arms. She began to cry, but none of the boys made a move except to put more distance between themselves and the action.

Full of newfound hubris, I stood my ground. Noticing me for the first time, Mike threw another loop of the lasso over my head. The die was cast. I pulled out my arms before he could tighten the noose. Then, stepping in close, I cocked my fist, adjusted my trajectory to the upward angle needed to reach his great height and landed a perfectly-aimed punch to his nose. I felt the cartilage give way as blood spurted forth.

Time seemed to freeze. Then the girl burst into tears and every kid in the vicinity began walking backwards rapidly. Mike howled and made a grab for me, and I did some backpedalling myself. Then I turned and ran—not even Rudy and Jesse together could face that maddened gorilla.

Looking back, I saw Mike's horribly contorted face and blood dripping down his tee-shirt as he half-screamed, half-sobbed, "Imo getchu! Imo getchu!" He chased me to a kickball backstop and I dodged behind it. We ran around the structure a couple of times; then the fight seemed to drain from him and his snarls subsided into blubbering. I was considering how best to take advantage of this development when I perceived over Mike's shoulder a dark blue suit and military gait—Principal Grapis himself striding across the playground. He took Mike by the arm and led him away, motioning for me to follow. This I did at a prudent distance.

"Wait here," the principal said to me as we reached the administration building. After a whispered conversation with the secretary, he escorted Mike to the nurse's office. From my seat in the waiting area I overheard the secretary calling Mike's mother, whom she apparently knew on a first-name basis.

Mr. Grapis returned and motioned me into his inner office. I expected to be suspended, probably with swats; nonetheless, I felt exultant—I had stepped up like a hero in the westerns and science fiction stories, like Tom Sawyer himself! But the principal neither hit me nor called my parents. He spoke in a vague way about violence being an unsatisfactory answer to our problems, but he seemed to be looking at me more fondly than otherwise. The conversation worked around to my studies, and we chatted about *Huckleberry Finn,* which he named as his favorite book. It became clear that no corporal punishment was forthcoming—on the contrary, he had to strain mightily to disguise his satisfaction with my chastening of Mike, the student who caused the school administration more work and frustration than all the other difficult kids put together. If publicity could be avoided, the harried faculty and staff probably would have taken up a token-of-appreciation collection and given me a box of candy and the rest of the day off.

I left his office in an exuberant state and returned to class a hero. I had reached the Jefferson pinnacle: boxer, academic star, playwright, and now a modern-day David. The tough guys showed awe and amazement that old Grapis didn't paddle or suspend me—on top of everything else, I somehow rated preferential treatment from the authorities.

I should have been content with my ascent from nowhere, but as in the TV news reports of Supreme Generals and El Presidentes of the third-world rising, I didn't handle success well. Over the next several weeks, without even realizing the change, I grew a chip on my shoulder, became a swaggerer, show-off, and dispenser of sarcastic comments. Outside of class, I carried myself like a TV western gunfighter, always ready for a showdown, which now rarely occurred as the result of playground disputes—it was all about position in the dog pack. I won three or four more bouts with my reputation as a giant killer doing most of the work in unnerving my opponents. Boxing caught on quickly among school fighters, but I never suffered worse than scratches and bruises. It began to seem that no one could beat me, and like a Prima Donna sports star, I grew ever quicker to anger and to retaliate against perceived slights.

The first blow to my reputation came from an instance illustrative of this lack of humility. I had signed up for the school band, choosing saxophone because next to the guitar (not one of the school band choices), the sax featured most prominently in rock and roll. Most boys played the trumpet and most girls the violin, each renting for five dollars per semester. My hipster saxophone cost fifteen dollars for the term, which Jay and Jane paid after only asking once if I were sure I wouldn't prefer the trumpet. Only two of us attempted the saxophone next to ten or so trumpets and a half-dozen trombones, so the teacher sometimes called in the reed men for special afternoon lessons.

I remember feeling irritated after one of these sessions because I wasn't excelling in music. I could have practiced more, but there were better things to do in the afternoons than run through scales from the elementary lesson book over and over. Why couldn't I pick up the sax and, using the "think method" as promoted by Dr. Harold Hill in *The Music Man*, blow whatever song I wanted to play?

Wrapped in these reflections, I neglected to watch where I was going on my way back to my regular classroom. Suddenly I bumped into a kid from class, an insignificant little nobody who wore suit slacks, and high-top tennis shoes, and sweaters with zippers. He was probably en route to speech therapy or some such embarrassment. After we collided I gave him a steely glance and returned to my fantasy of dazzling everyone with my effortless sax playing.

But suddenly I stopped. Did I hear the little pipsqueak yelling something at my back?

"Watch where ya goin', you big showoff!"

I turned slowly. "Shut up!" I suggested, with a meaningful glare, but he stood his ground. His flushed face and twitchy demeanor suggested that I must have been the last straw in a trying day — or maybe he had cracked under the Jefferson strain, like a convict in the prison movies who suddenly hurls himself at a phalanx of armed guards.

"You shut up!" he screeched. "Go an' comb your greasy hair ten more times today!"

It was true that, in order to keep my recently grown flattop with fenders coiffure in perfect condition, I regularly employed a comb I carried in my back pocket. The mere mention of the act brought on an automatic urge to pull out the comb, but I stopped in mid-reach.

He didn't flinch when I raised my hand; rather, he pointed at my fingers and laughed almost hysterically. "Lookit all the rings! Only girls wear rings!"

He was referring to the three cheap and flashy items I bought back in Manhattan Beach and had lately resumed wearing, two on my left hand and one on my right. I glanced at them myself now: one a fake gold signet with a filigree R inset, another an imitation high school class ring, the third a faux gold snake with ruby eyes. Suddenly they seemed affectatious even to me, but I didn't have to listen to any such static from this little runt. "Shut *up!*" I advised even more firmly.

He dodged behind a pole and actually stuck his tongue out at me. "*You* shut up, you—" he began, and I lunged at him.

He showed remarkable speed as he took off down the sidewalk fronting a wing of classroom buildings. I pounded behind him, murder in my heart. As we rounded the corner, he looked over his shoulder, his previously flushed face ghostly white. Apparently his manic courage deserted him as I began to close the gap.

He stumbled, fell down, and as I caught up he gave me the wide-eyed look a mouse gives a descending hawk. I fell upon him, straddled his chest—and suddenly he was bleeding from the nose, both nostrils pouring red. I looked down, confused—I hadn't hit him yet, hadn't even raised my fist.

But I didn't have time to consider the matter; a male teacher I didn't know pulled me off the bleeding boy and held me with one hand while he blew his silver whistle. Another teacher from an adjacent room helped the kid up and gave him a handkerchief. And within seconds the principal bore down on me like a maddened elephant—he grabbed me by the bicep and pulled me along to his office, shaking me as we went, my feet barely touching the ground as I struggled to keep up.

"WHO DO YOU THINK YOU ARE?!"

He kept yelling this rhetorical question, which I recalled from ancient days at Park Western when upstart Raymond had been subject to it and similar violence. I couldn't get a word in until we entered his office, whereupon I blurted out, "I didn't even hit him! I didn't!"

The principal's face looked almost as red as the kid's had been. "You mean to stand there and tell me he just bled *spontaneously?*"

This was a nightmare. Since I bloodied Mike's nose, he typecast me as a nose destructionist, like the mafia guys in the movies who specialize in killing people by sticking icepicks in their ears.

"I dunno! He just…"

"Butter wouldn't melt in your mouth, you little—"

"I didn't hit him! He just started bleeding! He's…" (I searched my memory desperately for the name of the disease suffered by my friend Marshall back in Las Vegas) "He's uh… he's one of those homo-pilliates or something!"

Grapis sat down, visibly struggling to contain himself, his fists clenching and unclenching. I probably escaped an immediate paddling only because he feared his own temper.

But I couldn't figure out what so infuriated him. I really hadn't hit the kid, a fact that would be determined shortly when the kid's mother affirmed him as a spontaneous nose bleeder. But even if I had hit him, the principal dealt with fighting every day, so why so monumentally upset at me? I surmise now that, by failing to punish me when I struck the first blow in the fight with Mike, Grapis blamed himself for creating a monster. After lecturing me rather incoherently and threatening me with suspension and paddling the next time I involved myself in a fight of any kind, he let me go. And as we shall see, I should have quit while I was ahead.

When I returned to my classroom ten minutes before dismissal, the tough guys were amazed after confidently predicted a paddling and absence of at least three days, the minimum suspension. And yet their admiration seemed tinged with reproach as the general public branded me an official bully for picking on the pathetic kid. My protestations that I didn't hit him didn't seem to matter. Sure, I would have hit him, but it hadn't actually happened. Frustrating! Not fair!

As I left school, a pudgy guy from one of the other fourth grade classes approached me. He too wore a flat top and fenders, but his cut looked ratty compared to the smooth perfection to which I'd restored mine on the way from the principal's office.

"Brian will fight you," he said, with a smirk.

I feigned boredom. "Who's Brian?"

"Come over to our backstop tomorrow." Their backstop sat kitty-corner from the one considered our turf.

"Is he choosing me off?"

"Come on over. He'll fight you." He gave his sneaky look again.

Good psychological warfare called for a statement to the effect that if his boy wanted to fight me, he could present himself for inspection at *our* backstop tomorrow. But the principal's threat to punish me if I involved myself in any further altercation still rankled. Grapis couldn't scare me! Nobody could scare me! I'd fight anybody, anytime I wanted!

I decided to go see this Brian.

CHAPTER THIRTY-FIVE

~ Global Parallels and Pariahs ~ In Over His Head ~ Retiring from the Ring
~ Playing War ~ An Unlikely Friend ~ "You Lied to Me" ~ Referential Mania

The events of the previous chapter occurred in October 1962; meanwhile, a similar drama (albeit on a somewhat larger scale) played out on the global blacktop. The Cuban Missile Crisis confrontation between the U.S. and the U.S.S.R., suddenly threatened to ignite nuclear war between the two superpowers. On Tuesday, October 22, President Kennedy announced the presence of Soviet missiles in Cuba. The next day he ordered a naval blockade of the island to begin at one p.m. Pacific time. Kennedy, who looked more like a Hollywood hero than any actors who later portrayed him in the movies, led the Free World home team, while Nikita Khrushchev, the squat, bald, shoe-pounding Russian premier, played the Iron Curtain villain.

As one p.m. arrived with no flinch from the Soviets, the metaphorical doomsday clock began to tick toward nuclear Armageddon (Begging the reader's pardon, but it's hard to resist the dramatic rhetoric of TV docu-dramas associated with this event.) At approximately the same time I was walking the length of Jefferson's blacktop, my destination the kickball diamond at the west end of campus. I proceeded without escort, partly to demonstrate my fearlessness and partly because, after the debacle with the spontaneous nose bleeder (a public relations nightmare as grave to me as Khrushchev's sponsorship of the Berlin wall a year before must have seemed to him), I lost some esteem among my own classmates. No matter. I didn't need any support, moral or otherwise.

But as I approached the rival backstop, the campus felt less like my domain—over here seemed a different school altogether.

Besides the ratty kid who proposed the fight, the rest of the rival fourth grade class looked more wholesome than my compatriots at the other end of campus. They dressed less hand-me-down and harbored no overgrown, emotionally unstable Mikes. Their young teacher, hovering nearby on lunch duty, looked brighter, more professional, and definitely more attractive than ours. Further, the general atmosphere of the crowd around the kickball game seemed less tense and belligerent than on our side. The young teacher had carved out a veritable West Berlin over here, and I felt both the deflation and determined defiance Khrushchev must have felt when he actually visited the West and saw what he was up against.

The kid with the flattop came smirking to meet me. "That's Brian," he said, pointing to the first-baseman of the team on the field.

I studied my potential opponent as I waited for the inning's last out. Without glasses I couldn't make out his facial expression, but his body language seemed to indicate self-possession to the point of haughtiness. He looked tall, which indicated a longer reach. He dressed like a square — slacks, button-up shirt, sweater, and black oxfords — and wore a neatly combed short haircut. He could have been a clothing model for Sears and looked more like a smart, athletic guy than a tough guy. Already I didn't like him.

When Brian trotted in from the field, Flattop stepped forward. "This is the kid who wants to fight you," he said. Actually, Flattop himself had proposed the fight, but I didn't correct him. It didn't matter at this point anyway.

Brian gave me what I took as disdainful glance. "How do you want to fight?" he asked abruptly. "Judo? Karate?"

My intuition up to this point told me that this fellow could be a formidable opponent, but now I saw that he was just another fourth-grade fool. The first James Bond movie premiered earlier that year, and seemingly every TV show featured an episode with a character who knew Judo and/or Karate. All boys fantasized about performing the dazzling throws and barehanded brick-breaking we saw on the screen, but in the real world only little kids and dummies claimed to actually know those esoteric martial arts skills. I restrained myself from laughing in his face and answered, in a calculatedly patronizing manner: "Let's just fight, huh? The ice plant. Right after school."

"The ice plant" (actually a hill covered with that flora and a few scattered trees) bordered the school grounds, but we considered it a safe distance from the principal's office. Several of Brian's classmates congregated at the appointed time, and a few of the tough guys from my class turned out as well. But somehow the feel of the crowd didn't seem in tune with me. The pre-fight chatter confirmed my unease: "He's got the reach on Ricky." "Ricky thinks he's so tough." "He's a dirty fighter—check those rings."

But I didn't need any cheering section. I put up my fists, and Brian took a similar stance, only more tentative, as did most of my opponents in transition from wrestling. I quickly took the initiative. Moving in to jab, I connected with his jaw. He pulled back in time to make it only a glancing blow. He stared back intently as I pressed forward for another opening.

"Principal!" someone yelled, and we instantly dropped our hands. I looked up. Yes, the blue suit was on the horizon. The spectators began to disperse; Brian and I melted into different groups.

I stole a look back as I sauntered away and saw Brian stroking his jaw lightly, seemingly in deep concentration. Now I struck a psychological second blow. "See you tomorrow!" I called jauntily, adding an exaggeratedly friendly wave for good measure. A laugh rippled through the departing crowd; I had won back my classmates and a few strangers besides.

When we met at the same place the next day, a large audience gathered and I determined to give them a good show. Moving in swiftly as before, I landed another left jab to Brian's jaw. Again he showed good reflexes by pulling back from full connection. But I continued to advance, swinging a roundhouse right at his midsection. A few weeks ago I had been a more tentative fighter; now I felt on top of my game and sublimely confident.

Suddenly Brian twisted sideways, grabbing my wrist as my momentum carried me forward. He seemed to turn his back on me, but before I could process this surprising move, I felt the pressure of his shoulder against my chest. And suddenly I found myself off my feet and flying over him, headfirst down the ice-plant hill.

During the second or so of my airborne experience, I deduced two things in primitive-thought shorthand: (1) I not only had the misfortune to meet one of the rare boys in the Western world who actually studied martial arts, but (2) I was also on the losing end of a judo throw, just like in the movies. It all made sense, I reflected as I made my descent—Brian's irritating self-confidence and Flattop's smirk as he set me up for this mess.

I skid-landed on my head, completed a summersault, and rolled into the nearest tree. Such a fall would break my neck now, but youth is supple. I stood up, dazed. More than anything I wanted to run home, but any such display would destroy whatever reputation that remained to me. Resolutely I staggered up the slope, brushing dirt and leaves from my clothes. As I made it to the top, fists raised, fortune tossed me a crumb: someone called "Principal!" and the group scattered. So today's battle had been almost a rerun of yesterday, right down to Mr. Grapis stopping the action. The only difference was that the match was over and I had lost.

No one joined me as I made my unsteady way home, my head still throbbing. Jay had been around the house the last several days in the afternoons; I could hear him and Jane in their room doing something with the fish. A TV news anchor droned in the background—but wasn't it too early for the news to be on? I continued straight to my room without announcing myself. I needed to wash my face and change my dirty clothes, but it felt good to stretch out on my bed in the dim light with my room's fish tank bubbling in the background. After a while my gaze fixed on my clay city of the future, gathering dust on the bookshelf since school began. One of the monorail bridges between buildings had fallen down, but I left it there.

What happened the next day at lunchtime leads me to conclude that I could summon more poise under pressure at age nine than I've exhibited from teendom on. Even in my mature years I tend to lose my composure in awkward social confrontations, but when I saw Brian in the cafeteria, I made myself walk directly toward him. A ring of spectators formed instantly around us.

Forcing a grin I said, "Hey, you really do know judo!" in a tone implying that the fight didn't signify anything else. I continued, "You gotta show me how to do some of that stuff sometime."

Everyone laughed good-naturedly at this, and Brian allowed a slow smile. Flattop probably goaded him into the fight against his better judgment, and being a square, Brian must have worried that using his skills in an illegal after-school brawl would get him into trouble. But apparently I did not intend to inform the authorities. "Are you okay?" he asked. "I could feel it when you hit the ground."

"Oh yeah, I'm okay. See you around, Joe Jitsu."[32] I grinned again as jauntily as possible and made my exit without eating. Staying

---

[32] Joe Jitsu, an Asian martial arts specialist, appeared regularly in the Dick Tracy cartoon series then current.

would have been anticlimactic, and anyway, maintaining my casual front had already strained my histrionic abilities.

Preoccupied with my own troubles, I didn't notice any extra tension that afternoon among the grown-ups on campus. But alert adults probably felt anxious indeed about the escalating Cuban missile crisis news as reported in special TV and radio bulletins all day. They knew we actually teetered on the brink of World War III, and at least some of them must have reflected that Redondo Beach sprawled uncomfortably close to the giant oil refineries and naval base at Long Beach. With such strategic targets so near, drop drills wouldn't help us much.

After school I avoided my usual cohorts. Instead I surprised a classmate, one of the actors from the Our Gang skit I directed. He, a non-contender in the fighting pecking order, tried to cultivate me previously, but I'd been too busy building my gentleman-gangster reputation. Now I agreed to come over to his place to play army. He belonged to the cult of military fanatic kids fairly common in those days—the 1962 version of today's dedicated video gamers. In a vacant lot near his house, he and his brothers showed me their pillbox: a large hole covered by plywood with dirt shoveled on top. We ran the standard World War II scenario: Germans vs. Americans. Russians were all about big bombs and bombastic speeches, not armies. We played a couple of hours, and all the killing and mayhem took my mind off my troubles.

At dusk I came home, and Jane met me at the door with a worried look. "Where were you?"

"Playing army."

Her smile seemed somewhat strained. "We might have a real war," she said. "With Russia. The President is coming on the news in a few minutes."

A real war might be kind of interesting; after all, I'd been practicing for it for years. But the doomsday clock didn't toll. Since the U.S. at the time maintained a massive advantage in nuclear weapons and Kennedy showed his willingness to fight, Khrushchev backed down. I didn't make the connection at the time, but JFK might have been Brian asking, "Judo? Karate?" to apprise the enemy as to what strength he faced. Khrushchev could box pretty well, but, unlike me, he knew he couldn't win against the other guy's firepower. I should have done more intelligence gathering before I maneuvered myself into a showdown.

The Kremlin abruptly deposed Khrushchev, but I faded more gracefully. My bullet-proof hubris would never be so impenetrable again; yet the corresponding drop in status amounted to a net relief. At heart I remained an introvert, without the natural instincts needed by the always-public, fast-track gangster. By adjusting my playground profile, I effectively retired from competition, yet maintained enough cachet to discourage the up-and-comers.

Less fortunate was Mike, the big guy who jump-started my career. Since his humiliation at my hands, every kid he'd ever picked on had challenged him. And after he lost several fights, even the girls were emboldened to drive him away when he annoyed them. A fearsome giant at the beginning of the semester, he became a has-been in less than two months.

I've always gravitated to companions who lower my social standing (and vice-versa), but perennial bad judgment doesn't fully explain what happened next. One day I found myself striking up a conversation with Mike, and for a few weeks I kept company with him more often than with anyone I'd known in Redondo Beach so far. No one could believe it—not my previous entourage of tough guys, not the kids who looked up to me intellectually, nor even the teacher, whom one might have guessed would applaud my showing some kindness to an outcast. Even Mike's parents, when we stopped at his house one day after school, seemed to think I was an idiot for associating with him.

I suppose they were right. We had nothing in common but a penchant for walking long distances around town. Mike didn't read, he knew nothing of fair play or sharing, and in our travels he could be an embarrassment or even downright dangerous. One afternoon we were taking his usual shortcut across a field on the way to his house, when suddenly six or eight guys from another school jumped us. Two of them held me while the rest wrestled Mike to the ground and took turns hitting and kicking him. I gathered from the accompanying dialogue that he had picked on someone's little sister. One of the avengers restraining me asked in genuine wonder, "What are you doin' hanging around with THAT guy?"

I didn't have a reasonable answer, but I kept up the unlikely friendship until a few Saturdays later. Driving home from the shopping center, Jane saw us along the highway and stopped to pick us up. I had told her about Mike months before: how he sassed grownups, used baby talk, and generally acted outrageously. I think my motive was to establish, should the principal ever decide to contact my parents, that Mike rated as a legitimate recipient for the punch in the nose I'd given him.

In reply, Jane exhorted me to refrain from keeping company with Mike. I assured her I would never have any associations whatever with such a spaz. But here we were in the car with the spaz talking a mile a minute, imitating cartoon characters and free-associating all sorts of obnoxious insolence. As previously noted, hyperactive children exhibiting such behavior in the company of grownups are a common sight nowadays, but in the early 1960s such temerity rarely took place. As he performed, Jane assumed the thoughtful frown that always set off warning bells in my mind.

I of course neglected on purpose to introduce Mike by name, but she knew. After we let him off at his house, the silence in the car became palpable. Then, with one of the sterner looks she'd ever worn in my presence she said, "You lied to me."

I hung my head and for once didn't try to alibi. What could I say?

My strange association with Mike tapered off soon afterward, and Jane didn't mention the incident again. In true motherly fashion, she continued to believe—against much evidence to the contrary—that she could trust me to be honest with her. Thus we see another parallel between my doings and global history: Jane's irrational conviction that I would never deceive her exhibited the same sort of reality disconnect some Americans displayed with the Soviet Union's chicanery for years to come.

But enough of what coincidentally Russian Novelist Vladimir Nabokov termed "Referential Mania" in his story "Signs and Symbols" ("… the patient imagines that everything happening around him is a veiled reference to his personality and existence.") The time has come to chronicle another Hill Family Evasion.

CHAPTER THIRTY-SIX

~ Sociobiology Among the Pumpkins ~"I Wanna Be a Bum" ~"Ricky's Dead"
~"Wonder What the Poor People Are Doing?" ~ My First Pusher ~ A Fish's Life

"You stick the hose through the mail slot, see, and when the water comes on, haul buns!"

These instructions were provided in a terse whisper on Halloween night, 1962, by the seventh grader who lived next door For a week I had been contemplating what to "be" for Halloween, but I discerned in time that the older neighborhood boys disdained costumes, preferring dark clothing for concealment and gym shoes for quick getaways. Their holiday mission was to make as much trouble as possible, and I tagged along as a sort of apprentice in crime.

A sociobiologist might explain our behavior in avian terms: taking our first flights from the nest to associate with other fledglings in a normal bird transition stage. If I comprehend the theory correctly, our hormones were percolating, inducing us to restlessness in the nest and such obnoxiousness to our elders that they would eventually push us out with a sense of relief.

Unaware of all such biochemical processes, we focused our attention on the aforementioned hose-through-the-mail-slot trick, plus throwing eggs, smashing jack o' lanterns, trampling flower beds, activating sprinklers when other groups approached, and running while laughing manically from grownups offended by such amusements. Swaggering after dark, pushing ahead of smaller kids at five-cent-candy houses, and stealing from porches of those naïve enough to leave boxes of treats outside and expect trick-or-treaters to take only their fair share—all were exhilarating adventures, much discussed in the ensuing weeks.

Around the same time I also made a friend my own age. Lloyd sprang from either Chinese or Korean heritage, but his style contrasted with the super-achieving Asian stereotype. He brought *Mad* Magazines to school and could look bored in a remarkably expressive way during lessons. He never did more schoolwork than absolutely necessary to avoid trouble. He disdained ball games and never tucked in his shirt.

Such rebellion intrigued me, but one late fall rainy afternoon Lloyd demonstrated a truly fascinating individualism. Our teacher, struggling to find something to occupy students during the indoor recess, began working the room, asking each of us in turn what we would like to be when we grew up. The rest of us said the usual: nurse, fireman, lawyer, etc. I chimed in with my usual "Doctor," since the medical field seemed the highest status occupation.

When Lloyd's turn came, he said, "I wanna be a bum."

Teacher looked nonplussed. "Why in the world would you want to be a — a person like that, Lloyd? Are you making a joke?"

"Nah. A bum don't have to work. Yeah, and they get free food all over town. All the pie they can eat. And you know those wall plugs in gas station bathrooms? The gas guys put them there so the bums can plug in their electric razors." He said all this in a sort of sepulchral deadpan. After a short pause, during which we all silently stared at him, he added in the same tone, "Real bums never grow a beard. Never."

As he spoke, I felt admiration for his straightface put-on of the teacher, but also a wave of nostalgia. I, too, had wanted to be a bum, or hobo, in the carefree San Pedro days when Linda took me trash picking in the alleys and when I'd dressed in raggedy clothes and sloshed through the gutters in San Fernando. I also recalled the doctors in action during my hepatitis months. In that moment, my doubts coalesced: the medical profession definitely held nothing for me.

After school I walked home with Lloyd. His family ran a junk shop in Torrance (in those days charities like Goodwill and the Salvation Army didn't have a monopoly on such endeavors), and among the shop's treasures I noticed some old aquariums priced at less than five dollars each. Back home I reported my find to Jay, and he promptly drove to the shop and bought three tanks, thanking me for the tip. As Lloyd informed me later, his dad also reacted positively to the transaction. My flashy getup initially branded me as the type of kid he wanted Lloyd to avoid, but I had proven good for business.

In the next week or two, I discovered that Lloyd was indeed a kindred spirit. He demonstrated a gimlet eye for pretension and hypocrisy among grownups, a skill I wished to cultivate. While he disdained my teen wanna-be hair and clothing styles, he saw my potential. We both fancied ourselves connoisseurs of pop music novelty songs, and many songs came forth to be appreciated that season. In addition to 1962's amazing advances in science, art, and culture, the year also brought forth "The Monster Mash" by Bobby "Boris" Pickett, a masterpiece of mimicry destined to reach number one and sell millions. Lloyd first alerted me to an equally brilliant composition, "She Got a Nose Job," from the *Mad Twists Rock and Roll* album. The single version could only be accessed as a cardboard insert in a *Mad* annual. When detached on the dotted line, the paper record actually played on a turntable. The original album, obtainable through mail order directly from *Mad*, contained many other such gems, including "Agnes, The Teenage Russian Spy," "I'll Never Make Fun of Her Moustache Again," and "When My Pimples Turned to Dimples."

I have forgotten much crucial information in my life, including my phone and social security numbers, and though I have a Ph.D. in literature, I can only recite a few great poems by heart. Yet after fifty years I remember the stirring lyrics of "She Got a Nose Job," the Cinderella story of a teenage girl with an oversize "schnozz," whom the teenage boy chronicler comes to love enough to marry and provide nose jobs for their children as well. Considering the popularity of "Monster Mash," I think it extremely likely that "Nose Job" would have also charted near the top if top-forty DJ's had shown the courage to play it.

Though we shared an appreciation for the arts, my friendship with Lloyd never fully developed. One impediment involved logistics: he lived two miles away, over the Torrance line. Another problem was that despite his beatnik sensibilities, his dad made him work at the junk shop after school and weekends. Considering the high aspirations of the typical Asian immigrant home, it must have been a stormy scene in the late sixties when Lloyd became a teenager. But probably the main reason Lloyd and I didn't have a close friendship had more to do with timing—we didn't begin our association until late November of '62, in the twilight of the Redondo epoch.

The latest evasion stemmed from the usual Jay and Jane restlessness, but we appeared to be settled enough until the actual departure day. For instance, we hosted Thanksgiving for the extended family, including Fran Faye and kids. That year's celebration is most memorable because, as the turkey was served,

Nanny smiled broadly and voiced a line from the grin-and-bear-it depression years: "Well, I wonder what the poor people are doing." In Nanny's honor, I have used this signature line every Thanksgiving since I became a head of household.

For Christmas we also hosted both sets of California grandparents, plus assorted uncles and aunts-in-law. In addition to impressive gifts all around (including the fifteen-speed bike mentioned earlier), our home display featured an aluminum Christmas tree with blue metallic ornaments. When plugged in, the tree turned full circle on a stand and played "Oh Christmas Tree" in electronic tinkling—the acme of '62 modern.

I had become inured to abrupt turns of fortune, but this holiday opulence caught me by surprise, for I already assumed from certain clues that leaner times lay head. For instance, I knew that sometime in late October or early November Jay had become so obsessed with the tropical fish—our little house contained twenty-eight tanks at the peak of the guppy phase—that he quit going to work altogether.

This decision fueled a marital disagreement of such magnitude that one day soon after Halloween Jay packed a few clothes, his shoeshine box, and all the expensive belt-driven air pumps for the fish tanks, then departed in frigid dignity. I'm unsure whether he meant taking the air pumps to be vindictive or if he merely viewed them as readily pawnable merchandise. But I do remember the strange, dead silence of a house with no fish tanks bubbling.

As our only car drove away, Jane told me that we would have to do the best we could to get along. She would get a job, but we might have to move back in with Nanny for a while. In retrospect, she seemed oddly serene considering she had no money, no car, no job, no man, three kids, and twenty-eight tanks of unfiltered fish on her hands. She interrupted our talk to check on Greg, who had taken to banging his head against his crib. I sat in the living room and wondered what next lay in store.

The meditation period didn't last long. A few minutes later I answered a knock and found Jay on the porch, hands in pockets and looking sheepish. "Is your mother home?" he asked, as if he were a door-to-door salesman.

"She's in the bedroom." Several months removed from those feelings I'd suffered when Rebecca McCain obsessed me, I could only marvel at the embarrassing depths that even grownups could sink under the influence of love madness.

"Who is it?" Jane appeared from the hallway and surveyed Jay impassively. He straightened his posture and crossed the threshold. She turned her back on him, and he followed her to the bedroom. I could hear them talking, then laughing. A few minutes later Jay came out to unload the car. He reconnected the air pumps, and that was that.

No one spoke of the separation again, but Jay stepped forth the next morning with mirror-shined shoes and landed a new job in Orange County. This time he rose to manager just in time for a Christmas bonus. But the new job and bonus were not the only factors in our surprisingly lavish Christmas. Jay and Jane also skipped paying December bills and rent and planned to ignore January obligations as well. They were hatching an exciting relocation plan, and thereupon it became necessary to begin 1963 with a covert operation.

Of course we could have simply skipped town after Christmas, but the new place wouldn't be available until January 12. So on New Year's Day when the landlord inquired about the back rent, Jay met him at the door. Oozing man-to-man integrity and promising a full settlement for both months, Jay declared that on Monday, 14 days hence, he would cash his first paycheck for the new job and personally deliver the full balance to the landlord's house. Of course he had already received his first paycheck, but some connection with the truth—he did have a new job and the snoopy landlord might have already seen him leaving or returning from work—helped to shore up the fabrication.

Jay instituted a family gag order on discussing the move, a caution not invoked since Glendale. So I returned to school after the Christmas break and walked around campus, looking my surreptitious last on Jefferson Elementary. But lest the reader feel sorry for me for having my barely-established roots ripped up yet again by a callous family, let me hasten to state that for once I looked forward to moving as much as my parents did. In Redondo I was an outlaw without portfolio at a school where I never felt comfortable and in a classroom both intellectually unchallenging and full of tension. Flexible flyer tragedy, ever-encroaching fish, hepatitis quarantine, judo boy—Redondo brought one unlikely crisis, discomfort, melodrama, or fiasco after the next.

The neighborhood scene had deteriorated as well. Sometime in the last week I inadvertently put myself on the wrong side of the volatile brother next door. With his father in earshot, I said something incriminating about some post-Halloween vandalism activities, and his dad slapped him around their front yard. Somehow the parental ill-temper became my fault. Thursday evening, across the chain link fence separating our houses, he proclaimed ominously, "Ricky's dead."

This announcement meant he would "pound" me the next time he saw me away from the safety of my home. A trouncing from a sixth grader would amount to no great shame, but my feelings were hurt by the proposition. This supposed friend had turned on me after our long history and Halloween bonding adventures, and all for one completely unintentional mistake. It amounted to yet another example of Redondo's capriciousness.

On the bright side, whatever trepidation I might have felt about starting over at a new school, and whatever regret came from never seeing Lloyd again, the disappointment the unreasonable kid next door must have felt as he saw the moving truck pull up late Friday night cheered me somewhat. Despite his dramatic pronouncement, Ricky would live after all.

As with previous and later moves, no neighbor, young or old, came to investigate after the truck arrived. They could only peek out their windows, wondering if we were spies, criminals, or government agents—why else would we be leaving without any warning? However, as Jay related later, he knew that by morning the spell would be broken and every curious housewife, grandpa, kid, and dad-off-work would descend upon the house to ask questions, so we must move all in one night.

Unfortunately for the swift pace demanded of this evasion, various work crises kept Jay past eight, and several maternal emergencies sidetracked Jane. We owned more furniture this time, and among Jay's twin half-brothers, only Eddie answered the call for help. To complicate matters further, Eddie declared he could only stay until midnight because his new job, a bread delivery route, started at dawn.

My primary moving job usually consisted of keeping out of the way, but this time Jay enlisted me as a truck loader, junior grade. After Jane put Trish and Greg to bed using pillows on the floor, she commenced draining and packing fish tanks, a time-consuming process. When Eddie yawned away at one a.m., we had loaded only three-quarters of our possessions. I did my share of yawning, too, and though Jay kept up a running stream of jokes and encouragement, I was practically asleep on my feet.

"Here," he said, handing me what looked like a miniature aspirin with a cross scored in it. "Swallow it whole; it's too bitter to chew."

"What is it?"

"Got 'em from a truck driver at the store. You'll feel better pretty quick."

He was right—in a few minutes I felt ... great! Not tired at all! Finishing the load seemed exhilarating, and our conversation grew unusually animated as we drove over to our new place in Huntington Beach. Jay told me in interesting detail about his motorcycle riding days and the time he'd spent a couple of weeks in a Mexican jail. I told him about some of my fights, including the one with Brian the judo boy. The incident seemed funny now, and he laughed along with me. Both talking at once, we arrived around three in the morning. I leapt for the curb and with unflagging energy carried my end of tables and couch, plus chairs and large boxes until we emptied the truck.

Around five a.m., as Jay headed back for the final load from the Redondo house, I stumbled off to sleep on the floor of my new room. I felt physically exhausted, but for some reason it took me a while to drift off—I saw cartoon visions when I closed my eyes, and the lyrics to "Do the Locomotion," "She Got a Nose Job," and "Monster Mash" were playing simultaneously and repeatedly in my head. I felt sore and disoriented the next day, but it all paid off a few years later. As a young teen, I could brag that I had experienced illegal drugs—in this case the infamous "cross-white" Benzedrine tablet—before I turned ten.

Dawn glowed in the east over Torrance as Jay approached the Redondo house. He found, in addition to the remaining furniture and boxes, all the fish tanks drained to an inch or two of water in the bottom. Most of the fish still needed to be transferred individually to the special cardboard containers, and the fragile tanks would have to be wrapped in sheets and blankets for transit. Jay loaded the truck until the first kitchen lights on the block flickered on; then he drove south as the sun rose. He crossed the Orange county line around seven a.m. as the first neighbors came scuttling over to the mystery house.

They found the oddball Hill family gone, but not without a trace. From memory, plus Jay's subsequent remarks and inventory of what actually arrived at the new house, I am able, based on process of elimination and much experience with Jay's fast-move methods, to reconstruct the scene as the snoopers probably saw it.

As the more adventurous neighbors ventured into the house, they could detect a particular odor coming from the kitchen. The refrigerator door was propped open: Jane had left it to defrost. But Jay neglected to transfer the frozen brine shrimp from freezer to ice chest, so the fragrant remains had oozed onto the kitchen floor.

Strewn everywhere were stray clothes, paperback books, knick-knacks, diapers, toys — the typical miscellany that usually surprises the mover by filling three or four extra boxes after everything seemed packed. Because of Jay's haste to leave by sunrise, probably enough for six or eight extra boxes still littered the floors of each room. The master bedroom floor also featured fish equipment Jay and Jane bought before they became real aficionados, including vibrating air blowers, dry food, ceramic divers, castles, and other aquarium decorations too amateur to bother with, plus scores of tropical fish magazines whose information Jay had already digested.

Neighbors who entered the property through the backyard gate instead of venturing inside discovered another interesting display. A trail of aquariums ranged along the side of the house like stepping stones. In the back yard proper, lawn furniture Jay and Jane acquired from Goodwill and Blue Chip Stamps scattered among weeds unmown since August. Other decorations included my old bike, a half-built go-cart, and several pairs of stilts; Greg's stroller, plastic pool, and push car; Trish's tricycle and caved-in dollhouse, plus other toys that didn't make the moving cut and several rusting industrial shelves Jay appropriated from work. (The shelves were meant for stacking more fish tanks in the house, presumably after removal of the living room couch. Jay argued that we never sat in the living room anyway, but Jane had nonetheless vetoed that plan.)

And the main attraction of the whole tableau, the piece de resistance responsible for gathering the neighbors in a head-shaking and tsk-tsking crowd, now spread out before them: hundreds and hundreds of exotic, colorful, prize-worthy fantail guppies, along with assorted black mollies, Siamese fighting fish, angelfish, neon tetras, dwarf curviceps, clownfish, seven varieties of catfish, miniature sea horses, jewel chichlids, Oscars, and other rarities — the whole eclectic multitude lying stiff, dry, and dead on the patchy brown and yellow lawn where, at sunrise, Jay had unceremoniously dumped them.

PART IV: 1963–65

Huntington Beach

Westminster

Tract Under Construction

Jay and Jane: Their First Home, 1963

Hill Siblings Summer 1963

CHAPTER THIRTY-SEVEN

~ Stumbling into Paradise ~ Surrounded by Indians ~ Home Improvement
~ K-Mart Genesis ~ Lost in the Inter-Dimension

Sign after sign on all roads leading to northwest Orange Country:
Own Your Own Home!
$200 Moves You In!
NO Down to Vets!
The latest Southern California land rush was on, and it came to pass that despite previous mistakes, bad decisions, and relatives' dire predictions, Jay and Jane veered onto the right on-ramp at the right time and found themselves the goldenest deal of the golden-opportunity decade. They joined blue collar and white collar families, small businessmen, and many Douglas aerospace workers in migrating to the Springdale tract, the latest of many such massive projects in the county. Springdale offered brand new four-bedroom, two-bath homes for $16,950 (those same houses valued in the $600,000 range when last I checked). The interest rate stood at 4% on twenty-year mortgages, and as advertised, $200 moved them in.

Of course my parents found it necessary to fabricate extensively on the income section of the mortgage application. They invented a higher salary, larger bank account, references, and housing history. Apparently no one bothered to check these claims, for Jay and Jane were granted a homestead on Oasis Drive. Right after the army of finish-carpenters and plumbers moved on and inspectors made sure the doorknobs turned and water flowed from the taps, each family in our construction sector crossed the threshold of its own linoleum-on-slab tract home, set on a uniform size plot of graded dirt.

The product sounds cookie-cutter in jaded modern retrospect, and even then Malvina Reynolds's song "Little Boxes" (a minor hit for Pete Seeger) popularized the phrase "ticky-tacky" for Eastern intellectual snide commentary on suburbia. But one could also look at the tract-home phenomenon from another angle. First-time homeowners appreciated each uniform dwelling and dirt plot as a blank canvas ready to personalize without landlord or worker housing bureaucrat interference. Repressed castle-keepers, heretofore confined in bland rentals, could at last express themselves with glorious abandon.

Thanks to easy credit (it must have been easy if Jay and Jane could acquire it) at the burgeoning home furnishing businesses, we installed within a week new gold carpet, floor to ceiling drapes, and matching couch and loveseat. "Working on the house" became the premier free-time activity of every able-bodied resident in the tract, and with the happy discovery that materials could be bought cheaply or on time payments, Jay proceeded over the next several months to build fences and flowerbeds, pour walkways and a patio, and turn the garage into a rumpus room. Wood paneling covered all walls in the house except the kitchen where Jay cemented a colored tile mosaic and one wall in the living room apportioned in elegant smoked mirrors. To complement the living room decor, he constructed an 8' x 4' walnut-stained coffee table, providing plenty of room for two or three enormous pottery ashtrays, each with slots for sixteen cigarettes, four to a side. The table also featured thick, short, faux-Corinthian ceramic legs, spray-painted gold to match the carpet.

Though focused on the house, Jay did manage to keep up with his paying job at the supermarket and appeared to be doing well at it, for a while at least. Meanwhile, furniture, appliances, tons of cement by the sack, potted banana trees, decorative concrete blocks, and other building materials poured in.

As the block beautification progressed, neighbors inspired one another. Next door to our right, Herman "Drew" Drolet and his wife Arlis, who moved in two days before we did, showed an inspiring zeal in their home projects and kept the pace for thirty years after we left. Drew was a full-blooded Indian from the Midwest, a tall, former college football player who sold built-in pools. He and Arlis were warm people, probably the best friends Jay and Jane ever had. Their four daughters, Cindy, Jeanie, Marci, and Dinie (short for Diane), were as friendly and unaffected as their parents. Drew installed our street's first cement pool in his back yard, and while the kids flocked there to swim, grownups up and down the block planted shrubs and seeded their lawns.

The tidiest landscaping in the first months belonged to the Verdimans next door to our left: Jim, a full-blooded Cherokee from

Oklahoma[33] and his bride, a pale redhead twice his size who later introduced me to Elvis's earliest albums. Jim worked as a Garden Grove city street sweeper and sold lawn equipment for his second job, so thanks to the employee discount, his self-propelled reel mower and power edger enabled him to maintain the sharpest-looking lawn on the block.

In those exuberant early days, Huntington Beach seemed a promised land. Grownups, kids, white-collar, blue-collar, mixed-race marriages—we all felt as happy as the Joads when they arrived at Steinbeck's socialist heaven Government Camp in *The Grapes of Wrath*, only this heaven required no housing committee or director and suffered no outside agitators. It was ours, all ours, to do with as we pleased. With gorgeous weather, plentiful goods, spacious dwellings, good neighbors, new schools for the kids, and no landlord, beneficent or otherwise, what was there not to appreciate? The millions of bags of steer manure for lawn dressing brought billions of flies to Orange County, but even this seemingly negative development provided neighborhood youth with a mission and a money-making opportunity at the going rate of one penny for each two flies swatted.

With all the credit and attending bills, money occasionally became a bit tight for grownups, but if you ran a little short between paychecks, the home finance companies were ready and eager to help. As I write this, a radio jingle for Seaboard Finance, a catchy number reminiscent of the Chiquita Banana, song plays in my head: *"We're renting mo-ney at Seaboard now!"* And the finance company clerks passed out the rentals in crisp new twenties, sometimes still in the bank wrapper.

And so much could be gotten for the money! K-Mart opened one of its earliest stores on Beach Boulevard in Huntington Beach, a colossal emporium set in a huge expanse of parking lot. Low prices and sales volume are the keys to large-scale marketing, and K-Mart proved itself the shining example of that winning combination: five gallon landscaping plants, only 76 cents! Shasta cola, a nickel per can in case lots! Elvis records, selling elsewhere for $2.98 (mono) and

---

[33] The block was not as heavily populated with Native Americans as one might surmise from our immediate neighbors; besides Drew and Jim, one other Indian family lived on our street (they moved from Kansas on the Verdimans' recommendation), but I don't remember any others in the whole tract. We did, however, have Norwegians, Hawaiians, Texans, Mexicans, Dutch, Australians, Germans, and even Bronxites within a few blocks.

$3.98 (stereo), only $2.76 and $3.33! From the first week we moved in, K-Mart fed us, entertained us, decorated our homes, and uniformed us: Jay's white shirts, Jane's Capris, my surfer-striped tees, Trish's jumpers, Greg's diapers—all at volume sales prices even before the Blue Light Special made shopping at the K even more exciting.

The only downside to K-mart came when Jay and Jane left us kids in the car while they perused the goods. We never knew when the whim would strike them to shop alone. What seemed endless hours of auto confinement would pass, and in the close quarters of our isolation I began to manifest latent bullying tendencies toward poor Trish and Greg. "Get over on your side and shut up!" "I'M driving the car!" "I'm dropping you off at the orphanage!" "Stop crying or I'll smash your face!" "Puny humans! NO ONE can stand against the Killer Robot!"

Jay and Jane may have been too aglow with their purchases to notice the tension when they returned to the car. In any case, the new house became ever more distinctively decorated, and within a year we were firmly entrenched in the Southern California good life. High time for some icing on the cake, and Jay provided it by purchasing (on easy payments from the local used car lot) the pinnacle of fifties culture, a 1959 Cadillac Fleetwood hardtop—and a pink one no less. The Caddy had served other drivers for five years, the equivalent of a fifteen-year-old car by today's standards, but its sweeping fins and jet blast taillights remained a highlight of automotive poetry. Elvis himself would have been proud of that car, at least when it was new in '59. As Jay cruised off to work, he no doubt gazed at his homestead and vehicle with a feeling of having arrived, as only a former East L.A. tenement youth could feel it.

But I stray from my chronological unfolding. One Saturday, back during our first week or two at Springdale when the future lawns still showed only manure, I took my first protracted exploration of the new domain. I hadn't made any real friends yet, but I fell in with the first kid I met on the street, eleven-year-old, small for his age, wearing old jeans and a faded tee shirt apparently handed down from several big brothers. He took the lead at first, for he said he knew the way to Tibbet's Family Market a mile or so away.

Oasis Drive marked the southern border of the Springdale tract, with the railroad line directly behind our back fence. After a block or so, houses stood partially built with no fences as yet, so we cut through and walked the train tracks a while, then crossed a former orange grove scattered with uprooted stumps. We came out in an ancient section of Springdale settled a whole year before. Here I first noted that all the tract streets were named after Las Vegas landmarks and casinos: Sans Souci Circle, Thunderbird Ave, Oasis Drive, etc.

Eventually we reached the little store where we shared a Hershey bar and an RC Cola, purchased with our combined fly-killer bounty. We began to retrace our steps and had made our way about halfway home when suddenly, on some odd impulse, I suggested we get lost. Literally. "We'll just start walking fast, see, and no looking where we're going."

My new friend seemed puzzled. "How come?"

"We can have a adventure!"

He looked as if he still didn't quite get it, but suddenly he smiled, showing crooked teeth. "Okay!"

I'm not sure now what I meant by adventure, but it probably involved getting away from the civilized world, as I'd last been able to accomplish in the wilds of San Pedro in 1958 and the Sylmar desert in 1961. Now and for the past few years, the streams with crawdads were being culverted. Sylmar still had its genuine desert and dirt roads—or did it? I'd been gone two years, and change came swiftly. All around this part of the Southland, contractors were bulldozing the big Eucalyptus tree windbreaks and orange groves to make way for houses. I'd seen a huge pile of tree stumps only a couple of hours ago. Soon there would be nowhere to get lost at all.

We set out through open fields, over chain link fences, across blighted groves, and vacant lots, being careful to pay no attention to the route. It felt exhilarating, for by temperament I was a non-attention-payer, forced in the numerous family moves to maintain some level of focus in new surroundings. Now at last I could soar free.

By contrast, my companion became more nervous as we found ourselves ever further from home and most definitely lost. He began to lag behind and look long down each crossroads. Finally he sped past me and planted himself in my path. "What way we go to get home?" he asked beseechingly.

"I dunno. We're on a adventure. Y' wanna give up?"

He followed reluctantly for another block but then stopped again. "C'mon, s' head back, huh?"

"Head back where?"

"Uh—down this way, I think." He pointed vaguely. "'S' go 'cross this field and get back home."

I felt in no mood to compromise. "I'm gonna walk till I see the ocean!"

"I'm goin' home." With a pessimistic but determined look, he turned in what he hoped was home's direction.

I continued across the field, relieved to be on my own and able to immerse myself in an elaborate fantasy involving space rangers battling for their lives on a hostile planet. Eventually I emerged from a culvert strip: a weed and gravel zone between tracts with large electrical towers at regular intervals. Their metal heights and dangling wires looked perfectly authentic for the imaginative teleplay in progress. I could see civilization's back yard fences from this inter-dimensional gateway, and eventually I found an entrance to a street of alien houses. This sector definitely seemed like worlds away from my neighborhood. I vaporized the last of the renegade extraterrestrials with my imaginary ray gun and stepped back through the teleportation gate.

As I found out soon afterward, I had made my way to an older section of Westminster, about two miles northeast of my neighborhood. As I, like a pre-teen Marco Polo, strolled boldly along the tree-lined street on a sunny winter Southern California afternoon, I felt a sort of hyper-awareness, probably born of equal parts hunger and excitement. This was worlds away from home, a realm of cement driveways instead of blacktop, trees full-grown and lawns thicker, larger lots, muted house colors, and all-wood siding. But about halfway down the block my prosaic self began to return. We set out before nine o'clock, and the lowering winter sun foretold an hour well past noon. I was hungry. And tired. With a sigh, I realized that the time had come to get back to my own solar system.

But how? The Hill house featured all the modern conveniences but a phone; for all their extravagant dedication to improvement, Jay and Jane never procured one at Huntington Beach. Their reluctance probably stemmed from a combination of being on the Pacific Bell bill-skippers blacklist and a desire to keep Jay's ex-wife at bay. But even if they had installed a home line and even if I could have found a phone booth on such a bucolic street, I wouldn't have dreamed of spending a whole dime to call home. Besides, the sort of attention that would follow any admission of getting lost on purpose would likely have negative consequences, while claiming I had gotten legitimately lost could limit my future wanderings. All things considered, it would be better, if at all possible, to leave one's parents out of this sort of challenge.

Accordingly, I approached a grey-haired man washing his car in a driveway. He looked like the dads on my block who worked at the Douglas plant, only older.

"'Scuse me, Sir." I didn't use "Sir" as a general thing, but I took a tip from the kids on the *Leave it to Beaver* TV show, then in its final season. This neighborhood reminded me of Wally and Beaver's environs, so the old-fashioned politeness seemed appropriate. "Uh, can you tell me where Oasis Drive is?"

"What's that, son? Oasis? Oh—You mean the new tract off Springdale? The one with all the Las Vegas street names?" (He pronounced "Las" as "Lass")

"I guess so."

"Well, how'd you get way over this side of town?"

"I dunno."

That seemed to satisfy him. He stepped into the open garage and came out with a ragged scrap of bath towel. "Here, help me finish drying, and we'll see if we can't get you home."

"Thanks!" I said, wiping the fender with a show of enthusiasm. His plan seemed excellent—I had no energy to walk much farther, much less pay attention to directions.

A few minutes later the Good Samaritan loaded me in his car as promised. He kept the patronizing conversation to a minimum as we drove, and seemed to understand when I asked him to drop me at a corner a few blocks from my house. I strolled home and enjoyed a late lunch before helping with some backyard weeding. Jay and Jane remained unaware of my adventure, a plus for everyone's serenity.

As for my walking partner, the old-fashioned kid who seemed more a throwback to San Pedro than a denizen of this New Jerusalem, I never saw him again. For all I know, he may yet be wandering, as he does in my memory, through the other-worldly culverts of Westminster, somewhere near the timeless Orange County galactic center of the known universe.

CHAPTER THIRTY-EIGHT

~ The Dawn of Music ~ Premature Teendom ~ Civic Growth Pangs
~ Social Groupings ~ Dwarf Sensibilities~ Lull Before The Delia

"Are you ready for NUUUMMBERR TEN??"

For what reason did I lie abed late on a Saturday morning in spring1963, sometime around my tenth birthday? I may have had a cold — with two three-pack-a-day smokers in the house, my siblings and I suffered regularly from respiratory reactions. Or I could have been avoiding duty — several major landscape projects were always under way at our new house, and Jay always assigned yard work if he caught sight of me. Or perhaps Jane had sentenced me to straighten up my room and I was girding myself to begin. Lately she showed less inclination to do the cleaning for me, though I explained to her that I faced heavy responsibilities at school.

Whatever the cause, I definitely occupied my room that morning, and I'm certain the white table radio Nanny gave me for Christmas in 1958 provided the soundtrack. I idly spun the little AM dial, stopping at the compelling voice of a KFWB Channel 98 disk jockey announcing the cream of the top forty countdown.

"Are you ready for NUUUMMBERR TEN?"

Some timeless gem began to play, perhaps "Walk Like a Man," "My Boyfriend's Back," or "It's My Party (and I'll Cry If I Want To)," which were all hit songs around then. Whichever hit it happened to be, the music grabbed my attention in a way never before experienced. I'd been listening with interest to pop music for several years; I kept up with the novelty songs and already counted myself an Elvis fan. But at that instant, a special radio frequency, perceivable only by pre-adolescents at a particular state of development, clicked my hormones into "teenager."

This psycho-chemical reaction immediately triggered a faculty for unprecedented concentration and memory. Boys who experienced the phenomenon in other cultures and eras began to make great strides in Greek or Hebrew, or in absorption of vast tracts of poetry or scripture. For my part, I nailed in the lyrics to "Mr. Bass Man," "Harry, the Hairy Ape," and of course, the transcendent "South Street," that paean to the hip teen scene in Philadelphia that somehow, through hyper-catchy rhythm, sexy chorus singers, comic-relief frog-voice bassman, and exhortation to *join us*, transmitted even into west coast suburbs all the exuberance and joie de vivre of being young and happy and free from school, parents, and responsibility.

Perhaps the most interesting aspect of the AM top-forty in the years before the so-called British Invasion was the eclectic playlists. Nowadays all is niche market: separate stations for every age-group and micro-distinction of pop music. But in the early sixties, everyone from precocious ten-year-olds through parents in their forties listened to the same stations, and anything unique could compete on the charts.

For instance, in succession that day I might have heard sappy Paul and sexy-voiced Paula, the Christian college students from Brownwood, Texas, singing "Hey Paula," followed by the peppy Folk-Pop Greenwich Village band The Rooftop Singers covering the 1929 blues/jugband number "Walk Right In." Or the poignant "Sukiyaki" by Kyu Sakamoto, a one-hit Japanese crooner; "Domi-nique" by Soeur Sourire, a French singing nun; "Deep Purple" by aging lounge singers April Stevens and Nino Temple; "He's So Fine" by the meat-and-potatoes girl group The Chiffons; and the up-and-coming songwriter Bob Dylan's "Blowin' in the Wind," covered by pre-fabricated folkniks Peter, Paul, and Mary. Most of those songs made number one in the first half of 1963, and all, despite their ori-entation in folk, do-wop, lounge, country, blues, or international, appealed to a wide range of listeners.

From that day forward, the white table radio hummed along each morning as I dressed for school. I put new batteries in my transistor and carried it with me to dial up during recess until Mr. Evans caught me listening in class and banned possession. I headed straight to the table model immediately upon returning home, listening for an hour or more while I read or puttered about my room. My 9:30 bedtime ceased as a point of contention with my parents; I would happily drift off to sleep with the radio volume turned so low that no one over thirty could have heard it from three feet away.

My then-supple brain wrapped itself around those songs such that even now, when I can't remember a phone number for five seconds or a line of a poem I've heard a hundred times, I recall every word, every chorus, every drum fill, every fade out riff of "Another Saturday Night" by Sam Cooke, "Do the Bird" by Dee-Dee Sharp, "Can't Get Used to Losing You" by Andy Williams, and scores of others from my first season of pop music worship. Soon I could recite the top-forty chart position of every song on the playlist for several weeks previous, and I handicapped the upcoming results like a race track tout. When "He's So Fine" made number one, it caused all the excitement of a twenty-to-one shot coming in — a girl group with no previous hits and no name stars or hot lookers in the group, yet passing all the favorites — unprecedented!

I wasn't the only unofficial adolescent in our household tuned in to the teen scene. Jane had always been a conscientious if not zealous housekeeper; now, in the afternoons, she ironed or folded clothes in front of the TV while viewing *The Lloyd Thaxton Hop*, a local version of Dick Clark's *American Bandstand*. Sometimes she danced along, with a studious air of keeping up with the latest innovations in her former profession. The show's air time coincided with kids arriving home from school, and more than once I came in to find her dancing around the living room in front of the TV.

"C'mon let me show you this step," she'd say, puffing slightly but fixing upon me the purposeful gleam she must have used on shy customers at the dance studio. But I always demurred. A few years later I would become a dancing fool, but as yet I remained an aesthete who hadn't quite crossed the threshold of genuine teendom, beyond which flailing around in public doesn't seem embarrassing.

We enjoyed family breakfasts that season, for Jay usually left early for work. He and I were too cosmopolitan to carry lunch sacks, so Jane didn't pack lunches as in the Luke days. But she bought pastries and brownies from the bread truck for treats and desserts, and we sat down to a hot dinner together every night with a good assortment of canned and frozen vegetables, meat loaf, "goulash" with noodles and ground beef, and steak or pork chops at least twice a week. The grownups occasionally enjoyed an iceberg lettuce salad with Roquefort dressing, but we kids never touched raw vegetables.

After breakfast, Jane walked Trish, now five years old, to kindergarten at Cook Elementary School. Cook, visible from Springdale Street across a huge field perfect for kite flying before it became another tract, condescended to absorb the Springdale kids for grades K-3 only. We older invaders in Grades 4-6 were bussed several miles farther, to Schroeder School off Bolsa Chica Avenue.

The tract surrounding Schroeder had populated two years before, but construction of the mandated new school lagged behind schedule. During the first few weeks of classes in fall 1962, Schroder teachers worked without lights, clocks, or thermostats, and without a complete roof over at least one classroom. When I arrived a few months later, the school structures were complete, but the lawn beyond the fresh blacktop still consisted of steer manure and grass seed. Along the sidewalk, staked strings with bits of rag at intervals kept us off the newly planted areas—in that place and time, to step over such barriers broke a taboo as sacred as the one prohibiting swimming after meals.

Schroder had been overcrowded even before the Springdale kids appeared practically overnight, which may have accounted for the locals' obvious sense of annoyance with bussed-in newcomers. They exuded a sort of came-over-on-the-Mayflower disdain for us Springdalians, looking upon us as what has been more recently called "trailer trash" because (a) we arrived after they landed and (b) our houses lacked certain amenities that put them in the more genteel class—items like shake roofs and block wall fences. While most of this class-consciousness only mildly interested me, I did notice that all my Schroeder friends seemed to have older parents, plainer cars, and gas-log fireplaces. And they lived on streets named after Ivy League Universities (Harvard, Yale, Cornell, etc.) instead of Las Vegas Casinos.

In any case, we of the Springdale horde were a force to be reckoned with. The day I enrolled as the fourth new student that week, Mr. Evans's class population hit the high thirties. Within a month it rose to fifty, with most of the new additions from Springdale. Like Irish immigrants to New York a century before, we lost no time in making our presence known to our more refined predecessors. Despite my growing teen sensibility and the general chill of the new surroundings, I strove to be active at Schroder. I remember baseball and flag football at recess, student council meetings and tonette lessons once a week.[34]

After school I hung out with neighborhood classmates and

---

[34] A tonette was a short plastic flutelike instrument sold for one dollar to students by an outside vendor who may have donated a kickback to the school. The purchase included free lessons from the salesman. Rather than notes, the songbook used numbers corresponding with the flute holes. As I recall and offer to readers who might find a tonette at a yard sale or antique store, the tablature for the only song we learned, "Mary Had a Little Lamb," went like so: 1-2-3-2-1-1-1/ 2-2-2, 1-1-1/ 1-2-3-2- 1-1-1/ 2-2-1-2-3.

followed the current pastimes: street ball, BB guns, and fort building. With all this activity, there were also plenty of solitary endeavors — books, records, radio, kite flying, long bike rides and involved daydreams. Drive-in movies had lately become the Hills' premier family outing, and Elvis kept busy cranking out his string of three-a-year singing action hero films suitable for all family members. My fantasies of that era usually featured me as a sort of young Elvis with super powers as well as the ability to summon an orchestra from thin air. While involved in these reveries I felt content with my own company, and neighbors were liable to see me ambling down the street wearing a glazed look, either making vague karate moves or lip syncing a song, or both.

My general pop-culture precociousness was abetted by the Huntington Beach school bus Master Route Plan. The Master Route Planners designated Schroeder the hub for all educational transport; students bussed in from two junior highs and two high schools; then, after a short layover, transferred to a connecting bus that conveyed them to their respective housing tracts. As a result I beheld upon exiting my school's front gate a panorama of Southern California teendom in all its early sixties, pre-Beatle, pre-Hippie glory. Listening to my transistor as I waited for the bus, I absorbed the styles and mannerisms of the fashionable high school set. Oh, to be a manly teen — tall, deep-voiced, in full hair plumage, with a studied slouch and six-inch span of white sock between the bottom of one's drainpipe white jeans and black Italian spike-toed shoes — it all seemed a pinnacle that a lowly fourth-grader could only admire from afar. But I determined to at least dress the part. Within weeks my last flattop with fenders grew into a greasy upsweep; I acquired undercuffed white jeans with zippers on the pockets, tab collar dress shirts (worn with crew-neck tee-shirt showing underneath), and red streamline sweater — no pockets, no collar, two buttons. My inch-wide belt buckled slightly to the side, and my slip-ons featured horseshoe heel taps. I transformed myself into a one-man in-crowd (as per Dobie Grey's contemporary hit song); the only difference between me and the real teens was a foot or so in height and a few voice octaves.

Those finishing touches would come in time … or would they? One of the high schoolers at the bus stop wore the face of a troubled teen on the edge, but he was a midget or dwarf, only as tall as a third grader. Stares and waves of giggles accompanied his hurried, self-conscious strut through the gauntlet between busses. From him I perceived hells below hells in the social universe. Could it happen to me? What if I stopped growing now—never any taller, feet never big enough for a pair of those Italian shoes not available in fourth-grade sizes … the horror!

I kept well back in the crowd when the little guy walked by—I didn't want to catch anything or be caught staring. But after he passed I pushed up front for the high school girls' fashion show. In their tight skirts, sleeveless blouses through which one could occasionally glimpse a bra through the armholes, one-inch black high-heels, and make-up seemingly applied by trowel, those beauties were like movie star goddesses, universes away from the frilly dresses, Mary Jane strap shoes, and white socks worn by most of the girls in my class. Around eighth grade the debs began to wear their hair with stylized, Dipity-Doo® enhanced bangs and a ratted bump in the back. The older and/or wilder girls piled up huge bumps of hair called "beehives."

Despite my advanced fashion awareness, I remained a grammar school midget to those exalted females. But thanks to Cindy Drolet, the sophomore next door who sometimes babysat Greg and Trish, I conversed with them occasionally. Cindy even loaned me her Dick and Dee Dee records and told her girlfriends in my presence that I was "cute." But I understood that she thought so in the same way she'd think a Chimpanzee in hipster clothes fit that designation.

As an aspiring teen, I became more interested in girls, but no girls my age were ready for a meaningful relationship—they all listened to Disney 78s passed down from their big sisters and wore frilly dresses, un-dipityed bangs, and freckles. That is, until Delia Thornton arrived—a portentous event still weeks in the future.

CHAPTER THIRTY-NINE

~ News Views ~ Losing Status ~ First Encounter With Archie
~ Diet Rite and Metracal ~ Charm School Black Magic
~ How to Tell If a Girl is Into You ~ Not a Cave Man

As I became hyper-aware of music and pop culture during spring 1963, I also began to follow national and world events via Radio KFWB's hourly newsbreaks. I remember the sound clip of President Kennedy at the Berlin wall, making his famous "Ich bin ein Berliner" speech. Vietnam, wherever that was, put in an occasional appearance above the headline surface. The astronauts continued to blast off regularly to great fanfare, though public interest peaked with John Glenn's first orbital odyssey in 1962. Gus Grissom's May 1963 multi-orbital flight marked the end of project Mercury, and space travel became non-news until the moon landing in '69.

Meanwhile back in the states[35], Martin Luther King, Jr. marched in Birmingham on my tenth birthday. The Birmingham bus boycotts followed, and Sheriff Bull Conner met the protesters with cattle prods, dogs, and fire hoses. National Guard troops moved in later to force Governor George Wallace to accept black students at the University of Alabama. I heard variant views on these events. Most teachers and adults I knew followed network newscasters on both TV and radio who presented the African American protestors as heroic figures and the local authorities as melodrama villains. But old guard Southerners like Daddy saw these confrontations as an ominous usurpation of states' rights destined to precede both a rising tide of anarchy and a new dark age, as it were. Jane and Jay generally concurred with this sentiment. But the only social question I actually cared about that week was whether Dion's "Ruby Baby"

---

[35] For non-scholars of novelty songs, this is an allusion to the spoken part of "Stranded in the Jungle" by the Cadets.

would make the top ten or stall at number 20. And I would have much preferred to shake hands with Ricky Nelson and Sam Cooke than with John F. Kennedy and Martin Luther King.

At Schroeder I struggled with being a lowly fourth-grader in a school where sixth graders ruled, unlike the unusual first-through-fourth arrangement in Redondo. And Redondo had been all about fighting, so my trained reaction to come out swinging at any playground dispute provided an unpleasant surprise to classmates who tried to mess up my hair or take cuts in the foursquare game. However, the unpleasantness ricocheted back to me when I used my method on bigger and older boys not so impressed with my bravado or pugilistic skills.

Fifth-grade Jimmy was a Filipino kid about my size, but older, faster, and a better boxer all around. In a two minute scuffle one afternoon recess, he outpunched me three blows to one, then observed with a silver-toothed grin, "You ain' so tough." The judgment hurt worse than the punches. Sixth-grader Archie, red-haired and temper-challenged, stood almost a foot taller than I and weighed half-again as much. He reminded me of Mike, my old nemesis/friend from Redondo, only larger and meaner. In an altercation over a foursquare game, I became coolly insolent and used the unfortunate phrase "big spaz." Archie suddenly pushed me so hard I literally left the ground and hit the blacktop rolling. He then stood over me, trembling, red-faced and practically foaming at the mouth until a couple of his friends led him away. I hadn't faced any such elemental force since the crazy gigantic nine-year old ordered five-year-old me "OFF HER PROPERTY!" back in San Pedro.

Again I felt less troubled by the bruises and scrapes than with the shame of not standing up to his fury, whatever the final outcome. But Peter, my first friend at Schroeder and as yet uncursed with teenage sensitivity, didn't hold my discretion against me. "That guy's crazy," he observed. "And you shouldn't mess with sixth graders anyhow."

Peter already knew that I, too, sometimes exhibited less-than-stable behavior: after an earlier playground argument between us, I'd challenged him to a fight, but he simply turned away. In my rage I faux-karate-chopped him on the back of his neck.

He turned back around, more puzzled than angry. "Whaja hit me for?"

I could think of no good answer. His patient wonder at my

violence prompted a rare effort to be conciliatory. We became school friends, even hanging out occasionally on weekends when I rode my bike the five miles to his house. I played a sort of Eddie Haskell to his Wally Cleaver, at least in the estimation of his mother, who always eyed my hair and clothes with an expression between alarm and disgust. She was what doctors now call "morbidly obese" and most notable to me as the first person I'd ever observed drinking the new Diet-Rite soda I'd seen advertised on TV. One Saturday as Peter helped unload her groceries, I noticed that she also consumed Metracal, the space age diet drink meal substitute; saccharin, before the FDA determined it carcinogenic; Contac one-a-day cold capsules; and other scientific breakthroughs yet to be assimilated into the Hill family shopping list.

Despite his mother's cutting-edge consumerism, I sensed Peter's shame at her jumbo size and sour temperament. Until then I more or less took for granted that Jay and Jane caused less embarrassment than most parents. Fate had burdened Jane with no size, weight, or other peculiarities (though I do recall a pamphlet around the house called "The Drinking Man's Diet" in which the author outlined a high-protein program similar to the Atkins program of this century). She could even make an Alabama accent sound good, and practiced no overt nosiness, nagging, nor violent mood swings.

Now that I am a parent and grandparent, I understand that Peter's mom had reason enough to give me the fish eye, but in fairness, some redeeming qualities did temper my Eddie-Haskality. I helped Peter with reading and encouraged him to sign up for the Saturday softball league run by the city recreation department. I also perhaps indirectly inspired the lad to good citizenship by becoming student council representative for Mr. Evans's class—though I must here confess that I took the position less from a sense of school spirit or civic responsibility than for the opportunity to leave class for official meetings one afternoon per week.

In any case, this political capacity brought about my first close-range observation of Delia Thornton. When Mr. Evans presented her in the front of the room—"All right, boys and girls, give me your attention. This is Delia, *another* new student from Springdale"—I hunched over my desk near the back of our overcrowded classroom. With my uncorrected myopia I couldn't have made her out distinctly if I'd wanted to, so during the introduction I hardly glanced up from drawing a spider web in the corner of my math paper. But two days later, as I presented my student council report in front of the class, my attention gradually focused on this new girl seated right in my line of vision. I noted her sheath skirt and sweater, a sophisticated high school ensemble that distinguished her from her female classmates. Her nose had freckles like theirs, but her freckles were subdued by modest powdering, and a hint of coral lipstick accented her thin lips. She had teased her hair into a little puff in back and it flipped at the shoulders, just like the older girls at the bus stop. Slim, with no remnant of baby fat, she sat with bare knees pressed together and cocked at a 45-degree angle, another high-school standard pose.

Delia caught me staring and met my gaze with what I perceived as a mysterious smile. The next recess I found myself gravitating to the girls' section of the playground, where I noted that while this interesting new classmate did participate nominally in the jump rope rituals, she exhibited a particularly grown-up walk. In an upcoming conversation, she attributed this elegant sway to Charm School, a six-week course in which her mother enrolled her the previous summer. The charm school mission focused on making motivated young ladies irresistible to young gentlemen. They learned to walk with grace by balancing books on their heads, used the same books as dumbbells for chest development exercises ("We must, we must, increase the bust"), and practiced the rudiments of make-up.

The program certainly worked on me. As Elvis put it in "It's Now or Never" a couple of years earlier: "My heart was captured; my soul surrendered." All third-grade feelings for Rebecca McCain seemed childish in comparison.

I longed to know Delia in a meaningful way, but as ten-year-olds, we were subject to certain cultural proscriptions. In the first through third elementary years, one could get away with boy-girl friendships, as I had ventured on several occasions. I could even visit Rebecca McCain at home. But at ten, when the hormones have only begun to percolate, the child resists the change within, and the resistance is manifested in disharmony between genders. "Boys are icky!" say the girls.[36] "Girls stink!" resounds from the boys.

But as a teenager in spirit, I resisted such provincialism. Delia also rode the Springdale bus, and the next day I connived a spot right across the aisle from her (strictly segregated seats: boys on the

---

[36] According to my granddaughter, "Girls rule; boys drool" is the equivalent in 21st century elementary schools.

right; girls on the left). Catching her eye, I beamed what I meant as a smoldering Elvis stare, and piped, "What street you live on?"

"Casino."

"I'm on Oasis. Right around the corner. Here, check out this cool song." I held my radio close to her ear.

Delia leaned over slightly. Just then the bus driver, a thin lady who wore a man's uniform complete with boots and bow tie, and whose face reminded me of Jefferson Davis in our history book (only without the goatee) — this lady, I say, looked in her rearview mirror and saw my arm extending into forbidden territory. In a foghorn voice, she commanded me over her shoulder to "Put that thing away or you'll lose it till the end of the school year!"

I withdrew the radio, embarrassed into silence. When we arrived at the first Springdale stop, girls filed off the bus first, as per the rules. By the time I disembarked at the end of the boys' line, I could see Delia's unmistakably provocative walk receding down the block. She may not have been hurrying, but she definitely did not dawdle. I stared after her with a sigh. While I would have preferred her to demonstrate a little reciprocal interest by waiting for me, standard procedure in the Elvis movies called for the female object of pursuit to vigorously resist initial advances, especially after a public discomfiture. So we were right on script.

From that day forth, I sought any opportunity to impress Delia. I combed my hair even more often and missed no chance to exhibit my pop music erudition. In the ensuing weeks she became more willing to chat a little on subjects like charm school, teen TV stars, and records, but I didn't reflect until much later that my new flame didn't start any of the conversations. In retrospect it should have been obvious that the chemistry didn't react on Delia's end. I should have lunged from the quicksand de amour before the more profound disappointment to come, but how, at age ten, could I have begun to understand the capriciousness of love?

Of course at some level I did know about relational chemistry, for I currently practiced on another the same arms-length, polite discouragement Delia seemed to be practicing on me. For weeks I had resisted the advances of a wan girl with pale red hair I'll call Mary, who sat directly behind me in Mr. Evans's class. I can't even remember the poor soul's real name, only that she embodied the antithesis of what I, the wanna-be teen, found alluring. Short and young looking even by fourth-grade standards, she wore little girl dresses and limp curls. She even talked with a slight lisp.

Despite my complete lack of encouragement, Mary made many overtures. She expressed admiration for my sweater, my answers in class discussions, and my student council reports. She even touched the back of my head from her seat behind me and remarked that she wished she had such nice naturally curly hair. Finally, she grew bold enough to invite me to her house after school, ostensibly to examine a nature collection that had something to do with insects.

I brushed the invitation aside, citing my need to take the bus home to Springdale. She didn't seem to get it: associating with her in any capacity would brand me as playing with the girls, and to visit her home would definitely compromise my status on the playground. I could suffer those insults for Delia's sake, but with Mary I had nothing to gain. Yet a few days after my initial conversation with Delia, wan little Mary managed to get me to her house. Spiking my usual objection, she claimed her mom planned to drive to Westminster for shopping at five and could drop me off at Springdale on the way. She then waited for an answer, her expression the epitome of mute yearning.

So, in a moment of tender-heartedness or perhaps some other character twist, I actually went. Her mother showed bright solicitude when she met me at the door, and to my surprise, her big brother turned out to be Tony, the sixth-grader school president and titular head of the Student Council on which I sat as a lowly fourth-grade representative. Tony greeted me with warm condescension, but even the proximity of such a luminary failed to ease my discomfort. I don't remember the nature display, and the ride home with Mary's mother was especially grim. She prattled on at length about all the wonderful things Mary had told her about me. I said nothing at all for five long miles.

In the ensuing days, I hedged, dodged, and made excuses for avoiding my relentless admirer. Sometime in May, Mary disappeared for two weeks, providing some relief. Upon her return she looked even more delicate than usual. One afternoon while Mr. Evans droned on about something way up in front of the class, I heard a soft moan behind me. I turned. Common decency overrode my resolution to never start a conversation with Mary.

"Are you okay?" I whispered.

Her eyes brimmed with tears and her lower lip trembled. "I hurt so bad!" she whispered back in hideously embarrassing confidence. "I had appendix and had to have a operation!"

I nodded sympathetically, but her pain, weakness, and naked desire for comfort overwhelmed my shallow ten-year-old soul. She left for the nurse's office a few minutes later, and I avoided her even more assiduously from then on, especially after I stepped up my campaign to attract Delia's attention.

After two weeks of dogged courtship, she finally granted a lukewarm invitation to the Thornton estate. We walked there straight from the bus stop, and Bonnie, Delia's tomboy third-grade sister, met us at the porch. Bonnie resembled Delia in nose only, and with her dirty blonde hair, jeans, and sweatshirt, she seemed as distantly removed from charm school as a girl could get. Her "Who's *he*?" provided a model of scorn. She might have blocked the door indefinitely, but the girls' mother appeared, a faded beauty with an ironic air. Delia called her "Mother."

"Bonnie, dear, why don't you go feed the poor, starving pooch?" said Mother. She then summoned Delia's father, and a prematurely balding, blue-collar-and-proud fellow came forth to take my measure. I don't remember much of the exchange, but he practiced edgy sardonica and my rudimentary social skills deserted me—I hardly looked either parent in the eyes and made a poor impression.

To my relief, we retreated to Delia's room. Within seconds Bonnie began scratching on the outside, first making kitten sounds, then exaggerated kissing noises. Delia merely crinkled her nose at the door, an anticipation of Elizabeth Montgomery in the TV show *Bewitched*, still a year away from its premier.

We had discussed music on our bus rides, and Delia now brought out her singles collection, a set of "forty-fives," the small, large-holed, usually one-song-per-side disks that played at 45 rpm. As she stacked them on the spindle of her little record player, I felt the exquisite but tragically fleeting sense of dreams coming true. I had somehow leapt the gap of years to become a teenager, hanging out with his girlfriend and spinning tunes, just like the older kids on TV.

I remember little of the conversation except that I probably expressed too much irritation with her sister. Bonnie stood outside the window, tapping on the glass to the beat. But I remember perfectly at least three records we heard: "The Stripper" by David Rose, "Let's Dance" by Chris Montez, and "Bobby's Girl" by Marcie Blaine. To check the spelling of Ms. Blaine's last name, I typed in "Bobby's Girl" into Google, and it came up on an ad for a 10-CD collection of "Malt Shop Hits." I perused the list of 200 songs and realized I remembered the lyrics to virtually all of them. But the three songs Delia played are in a vivid memory category by themselves. "The Stripper" is an instrumental, but every nuance of the song and every second of "Let's Dance" and "Bobby's Girl" are forever branded on my brain.

Speaking of the internet, a recent article for teens on one of the browser home pages listed "Five ways to tell if a girl is into you." They are as follows:

1. She tilts her head
2. She instinctively mirrors your actions
3. She twirls her hair
4. She gets a visible glow
5. Her pupils dilate

Conversely, the five signs a girl is *not* into you are, according to the article:

1. She crosses her arms
2. She places her bag between you two
3. She speaks very rapidly
4. She offers you a chin-up smile
5. She strokes her neck

Memory of my golden afternoon with Delia has faded somewhat with the decades, but aided by this article's timeless guide to attraction, I can picture us sitting in her room, the record case between us. Delia exhibits no glow whatsoever; her complexion is icy white, her pupils mere pinpoints, and her head absolutely un-tilted except for an occasional chin-up smile as she speaks very rapidly and does the opposite of whatever I'm doing. She resolutely keeps her fingers from her hair but alternates between stroking her neck and crossing her arms tightly.

I left after an hour or so and did my best to think positive, but the pessimistic undertones of this effort were prescient: though I would pursue Delia all the way through sixth grade, that afternoon in late spring of '63 marked the only time I ever crossed the threshold of her salon/boudoir.

According to a schoolmate I talked with some years later, Delia became smitten at age sixteen by a dashing gentleman of the biker persuasion. She ran away from home to live with the fellow and soon afterward gave birth to a child. This supposedly took place in 1969, eons later in cultural time than 1963. If this uncorroborated gossip is true, then, like Joanie Summers who'd scored a hit in 1962 with "Johnny Get Angry," Delia probably already "want[ed] a brave man, a cave man" in her formative years. Alas, I was but an aspiring teeny-bopper in red sweater and white pants with zippers on the pockets.

Delia never alluded to the Joanie Summers song[37] in any of our conversations, but she did express at length her admiration for Paul Petersen, resident teen on the Donna Reed show. Petersen, nowadays described as "grandfatherly" in press releases, is president of Minor Consideration, an advocacy group for exploited young actors. But Delia's fascination during his exploited period should have tipped me off, too — Petersen possessed a dark, pouty young Italian look just the opposite of my freckles and blond curliness. In pathetic moments in the months ahead, I would imagine myself as Petersen, cruising into Huntington Beach from Hollywood, tooling down Casino Street to sweep her into my sports car.

In real life, as the Ira Gershwin lyric says, I couldn't get started with her. But I had begun to accomplish something, at least. In older pouty Italian Frank Sinatra's parlance, I was learning the blues.

---

[37] On the plus side, "Johnny Get Angry" has a brilliant, tongue-in-cheek production, including an instrumental break which features a double-tracked kazoo belting out the melody over a lush string background. Well worth a listen on YouTube.

CHAPTER FORTY

*~ The Sick Rose ~ That's All Right, Mama ~ Comedic Connoisseurs and Their
Detractors ~ Journalism Redux ~ Moving While Standing Still*

More to come on Delia and what seemed then the most tragic love
affair of all time. Looking back, the overall irony is that through two
years of self-propelled tragedy I remained callously unaware of
causing others to suffer the same pangs of unrequited love I suffered
myself. Little Mary in Mr. Evans's class, then Roberta, Gwen, Junie —
all, as will be told, were perfectly nice girls who developed crushes
on me during the next two years in Huntington Beach. With any one
of them I could have passed many hours in pleasant companionship,
but I never gave them a serious thought as I beat my head against
the wall of Delia's affection or lack thereof.

I did have a few other interests besides love in that spring
of my eleventh year. I began to invest in what would become a
relatively extensive LP collection, usually purchased at K-mart, but
occasionally, in the case of older albums, ordered from the thick
catalogue at the Westminster record store. In solitary pursuits I
read boys' adventure books, comic books, teen magazines, and an
occasional Freddy the Pig for old times' sake, usually while listening
to records. But as my short stretch at Schroeder played out and the
season turned from spring to perfect Huntington Beach summer, I
harbored a small but chronic bittersweet pain, an ache no song or
book could assuage. Had I been a young literary scholar like C.S.
Lewis at age ten, reciting Romantic verse to myself as I wandered
lonely as a cloud through vacant lots and blooming wildflowers, I
might have become convinced that William Blake anticipated my
pain with "A Sick Rose" and I could have felt all the more tragically
Romantic for it:

Oh Rose, thou art sick
The invisible worm
That flies in the night
In the howling storm
Has found out thy bed
Of crimson joy
And his dark secret love
Doth thy life destroy

But since I had already contracted enough of the tragic-romantic virus without deep poetic encouragement, it's probably best that I spent most of my free time learning pinball at the bowling alley, reading *Teen Screen*, Archie and Superman comics, and *Mad* Magazine at the liquor store, or studying early Elvis and poker at the Verdimans' house. None of my new friends knew my secret sorrow; or if they did, they refrained from belaboring such folly.

Several guys around my age lived within a couple of hundred yards' radius, so teams, gangs, and armies sprang up that spring on Oasis Drive. Next-door neighbors Bobby and Carl Verdiman had a basketball hoop on their garage and liked to organize street-baseball games. Their mom carried even more extra poundage than Peter's mother, but Mrs. Verdiman always seemed more cheerful and entirely unselfconscious. She drank beer out of the can, sang along with "Hit the Road, Jack," and taught us the fan shuffle with cards. She refereed as we learned to play poker with our fly-killing pennies, and she often drove us to the theatre in Garden Grove, beginning when the first Annette Funicello and Frankie Avalon beach movies debuted that summer. She would crank up the radio for a song she liked, and every time I hear the Rolling Stones' "It's All Over Now," which came out during my second Huntington Beach summer, I remember her beating out the rhythm on the dashboard. But I owe Mrs. V my biggest debt of gratitude and affection for introducing me to Elvis Presley's early efforts.

Though I knew all the lyrics to several Elvis albums released since 1960, I had never heard any of the Sun recordings from 1954-55. Radio stations rarely played "oldies" then, and no one I knew had any Elvis albums I didn't own. But one day Carl, the younger Verdiman brother, heard me say something about Elvis and led me to their "den." The Verdiman four-bedroom house contained a den *and* a spare bedroom because the three boys (Carl, Bobby, and

"Peanut," their four-year-old brother) roomed together. I'm unclear if this arrangement stemmed from Jim and his wife's dirt-poor background, his Indian heritage, or general Kansas sensibilities, but so it went.

Carl showed me his mom's Elvis collection, featuring some albums I'd never seen. While Elvis served in the army, RCA released the old Sun sides on two albums: *A Date With Elvis* and *For LP Fans Only*. Side one of the latter featured "That's All Right, Mama" plus "Mystery Train" and other early gems, but I didn't get to them right away—I played "That's All Right, Mama" again. And again. My reaction followed that of Dewy Phillips, the Memphis DJ, when he first got hold of the single in July 1954—he couldn't stop playing it on the air, and no one listening to the station wanted him to stop. Something magical came out in nineteen-year-old Elvis's vocal, the way he sang the phrase "That's all r-i-i-ght" with a sort of diphthong trill—and the band provided the perfect accompaniment. The whole package came across as aged but ageless, hypnotic, compelling, completely original. In the last chapter, calling "South Street" by the Orlons "transcendent," may have been a bit sarcastic, but "That's All Right, Mama" was and is transcendent without any quotation marks whatsoever.

Carl left the den after the fourth or fifth reprise of the song, but I didn't take the hint. When I finally came out an hour or so later, Carl and Bobby had departed to play baseball. Mrs. Verdiman reclined on the couch, watching a soap opera and drinking a beer. "You like ol' Elvis, huh?" she chuckled. "Well, you can come over and play them records any time."

The next day, figuring Mrs. V must be partial to Indians since she married one, I brought over my worn copy of "Flaming Star," from the soundtrack of the film featuring Elvis as a half-breed.

"Well, look a that!" she beamed. "I seen the movie, but never heard the song but the once."

Of her two offspring in my age group, Carl looked most like an Indian and had the more serene disposition. Bobby's complexion was almost as pale as his mom's, but he usually exhibited the truculent Indian sensibility seen in the cowboy movies, when excitable young braves repudiate the treaty and start an uprising. Quick tempered, always competitive, always ready to take umbrage, Bobby seemed to seethe, even in repose. Our first fistfight occurred early on over a basketball disagreement. We boxed for a few minutes; then I caught him with a left-right combination to the mouth and ear. He turned and walked into his house without a word, conceding the match.

Spectators at that fight included my Uncle Barry, Bobby's young uncle, and both his parents. Contemporary parents reading this might wonder why the grownups or older kids didn't stop the action, but no sensible person in those days would interfere with youthful combat as long as observers judged the bout as "a fair fight" and no one bled overmuch. Due in large part to that policy, Bobby and I were able to make up on the surface and continued to hang out in the same circles. Mrs. Verdiman acted as if the incident never happened, but Bobby apparently burned with resentment for years, as we shall see.

I had a much warmer relationship with Benjy Allard, who lived across the street and a few doors down. Benjy was my age and grade, but a head shorter, a sort of Mickey Rooney of the neighborhood, with the classic short guy's eagerness to please and anxiety about being judged for his height, but with none of the chip on the shoulder which often accompanies the short-guy personality. His dad worked at the Douglas plant and dealt strictly with his six kids. They did daily chores, attended church all Sundays, and called their parents "Sir" and "Ma'am."[38]

When anyone disagreed with Benjy, he heard taunts of "shorty," "shrimp," and the like, but I never called attention to his stature. I would do even worse, as I'll recount later, but for the first year at least we were close friends.

One afternoon we began swapping dirty jokes. Both of us knew several standards: "Johnny Fuckerfaster," "Fo' a Nickel Ah Will," "Chimes," etc. and we enjoyed comparing variations as well as learning new material. The session turned into a sort of joke marathon, starting at my front yard, continuing up the street, and concluding on the side of his house, where, caught up in mutual hilarity, we laughed uproariously at even mildly funny turns.

Unfortunately, we reached our noisiest right by the Allard bathroom window, and his dad overheard us. He sent a little brother out to tell Benjy to come in and me to go home. My partner in smut gave me a stricken look as he marched in to his doom. He told me

---

[38] As the sixties progressed, I saw less and less of this old-school family dynamic; by 1969, only one family I knew kept those traditions, and they were Mormons who didn't drink cokes or iced tea, either. (See the Mormon *Word of Wisdom* for other dietary particulars.)

later that he expected his dad to beat him with a belt; but instead he drew a suspended sentence with no TV for a month. Mr. Allan also pronounced me officially persona non grata in their home, though he used different terminology. My main concern was that my folks would get wind of what apparently constituted a big deal to all grownups except Redd Foxx, but parents seemed even more reluctant in those days than they are now to confront other parents with their children's behavior.

Exceptions to this general rule occurred, and I had the misfortune to experience one when I acquired my first paper route. I actually ran two paper routes in Huntington Beach, and both came as the result of someone asking me if I wanted a job. Such good fortune provided the neighborhood kid version of the instant-movie-star legends: nobodies like Lana Turner happened to be in the right place at the right time with the right looks. The parallel is that, like movie stardom, paper routes involved sudden wealth, arcane skills and wide exposure.

My first big break came one Saturday morning as I pulled a wagon down Oasis Drive. The wagon belonged to my little brother Greg; I became involved when Jane sent me to fetch it from the corner where Greg and Trish abandoned it. Five-year-old Trish had pulled two-year-old Greg a whole block, then panicked and ran home, with Greg toddling behind her. As I made my way back, immersed in the tinny sounds from my transistor, a car pulled up and matched my speed. A guy about thirty hunched over the wheel.

"Hey," he shouted out the passenger window, "You live in this neighborhood?"

"Yeah."

"How old are you?

"Ten."

"You want a paper route?"

I hesitated no more than a microsecond. "Yeah!"

I soon learned he worked as district manager for a Huntington Beach local daily and also distributed weekly advertising sheets. His neighborhood paperboy had quit a few minutes ago, and I happened to be the first kid he saw after receiving the resignation. If he didn't find a new boy, he would have to deliver a bale of adverts himself. But here was a kid with a wagon, and thus began my career in journalism.

The wagon worked well for delivering adverts to each house, and

I rode my bike for the early morning regular newspapers, delivering to customers on all the Springdale blocks. Luckily I met few drivers on the road at 6:00 a.m., for I still couldn't reach the pedals from the seat of my fifteen-speed racer. Also, the newspapers in the bags I wore front and back made me even more prone than usual to wild veering and crashes into parked cars.

On Saturdays I enlisted Trish and Greg for the adverts and sent them to the porches while I kept watch on the wagon. I delivered everything myself after Greg and Trish lost interest, and I woke up faithfully every morning for the dailies. Unfortunately, a few days after I received my first month's pay of twelve dollars, a parental edict forced me to give up the route because I almost literally ran into one of the exceptions to the parents-don't-interact-with-other-parents norm.

Riding my racing bike back from a comic book run and undergoing the usual trouble with steering straight and stopping, I started across a busy intersection, right in the path of a car. The driver, a young dad, stopped in time, but followed me when I rode away. I've always wondered why I pedaled directly home when I could have led him on a wild goose chase until he gave up. I suppose the strangeness of a grownup relentlessly following me while he bawled recriminations out the window put me off my game.

Unfortunately, when we arrived Jay was in the front yard, digging a posthole or something. The driver stepped from his car and gave a dramatic account of the incident, concluding with, "He didn't even look! I could have killed him."

I could almost see the wheels turning as Jay considered what to do: should he take the complaint as an insult to his parenting or play the firm parent? He opted for the latter, decreeing on the spot I couldn't ride my bike for a month.

"But I gotta ride the bike for my paper route!"

"Too bad, Charlie. If you can't watch where you're going, you'd better stay off the street."

I could almost see the moneybags flying away. When the district manager showed up the next morning at six a.m. with the papers, he met with yet another abrupt resignation Seeming to take it personally, he slouched to his car, muttering, "Where am I gonna get another kid at this hour?"

The above scene took place in June, a couple of weeks before school let out and the same day Mr. Evans informed our class that we Springdalians wouldn't be coming back to Schroeder for fifth grade. We would instead attend the new Springdale Elementary, under construction around the corner from Delia's house on Casino and scheduled for completion by late August.

All concerned parties were pleased with this news: the Schroederites wouldn't be so ridiculously overcrowded next year and we Springdalians wouldn't have to be gypsy bus riders. Starting over at a new school every few months had been standard operating procedure for me, and this time would be much easier; I could stay in the same house and keep some of the same friends. True, Peter, Linda and Caroline (more on the last two later) would fade from my life, but Benjy Allard, Delia, Harlan the Norwegian, Cajun Gary Hallideaux and other transplanted locals would ascend. I remember reflecting that things on the whole were looking up. I didn't have my paper route anymore, but then again I wouldn't have to get up at five-thirty — and who wanted to work anyhow as summer '63 unfolded and surf music engulfed the world?

CHAPTER FORTY-ONE

~Hawthorne's Favorite Sons ~ Fashion Scabs ~ Hawaiians in Exile
~ Cheerleaders ~ A Platonic Padre ~ The Golden Idyll

Though "Surfin' USA" peaked at number three on the national charts back in April, the song still rated constant play in L.A. through June, especially on KFWB Channel 98, where the Beach Boys reigned as royal locals. Surfing indeed constituted the Only Life that summer, and Huntington Beach occupied Surfin' Universe Central.

Though I had never actually touched a surfboard, I internalized the surfing state of mind through music, fashion, and skateboard. I employed the latter in "sidewalk surfin'," to use prematurely a term scheduled to enter the popular idiom a year later when surf music duo Jan and Dean released a thus-titled single. My skateboard counted among the first mass-produced models; I purchased it secondhand for fifty cents and spray-painted the deck black with a silver stripe down the center—Jay showed me how to use masking tape to get the stripe straight. Most kids rode hunks of two-by-four with shoe-skate wheels nailed on, but all boards, custom or handmade, still rolled on metal skate wheels that stopped dead upon encountering any obstruction larger than coarse-grain sand. Scabbed knees were common fashion accessories around the neighborhood.

Thanks to Jane and neighborhood moms Mrs. Verdiman and Mrs. Kalani, our designated beach shuttle drivers, the local guys got to the beach almost every Saturday and more often during the summer. Depending on whose husband was off work to leave the family car available, one of them would drop off five or six of us young-surfers-who-don't-actually-surf at the Huntington Beach pier, then pick us up several hours later, usually at the downtown post office parking lot, a few blocks from the beach.

The Kalanis, Dan (14), Gary (12), Wayne (10), and their mom, Hawaiians all, migrated to Huntington Beach from Oahu. For some

Native Islanders I've met since, moving to Southern California is the coming-down-in-the-world equivalent Californians might feel if forced to move to North Dakota, but the Kalanis didn't complain. The family previously lived in a one-bedroom apartment in Honolulu where the boys attended a school that, for violence and general chaos, made my Redondo Beach elementary sound like a Montessori. These Hawaiian brothers had never surfed either (Dan: "Boards cost like fifty bucks!" Gary: "Yeah, and the locals kill you if you even look at their break!"), but all three of them excelled at body surfing. Once every couple of weeks I'd be invited to pile in the family station wagon with the Kalanis for Hawaiian feasts and moonlight swims at lifeguard station 17. Those nights shimmer magically in memories of beach fires, warm water, and glowing phosphorescence on the waves. Dan could spot the dark swells coming; when he yelled "Outside!" we'd turn and start swimming until the wave roiled us in the dark surf, from which we'd emerge in moonlit whitewash long seconds later.

I learned much surfing terminology and general urban Hawaiian lore from the Kalani boys. I would follow Dan to the little surf shop across from the pier after our beach sessions. The shop became a revered legend when Huntington Beach transformed from small beach town to mega resort. When I returned almost fifty years later, the streets and pier teemed with visitors from all over the world. I witnessed an MTV special filmed by the pier, then turned down the old main street, shuffling past chic restaurants and bikini boutiques, wondering what happened to the Woolworths, the music store, the family restaurant. Only the old post office remained standing.

But back in 1963, while I occasionally glanced into the back room of the surf shop where the board shapers worked, I saved most of my attention for the decals in the glass case up front, comic surfer cartoons with captions like "Pray for Surf." These art objects were pricy, fifty cents each, but they looked twitchin' after Dan and I dipped them in water and carefully smoothed them onto our bedroom windows facing out. Again following in Dan's footsteps, I bought both Beach Boys albums. Current social critics sometimes cast the Wilson clan as opportunists interloping on native culture, but the Kalanis didn't trouble themselves with such distinctions at the time. Dan owned every record available with anything to do with surfing—Dick Dale, The Challengers, even the schlocky ones like *Surfin Pajama Party*.

As pop culture would have it, I looked more like a surfer (at least by Hollywood surf movie standards) than any of the Kalanis. Recently I had adapted basic surf coiffure, accomplished by parting my blonde hair on the side with no wave in front at all. Instead the hair swept across the forehead, Hitler style, and every few seconds the surfer flicked it back from his eyes with a practiced head toss. I quickly became an expert at this maneuver and faithfully adhered to the surfer uniform code: striped tee-shirts, Saint Christopher medal on a chain, cut-off white jeans. When I looked at the back of the Beach Boys' first album, it seemed to me that I could pass for a younger brother of Dave Marks, the blond, fourteen-year-old Hawthorne neighbor of the Wilson family.

The photos on the back of the albums showed the Boys singing and playing in their bare feet, for of course none of us surfers would be caught dead wearing shoes, a fashion decision bound to add yet more scabs to our sidewalk surfin' contusion collection. Actually, I did wear shoes a couple of times a week when I rode to Schroder to play baseball — but I carried them with me to the games, hanging on the crowded little racing handlebars with my Padres team shirt and transistor radio.

In reverie I'm pedaling to a ballgame right now ... It's a five-mile ride to Schroeder, where the teams meet. My transistor trills "Surfin USA!" through its tinny little speakers as I turn right on Bolsa. Taking a break from peddling, I shift myself backward to the tiny seat (I'm still too short to sit and pedal at the same time), and I imagine jet blasts streaming from the curved racing handlebars as I rocket a thousand feet above the cars.

Five miles down busy roads is way beyond the parental permission range of other Springdale kids, but for the past year or so, my folks and I have operated on a "Don't ask, don't tell" footing with my wanderings. After a short hiatus when I was grounded for riding in front of the car, the system unofficially resumed. Jay and Jane gave me the two dollars for my Padres team tee-shirt, so they know I am getting over to my remote school somehow, but as long as I (a) don't trouble them for a ride and (b) get back safe by dinner time, they don't inquire as to the particulars, and they wouldn't think of coming to a game, thank goodness. We were all too cool for that sort of all-around embarrassment.

Another right turn and I'm in the Ivy League street names tract.

Peter, my only friend in this neighborhood, skipped the second round of summer league games to go on vacation with his parents, but I persist. I'm not the captain of the Padres—a fifth-grader who looks like Larry Mondello on *Leave it to Beaver* has that honor—but I hit consistently and am the best pitcher. The coach, a junior college student earning summer credit for his efforts, switched me from the outfield because I had no glove of my own and pitchers don't have to catch much. Only about half the guys actually own gloves, for good ones cost fifteen or twenty dollars. Outfielders who do own gloves customarily leave them in the field when they come in to bat, but I've yet to find a left-handed glove owner on any of the teams. By necessity I and the one other southpaw in the league have learned to catch with a right-hander's glove on our left hand, after which we have to grab the ball from the glove pocket with our right hand, pull off the glove while continuing to hold the ball, and switch the ball to our left hand before throwing it. Unfortunately, this complex routine doesn't work so well in double plays and other clutch situations where every second counts.

Our games don't usually attract many spectators, but today I have my own cheering section: Carol and Linda, two Schroeder neighborhood girls and my former classmates in Mr. Evans's room. They have wandered over to the field from the weekly ten-cent movie in the cafeteria-turned-rec-room. The film is usually a grainy print of *A Christmas Carol, Old Yeller* or some other ancient family fare, but the admission price is right and the PTA sells bags of popcorn for a nickel.

Batted home by a teammate, I'm rounding third in the bottom of the ninth, about to score the winning run, and right there along the third base line are Linda and Carol doing a parody of cheerleading, shaking imaginary pom-poms and yelling "Five, ten, fourteen, eight! Who do we appreciate! Ricky! Ricky! Yaaaaaaay, Ricky!" Their smiles show they are being friendly rather than mocking, which seems extra nice coming from Schroeder locals.

After the hand shaking ceremony with the other team, I wander over to chat. The conversation proceeds awkwardly at first, but when I do an imitation of Mr. Evans's scowl and crouched-over walk, the ice is broken. Awash in nostalgia, we recall those younger days of a month ago when we were fourth graders. They ask about a couple of Springdalians; then Carol says, "Have you seen Delia? She's so stuck up!"

Linda concurs. "Delia thinks she's sooo sophisticated. You don't still like her, do you, Ricky?"

I shrug as if to say, "I never even noticed her in the first place; why would I like her now?" But the mere mention of Delia's name sends a pang through me. I haven't set eyes on the object of my tragic affection in over a month, though I've contrived to ride my bike past her house almost daily. She must be attending advanced charm school or something. In an odd, poignant nineteenth-century novel sort of way, I remain nobly (though silently) loyal to Delia, even as I chat with these two friendly girls. Then Linda makes a bold move, considering the unwritten rule that boys and girls don't hang around together.

"Want to come over to my garage? We can play Clue."

Carol adds, "It's better with more people."

Both girls live on Yale Circle, a block from the school. I've mentioned before how the Schroederites, with their shake roofs, fireplaces, and block walls, viewed with some condescension us Springdalian latecomers who dwell on streets named after Las Vegas casinos. But I feel no snobbishness from Linda and Carol; on the contrary, they seem to genuinely like me. At first I wonder at their interest, but then I modestly deduce that to them I am an exotic of sorts: a widely-read wanderer who's lived in three states, a baseball star, and an accomplished surfer—which again only requires knowing more than most kids about surf music and owning a few surf decals.

As we stroll to Linda's garage I am more than happy to play the role of the devil-may-care adventurer, unfettered by parental restrictions. The baseball league games are twice or three times a week, and Linda and Carol meet me at all games thereafter. My teammates tease me a bit about my "girlfriends," but I don't let it bother me; these boys are business associates, not friends. The college-age coach says, "Man, you're a stud—two chicks at a time!" But there are no romantic feelings, jealousies, or flirting between Linda, Carol, and me. I can't decide which of the two I like best, and it doesn't seem important. I feel perfectly comfortable in their company; they hardly giggle at all and rarely give each other private girl-looks.

Linda is fair-skinned, with light brown hair and an open smile, Carol, a little more filled out, has reddish, curly hair and freckles. The worldlier of the two, she chews Dentyne gum and says she has a boyfriend in North Carolina. "His big brother surfs," she reports, "but the waves aren't as good out there."

Linda's mom provides snacks, but I never meet the woman and never set foot inside either of the girls' houses—Linda always brings the cookies, peanut butter sandwiches, and Kool-Aid out to the garage. We invariably play Clue, with its adult-like scenario, sophisticated characters, and a murder to solve. I begin biking to the Schroeder tract even on days when no ball game is scheduled, and the three of us spend many a sunny afternoon in the shade of the garage, chatting freely as we move our pieces around the board and try to guess the murderer.

In contrast to the Candyland sessions with the little girl back in Glendale, the game is secondary for sophisticates Linda, Carol, and me. The conversation never flags between moves, and we appreciate one another's humor. The radio regularly plays Jan and Dean's "Surf City" and "My Boyfriend's Back" by the Angels, and "Surfin' USA" spins every fifteen minutes or so. For the hourly newscasts the DJ puts on a more solemn voice and drones about a giant civil rights march on Washington, a nuclear test ban treaty, or a monk setting himself on fire in Vietnam. As we wait patiently for the songs to resume, I expound on music and Carol and Linda match me in goofy repartee about TV shows.

Free from peer pressure and the tyranny of the school crush, these midsummer days blossom into a memorable idyll, the rare kind possible only in the twilight of childhood, before the wild aurora of adolescence blazes out any chance of genuine friendliness between the sexes. Eventually I drop all my worldly-wise pretension and they stop giggling altogether. Ours is a sort of platonic shipboard romance with not one disagreement, misunderstanding, or awkward moment.

Were we able to continue in school together come fall, either Carol or Linda could become a non-tragic official girlfriend, the perfect antidote to Delia. But Carol's family plans to move back to North Carolina in August, and, since the Springdalians are supposedly getting our own campus, I know I won't see Linda much once school takes up.

But none of those facts yet exist — the time is now and we are here in the garage on Yale Street in perfect psychic tune, quaffing perfectly sweetened Kool Aid and munching perfect peanut butter sandwiches while the Beach Boys serenade us in the sweet growing-pain-less bliss of endless summer 1964 ...

CHAPTER FORTY-TWO

~ Bliss: Easy Come, Easy Go ~ Failed Enterprise ~ Learning the Route
~ Chop Shop ~ Stolen Security

The idyll with Linda and Carol ended toward the close of August, in the weeks leading up to Martin Luther King's "I Have A Dream" speech in Washington. I had achieved my own dream of acquiring my second paper route, this time an afternoon delivery (plus Saturday mornings but no Sundays) with the Huntington Beach *Daily Pilot*. Caught up in this new venture, I left off riding over to the girls' neighborhood for what I vaguely supposed would be only a few days. I didn't realize at the time that I would lose friends forever; such loss only happened previously when the family moved. After a couple of busy weeks learning the paper route, school took up again and further distracted me. With one thing and another, I never saw Linda or Carol (or good old Peter) again.

The reason I needed the paper route boiled down to my role as a junior consumer, me doing my part to keep the economy strong. Comic books, Elvis records from K-Mart, surf decals and the like all cost money, and my allowance had stalled at seventy-five cents for the past couple of years. Clearly I must increase my income—but how? The fly-killing bonanza had passed, and bottle collecting was unreliable. Despite my general distaste for lawn maintenance, I determined at midsummer to start a gardening business. Borrowing the family machine one weekday in late July between trips to Schroeder and the beach, I had mowed four lawns on the block at fifty cents each, edging and sweeping not included. My customers were housewives with no children old enough to work or whose husbands relegated lawn maintenance to the general category of women's duties.

Earning two whole dollars in one afternoon from these oppressed ladies inspired a business expansion: the next Saturday I teamed with next-door neighbor Carl Verdiman and his high-school-age uncle visiting from Garden Grove. Like Jay's brother Barry, this young uncle seemed on the slow side developmentally, and his willingness to join the venture proved it. Carl's other contribution to the business was more substantial: the Verdimans' King O' Lawn gas-powered edger. Carl's dad Jim, who worked at the King O' Lawn store in Garden Grove, had recently acquired an unprecedented second edger by buying a trade-in and refurbishing it in his spare time.

Not that Jim had much spare time. The King O' Lawn store provided his second job, a noon-to-four, part-time shift after working 1 a.m. to 9:30 a.m. as a street sweeper in Garden Grove. Pop sociologists nowadays report that the economy has slipped backwards somehow from the good old days of the fifties and sixties when the father's income sufficed to support a family. But many dads in working-class families held two jobs while their wives stayed home to run the household. Even white-collar men sought second paychecks: all through the sixties I knew teachers who moonlighted as liquor store clerks in the evenings and as shoe salesmen or construction workers in the summer. Jay managed to avoid a second job by flogging Blue Chip Stamps and arranging out-the-back-door acquisitions. Plus, retail clerks in those days earned double-time for Sunday and triple-time for some holidays, and Jay knew how to pull the overtime strings. In any case, none of us kids saw our fathers often, a convenient turn of events when we made first attempts to grow our hair over our ears or commandeer the family lawn equipment for commercial purposes.

The Verdiman edger became a key item in our business plan, for in the Springdale tract most people didn't pursue lawn maintenance beyond weekly mowing. Those who did edge their yards used a hand tool for the purpose, basically a broom handle with a spiked wheel on the end. Edging this way was a tedious process with a ragged result. Considering the general distaste for the hand edger, Carl, his uncle, and I envisioned great riches at a dollar per house for a professional lawn makeover. One of us would mow, one would edge, and one sweep. The first one done would run ahead to line up the next customer while the other two collected the dollars and transported the equipment to the subsequent worksite.

I'm not sure why this model of initiative and efficiency didn't pay off. Perhaps the visual of one full-blood Indian (the uncle) one half-breed Indian with a butch haircut (Carl) and a white kid with a striped shirt and blonde Hitler hairdo seemed too exotic for the neighborhood. It could also have been fear of liability—people seemed less litigious then, but the look of our crew could certainly have engendered caution in prudent homeowners. For one thing, in keeping with general summer custom I wore no shoes. Also, Carl (age nine but small for his age) appeared to be about seven and he insisted on pushing the edger, an activity which, with no guards for the belt, exhaust, or blade, constituted a serious injury waiting to happen. But I suspect the main impediment to riches was simply that most housewives felt trepidation at parting with a whole dollar without consulting their husbands.

Whatever the cause of our business failure, we walked around all afternoon with no customers and finally disbanded the partnership, not altogether amicably. Carl's cousin insinuated that, in order to inveigle them into a hopeless venture, I'd fabricated the story of mowing four lawns the last time I'd gone out.

"You lie, man. You didn't mow no four lawns!"

"Did too! Didn't I, Carl?"

"I dunno. I didn't see you."

So that's how it was. I had assumed Carl and I were next-door-neighbor homeboys, but apparently I had fallen in with clannish Indians. Without another word I turned my mower toward home.

That burst of ill-conceived entrepreneurial energy took place just before the end of baseball season and the Clue marathons. Then the August doldrums began to creep in, the feeling of waiting offstage for the new school year to begin. As fifth-grade and its regimentation approached, the summer sun had tanned me to the peeled nose stage and my barefooted-all-summer calluses would withstand anything short of a straight shot from a roofing tack. But beach trips and long bike rides to Schroeder became less frequent; I wallowed in my last days of freedom from time constraint, rising from bed later, eating a sugar cereal or even ice-cream brunch, sometimes listening to the radio all morning.

I also delved deeper into escapist reading. Our TV had broken, and rather than pay ten or fifteen dollars to fix it, by-then chess aficionados Jay and Jane let it sit. One day while driving past the downtown public library, they decided to go in. Jay remembered Tarzan books from his youth and checked out a few. Soon Jane and I joined him as enthusiastic fans of the ape man's jungle adventures.

Fifteen of the 25 novels in the series had the same plot: Tarzan happens upon a lost civilization, usually somewhere in Africa. Myriad exotics populate these outposts, including lost tribes of Romans, epileptic first-century Christians, descendants of ape and homosapien unions, Mayans still practicing human sacrifice, twelve-inch tall warriors, etc. Within a few days, Master linguist Tarzan learns their language and becomes embroiled in a political struggle between good and evil factions. But each variation on this plot turned out to be so exciting that I didn't mind the general repetition at all.

After one reading debauch in late August, I finally left the house at 3 p.m. At 3:30 I had gotten no farther than the chair-high post fence in front of our lawn. There I sat, a picture of youthful torpor, eating a peach and daydreaming about *Tarzan and the Jewels of Opar.* In that adventure Tarzan had won (in addition to the jewels) the admiration of magnificent naked High Priestess La, who declared herself his for the taking. The ape man resolutely remained loyal to his wife Jane, but the more he tried to keep his distance from La, the more she seethed with lust for him.

Unfortunately, Tarzan's playing-hard-to-get method of attraction didn't work so well for me. I hadn't seen Delia all summer, and she didn't seem to be plotting to kidnap me or to utilize any of Priestess La's other methods of getting the ape man's attention.

My reverie involving enhanced versions of those other methods was interrupted by Mike, a twelve-year-old paperboy for the *Huntington Beach Daily Pilot,* who peddled onto the sidewalk. After some opening remarks, he made it known that an exciting business opportunity would soon come available.

"I'm startin' eighth [grade] and goin' out for football," he said. "I gotta split my route so I'll have time to do it after practice. Last summer, I had like 25 customers; now it's over fifty. The new guy gets 25 on the south side."

Sensing a break in my fortunes, I ventured: "I used to deliver the *Telegram* and ad papers."

As Mike explained, the *Telegram* boys were merely hired hands. But the *Pilot* team member ran his own business, essentially managing a franchise. He bought product from the company wholesale and sold the papers at a near-retail monthly rate. Out of the profit, the operator bought his own rubber bands, plastic rain wraps, and canvas paper carrier bags. But each new customer meant more money and more opportunity for tips.

"So, how much you get a month?" I asked with an air of intense casualness.

"After all the bills and shit, around thirty bucks. Plus ten bucks or so in tips at Christmas."

Half of such a fortune would provide something like a 1000% rise in income. Standing up from my slouching seat on the fence, I stood before Mike and professed a fervent interest in the job.

"Well, I'll take it, I guess."

He gave me a searching look. "How old are you?"

"Almost eleven." (I had only eight months to go.)

"They like guys to be twelve already."

"I never missed a day on my other route. Had to quit when the boss moved to Africa." Excited by the opportunity, I blurted whatever came into my head. "He was a arkaologist or something."

Eventually, Mike allowed himself be talked into introducing me to Mr. Simmons, his district manager. Simmons, a lean, taciturn Kansas immigrant, had scratched a living with the *Pilot* for the past five years. He seemed kindly enough but stated frankly his preference for boys twelve or older. But when Mike announced that his last delivery had to be Saturday three days hence, Mr. Simmons said, "All right, we'll try you out if your parents are okay with guaranteeing your bill."

For all my confidence and resolution, I wondered how the parental permission requirement would fly. But over dinner that evening Jay and Jane gave their blessings. I suspect now that Jay regretted his snap decision to take away my previous route.

The immediate task was to find a serviceable vehicle for the job. I still had the Royce Union fifteen-speed racer, but though I had grown an inch or so during the vacation months, I still had difficulty sitting on the seat while peddling. More importantly, the bike had no luggage rack on which to hang the dual cloth bags for the papers, and the racing handlebars were too small to put the bags up there. I had been unaware of paperboy cultural proscriptions when I had the *Press Telegram* route, but I now knew that sophisticated kids considered hanging the bags over one's head (as the unit was designed to be carried) as ridiculously old-fashioned as wearing a bow tie. I've since read accounts of lads in the Midwest who apparently even *walked* their paper routes wearing the bags, but no West Coast paper boy in the 1960s would have thus shamed himself.

Mike assured me he could find a decent bike for no more than five dollars, so I borrowed the sum from Jane on the strength of future income. After shadowing Mike on his last day on the south side route, he rode me tandem on his luggage rack to see his friend Eddie. I'm uncertain whether I recall the lad's name accurately or if I remember it as Eddie because he resembled Eddie Haskell, the bad kid on the *Leave It To Beaver* show. This real-life Eddie was fourteen or so and more sinister than the one on TV. He lived in the outskirts of Westminster, on a street of pre-tract houses with large, unkempt yards, a neighborhood infamous for juvenile delinquents who packed BB guns. They not only blasted each other with these weapons, but purportedly took pot shots at strangers.

Eddie exuded a sense of danger, but with Mike as my sponsor he treated me with friendly condescension as he led the way to a sort of chop shop he ran in his back yard. As Mike had explained earlier, sometimes Eddie bought broken bikes cheap, fixed them, and sold them at good profit. But mostly he stole bikes, dismantled them, and piled the parts in the weedy expanse behind the detached garage.

Mike explained my requirements, and Eddie retrieved a frame, chain and wheels from the pile. He pointed to a tangle of handlebars and seats. "Take yer pick!"

I chose a not-too-rusty set of bars and an ancient but comfortable Schwinn seat. While Eddie expertly assembled the parts, I listened to him fill Mike in on the latest development in the neighborhood BB gun wars. Someone had supposedly been shot in the eye during last night's battle with the guys on the next block.

"The punk might need some kinda operation."

Mike looked impressed. "No shit? Did *you* shoot him?"

Eddie rolled his eyes in a parody of innocence. "Not me. I was at the show at the time, and I can prove it."

The assembled bike wouldn't win any beauty contests, but it had both a luggage rack and handlebars capable of holding a delivery bag. Eddie's asking price was four dollars, but Mike bargained on my behalf.

"Give it to him for two bucks—he's gotta buy rubber bands and shit."

"Okay, Ricky Nelson. For you, two-fifty."

I felt a flush of gratitude to Mike. While true that I had to purchase a bag, rubber bands, and other tools of the trade, I wouldn't have to pay immediately; the cost would be added to my first bill. Thus

I could ride to the bowling alley on my new bike and spend the other $2.50 from the loan. I proceeded to do just that and passed the afternoon on the lanes and pinball machines, contemplating my future riches.

A few Saturdays later at the same bowling alley, I made one more related purchase from Eddie. I had completed my first route collection and was flush with cash. Eddie, on the other hand, had blown all his money on pinball, and now he burned with the compulsive gambler's urge for further play. Intuiting my well-funded state, he proposed a security system for my work vehicle, which I now rode exclusively while the fifteen-speed gathered cobwebs in the garage.

"You get your bike kiped, how you gonna do your paper route?" Eddie asked rhetorically. "Lotsa thieves in this town."

He then assured me that for thirty cents (the price of three games of pinball and a candy bar) he could supply me a used combination bike lock guaranteed to insure my peace of mind. "The combo lock is what you want. No keys to lose, no hassles."

As a man of growing wealth, security had become a concern. "Yeah, okay. Where's the lock? We gotta go back to your yard?"

"Nah." Eddie preceded me to the bike rack out front. After a quick scan of the area, he knelt and began manipulating a combination lock on one of the bikes. The mechanism employed rotating disks, so he proceeded to feel his way, lining up the numbers by gentle pulls and twists. A kid about my age walked by and gave Eddie a curious look. Eddie felt the gaze and turned slowly, showing a coldly murderous expression. The kid edged away. In less than a minute the lock succumbed. "The combo is 9643. That'll be thirty cents," Eddie grinned, hanging the chain over my shoulder.

I had no great qualms about buying the stolen merchandise, but along with the bargain price came trepidation at leaving my bike unattended anywhere again, even when locked. But despite such unease, things were definitely looking up that September. With fifth grade underway, I could gaze upon Delia regularly again. And she could gaze upon me with more interest—not only as a surfer, gambler, musicologist, and guy who gets around, but also a business owner and man of means.

CHAPTER FORTY-THREE

"Ricky? You in here?"

"Yeah. What's up, Johnny?"

"The president's been kilt or somethin'. It's on TV."

Like almost everyone else between eight and eighty at that time, I remember the moment on Friday, November 22, 1963, when I heard about the Kennedy assassination. The news found me in the boys' bathroom at Gill Elementary School. The contractors had failed to complete our Springdale campus on schedule, so we gypsies were bussed en masse to Gill, an even more distant and upscale facility. I was in the bathroom because our teacher Mrs. Taylor, no mindless disciplinarian, believed in trusting her students to use the facilities without passes or special permission. Taking full advantage of her enlightened attitude, I usually finessed the long stretch between the 9:30 recess and noon lunch with at least one leisurely hair-combing break.

I found it necessary to keep up appearances because between September and November I established myself at Gill School as what is now known in urban circles as a "playa"; i.e., one who is competitive and gregarious, who dresses fashionably and assumes a leadership role. Big kid Johnny looked up to me the way big palookas used to look up to little Edward G. Robinson in the gangster movies. When the principal announced the tragedy, Johnny figured I'd want to be in on the action, and he knew where to find me.

"Kennedy and some other guys got shot," Johnny continued. "Miz Taylor is crying."

The report seemed unreal, somehow — the president assassinated, like Lincoln? Such profound events only happened in history books, and besides, even in fifth grade, you can't believe everything you hear. "Let's go check it out," I said casually, and led the way back to the classroom.

By the time we arrived, the somber TV newsmen outside the Dallas hospital were speculating that the president might not survive. Schoolwork forgotten, we watched unfolding events on the little TV, heretofore used exclusively for Spanish language lessons once a week. Before this day, we didn't actually know much about John F. Kennedy. Comedians like Vaughn Meader and others did impersonations of the Kennedy brothers, usually exaggerating their Massachusetts accents and making them say things like, "I do not sound like Bugs Bunny! Bugs Bunny sounds like me!" But the photo montages gave us a quick education on the young, heroic P.T. boat veteran, the author of *Profiles in Courage*, the dynamic leader of the Free World.

Some of the girls followed Mrs. Taylor's lead in crying, but Delia seemed as cool and collected as ever. She had conversed more with me lately, but now wouldn't meet my gaze. The TV kept showing the same clips, and the whole scene felt constricting and uncomfortable. Restlessness overcame me, so unnoticed by Mrs. Taylor, I took another stroll toward the bathroom.

On impulse I kept going past the "boys" sign, walking purposefully so no one would stop me. I glanced into several classrooms, each with its TV on. Many girls and more than one teacher cried openly; I found the one exception in the other fifth grade class made up of Gill neighborhood locals. Their teacher used to insult his elite charges by comparing them to the "goofuses" in Mrs. Taylor's class. They had also hung a sign across the front of the room: "THIS IS THE BEST CLASS IN GILL SCHOOL." The students sat dry-eyed, hands folded on desks, watching the news coverage. The teacher stood attention-straight by the door, arms akimbo. He glanced at me as I passed, but he didn't seem quite focused and said nothing officious.

I returned to my classroom in time to hear the principal over the intercom announcing school would be closing for the remainder of the day. Busses came right after lunch to take us home, and when I arrived, even Jane looked troubled. She said later that she felt guilty because, after voting for Kennedy in 1960, she came to dislike him, especially in the last year. Many other citizens felt discontent with Camelot. The economy had taken a bad turn. Both liberals and conservatives were dissatisfied with JFK's approach to civil rights, and his missteps in the Bay of Pigs incident angered people from all sectors. Most commentators gave him scant chance of winning a second term.

Nowadays most political historians would seem to have forgotten those pre-assassination attitudes toward JFK, and certainly no one on or off TV spoke of them that afternoon. Networks and local channels preempted regular programming, and every reporter in the country seemed to be milling about in Dallas. By mid-afternoon the media officially pronounced President Kennedy dead. Walter Cronkite shed tears on camera as he spoke the words.

I watched the coverage with Jane for over an hour, then exited to fold my papers. The headline of the afternoon *Daily Pilot* read KENNEDY DEAD—SHOT IN TEXAS. As a Lincoln buff, I immediately saw some similarities: the lone gunman and his incredibly good luck, plus the lax security seen only in hindsight by the officials. Later when the urban legend mills started grinding, the complete list of Kennedy/Lincoln coincidences was striking. A half-century later, they still seem eerie:

Lincoln[1]	Kennedy
Lincoln elected to Congress in 1846.	Kennedy elected to Congress in 1946.
Elected President in 1860.	Elected President in 1960.
Wife lost a child while living in the White House	Wife lost a child while living in the White House.
Lincoln shot in the back of the head in the presence of his wife.	Kennedy shot in the back of the head in the presence of his wife.
Lincoln shot in the Ford Theatre.	Kennedy shot in a Lincoln, made by Ford.
Shot on a Friday.	Shot on a Friday.
Assassin, John Wilkes Booth known by three names composed of fifteen letters.	Assassin Lee Harvey Oswald known by three names composed of fifteen letters.
Booth shot Lincoln in a theater and fled to a warehouse.	Oswald shot Kennedy from a warehouse and fled to a theater.
Booth killed before being brought to trial.	Oswald killed before being brought to trial.
Lincoln's successor Andrew Johnson, born in 1808.	Kennedy's successor Lyndon Johnson, born in 1908.

[1]Chart from www.school-for-champions.com/history/lincolnjfk.htm. All the above are actually true; Kennedy even employed a secretary named Lincoln, though Lincoln had no secretary named Kennedy, as was widely repeated along with the rest of the amazing assassination tie-ins.

Gill School segregated Springdale students from the locals; our fourth-, fifth-, and sixth-graders occupied three classrooms of an outer building. In order to fit us in, class sizes throughout the school increased, a policy that Gill teachers and parents found annoying. Springdale parents, teachers, and kids also complained about the new developments, but I took it all calmly, being used to a new school at least every fall. Besides, the moment I stepped off the bus on the first day of classes, I began my ascent as a man of note in academic, social, pugilistic, and artistic endeavors.

The reputation of being ruffians and worse preceded the Springdale contingent. Our girls hated the unfeminine notoriety, but we boys enjoyed the instant elevation on the tough guy scale. Rumors intimidated students from the BEST CLASS IN GILL SCHOOL in advance, providing us a psychological advantage in disputes. I could still outbox almost anyone my size, and a few decisive wins during the first few days of school cemented my reputation as a dude not to be messed with.

And dude I most assuredly was. My white pants were fashionably tight, and I sported turtleneck dickies under my striped tee-shirts or dress shirts. My feet grew enough over the summer to wheedle Jane into buying me a pair of tapered-to-a-square-toe Italian shoes, and they almost fit me. My return-to-school surf coiffure, a wild amalgam of Elvis and the Beach Boys, waved and swooped at the same time. Naturally my peers accepted me as the top surfer in school. I had yet to surf, but who needed to ride a board when I knew all the songs, wore the clothes, and brought my single of "Surfer Joe" by the Surfaris (with "Wipeout" on the flip side) to class? Mrs. Taylor, who would soon buy one of the new Ford Mustangs and thus prove herself sympathetic to contemporary culture, let me play the record after lunch and I lip-synched it like the teenagers did on the *Lloyd Thaxton Hop* — to her amusement and the class's amazement.

Besides my efforts as a tough guy, surfer, and fashion plate, I became a commercial artist as well. During lazy afternoons between Tarzan books, I learned to copy the cartoon surfer guy trademark featured on the Murphy Surfboards decal. This iconic character had a perfect slouch and a slouchy surfboard to match, baggy trunks, and a lobster attached to his leg. At school I drew this character as incessantly as I'd drawn the house-through-the-seasons in first grade, and my copyright infringement so impressed my classmates that I started a small business, charging a dime to draw "Murphy" on notebooks.

Furthermore, I found myself in the right place at the right time on the academic front. The Gill School principal had a Master's degree in reading pedagogy and some advanced ideas on the subject. She decreed that all fourth to sixth grade students be skill-tested and assigned to level-appropriate reading classes. This meant we would actually walk between rooms for one period, like the big kids did in high school. I became one of two Springdale fifth-graders sent to the top group, and judging from the reaction of teachers and parents, this assignment rated as the local equivalent of a Rhodes scholarship. When I brought home the mimeographed explanation of the project, even Jay seemed impressed.

But even more importantly, the principal was impressed. She made a royal visit to the special class to predict our success in higher education and invited the advanced readers to visit her office in groups of five for tea and personal congratulations. Unfortunately I returned to her office a short time later, accused of alcohol abuse and disorderly conduct.

My descent from respectability began one October morning at the bus stop in front of Scotty's house. The bus ran late, and we all wondered if it had broken down again—we'd waited for over an hour one day the week before. Some of the boys started a game of tag, accidentally bumping the girls as often as possible. I stepped back with Scotty onto his lawn while he finished a joke in progress. Scotty belonged to the lowest reading group and seemed to be in perpetual trouble, but our bond of humor transcended any academic, social, or fashion gap between us.

"You wanna see my pet rats?" he offered. "I ain't spozed to bring anyone in, but my old lady don't get up till noon anyhow."

Rather than attempting more cool witticisms that Delia would only pretend to ignore, I followed him in the house. The odor of cigarettes and stale booze met us at the door. Kitchen chairs, dining table, counters, coffee tables—every flat surface in both areas was littered with empty or half-empty bottles and overflowing ashtrays. We passed through to Scotty's room and looked at the rats, eight of them huddled in a cage. He said they drank warm beer; to prove it, he poured some from the dregs of a can into a saucer and placed the saucer in the cage. Sure enough, the largest two of the group rushed forward eagerly.

On the way outside, I saw a half-filled bottle of Ripple wine on the counter. On impulse, or perhaps inspired by the rats, I picked it up and smelled it. Scotty's eyes widened as he glanced toward the hallway. He then followed nervously as I took the wine out to show the kids.

Approaching Delia and the other girls, I staggered in the manner of TV inebriates and brought the bottle to my lips. Ripple tasted like warm soda pop with isopropyl alcohol added, and I wondered how any grown-up could actually drink the stuff—but I swallowed a small amount and rubbed my stomach to pantomime how much I liked it.

"Y' wanna lil' drink, lay-deeze?" I said in my best Otis (town drunk from the Andy Griffith show) homage. Scotty also took a small sip and matched my impersonation with an elaborate stagger of his own. The girls recoiled in horror, and none of the other boys were brave or foolish enough to follow suit. Feeling like a daredevil supreme, I took another small sip for authenticity while pretending to gulp from the bottle.

A few minutes later the bus rumbled around the corner. Scotty tossed the bottle in the overgrown bushes on the side of the house and we sedately climbed aboard. The whole act amounted to one more bootless demonstration to Delia of how fearless and cool I could be but really wasn't, and I forgot it by the time we arrived at school.

Forty-five minutes later a monitor delivered a message to Mrs. Taylor: I must report to the Principal's office immediately. Scotty had gotten a summons a half-hour before, but since he went to the principal's nearly every day, I didn't connect the dots.

As I approached headquarters at an unhurried pace, I saw Scotty coming out.

"I got suspended," he said hoarsely. "Two weeks. The girls finked on us. My old lady's comin' to pick me up." He sighed. "I'm dead."

I shook my head in disbelief. How could the girls—how could Delia!—be so perfidious? If I were suspended, I'd have to give up my paper route and I'd probably be grounded for who knew how long—this kind of trouble was unprecedented.

I had to think. Looking at Scotty's uncombed hair, ragged jeans, and miss-buttoned shirt, a plan occurred to me and I retraced my steps to the boys' bathroom. Drawing my pocket comb, I flattened my hair into a more subdued wave. I stuffed my turtleneck dickie in my back pocket, buttoned my top shirt button, took a deep breath, and marched to the principal's domain. For the first time in my life,

I wished I'd brought my glasses with me. The secretary waved me into her office, and the old administrator, expressing quiet dignity and firmness, said, "Do you know why you are here, Richard?"

I nodded, matching her tone with all the body language of chagrined honesty. She said that Scotty coming to such a pass did not surprise her; he had been in no end of trouble before. "But you, Richard—you're in our honors reading class, and you seem such a clean-cut young man."

I proceeded with a bravura performance, dodging and dancing around the truth. I didn't exactly put the blame on Scotty, but rather allowed my clean-cut sincerity to imply that he initiated the incident. As I reasoned to myself, my statement neither tattled nor accused; but in any case Scotty had already been suspended, so I couldn't hurt him by protecting myself.

"No Ma'am, I've never been in ANY trouble before at school, ever!" I lied, hoping Her Principalship didn't have any of my Redondo records on file.

I must have been convincing, for she let me go with a mild scolding, not so much for drinking, but for associating with questionable playmates. No call to the parents, no staying after school—and I exited the office just in time for recess. Classmates gathered round to hear of my miraculous escape. It would seem my good fortune could rise no higher, but they soon took yet another upward leap. I, the premier surfer of the fifth grade, would presently have an opportunity to actually go surfing.

CHAPTER FORTY-FOUR

~ Circumstantial Evidence ~ Actually Surfing ~ Down a Peg
~ Crafty Norwegians ~ Monday Off?

Employing circumstantial evidence, a case could be made for the proposition "There is no justice in the Universe." Exhibits might include the following: on a lovely Autumn Saturday, poor Scotty probably remained confined and/or sore from corporal punishment; meanwhile I, the one who actually initiated the drinking that incriminated him, journeyed to the beach and actually *surfed*—on a real surfboard in the Pacific Ocean.

I experienced this memorable morning with Clifford, one of the class tough guys, who, like Johnny, was a year older than the rest of us due to repeating a grade. Before my interrogation by the principal, Cliff disapproved of my flashy clothes and good grades. But then he heard that I'd gotten drunk at the bus stop and snarled at the principal, "You ain't swattin' me! You gotta have my parents' permission!" (The tale grew more exciting as it spread through the school.) The snarling part so impressed Cliff that he invited me on a beach trip with his big brother and the brother's high school friend.

On Saturday the three of them picked me up at seven a.m., the hour when real surfers head for the waves. The sun shone brightly but I shivered a little in my tee-shirt and cutoffs as we drove south in an old Ford station wagon, with air blasting in through a few missing windows and its glasspack mufflers roaring sweetly.

At the time, much of the Orange County coast remained undeveloped, but housing marketers and city zoning would soon move in. Meanwhile, most of the shoreline remained open, unpatrolled, and lifeguard-free. Somewhere in Seal Beach, Cliff's brother parked behind a few other decrepit cars on a sandy shoulder overlooking the ocean. The big guys unloaded their boards and joined several surfers already in the water.

Cliff and I body-surfed for a while, then built a sand castle near the tide line while we kept an eye on the waves. In those days surfers seemed to be more into the fun tricks of the sport—hanging five, walking the nose, switching boards in mid-wave—all the goofiness disdained by dead-serious shortboard shredders in the new millennium. I appreciated the show, but it never crossed my mind I could actually participate in this big kid activity—not even Dan Kalani, all of fourteen years old, had actually ridden a wave.

But when Cliff's brother and friend left the water, Cliff casually asked if we could use their boards. To my surprise and delight, they consented. As if in a dream I followed my new pal's lead in half carrying, half dragging my board to the water. And wonder of wonders, within a few minutes I actually stood up on a shore breaker wave! Of course it helped that I was still less than five feet tall, which made the 1963 longboard the relative size of an Indian war canoe. But in any case I felt the sublime sensation of the wave propelling the board. Completely forgetting my coolest-guy-in-the-fifth-grade dignity, I exulted, "Cliff! Look! I'm SURFIN'!" right before the fin dug into the sand in six inches of water. I didn't ride a wave again for many years, but I didn't need to—I had climbed Everest, landed on the moon, found the fabled Jewels of Opar!

With confidence buoyed by supreme good fortune, I determined to tie up a loose end in my social life. I made my move the next Monday at school when, at the first recess, I approached my objective.

"Hi, Dee."

"Oh. Hi, Ricky."

"You want to go steady with me?"

"Go … steady?" Delia seemed stunned, and I felt gratified to see her less-than-poised for once.

I'd learned of "Going steady," a junior high and high school phenomenon, from eleventh-grader Cindy next door. Of course all the girls from fourth grade on knew all about it, but before my audacious proposal, no one in the elementary school, not even the sixth-graders, had thus far experienced the ultimate charm school validation of publicly declaring for a boyfriend or girlfriend.

"Yeah," I said as casually as I could. "Here, I bought this for you." I proffered a yellow and white genuine sterling silver Saint Christopher medal acquired at the Westminster hobby store. "Christophers" had somehow become the surfer totem of the era, and high-schoolers wore them to signify a betrothal, just as 1950s teens had worn class rings on chains around their necks.

Dazzled by the opportunity to look like a high school girl, Delia consented to the union with a, for her, relatively enthusiastic nod. "Fasten it for me?" she turned and held her hair above her delicate neck. As I clipped the little O-rings together, I could feel her closeness, smell her hairspray. The world seemed suffused with light; my exultation knew no earthly bounds.

In addition to pointing out the lack of justice in the world, circumstantial evidence also suggests that it is difficult to maintain perfect happiness in this mortal coil. I declined Cliff's invitation to another surf trip the next Saturday; I thought Delia and I might lounge around her room and listen to some records, or if her sister were too bothersome, take a walk together. But no one answered my knock at her door—an extremely odd occurrence for a Saturday at Springdale, when property owners usually busied themselves with home improvement. From the state of supreme serenity and confidence I'd felt walking over to Casino Street, I found myself descending rapidly into morbid reflection, the telltale mood-swing of love. What if her family skipped town without warning, like mine always did? What if they were in there hiding and laughing at me? My confidence fled before a flood of suppositions and premonitions. I returned home to brood, choosing the records from my collection with lyrics most concerned with romantic troubles, misunderstandings, and betrayals.

My worst fears seemed borne out when Delia didn't show up at the bus stop on Monday morning. Now I felt certain that her family had skipped town.

But here she stood outside of our Gill classroom, glancing around nervously. I approached with the most confident smile I could muster. "I didn't see you on the bus," I ventured. "I thought you got sick or something."

"I woke up too late. My mom drove me so she could yell at me."

"Where'd you go Saturday?" I asked this with a painful attempt to sound casual.

"To my aunt's. My mom made me." Silence for a moment, then

she blurted, "I can't go steady with you. I'm not allowed to go steady with anyone!"

The background for this news came out in monosyllables. Essentially her mother forbade our romantic understanding and furthermore decreed that Delia must return the Christopher. "So, here," Delia said, holding out the medal and not quite looking at me.

"It's yours," I mumbled, heart sinking. "It's a present ... real sterling silver—"

"No, I don't want it—I *can't* go steady. Here!" She thrust the medallion at me and hurried into the girls' bathroom, her little heels clicking.

I stood holding the Christopher, feeling the slow crumbling of my dream sand castle. Then my despair twisted into resentment. Why had she given up so easily, complied with adult orders so quickly? Why couldn't she have argued more, threatened to kill herself, or run away? Considering what I knew of her temperament, I didn't expect such dramatics, but still. In my summer reading, once Baltimore belle Jane Porter had warmed up to Tarzan of the Apes, no parent, villain, or even landlord willing to forgive the family debts for her hand in marriage could, to paraphrase Motown singer Mary Wells's smash hit of a few months later, lessen her affection for her boyfriend. Well, one thing was certain: with the exception of the top-forty songwriters, no one could know my sorrow.

The advanced reading class provided some distraction in the raw days that followed. The teacher, a retired college professor, never wore a tie and only shaved every third day or so. At the first class meeting, he spread out on two side tables a few dozen hardbound books without library markings. Then he said, approximately: "Ladies and gentlemen, these are from my private library. You may choose any of them you desire, and you may take your choice home with you so long as you treat each volume with the utmost care."

I started with the fattest book on the table, which happened to be *The Royal Road to Romance*, a 1920s travel journal by Richard Haliburton. The flamboyant jazz-age adventurer's account of his extensive world sightseeing featured an over-the-top effusive style. Haliburton packed each chapter with exotic scenery and devil-may-care bon mots like, "Let those who wish have their respectability. I wanted freedom, freedom to indulge in whatever caprice struck my fancy, freedom to search in the furthermost corners of the earth for the beautiful, the joyous, and the romantic." Sounded great to me, and still does. My lifelong love of travel and travel writing may have crystallized with *The Royal Road*. Next I read *Magic Carpet,* an unfinished sequel in which Haliburton chartered what people then called "an aeroplane" to circumnavigate much of the globe.[39] After several more fascinating adventures, the plane ran into a storm somewhere in the South Pacific and never returned. It seemed a tragically fitting end for an adventurer.

For my next reading project I chose a straightforward account of explorers at the North Pole, but the authors never cleared up the question of why anyone would go there when he could be swimming the Hellespont or sailing past the site of the Colossus of Rhodes in the moonlight. But travel was travel, I supposed. I also signed up on the wait list for *Moby Dick*, that leviathan of a novel, but the only fourth-grader in the class kept it most of the semester.

The old teacher conducted the course as if we were college students. He addressed us by our last names, appending "Mister" or "Miss": "Miss Jones, thank you for the summary. Now please give us your thoughts on Captain Ahab's motive for his pursuit of the white whale." He also evaluated our writing at the college level. Though we all ended up with A grades on our report card to reflect our placement in the gifted class, he marked our book reports as he would for university sophomores in an Intro to Lit course. None of us ever earned better than a C-. I received all Ds, a record better than some sixth graders. My friend and fellow fifth-grader Harald actually received an *F minus*, the only time in my educational career I've seen that particular grade applied.

Despite this dubious distinction, Harald did well in all school subjects except P.E. He distinguished himself as both an avid reader and a musician, proficient on the accordion and French horn. His parents brought him from Norway as an infant, and in the custom of the day, the immigrants discouraged their aspiring American child from learning his native language. His mother spoke English with reasonable fluency, but his dad learned only the basics. Consequently, father and son could barely communicate.

---

[39] This book has gotten around, too. I began writing about my California childhood at a friend's house in Oregon, and over the past eight years I've continued in planes and airports across the continental USA, in various lodgings on four Hawaiian Islands, on a night train to Vienna, in a park in Jerusalem, in cruise ships off the coast of Mexico and the Mediterranean, on a ferry across the Irish Sea, and on trains across the UK and Europe. This chapter began on a beach in Korfu, Greece and continued in Venice and Kortula, an island off the Croatian coast. I fine-tuned the complete manuscript in Rio de Janeiro, Santiago, Easter Island, four Tahitian islands, Fiji, New Zealand, Australia, Bali, and Taiwan. Thanks Mr. Halliburton, and may your bones rest in peace, wherever they ended up.

Since Harald weighed in on the portly side and couldn't fight or play ball, he didn't set the Springdale social world on fire. But he liked books and lent me several—he even gave me his spare copy of *Black Beauty*, a volume highly recommended by the girl back in third grade who loved horses. With Harald I figured out how to play chess, using checkers with nametags for pieces, thus starting Jay and Jane on their chess binge. Harald also excelled in building model cars, which I hadn't tried since the Black Widow days in Glendale.

Model ships had their day, and model airplanes were the rage through the 1950s; but by the early sixties, ninety percent of the model market retooled to automotive. The Revel line of current Detroit replicas cost $1.50 each and offered the choice of assembling the car stock (like the real cars on the street), custom (with features like bubbletops and side pipes), or competition (bigger tires, less chrome, racing decals). Harald usually opted for straight stock, and I built mine wild custom. I fancied myself the creative one, but his cars invariably looked better—I rarely managed a tight alignment between body and frame, and the glue invariably seeped from the cracks, which made for lumpy joints. My attempts at auto painting and detailing also came out decidedly lumpy.

Harald and I remained close for several months before a dispute over something led to my walking on his rock garden, which led to righteous fury and verbal admonitions from him. I retaliated by calling him "fatso," which effectively ended the friendship.

The rock garden that caused all the trouble came into being on the Saturday preceding the Kennedy assassination. I remember standing outside his house, watching as he picked up bits of glass and cigarette butts on the lawn area, which remained in its original-purchase, hard-packed dirt state. In a neighborhood where exhibiting a presentable lawn was high priority, the Norwegian family's unlandscaped yard had become a scandal.

But not for long. Harald kept looking down the street as we chatted about his family history. Upon arrival in the U.S., his parents first joined an informal Norwegian colony in Whittier, Richard Nixon's hometown. They lived two or three families to a house until eventually the several family units bought their own homes. According to Harald, all the men were gruff and quarrelsome carpenters, but they agreed on at least one thing: front yards should be landscaped as rock gardens.

"What's a rock garden?"

"Trucks'll be here soon," Harald assured me. "Then you'll see."

A few minutes later, two pickup trucks and two cars arrived. Several men disembarked and began working at the desperate speed of German army prisoners, which some of them may well have been in their younger days. First they dumped loads of sand and raked it level, then piled more sand to form two mounds in the yard. Next they spread thick plastic over the expanse of sand, cutting slit crosses to insert one-gallon-size cactus and yuccas on the mounds in geometric patterns. Two pickup loads of river rock followed, and the men raked the smooth stones evenly over the plastic.

The entire process took less than two hours. As I watched from Harald's bedroom window, the import of the rock landscape dawned upon me. No weeds could grow through the plastic, and Huntington Beach's heavy morning dew would provide sufficient moisture for the cactus and yucca. *And there was no grass to mow!* Unlike the rest of the males on Oasis Drive, neither Harald nor his dad would henceforth have any yard chores whatsoever. I recognized a brilliant scheme…but it somehow seemed unfair, not playing the suburban game. To this day, when I see a rock garden front lawn (and they seem to be catching on in this age of water restriction), I always wonder if crafty Norwegians were behind it.

The following week brought the President's assassination. Even Jane cried at the TV image of little John-John saluting his father's casket. After that iconic moment, the deification picked up speed. According to the *Pilot* and Walter Cronkite, Kennedy's presidential status rivaled Washington's and Lincoln's. By Tuesday or Wednesday of the following week, stores carried hastily-pressed LP records of Kennedy's speeches. Within five days of his death, U.S. mint designers completed a prototype for the Kennedy half-dollar, and in January 1964 the Denver mint put the coin in circulation. In December Idyllwild Airport in New York became Kennedy Airport, and soon afterward, Cape Canaveral, the site of all manned rocket launches, was re-christened Cape Kennedy by executive order of President Lyndon Johnson.

The only hint of irreverence I saw that week — or that decade — took place during the long weekend immediately following the tragedy. Schools and government offices shut down Friday, and almost everyone stayed home to watch the news coverage. The next day, Saturday, I woke up late and turned on the radio. Like all other media, KFWB pre-empted everything but coverage of the assassination and its aftermath. The police had captured a suspect, Lee Harvey Oswald, a name that stuck in my mind immediately because it seemed sinister and sneaky—the perfect name for an assassin. I listened a while, then left to deliver my papers, peddling through the quiet tracts and across almost deserted Springdale Avenue.

Kids stayed indoors most of Saturday and Sunday. Following another executive order, Monday became a national day of mourning, with all schools and government offices closed. Mournful as we felt during telecast of the funeral, by early afternoon cabin fever began to set in among my age group. Next door dad Jim Verdiman, one of the city employees excused from work, drove several of us to the park in Westminster to play baseball. There we met Jim's friend and fellow street sweeper Mr. Russell, who always called Jim "Tonto" after the Lone Ranger's faithful Indian companion.

"Well, Tonto, you goin' in to your store this afternoon?" Mr. Russell referred to Jim's second job as a King O' Lawn salesman.

"Nah," said Jim, pulling on his mitt. "The old man told us to take the day off. Whole country's gone nuts, he says."

Russell snorted. "Got that right."

The two dads each captained a team and chose up sides among the kids. As usual, Bobby Verdiman tried mightily to outplay me. Noting his ongoing success, I began to affect an air of being too sophisticated for baseball. While waiting my turn at bat, I pulled out my transistor radio to demonstrate my coolness. Suddenly a special bulletin interrupted the droning coverage: "Lee Harvey Oswald fatally shot in Dallas police station by 'unknown gunman.'"

I relayed this information to the ball players, and Jim walked over to listen to the radio for a minute. "Hey Russ!" he yelled across the diamond. "Somebody just killed that Oswald prick."

A slow grin spread across Mr. Russell's face as he walked in from third base. "Well, Tonto," he said, "does this mean we're gonna get tomorrow off, too?"

This witticism sounded shockingly flip—even approaching blasphemy, given the national mindset of the past three days. But it also brought a revelation of sorts to my limited ten-year-old sensibility: not everyone responded fully to the emotion manipulators and opinion makers of the media—Walter Cronkite told us what we should be feeling, but we needn't exaggerate our compliance.

So between Richard Halliburton, the Brill Building songwriters, and Mr. Russell, my consciousness was expanding in interesting ways.

CHAPTER FORTY-FIVE

~ Xmas Cheer ~ Bully ~ Knit-Tie Inklings of the Counterculture ~ Froggy, Ugg and Base Five ~ The British (Wallet) Invasion

"Hey, Mom, Dad. Thought you weren't going to make it!"

Smiling, Jay hands large drinks to Ed and Eileen as they enter, then leads them to open chairs around the tree. The 1963 Hill house Christmas Eve celebration is already in progress. All of our Southern California relatives have made the long drive to Orange County to honor Jay and Jane's shrine to good living. Treading the gold carpet, surrounded by the smoked mirror wall and walnut veneer wood paneling, all the guests marvel at Jay's well-stocked bar and admire his workmanship on the giant coffee table. Such splendor provides a fine backdrop for further "oohs" and "ahhhs" at the seasonal additions: a ceiling-high, white flocked tree and a mountain of wrapped presents.

Ten minutes later Jay brings Eileen another double martini and Ed another triple scotch on the rocks. Ed usually has his first scotch of the day at three p.m. when he gets home from an afternoon of surreptitious beer drinking at the butcher shop. Tonight, however, Ed had to drive, so Eileen kept him relatively dry until the party. She usually takes the wheel, but, as she tells Jay, she is developing cataracts in both eyes and her night vision is gone. That's why they arrived late. "He'd kill us driving drunk, but he drives like an old woman when he's sober," she explains.

I hear the conversation and observe that Ed is paler and more tremulous than usual, but I am primarily focused on the huge electric sunburst clock on the wall. Eight-thirty, twenty minutes from now, is the pre-agreed-upon start time for opening presents. At last the moment falls and we tear into the festive wrappings. Ed has been focusing on his drinking, and now, after two extra-stiff ones, he begins to feel better, even expansive.

"Man, lookit that—all the presents these kids got here," he exclaims to no one in particular. "Jever see s'much loot?"

Nearby heads shake politely. Ed aims a bleary grin at me as I begin to open what proves to be my favorite gift of the evening. "Well, lookit that! Let's *hear* that *hi*-fi, man!"

He is referring to the new portable record player, about the size of a small vanity case. The unit has a stylish burnt orange and cream Naugahyde covering and features speakers on both sides so the music from separate tracks shoots out in opposite directions.

"It's a stereo, Dad," remarks Jay, taking Ed's not-quite-empty glass from the old man's hand. "They have a special double needle to pick up the two stereo grooves. Here, let me get you another Chivas."

With a practiced thumbnail I open the shrink-wrap seal of *Elvis's Greatest Hits Volume III* (one of the albums I received as a lead-in gift to the stereo) and put it on the turntable I've already plugged into the nearest outlet. As I strain to hear the music over the general party noise, Jay returns with Ed's scotch, smiling, even glowing in his magnanimity. He occasionally takes a sip of one of the two drinks he'll have most of the evening before switching to coffee. "Here, Dodie," he says to his brother Eddie's wife (the one who would later run off with Freddie). "Let me top off that B&B—Eddie will thank me for it later when you get loose and want to play."

Dodie has never tasted a Benedictine and brandy. She's dazzled by her big brother-in-law's attention and giggles at his risqué remarks. Jay works the room, not neglecting Jane. B&B is her favorite drink, and Jay has served her two. He struggles with conflicting impulses here—his seeming obsession to get everyone drunk and his caution at having to deal with her tendency to belligerence and maudlin weepiness if she has one too many. She is high, but mostly on the happy scene: since Thanksgiving she and Jay have sat up nights, making lists and discussing what presents the kids would like. Jane genuinely loves providing the embarrassment of riches, and all showing-off aside, Jay is basically a generous guy. But of course they both bask in the universal family admiration, or what passes for it.

All of the guests bring presents for Greg, Trish, and me, but from Jay and Jane exclusively we each receive more than any three other kids on the block. Besides the portable stereo, I get *Elvis's Greatest Hits* Volumes II and III (I already own volume I), a carom board (a sort of junior pool table), a dart board, and a CO_2 BB gun. In addition Nanny provides a complete sleep wardrobe and underwear ensemble, brought to us through her substandard Broadway wages and employee discount.

Trish and Greg also make out well, though four-year-old Greg almost lost one present when, excited beyond all restraint a few days before the big night, he tore off its wrapping paper. I've since known other families who, as a sort of emotional safety valve, allow their children to open one present prior to the official celebration. But in our household, the daily ratcheting up of anticipation, with more and more presents visible each morning leading up to The Day, evolved into a ritual such that breaking the tension is a sort of sacrilege. Greg received a stern admonishment and the present disappeared. But after a day or so Jay and Jane rewrapped and restored it to the pile under the tree.

I am peripherally glad to see all the gifts Trish and Greg have received because I know I will be able to play with any that spark my interest. But this sibling privilege includes no reciprocity clause — woe be onto Greg and Trish if I ever catch them operating my stereo or touching my carom set. This memory brings up the facet of my childhood character I am least proud of and is the first thing I would change if I could go back in my life and change anything. I had never been a warm older brother, but from around this time (age ten or so) until I turn thirteen, I am at best coldly indifferent and at worst a tyrant. I play too rough, turning pretend wrestling matches into painful "accidents," and explode into temper tantrums when either sibling invades my sacred room space. Worse yet, I get the bully's charge from striking fear into them.

Looking back, I can't satisfactorily explain this shameful behavior. One pop psychology line postulates that secure families spawn bad sibling relationships and vice-versa: kids who are afraid of their parents tend to stick together and protect each other, while kids who feel comfortable with their parents are always in conflict with one another. Another clinical exploration might focus on my emotional state at the time: the strain of spinning all the social plates at school, striving to be first in everything while feigning indifference, but always full of unacknowledged fear of someone overtaking me — perhaps all this insecurity had something to do with picking on the ones I could best get away with picking on. Or perhaps I was just a rotten kid, as practical psychologist Jay might have phrased it if he'd known the extent of my bullying.

Fortunately for my tormentees, I had so much activity in my

life that I ignored them most of the time. As Christmas passed and 1963 ended, my paper route expanded almost daily and I sold subscriptions in the evenings (more on that later). Springdale School, under construction for many months and delayed for its scheduled fall debut, finally opened in January 1964, allowing Mrs. Taylor's class to shake off the snooty dust of the Gill campus. Springdale's brand-new classrooms featured counters for science experiments and an intercom system that played the National Anthem each morning. Best of all, we were no longer interlopers; Springdalians all, we trod a home campus at last.

In March our young vice-principal Mr. Prine organized a lunch break baseball league, and I was elected captain of the team we named the Stingrays, after the sports car. On the artistic front, the new music teacher trained a choir authorized to perform at the all-city Spring Sing-Off, and I became a marginal participant, hovering somewhere between soprano and alto. We didn't win any prizes, but our two bittersweet songs, "Big Rock Candy Mountain" and "Yellow Bird" can even now stir melancholy when I hear them.

Those songs provided the closest link to folk music that I knew of in those days, unless one counts Peter, Paul, and Mary singles like "Blowin' in the Wind" and "Puff the Magic Dragon." But early on at Springdale, while Mrs. Taylor took off several days for a family emergency, a stranger exposed us to both folk music and the progressive educational movement that would, in a few years, explode into the Counterculture.

The perpetrator of this subversion was our substitute teacher, Mr. Washburn (no relation to my first-grade teacher at Callahan Elementary). He looked like a WASP version of Woody Allen: short, thin, horn-rimmed glasses, hair parted on the side and falling over his forehead. But his personality didn't match the first impression. He arrived each morning in a convertible MG Midget and circled the teachers' parking lot twice, straight pipes roaring, before parking and vaulting over the door. In those days, the standard male teacher uniform consisted of shiny black shoes, dark suit, white shirt, and solid color tie, but Mr. Washburn wore old brown loafers with a rumpled sweater over his blue shirt, and a cavalierly-loosened knit tie. Going through a doorway, he would suddenly reach up and swing by his fingertips. He flirted openly with the fourth-grade teacher next door, giving her mock-smoldering looks. He even kept his hands in his pockets when he talked to Mr. Hysler, our principal.

Like Principal Grapis at Redondo's Jefferson School, Mr. Hysler, with his crew cut, marine-gone-to-fat build, and Nixonian five-o'clock shadow, looked as if he came straight from Central Casting. But even Mr. Hysler seemed charmed by Mr. Washburn, for I observed them smiling and even laughing together once — the only time I'd ever seen any principal amused at anything.

For all his shenanigans, Mr. Washburn held serious ideas about education. Ignoring the custom of having classes line up at the end of recess and march quietly into the room, he simply waited for us to come in from recess on our own. On his first day he called us up individually for a chat. "What would you want to learn more about if you didn't have to go to school?" "What books have you read lately besides school books?" He even made notes as he listened. During these one-on-one interviews, the rest of the class could talk all we wanted and walk around the classroom, a state of anarchy thus far reserved for last-day-of-school parties.

One day Mr. Washburn spent a couple of hours on the concept of Base-5, a staple of the "New Math" beginning to work its way into school curriculums. Starting with an amusing impersonation of a one-legged caveman named Ugg, Mr. Washburn explained base 10 as merely a subjective system: if one-legged Ugg with only five toes to count on had prevailed, Base-5 would be the standard notation. Six objects would be written as 11, fifteen objects as 30, and so forth. According to conservative California educators like Max Rafferty, whose occasional op-ed pieces I read in the *Daily Pilot*, this primer in subjectivity may well have been the subversive aim of New Math's promoters, but it all seemed interesting to me.

That afternoon Mr. Washburn led a discussion about what makes people biologically and psychologically different from animals. The next day we spent an hour or so learning and singing the old folk song "Froggy Went a Courtin'" while he accompanied us on guitar. I'd never seen a teacher play guitar before, but had any other teacher tried such a sing-along, the lesson would have fallen flat — the song, after all, narrated the doings of "froggies" and "mousies" and we were practically teenagers! But Mr. Washburn explained in context the eerie strangeness and casual violence of the song. He expounded on the glimpse it gave us into the attitudes of the last century — the way those ancient people actually thought rather than the way they act in Western movies.

Elsewhere in 1964, Ken Kesey's Merry Pranksters ingested

massive doses of LSD, Bob Dylan had just written "Mr. Tambourine Man," and Berkeley students revved up the Free Speech Movement. Our exposure to Mr. Washburn for a few days brought us as close as we came to the current tide of nonconformity, but this proto-hippie Johnny Appleseed made a lasting impression. Mrs. Taylor must have felt a bit envious when she returned. We all told her about Ugg and how we didn't have to line up outside and Mr. Washburn's MG and could she play the guitar? She smiled politely through it all, then put us right back on fractions and memorizing the parts of a lima bean.

But not even Mr. Washburn could commandeer the cutting edge for long. Soon after he introduced us to folk music, a truly monumental pop music event swept away all that had gone before. I'd heard a snippet on KFWB around the first of February, something about a new group from England scheduled for three appearances on the Ed Sullivan show, beginning on the ninth of the month. This bulletin amounted to odd news, indeed — the only group from England to ever crack the U.S. pop charts had been the one-hit band who recorded the instrumental "Telstar." Our groups went to England; their groups — if the odd little country possessed more than one — generally stayed there. Pop stars Cliff Richard and Tommy Steele sold multi-millions in Britain, but nobody ever heard of them in the states.

Then the Beatles arrived in America in February 1964 and took over the pop song world literally overnight. Later that year KFWB called the band the "KFW-Beatles" and played their records as incessantly as any station in the country. But KFWB initially practiced caution. I don't think I even heard "I Want to Hold Your Hand" until I saw the Sullivan show that memorable first night when 73 million other Americans tuned in.

I soon came to know (and still remember) most of the Beatles' songs by heart, but at first their overnight sensation puzzled me. It's interesting to recall first impressions before I became steeped in the accepted norms of pop music. Compared to the usual run of teen idols, Ringo looked like a gargoyle, and John, Paul, and George oddly androgynous, arrayed in their matching collarless suits and hairdos. Their staging seemed stiff with the three vocalists tethered to two microphones. Performers didn't have stage monitors in those days, so two harmonizers stepping up to one microphone helped them hear one another and stay on key, but at the time I thought each singer should have his own. Furthermore, their sound, especially "I Want to Hold Your Hand" seemed tinny, and their pronunciation ("Oh yah, Ah — tellya schomthin' — I think you un-da-stchand") vaguely Teutonic. I learned later that they honed their craft performing in Hamburg, Germany strip clubs, an experience possibly influential on their early style. Before I knew this facet of Beatle history, their German version of the song, "Komm Gib Mir Deine Hand" came out on their album *Something New*. I remember thinking then that it sounded more natural in Deutch.

But despite my initial diffidence to the Fab Four, I watched all three Sullivan show appearances and dove into the high tide of Beatlemania that followed. The music really was extraordinary once one became comfortable with the style. The band expanded artistically with every record release, and the records (and number one singles) kept coming.

According to some psychologists, the Beatles' abundance of talent and charisma did not fully account for their immense popularity. Specialists not already focused on the "Why do older siblings pick on their juniors?" question theorized that all the hoopla came about as a reaction to the horror of the Kennedy assassination only eighty days before. In this postulate, Beatlemania triggered a corporate emotional release which put closure to the tragic loss of a beloved leader.

Certainly the timing was close. The mass Kennedy mourning had begun to wane when the Beatles hit, but the media had successfully primed us to focus, to adore, and to buy hastily distributed consumer goods. K-Mart featured albums of Kennedy speeches, quickie bios and reissues of JFK's ghostwritten books, Kennedy photos suitable for framing, etc. — and all paved the way for mass consumption of Beatles goods. But while JFK worship remained primarily national and permeated with sadness and tragedy, the Beatles phenomenon provided a global, happy spending catharsis. Within a week of the final Sullivan appearance, K-Mart began promoting a whole line of Beatles posters, wigs, cards, bobblehead dolls, and discount copycat albums like *The Beatle Beat* by a group called the Buggs. The Liverpool Lads (as the British Press tagged them) became a consumer orgy for the population bulge of teens and preteens in the same way hula hoops or coonskin caps had been the objects when the same age-group was younger.

I did my part as young consumer, purchasing the four LPs that appeared almost simultaneously: *Meet the Beatles, Introducing the Beatles* (on VJ Records), *The Beatles with Tony Sheridan* (some odd recordings from their Hamburg days), and *The Beatles Second Album*, a collection of songs culled from the English versions of their albums, which were always two or three songs longer than their continental counterparts. Using this method, for every three EMI albums the Beatles put out in England, Capitol Records could sell four in the states.

New Beatles singles hit the charts weekly—at one point they owned numbers one through five on the top forty. Youth from ten to twenty dutifully bought the albums as well as the singles. Beatles cards, packaged five for a nickel with bubble gum, became as popular among pre-teens as the music. Everyone I knew in the fourth, fifth, and sixth grade bought and traded these totems, trying to get all 188 cards in the three-series total. Complicit in my consumerism, Jane provided a K-Mart giant 5x3 foot Beatles poster, as well as another large one commemorating the famous Royal Albert Hall show in which John Lennon quipped, "Those of you in the cheap seats can clap your hands; the rest of you rattle your jewelry."

Meanwhile back in England, young hustlers like Andrew Loog Oldham (manager of the Rolling Stones) followed Brian Epstein's lead, rounding up any reasonably proficient band willing to skip a few haircuts and hop on the first plane to the states. Within a month of the Fab Four debut, the Dave Clark Five (from London's Tottingham district) played two Sullivan shows. On the strength of their Beatlesque sound, button-at-the-neck dentist shirts, and high-heeled boots, they too sold millions overnight. The Rolling Stones followed a couple of months later—I saw their first appearance on the Red Skelton show. The venerable comedian showed naked astonishment at the sight of them: the band members' hair flowed over their ears! But ever the professional, Red regained his poise and ad-libbed, "All these English groups are going to get together and have a dandruff convention."

The Stones' R&B cover versions and lively originals sounded more elemental than the Beatles, and I became an immediate fan, the first person I knew to buy their debut album. But other groups competed for attention: Gerry and the Pacemakers, Freddy and the Dreamers, Billy J. Kramer and the Dakotas, The Kinks, Manfred Mann, the Nashville Teens, the Animals, et al. seemed to arrive en masse. We experienced a British invasion, all right—of our parents' wallets. Andrew Loog Oldham declared, "The Rolling Stones are not just a band—they are a way of life." And as the new pop music explosion dovetailed with exploding consumerism, he was right on the money, as it were.

CHAPTER FORTY-SIX

~ So Long, Buddy ~ Renting Money ~ She Loves You ~ Family Diaspora
~ Flying Saucer, Solar Systems, & Little Stars

One Saturday in March, 1964, the family gathered in the kitchen over fried powdered sugar donuts, one of Jane's Southern legacy dishes. Arlis Drolet from next door knocked, then came in looking uncharacteristically grave.

"Jane, somebody's calling you from Alabama."

We never had home phone service at the Huntington Beach house, but in the days when only two of three families opted for phones, long distance operators would, under certain circumstances and if they were provided with an address, ring through to the nearest neighbor with a critical message.

Jane, her face a mask of apprehension, followed Arlis. I came behind more slowly and stopped on the sidewalk between the houses. Jay stood on the porch, arms crossed and grim-faced. We didn't have long to wait. I had never seen Jane seriously upset before, but now she ran sobbing across the Drolets' lawn and stepped over our low white fence. When I reached the porch she was crying in Jay's arms, but reached out to me as I approached, sobbing, "Daddy's in Heaven!"

I never heard any details of Daddy's passing, except that it came peacefully in his sleep a week short of his seventy-fourth birthday. Did he work as a night watchman until the end? Had he gone to bed in the morning after cleaning his gun, as usual? I only knew he was gone — the old fellow born in 1890 who loved me as unconditionally as he'd loved Jane, the gentle, surrogate father who'd whittled me swords, took me shooting, and called me Buddy.

Jane quickly pulled herself together to attend the funeral. The next morning she told me I could skip school and accompany her as she made arrangements. Financing the trip south involved an all-day operation, since, adjusted for inflation, airfare to Birmingham cost at least three times more than now. While the Hill family shrine to good living featured a pink Cadillac, mammoth coffee tables, smoked mirrors, wall-to-wall carpets, and high-end liquor brands, all those accoutrements were handmade, bought on credit, or stolen from Jay's workplace. He and Jane never opened a savings account, and the checking balance hovered near zero. Almost no one in their financial class carried a credit card then; the limited market (BankAmericard, American Express) catered to people with, solid credit, long-term jobs, and genuine references.

While we visited two pawn shops and a finance company, Jane told me stories of Daddy's generosity, his manliness and fortitude. She loved him deeply, but I think she also felt guilty for leaving him and not contacting him more often. She rarely wrote letters; Daddy may never have written one. Long distance phone calls cost an hour's pay per minute, so most people restricted them to major holidays, emergencies, and birth or death announcements.

I felt strangely numb as she talked — and guilty for feeling that way. Daddy had been four-year-old Ricky's hero, but I'd only spent a few intermittent weeks with him since. Remembering the way he called me Buddy set off something akin to sorrow, but mostly I felt disassociated, as if I were playing a part in some TV movie. Meanwhile, we trekked from shop to shop, pawning luggage and jewelry, stopping last at Seaboard Finance. For a rapacious interest rate, Seaboard, the loan agency with the catchy, faux mambo radio jingle about "renting money," allowed Jane to "rent" the rest of the funds she needed for the trip to Alabama. And added one more monthly payment to all the other bills.

We stopped at a fast food place for a late lunch of hamburger and malt for me, fried shrimp and coffee for her. I wanted to commiserate with her, but having experienced so little real sorrow in my life, I felt at a loss as to how to express it. I settled for a downcast silence.

The winter sun dipped low by the time we finished eating. When we stopped at Springdale Elementary to pick up my homework, I assumed that everyone had gone home except the teachers. But entering the gate, I literally ran into Delia, my heretofore primary source of heartache. She held two large shopping bags stuffed with red, white, and blue crepe paper. Alluring as ever, she stepped back, adjusted her bags, and looked me up and down. "What happened to you?"

I had left my shirt untucked and hair uncombed, the outer trappings of ritual mourning. "My grandfather died," I said quietly, with an undercurrent of drama.

Delia's face showed no emotion — or did I detect a subtle expression of sympathy there? In any case, she said nothing and seemed disinclined to tarry.

I pointed to the shopping bag. "What's all that?"

"Keith is moving away. He told the class this morning." Delia said this with a hint of impatience. Then she showed me her junior Mona Lisa smile. "So us girls that like him gave a surprise party. Mrs. Taylor let us go home for lunch and bring stuff back."

Us girls that like him? I felt viscerally numb to Daddy's death, but this news brought a sharp pang. Delia, the ice princess, had actually warmed to a guy, and the guy wasn't me. Keith belonged to a military family that relocated almost as often as the Hills. While I recognized him as a likable kid, he simply didn't register as Delia's type. After all, he knew nothing of pop music. He dressed indifferently and probably never even heard of Paul Peterson. How could she possibly be attracted to him?

I mumbled, "See ya tomorrow," and wandered back to the car.

Jane probably took my stricken look for mourning. She was correct, more or less. When we returned home I proceeded directly to my room and turned on my little stereo. It sat on a K-Mart gold-painted metal rack with slots for thirty or forty records underneath. My twelve Elvis albums lined up in chronological order on the left; four Beatles LPs moved out from the right in reverse chronological order, with several 45 rpm singles in the middle. I chose *The Beatles Second Album*, and put on the side with "She Loves You." No one, I reflected tragically, would be saying that to *me* anytime soon. Staring at the stereo, my thoughts wandered back to the Christmas party where I'd received it and how step-grandfather Ed teased me about all my "loot." I looked around the room at my BB guns and posters, my dart board and pennants from all the fun places I'd been. I thought of Daddy, but the happy scenes with him were hazy and the rest painful to recall. As I turned the Beatle record to side two, my musings returned to step-grandpa Ed and I remembered how he had looked that Christmas Eve when I'd first gotten the stereo — before he poured down several drinks to take off the ragged edge. His starkly miserable expression had been a perfect illustration of how I felt right now.

Next morning Jane left for the funeral, and over the next four or five days, the neighbors took in the Hill children for care and feeding, having spontaneously offered their hospitality when they heard of Jane's loss. Trish dispatched to the Drolet family on the right, Greg to the Verdimans on the left (he and Peanut were playmates and the same age), and I to the Kalanis across the street. The moms also took turns sending home-cooked dinners over to Jay — no suburban wife in those days supposed that a working father bereft of spouse would be able to take care of kids or even cook for himself.

I hadn't been away from home since summer camp, and I now felt the same disconnected sensation I'd undergone then. *The Twilight Zone,* Rod Serling's offbeat science fiction fantasy TV show that ran from 1959 to 1964, did much in the post-*Journeys to Bookland* phase to baptize my imagination. When I exited the Kalani home in the morning on the way to school, it felt strange to look across the street at what I knew on one level to be my home … and yet (segue into eerie Rod Serling voice-over): "The yellow stucco and the new white post fence emanated the sense of someone else's home — a house of … *strangers.*" The second morning I watched Jay leaving for work in the Cadillac. Preoccupied with lighting probably his fourth cigarette of the day, he didn't see me. He seemed like a *stranger,* too. All sorts of *Twilight Zone* scenarios came to mind, parallel-world stories, and the like. What if … every day I saw a completely different person drive away from the yellow stucco house in the same Cadillac …?

As a guest of the Kalanis, I grew to know Wayne, Gary, and Dan better. They reigned as the first, second, and third toughest guys on the block, but while I slept in their home, they treated me more like a cousin than a guest. Their mom, the only person the formidable Dan feared, went out of her way to make me feel like a family member. She even ordered me to brush my teeth.

Fred, the boys' latest stepfather or reasonable facsimile, seemed a mysterious figure: an old fellow who looked much too gray, bespectacled, and Caucasian to be part of such an exotic family. The boys' mother met him after she'd brought her sons to the mainland, and they pooled their money to come up with the $200 down payment on the house. Wayne shared with me a few of Fred's stories of being a hobo during the thirties and forties. To my great surprise, one of these tales independently corroborated my old Redondo Beach pal Lloyd's story about gas stations having outlets in their bathrooms to provide power for bums' electric shavers. I had assumed that Lloyd made that one up, but apparently it was a genuine fact.

Wayne owned one LP: *Neil Sedaka's Greatest Hits,* probably a hand-me-down from his mom. I soon took over operation of the record player, picking through the cuts on the Sedaka album and using the method I employed with Elvis—play a group of songs incessantly until you know them by heart. One night, after an hour or so of Neil's slick pop renditions of "Run Samson Run," "Right Next Door to an Angel," and "Calendar Girl," big brother Dan stomped through the door and tore the LP off the turntable.

"Flying saucer!" he announced, then flung the record across the room. Wayne, the baddest guy in the fifth grade (I had decisively lost my only fight with him a few months before), looked at me and shrugged. Dan then put on a Surfaris album, led off with "I'm a Hog For You, Baby," definitely worlds away from Sedaka's smooth approach.

When Jane came home from the funeral, she seemed as cheerful as ever—I don't know if she felt as well as she acted, but she did her best to "move on" as they say nowadays. Meanwhile at school, Mrs. Taylor started us on our first long report, which, perhaps inspired by tales of Mr. Washburn's progressive methods, involved lots of individual research and free-work time. We welcomed this innovation because it allowed for wandering around the room and talking indiscriminately. I chose Astronomy as my report topic and spent several hours copying the Encyclopedia Americana articles on the solar system, for our class was learning the virtues of brevity and discernment by choosing which paragraphs to copy.[40]

Jay's stock rose with me as a result of the report. In my view, an impressive cover was a major feature of the project. On the morning of the assignment due date, I was still struggling with the title lettering. After botching two new ten-cent covers, I asked Jay for help. He paused in his rushing for work and took the time to write "ASTRONOMY by Richard Hill" in fine calligraphy on the folder. He drew the A in Astronomy larger than the other letters and with a flourish rivaling the A in the *Action Comics* or *Tales to Astonish* logos.

Convinced that this beautiful letter A contributed significantly to the A+ grade received on the report, I temporarily felt as warmly toward Jay as when he'd helped me make the Valentine and envelope way back in Las Vegas. But his stock dropped again shortly afterward at Springdale School's first Open House. My authority-shy parents

---

[40] With the advent of the Internet this research method seems to have resurged among high school and college students.

rarely showed for extra-curricular functions, but Jay arrived with Jane, charmed Mrs. Taylor, and generally appeared interested. Then, as he thumbed through my best papers displayed on my desk, he commented that I needed to do neater work.

I had made certain to collect my neatest work, so I asked him what he meant.

"Well, look at this one," he said, holding up a math paper. "You drew stars all over the page. That's little kid stuff."

His obtuseness struck me dumb. Did he really think I would randomly draw little stars on a fifth-grade paper? As in the textbook, the stars denoted extra credit problems, which were not otherwise numbered. But the real issue boiled down to this: I had deliberately placed on my desk the math papers with extra credit precisely because they demonstrated my zeal in improving the one area of study I didn't excel in. To be completely forthcoming, I'd done those extra credits because they were proto-"New Math" think pieces that reminded me of the now-legendary Mr. Washburn. But the everlasting *point* was that I had *done extra credit*! I had taken initiative, completed more work than necessary — the very behavior grownups always encouraged!

But before I could gather my wits for an acid rejoinder, Mrs. Taylor appeared and began talking about my good work and how I could do even better if I would focus and put in more effort. This obnoxiousness left me speechless, and the moment for retort passed. But the memory lingered: for forty-four years afterward I would occasionally recall Jay's unwarranted accusation and imagine going back in time to the fifth grade so I could look him in the eye and state firmly, "Those little stars are NOT doodling. They denote EXTRA CREDIT problems!"

But when my final chance came to set him straight, just before the orderly wheeled him in for his last heart operation, I declined the opportunity. Modern psychologists who advocate Speaking Truths and Setting Boundaries might disagree with my decision, but in that last conversation a few months after I turned 55 and we were both technically senior citizens, I simply told Jay I loved him. He replied, "I love you, too." And that final exchange crossed all manner of boundaries and erased any remaining little stars.

CHAPTER FORTY-SEVEN

~ Anger Management ~ Allied with the Axis ~ Shirley Temple Meets The Psycho
~ Murky Guilt ~ A So-So Party

Closure takes time, and psychological equilibrium proved scarce that spring of 1964. Every time I saw Jay, the little stars misunderstanding still rankled more than I would admit. And perhaps my grandfather's death upset me more than I remember, or maybe something about my last conversation with Delia bothered me at a deeper level than I cared to acknowledge. In any case, one late afternoon a week or so after Jane returned from Alabama, temporary insanity descended upon me.

By way of prelude, I had earlier that day visited Delia's heartthrob Keith. Due to a 30-day delay in his father's military transfer, he remained in town after his female admirers put together their party for him. As noted previously, Keith impressed one and all as a likeable guy, a tall, fifth-grade Gary Cooper type. So despite the fact that he had somehow stolen Delia's affection from me (assuming for the sake of argument that she possessed any affection to steal), I couldn't work up a grudge against him — at least not a conscious one.

Keith and I didn't usually keep company, but as I threw the last of my papers on Thunderbird Street, I saw him in front of his house. I rode up the driveway and, after a friendly greeting, he showed me the customized bike he'd been working on in the garage. In the mid-sixties, Detroit turned out instant classics in Thunderbirds, Mustangs, Stingrays, and XKEs, so custom cars seemed hardly necessary, but an artistic hot rod always elicited admiration. Likewise with bicycles: the innovative Schwinn stingrays and Varsity ten-speeds of that era were splendid, but a sharp custom bike generated its own cachet. Keith's set of wheels featured fancy lights, a battery-powered horn, and a seat with cartoon wolf logo. Its wide white sidewall tires and small frame looked particularly stylish with an extended seat pole and butterfly handlebars.

Suitably impressed, I invited Keith to my place to see my CO_2 BB gun, then the top weapon among fifth-graders. As we parked our bikes in my driveway, Benjy Allard happened along. The day before he had committed some slight against me—so slight I can't remember anything about it now. It must have been trivial even then, for Benjy seemed unaware of its commission as he approached with a smile and a witty remark.

At that juncture I proceeded to go insane. Without premeditation I rushed up and began to berate him. His uncomprehending look infuriated me. I pushed him. He tripped and fell, and I stood snarling over him. In shock he stumbled to his feet, stuttering, "What—what'd I do?"

I told him incoherently what he'd done; then I pushed again, harder. I didn't progress to actual blows, but only because he didn't fight back. When he tried to leave the scene, I pushed him from behind and he sprawled on the ground and began to cry.

Could I have been showing off for Keith? If so, it didn't make sense. I would have bet in advance that he wouldn't approve. Now he stood by—characteristically calm, not interfering, but obviously troubled.

So was the showing off for someone else? By this time the Drolet sisters, the Verdiman brothers, and several other neighbor kids had gathered to watch, but I barely registered their presence. Anyway, pushing Benjy around demonstrated no great strength or bravery. Besides, I had never picked on anyone to show off before; I even refrained from meanness to Trish and Greg in public. Could I have been acting out my sublimated anger at Delia and Keith? Or my repressed rage at Daddy's death? Of course, nothing of the sort occurred to me at the time; I felt only blind fury—the first since I chased the kid with the nosebleed back in Redondo.

Keith might have stepped in on Benjy's side any minute, and I wonder now how such a turn would have affected my unbalanced state. Would I have attacked him, too? But before the situation obliged Keith to commit himself, help arrived from another quarter. One of Benjy's four little sisters had witnessed my attack and ran to find big brother Roy Allard. Roy, a serious kid who played on the Huntington Beach High tennis team, regularly attended Dodger games and wanted to be a minister. He came running with his best friend Martin, another ninth-grader who lived across the street. Martin's dad served as pastor of the Allard family's congregation.

Roy interposed himself between me and Benjy. When I snarled something insulting, he began to push me while lecturing on picking on people my own size—a bit hypocritical, I thought, since he stood a foot taller than I. I brought this observation to his attention, and he turned bright red. "You're just a little smart aleck, Ricky, and nobody likes you!"

I backed away from his onslaught. Benjy continued to sob. Roy's friend stood by Keith, both of them watching. It occurred to me then that Keith might have helped *me* in this two-on-one scene, but then I wondered if he thought me as reprehensible as Roy accused me of being. As this unpleasant possibility crossed my mind, Roy gave me a final shove. He and the preacher's son then led Benjy home, their arms around the little guy's shoulders.

I turned to see Keith peddling away down the street. The rest of the onlookers rushed in to surround me. After a couple of minutes of listening to me berating Roy and justifying my actions, the neighborhood kids also wandered off, not, it would seem, fully convinced of my righteousness. I looked around for a sympathetic face. Across the street, Dan and Gary Kalani stood in their driveway, murmuring quietly to one another. Then Dan jerked his head to indicate that I should come over to them.

I would like to report that I instead ran after Benjy to apologize or at least retreated for home to think things over, but neither of these options occurred to me. I crossed the street and followed Dan and Gary to their side yard, where they put their arms around me, football huddle style. Then they told me what the play was going to be.

The next afternoon around 4:30, after finishing about half of my paper route, I circled back to the Kalani house. After terse greetings, all three brothers and I crouched in the side yard, with Wayne as lookout. After a few minutes, the late bus for high school kids on sports teams or other after-school activities arrived at its usual stop a block down the street. Roy Allard and his friend Martin were exiting by the bus's front door steps as Dan and Gary reviewed my role in the imminent action.

The Kalani brothers felt about Roy and Martin the same way Tom Sawyer and Joe Harper felt about Albert Temple and Willie

Mufferson in *The Adventures of Tom Sawyer*. In the kid world, whether it be Missouri 1845 or Huntington Beach 1964, neighborhood goody-goodies were considered traitors in the struggle against grownup oppression, and thus fair game for harassment. Dan and Gary would have already been regularly chastising Roy and Martin, except Mrs. Kalani absolutely forbade them to start any fights. She brought her kids to the mainland partially to get them away from the urban gang culture of Honolulu, and she set about resolutely to "raise them right."

Some examples will illustrate her determination. When Mrs. Kalani caught Gary starting a fight with a schoolmate, she grounded him for a month. When Dan drew a school suspension for smoking, she grounded him for a month AND whipped him with a belt. The most fearsome fourteen-year-old in town took it meekly, even though he outweighed her by eighty pounds. When Wayne received two F's on his report card, she marched to the school and demanded that the principal hold him back to repeat fifth grade, even though they would have "social passed" him if she hadn't insisted.

So the Kalani boys knew their mom meant business, and they generally avoided any behavior that would upset her if there were a chance she could find out about it. Beating up on neighborhood nerds for fun definitely fit that category; however, the recent scene between me and Roy and Martin presented the perfect opportunity: they could claim honorable retribution against two big haoles (Hawaiian for "foreign devils") who recently ganged up on poor little Ricky, the Kalanis' recent guest and honorary family member.

All I had to do, Gary explained as we peeked around the side of the house, was approach Roy and Martin, now off the bus and strolling down the sidewalk.

"Walk right up to 'em and say something smartass," whispered Gary.

"What should I say?"

"You're a smartass. Think of something."

"Huh?"

The targets were getting closer. Gary hissed, "Call Allard a fag."

"What's a fag?"

"A mahu, a queer. Call 'em a couple of skinny-ass faggots and get 'em to chase you this way. We'll do the rest."

The plan worked perfectly. As I swaggered up the sidewalk, Roy and his friend stopped and watched my approach curiously. Martin gave me a stern look and started to say something, but I cut him off. "You queers don't scare me," I said, in my best cowboy movie villain soprano growl.

Martin stopped in mid-syllable and Roy's face turned bright red. It took them a second to react, and as they lunged, I turned and ran. They were closing fast as we passed the Kalani house, but as I felt Martin's hand grabbing at the back of my collar, Dan and Gary set upon them. In case their mom happened to be watching out the window, the Hawaiians punctuated the ensuing punches and kicks with, "You wan' beef? Pick on somebody you own size, huh!" "Mess wid our bruddah, huh, you mess wid us!" and other righteous exclamations. I stood with younger brother Wayne at a safe distance until Roy and Martin were allowed to limp away, accompanied by derisive comments from their conquerors.

Presented with apparently unimpeachable evidence, Mrs. Kalani backed Gary and Dan in their humanitarian endeavor. The brothers strutted about, well-pleased with the whole business, and I had achieved revenge on Roy, but personal and intra-neighborhood repercussions accompanied the victory. The Oasis drive political map became, for a month at least, as sharply drawn as Europe in World War II: the Axis powers included various ethnics, including the Kalanis and Verdimans and the other Indians down the street); the white "bad kids," comprising Kevin, the always-in-trouble kid from the single parent home (more on him later); and the Cadillac-driving white trash, as represented by my family, who supported me after they'd heard Mrs. Kalani's version of the fight). The Allies were composed of the church-going neighbors of the Allards and other whites on the block.

By dint of their all-female offspring, the Drolets remained neutral and managed to stay out of the crossfire. Little came of the charged atmosphere except gossip, but the incident generated plenty of that. Some of the parents continued off speaking terms long after everything blew over with the kids.

But I'm getting ahead of the story. Rather than feeling an ongoing sense of triumph after the incident, depression set in. I always considered myself a fair fighter and a stand-up guy whom friends could trust. But now I felt like one of Vic Morrow's gang of vicious juvenile delinquents in *King Creole*, the 1958 Elvis vehicle I'd seen recently on the KHJ Channel 9 Million Dollar Movie. The young hoods who inveigled Elvis into the gang weren't at all romantic—they were cruel punks who beat Elvis's screen father nearly to death. It became clearer and clearer to me (the last to know) that I attacked Benjy for no good reason. Furthermore, I knew Roy and Martin, whom I'd led into a premeditated ambush, hadn't done anything wrong in stopping me—if anything, I could take a lesson from Roy in how to be a protective brother. I had sunk so low as to even regret my callous treatment of Trish and Greg.

If only I could go back and start over, or if Benjy would let bygones be bygones somehow without my having to admit my fault or apologize. In those days and through my teen years, I held to the creed that being wrong was bad enough without having to admit it. But when I saw Benjy at school, he kept as much distance as possible between us. Meanwhile, mob fever rose quickly: Wayne Kalani and Bobby Verdiman promoted further action against Benjy and anyone else in the fifth grade who wanted to stand with him. By default I became the linchpin of the whole business—the axis powers expected me to start the neighborhood war by baiting Roy or attacking Benjy again.

But I had no heart for any of it. If only bygones could be bygones … but I had no character tools or cultural framework in which to make the necessary amends. However, I did have a cynical awareness of my always-precarious standing in the neighborhood pecking order. If my current ally and perennial nemesis Bobby Verdiman detected any inclination on my part to reconcile with the Allards, he would perceive it as going soft. He would then lose his fear of my speed and boxing prowess, the fear that had so far given me the edge over his greater size. And woe be upon me if I found myself on the wrong side of the Kalanis. So I said nothing and continued my feeble effort to work up a grudge against Benjy, or Roy, or anyone.

The fourth morning after the fight brought a perfect twist to the saga. I walked to school in a dark mood, moping down deserted Oasis Street, not caring that I was late to school and would probably have to stay after as punishment.

Behind me rang a little girl's voice. "Ricky! Wait!"

I looked up to see I had just passed the Allard house. And here came Beth Allard, one of Benjy's little sisters. No guys paid much attention to their friends' younger female siblings, but Beth, with her curly hair and cheerful disposition always reminded me of Shirley Temple and I'd been gruffly friendly with her before. I turned, dreading that she would say something recriminatory. My spirits were low enough already without having to endure a little girl making me feel even worse.

"Ricky, Benjy forgot his lunch. Can you please bring it to him?" Beth held the lunch bag out to me, smiling like Shirley charming the gangsters in her movies.

Had no one told her about the fight? If she did know about it, was she attempting to make me feel guilty? I couldn't bring myself to snarl at her, and I couldn't explain that her brother preferred to avoid me. I couldn't even make myself turn away. Finally, without a word, I took the lunch and continued toward school.

The bag had Benjy's name written on it, so I could have left it by the classroom door. But like an embezzler returning to a bank with half the money he stole or traitor walking into military headquarters with a signed confession, I made my way to the playground. Benjy saw me coming. His lip trembled a bit, but he stood his ground.

"Your sister gave me this. You forgot it," I said, thrusting the bag at him.

He took it, and stood staring at me. In the kid movie version, he would have smiled and stuck out his hand to shake. The soundtrack violin music would swell and we'd stroll out to the baseball field arm in arm.

In real life he did say, haltingly, wonderingly, "Thanks." But his look spoke this more clearly: "We may associate with one another socially again at some point. But I will never be able to trust you."

I walked away. What could I say? I couldn't trust myself either.

My eleventh birthday party took place a few weeks later as a sort of grand opening for the newly walnut-paneled garage Jay had transformed into a rumpus room. The rumpus room constituted a major home improvement in those days, adding two-hundred square feet to the living space and proclaiming that leisure and entertainment superseded the provincial desire to keep one's car out of the weather. Speaking of weather, rain poured on the party day, and the festivities were correspondingly low-key, nothing like the authentic teen bash I would have the next year, featuring girls, dancing, and even kissing games. At the 1964 eleventh birthday, my guests and I merely listened to some Beatles, Herman's Hermits, and Kinks records; ate cake and ice cream; and played a few retro games, like drop the clothespin in the milk bottle. I don't recall the full guest list, but I do remember that the older Kalanis, Bobby Verdiman, Benjy Allard, and Delia were conspicuous in their absence.

So as I embarked on my twelfth year, I may not have quite sunk to Oasis Drive Pariah, but I was definitely not in Keith's strata of popularity. Speaking of Keith, he didn't attend the party either. After causing me all that trouble, he moved two weeks ahead of the revised military schedule, leaving his girl fan club inconsolable.

CHAPTER FORTY-EIGHT

~ Deep Pockets and Business School ~ Forsaking Larceny
~ Magic Kingdom Lone Wolf ~ Touring Frisco ~ I Missed the Dead Before
You Missed the Dead ~ If It's on the Menu...

For all my social trials in the closing months of fifth grade, I had one consolation that has seemingly soothed many a troubled soul before me: I was rich.

How rich? In the early sixties, allowances paid to middle-class children my age probably averaged fifty cents per week. I had earned that much for the past two years in exchange for garbage detail and basic lawn care, but had recently been granted a liberal cost of living adjustment to seventy-five cents. This amount provided more than sufficient funds for a reasonable social life,[41] but compared to my other sources of income, I considered it mere pocket change.

My paper route provided the bulk of my new wealth. Across Springdale Avenue, in fields where, in the misty past of early '63, we used to fly kites among the frogs and wildflowers, gigantic housing tracts full of new *Daily Pilot* customers sprang up rapidly. By summer 1964 my route grew from twenty-five subscribers to more than a hundred, and I earned eighty or more dollars per month. As we shall see, I had yet additional sources of income, but my base pay exceeded the income of most boys my age by something like 11,000%. Extrapolated to the adult world in modern times, I would be in the top federal bracket and paying wealth surcharges on my state income tax. But of course I paid no taxes and had no living expenses. My parents supplied food, clothes and miscellaneous necessities, and I continued to receive my allowance. Some paper boys' parents forced them to bank half or more of their monthly

---

[41] Some 1964 prices: candy bar, five cents; comic books, twelve cents; movies, 35–50 cents.

earnings for school clothes, college fund, etc., but Jay and Jane, who never saved a penny, rarely placed financial strictures on their kids that they avoided themselves.

So, by any local standard I was moneyed, affluent, well-to-do, flush, and in the chips. But as any small businessman (I stood around 5'1" at the time) will tell you, wealth demands sacrifice. Every weekday afternoon and Saturday morning I forsook pickup ballgames, TV (including the *Lloyd Thaxton Hop* and Felix the Cat reruns), and general lollygagging. Instead I came straight home from school and proceeded directly to folding the inevitable stack of papers Mr. Simmons delivered to my driveway. I then heaved the paper bag over the handlebars of my old bike, and come rain, illness, or tempting recreational opportunities, I pedaled steadfastly from five to ten miles, which took two or more hours per day as the route expanded.

Only once in eighteen months did I miss delivering my papers. That rainy day I had strep throat, so Jane forbade me to leave the house. I had to get the route done somehow, so with the enticement of three dollars, I enlisted Carl Verdiman, my next-door neighbor and former landscaping business partner.

An hour later Carl returned, soaked to the skin and bearing the lurid tale that "Some big guys pushed me off my bike and stole all the papers!"

"What?! I gotta pay for those papers! They took them ALL?"

"Uh, I delivered all the ones up to Calneva."

So he had worked for twenty minutes, tops. "What'd the guys look like?"

"Big guys ... ninth-graders, prob'ly."

Carl became more evasive when I pressed him for details. I called Mr. Simmons, expecting him to as furious as I was, but he only chuckled and said he'd be right out to help me.

Jane recognized that a man had to do what a man had to do, and didn't attempt to impede my duty. She gave me a fresh tin of Sucrets throat lozenges and I went through several of them as I sat in the back of his station wagon, folding papers and putting them in wax paper bags. Mr. Simmons could fold and bag as he steered the car in the rain and threw papers from the windows. He said he'd heard the same story several times about guys beating up the sub and stealing the papers. "Boys who lie like that will never have what it takes," he said.

This was of course an indirect compliment; he saw me as a lad with initiative and a strong work ethic. But these attributes were not the sum of my character. A general lack of inherent or ingrained moral values left me vulnerable to the temptation for easy money. For instance, sometime that season I began, even as I pedaled along my suburban streets looking the perfect portrait of all-American industrious youth, to devise a Jay-like embezzlement scheme.

The accounting system for paper routes worked as follows: when subscribers signed up, Mr. Simmons would bring two items: a "pink slip" for each containing their name and address information and a blank customer card. The card had a space to fill in the customer's name and address and rows of tear-off receipt stubs for each month of the year. During my monthly collection, I gave tear-off stubs from the cards to make each transaction official.

A plan for getting around this system began to germinate when Mr. Simmons began leaving ten "samples" each day — i.e., extra papers for me to distribute to potential customers in the new houses. Well, what if I solicited legitimate new customers from five of the samples and used the other five for an even more profitable venture? I could start by reporting falsely that I had lost, say, five blank receipt cards. Then I could sign up five new customers using those blank cards and not notify the company at all. Then each month I could use five samples to service five shadow customers and collect $1.25 — the full subscription price — from each one. I could then give the shadow customer an official monthly receipt stub from the bogus card, and all would look official.

Thinking through this scheme made me feel as proudly crafty as "Doc" Riedenschneider, criminal genius in the 1950 caper movie *The Asphalt Jungle*, a heavily-edited version of which I had seen recently on TV. Within a week I set the plan in motion. Casually, I asked Mr. Simmons for additional customer blanks, saying I must have misplaced some. He complied, seemingly without suspicion, and left the usual extra ten papers for samples. So far, so good. But as I peddled toward the new housing tract where I would distribute the samples and sign up the bogus customers, my larcenous resolve began to falter and the samples seemed to glow radioactively in my extra-full paper bags. I remembered Mr. Simmons's kindness on the day I got sick, when he drove me in the rain and said I had what it took. Then I imagined the look on his face if he were to discover my deception.

In addition to moral considerations, I began to see some flaws in my master plan. What if one of my shadow customers called the office about a delayed paper? Mr. Simmons would know instantly what I'd done. And even if the ruse worked perfectly, I'd have to keep two sets of records and lie to Mr. Simmons about the samples every week. Five bogus customers at $1.25 per month profit vs. five legit customers at sixty cents plus the order credit or cash I would get for signing them up … I realized my grand heist would net me only three dollars a month. And I would still have to deliver and collect for the extra papers to get my money. Furthermore, if one of the bogus customers absconded without paying, I'd lose the whole $1.25!

But wait—what if I serviced ten or fifteen bogus customers for credit? Then I could make some real money! And if I couldn't cadge enough samples from Mr. Simmons, I could for a dime get a whole stack of them from the honor-system newsstands at gas stations and liquor stores. Yes … but that would be getting into serious criminal activity, the kind that sent guys like Eddie the bike thief to juvy (juvenile hall). But then again, if I were careful with stealing the news rack papers, I wouldn't have to worry about Mr. Simmons being suspicious of the extra samples…

I pedaled along, poised on the slippery slope of criminality. Then Jay's moral guidance shined forth. I remembered his maxim: "Steal, but don't be greedy" and realized that too much risk for such little gain would be stupid. I scratched my grand caper and gave Mr. Simmons the extra blank cards the next day.

"Found the other ones," I said, averting my gaze as I handed them back.

"Good." When I glanced up, Mr. Simmons's face wore what seemed to be a searching look. "It's not smart business to have blanks laying around."

Soon afterward, a new income avenue opened up to net me much more than petty larceny would have. Beginning in early '64 I gave up evening TV, often depriving myself of the essential music showcase shows *Shindig* and *Hullaballoo,* which featured all the best British and Motown artists—I even missed the Beatles' only appearance on Shindig. I made this great cultural sacrifice for a highly lucrative second job, working from 6:30 to 9:00 three or four nights a week with Mr. Simmons's team of mostly-teenage subscription solicitors.

New Orange County homeowners kept pouring into the freshly-minted tracts, and the latest neighborhoods provided fertile fields for door-to-door subscription harvesting. Mr. Simmons would drop us off in some virgin territory — Huntington Harbor, say, or Fountain Valley, and we set forth, carrying enticements to subscribe. These included imitation-bone handle steak knives, imitation-leather memo books, and the like. We had seasonal items like plastic table top Christmas trees and stuffed Easter Bunnies, and customers could also opt for a free one-month subscription. But the steak knives remained the big draw.

My sales persona developed into a friendly, sincere, "upstanding young man" approach I could portray much better in sales presentations than in genuine personal relations. The method seemed to work; though I was the youngest member of the crew, I nonetheless became one of two top producers in the district, nightly pulling in an average of five new "orders," each exchangeable for a fifty-cent cash payoff, prize redemption points, or credits toward company excursions.

Competitive lads made up the crew, but Mr. Simmons promoted a team spirit. At quitting time each night, he would drive us to the local burger place. Depending on our overall sales, he would treat us to cokes, or cokes and fries, or even burgers, fries, and malts if we'd had a particularly good evening.

I never traded in newspaper subscription orders for their fifty-cent cash value, for I had plenty of cash already. Occasionally I would opt for the prizes chosen from premium books reminiscent of Blue Chip Stamp catalogues, only geared to the boy market. The book featured everything from impulse, one-order purchases of giant candy bars to full-dress bikes for 100 orders. But our special paperboy excursions provided the best deal of all. Someone in the *Daily Pilot* office worked hard to arrange the trips, and in retrospect, I think the company actually did feel affection for their young workhorses. A mere six orders — cash value, three dollars — would convey us by luxury bus (well, nicer than school busses, anyhow) to Disneyland in nearby Anaheim. The "Magic Kingdom" shined like Mecca to us kids, and it seemed almost sacrilegious that my current family had never been there.

Thanks to the *Pilot*, I made several pilgrimages in 1964-65. Excitement would mount as our bus pulled into the vast Disneyland parking lot. We pocketed the pea shooters with which we'd been blasting passing cars all along the way and leaned forward eagerly in our seats. The *Pilot* managers distributed admission and ten-ticket books to each boy, then added a dollar in cash for lunch. (Yes, in those days a dollar would actually buy a burger, fries, and coke at Disneyland.) Then our ostensible chaperones turned us loose on the Magic Kingdom with no adult supervision whatsoever. I suspect they may have spent the afternoon in the Disneyland Hotel bar until time to drive home—they always seemed pretty jolly on the way back.

On the first trip that summer I fell in with some older paperboys from Costa Mesa who cared little for standard Disneyland amusements. With me in tow, they first terrorized Main Street with bean shooters, then purchased chewing tobacco at the cigar store and proceeded to Tomorrowland to ride the skyway cars, spitting tobacco juice on the people strolling below. (The eventual corporate decision to remove skyway cars from the modern Disneyland may have been at least partially inspired by those antics.) But however fun, continuous troublemaking seemed to me rather limited in scope. Beginning with my second visit, I became a Disneyland lone wolf, roving the park with imagination on full blast as childhood reading comingled with elaborate time-traveler fantasies. As I passed into each different "land"—Tomorrowland, Jungleland, Frontierland, etc. I spent more time wandering and daydreaming than I did in the long lines for rides.

Pilot orders also conveyed me to other Southern California wonders I would never have seen otherwise. These included Knott's Berry Farm in Buena Park and two now-extinct amusement parks: Nu-Pike in Long Beach and P.O.P. (Pacific Ocean Park) in Santa Monica. Both venues had dangerous roller coasters, and Nu-Pike featured a seedy row of tattoo parlors filled with drunken sailors and their girls—a fine opportunity to expand my social awareness. In December, for only four orders, we bussed to Santa's Village in the San Bernardino Mountains. The primitive rides at the Village couldn't compare with Disneyland's state-of-the-art attractions, but no matter—the hick place had actual snow on the ground! No Minnesota kid ever drew as much entertainment from a long winter of snowball fights as we season-deprived Southern Californians enjoyed during one freezing afternoon.

The acme of *Daily Pilot* trips took place early in 1965: a plane ride to San Francisco followed by a guided tour of the city and two deluxe meals—and all for only thirty orders ($15 cash value). Since only the elite sales personnel of mostly fifteen- and sixteen-year-olds could afford such a big ticket excursion, the adventure and status value compares relatively with the ostentatious tours of the Amazon, Himalayas, or Antarctica so popular now with young millionaires.

I was the youngest tycoon on the plane; sixteen-year-old Norman, my only rival for top order producer, also represented Mr. Simmons's district. These days, one can observe forty-year-old men wearing low-slung cargo shorts and backwards baseball caps as they ride their skateboards; in the mid-sixties about the same percentage of sixteen-year-olds strove to act as if they'd never been kids. Norman typified this fast-vanishing breed—he disdained rock and roll, voluntarily kept his hair short, and always wore a tie when he solicited door to door. He even put on a tie for the San Francisco trip.

Mr. Simmons and Norman picked me up at 6:30 a.m. and we met the other districts' high rollers at LAX a couple of hours later. Storm clouds covered the state, and the prop plane ride to San Francisco seemed rougher than the rickety Nu-Pike rollercoaster. Even the stewardesses looked uncomfortable. I had just lifted my coffee cup (the pretty women served us the hard stuff like we were grownups!) when the plane took a deep dip. The coffee shot up in an arc and seemed to hang suspended in midair for an appreciable time before splashing in Norman's lap. He was already airsick and the extra stimulation didn't help his disposition.

The rest of the trip maintained this level of excitement. A tour bus driver who, with his shaved head and rotund shape, bore a striking resemblance to Uncle Fester on *The Addams Family* TV show, met us at the airport and whisked us around the city. From the bus window, I employed the little camera I'd bought from the paperboy prize book to take four or five rolls of out-of-focus photos, including at least ten long views of the Golden Gate Bridge. A group shot or even a photo with a person in it never occurred to me.

On an interesting counter-cultural note, our visit roughly coincided with an historic moment: the Grateful Dead (then known as the Warlocks) played for the first time at McGoo's pizza parlor. We passed that establishment in our tour of the city; I noted it then because of the name association with Mr. McGoo, the blind old man cartoon character voiced by Jim Backus. In two years, "Frisco" (or "Frasco" in hippie dialect) would surpass Disneyland as the next Mecca for youth, and the more unstable lads among us would transition from Mickey Mouse and Main Street to the Grateful Dead and Haight Street. The Dead would also be instrumental, as it were, in killing AM radio as we knew it. Unfortunately I missed my chance to see the band during their poor and struggling period. Even if I had been free to roam on my own during the San Francisco tour, I had no time or inclination in 1965 to hear musicians who didn't appear with the Shindig dancers in the background.

Instead, prior to an afternoon at the zoo (where I took two rolls of out-of-focus animal photos), we lunched at Cliff House restaurant near Seal Rock. Then, to crown the day before our late return flight, we rode the cable cars and had dinner at legendary Fisherman's Wharf. The restaurant menu ran to several pages of ocean exotica, but I looked in vain for the only seafood I even remotely liked: processed fish sticks as served in the school cafeteria. However, anticipating my antipathy to clams, squid, and swordfish, the last page of the menu listed spaghetti and meatballs. My order seemed reasonable to the waiter, but prompted derision among the older guys at the table.

"Look, sonny," said Norman the premature adult. "When you're in a famous seafood restaurant, you're supposed to order seafood."

"Oh yeah?" I countered. "So why do they have spaghetti on the menu if you're not supposed to order it?"

He rolled his eyes as if to say there was no use talking to such an infant, but I remained supremely satisfied that my logic was superior, even if he did have a deep voice and wear a tie.

CHAPTER FORTY-NINE

~ Living La Vida Rico ~ Nice Cookies ~ Collecting First Editions
~ Sic Semper Barberous ~ Hot Weltschmerz

To continue my somewhat wistful account of the one time in my life I felt comfortably wealthy, I recall that when the 1957 movie *Around the World in Eighty Days* netted many millions for the already-rich producer Mike Todd, a famous columnist reported that Todd opined, "How am I gonna spend all this loot?" By the end of summer 1964, I faced a similar dilemma, for in addition to the large sums I earned from my paper route and selling subscriptions, I began to amass even more wealth as a high-rolling neighborhood gambler.

A year or so before, Mrs. Verdiman taught the Oasis Drive boys how to shuffle cards and deal various incarnations of poker. I practiced my fan shuffle assiduously, and with the Verdiman and Kalani brothers played rounds of five-card draw and seven-card stud (jokers and deuces wild), plus low-ball, seven-card baseball, and no-peekie, with an occasional round of blackjack. I usually won more pennies than I lost in these games, but when my new friend Kevin arrived, my gambling income skyrocketed.

Right before the end of the school term, Kevin and his mom moved into a rental three doors down on Oasis Drive. The neighborhood had begun to turn over residents who couldn't keep up their mortgage payments, and investors bought a few houses for rental property. Kevin, though a year younger than I and a mere fourth-grader, stood taller than any kid in school. Short tough guys would cross the street to shove him around, and, though always ready to initiate other trouble (usually vandalism and petty theft), the gentle giant never fought back. This pacifistic approach to conflict did not run in Kevin's family: his dad and various step-dads showed themselves as violent types before they departed, and his seventeen-year-old brother currently resided in juvenile hall for an assault conviction.

Kevin's mom, who worked nights as a cocktail waitress,

reminded me of the women in Jay's *Stag* magazines. She doted on her huge baby boy and routinely gave him at least fifty cents a day from her large tip change jar in the living room. When seven times the typical neighborhood allowance wasn't sufficient for his needs, Kevin helped himself to handfuls of coins from the jar. He actually jingled when he walked.

Thanks to this steady income, Kevin could keep up with my rich lifestyle. At Tibet's market, other kids would eke out their allowance for small cokes and penny candy, but big spenders Ricky and Kevin always went first cabin: quarts of Dr. Pepper for me and Dad's Root Beer for him, plus family size bags of peanut M&Ms, giant Mr. Goodbars, 39-cent packs of pistachios, and fifteen-cent sticks of beef jerky.

We consumed these delicacies behind the store or back at the Hill garage-turned-rumpus-room, and in either location I always kept my poker cards handy. We played high-stakes games, and pots could swell to a dollar or more. Kevin knew even less than I did about elementary poker strategy, but if I cleaned him out (as I usually did), he would simply repair to the change jar at home, so I could usually count on him for five to ten dollars a week to add to my other sources of income. Mike Todd had nothing on me.

One Saturday afternoon sometime in late summer or early autumn 1964 stands out as the perfect illustration of those flush times, but also provides a reminder that money does not necessarily buy contentment.

I'd finished my paper route by noon and returned home to prepare for adventures on the town. While combing my hair and arraying myself in period finery (tight white pants, short-sleeved black turtleneck shirt, elastic-sided Beatle boots), I scanned my room with the satisfaction of the self-made man, junior grade. The record rack below the stereo now stood current with Elvis Presley LPs: everything in the RCA catalogue, from Elvis's first album through the *Kissin' Cousins* soundtrack. In addition to all available Beatles albums, I owned multiple LPs by the Rolling Stones, Dave Clark Five, Beach Boys, and Herman's Hermits. I owned a growing collection of singles as well: Kinks, Lesley Gore, Supremes, Petula Clark, et al.

But any visitor to my room could discern that my interests ranged beyond music. Next to the regulation dart board on my wood-paneled wall hung my 30-pound-test bow and quiver of arrows, with which I practiced archery for a short time. At Jane's urging a few months before, Jay had taken me on our first father/son outing since I'd accompanied him to work in the Sylmar days. We went to a venture in Westminster called Robin Hood Lanes, where archery enthusiasts could shoot at targets placed on bales of hay at the end of former bowling lanes. To retrieve the arrows, the space-age archer simply pushed a button, and an electric carriage brought the whole operation forward on wheels that followed the tracks of the old bowling alley gutters.

Getting back to my room and moving technologically forward in the weapons line, my BB rifle and pistol hung on the wall between the bow and Beatle posters. These top of the line guns employed CO_2 cartridges for maximum power—none of your have-to-pump-it-fifty-times cheapos for me. Gadgets, magic tricks, practical joke items, decals, and model cars covered every surface, along with ticket stubs for movies and amusement parks, two giant Hershey bars and a one-pound Sugar Daddy sucker purchased with *Daily Pilot* subscription orders, and of course my vast but unorganized comic book and *Mad* collection.

This day, a half-empty box of Girl Scout cookies added to the jumble. I had acquired the box on my paper route earlier that morning. Angling from street to sidewalk for a porch shot, I spied two Girl Scouts, in uniform with shoulder satchels, leaving a porch down the block. My dim vision couldn't make out their features, but I knew the general shapes of Delia Thornton and Pattie Grant. Pattie towered over most of the boys in the school, and her green uniform hung on her lanky frame. Delia's longer hair and more interesting gait were achingly familiar, and her uniform fit better. She didn't compare with Kevin's mom as yet, but the object of my devotion had begun to take on new dimensions.

I rode up to meet them at the sidewalk and, in the manner of a fellow professional door-to-door salesman, inquired about their line of goods.

"Girl Scout cookies," Delia replied politely enough, but her half-smile seemed to add, "Which should be obvious."

Pattie, showing fine aptitude as a glass-ceiling-breaking marketing executive, began pulling boxes from her shoulder satchel. Balancing her inventory on one arm, she ticked off the merchandise: "Thin Mints, Samoas, and Trefoils, and they're only sixty cents each. How many boxes would you like, Ricky?" She probably meant the question as banter; we both knew that kids never bought sixty-cent boxes of cookies—such items we considered groceries, i.e. for parents to purchase and kids to eat.

I shrugged with studied casualness, and then pulled my bankroll from the pocket of my white jeans. Said roll, secured with a 1904 Morgan silver dollar money clip purchased recently at the coin collector store, consisted of a lucky two-dollar bill, five crisp new one-dollar notes, a five, and a ten, folded with the ten on the outside. I peeled off two ones and handed them to Pattie. "I'll take one of each."

"Three boxes? Really?" Pattie's tone had lost all irony. At my nod, she handed over the cookies and began to dig in her pockets for change.

"That's all right," I said, dismissing the twenty cents with a casual wave.

I thought I saw Delia's expression take on a slightly heightened interest, but she had nothing more to say. Having made my impression, I mumbled "S'long" and pedaled away, opening a cookie box as I rode.

My primary motive for the purchase had been to show off, but I genuinely enjoyed Girl Scout cookies, and on my route I'd eaten all I'd bought except the half-empty box on the dresser. The dresser's top drawer overflowed with pennies, nickels, dimes, and a few quarters, plus un-cashed subscription orders and several worn one-dollar bills. But all this legal tender amounted to small change next to the cache I had secured in a miniature safe acquired from the paperboy catalogue ("With real combination lock! Only three orders!"). This strongbox hidden on the closet shelf contained around a hundred dollars, plus my most valuable coin collection items and keepsakes. And the wad of bills I'd flashed for the girls that morning? Petty cash.

I pocketed the funds and put the finishing touches on my hair. Eventually I made my way toward Springdale Street, riding my old paper route bike. My choice of transportation seems odd now — as if, instead of buying a brand new Cadillac when he became rich, Elvis had cruised around Memphis in his pre-fame Crown Electric Company truck. Wal-Mart founder Sam Walton invites closer comparison; he is said to have actually driven an old pickup truck around Bentonville, Arkansas, even after he became a billionaire. I can't speak for Sam's motives, but I have some idea of mine. I could have afforded a Schwinn Stingray or ten-speed with no parental subsidy, but my pop-culture sensor was beginning to pick up traces of pre-hippie reverse snobbery, the attitude that would soon manifest in the ragged-jeans counterculture. Thus I could exhibit low-rent coolness in riding my old junker, and I didn't have to worry too much about Eddie and his chop-shop pals making off with it.

Had I run into a friend or acquaintance, I would have invited him to join me downtown, but most of the guys had already set forth on their day's activities while I finished my paper route. I usually preferred going solo anyway, since I tended to ride farther and spend more money than anyone I knew. Plus, friends tended to get impatient when I took the time to read a whole magazine or several chapters of a paperback book at the liquor store.

My first stop was the Westminster Bowl, where I availed myself of their three-games-for-a-dollar special. Because of my poor distance vision I couldn't read the alley numbers, so to find my assigned lane I manually counted from the left end of the building. Even squinting I couldn't see the pins as distinctive entities, but I could aim with reasonable accuracy at the blur of white and red at the end of the lane. Between frames, I refreshed myself with a large vanilla coke, and after turning in my rental shoes, I dropped a couple of quarters (at three games per) on pinball. On this day I paid full retail for the games because Eddie wasn't around to provide a discount. He and his pals sometimes came early and placed four ashtrays under the legs of the pinball table. One would then act as lookout while another, usually Eddie, went to work. The modification slowed the ball down considerably, making it easy to rack up the maximum twenty free games in no time. They would then remove the ashtrays and sell the games to passersby at five for a quarter.

I rode on to Grant's department store, where I fed a few dimes into the shooting gallery. With distance not a factor and much weekly practice, I could usually approach the maximum 900 points, but this machine offered no three-for-a-quarter discount nor free-game incentive, so I didn't linger. Next destination, the liquor mart for the Marvel comics I'd recently begun to collect in earnest. I bought nearly a dozen titles a month, plus double-priced summer annuals.[42] Marvel characters weren't merely superheroes; they acted like real people: they lost their tempers, didn't always get the

---

[42] From memory: *Fantastic Four, Spiderman, The Avengers, X-Men, Tales of Suspense* featuring Iron Man, *Tales to Astonish* featuring Giant Man and The Hulk, *Journey into Mystery* featuring The Mighty Thor, *Strange Tales* featuring the Human Torch and Dr. Strange, *Sgt. Fury and his Howling Commandos, Daredevil,* and an occasional western title from among *Two Gun Kid, Rawhide Kid,* or *Kid Colt.* The only Marvel comic I disdained was *Millie the Model.* All titles, including *Millie,* were written by Stan Lee with help from the artists.

girl, and sometimes found themselves outsmarted by the villains —
yet they were ready in any situation to provide the sort of quick
wisecrack that seemed perfectly brilliant to preteens.

Until fifth grade I generally preferred DC Comics over Marvels,
but everything changed when I read *Fantastic Four* # 25, "The Thing
vs. The Hulk" in, of all places, a barber shop. The Stan Lee and Jack
Kirby story exhibited Marvel at its zenith, but the issue was already
two months old and no longer available in stores.

I simply had to own it. First I offered the barber on duty a nickel,
the then going rate for used comics.

"A NICKEL?" he repeated in his exaggerated East-Coast manner.
"Nadda chance."

"Okay," I said patiently. "I'll give you a dime."

"Look, kid, the magazines are there for customers. That's why we
buy 'em. You wawk off wid 'em, the customers got nuttin' to read."

The item under consideration was the only comic book among
the sports pages and men's magazines, so some other kid probably
brought it in and forgot to take it home. But I didn't argue. "Okay,
I'll bring you another comic book to trade."

"Awright." He grinned avariciously. "But it's gotta be a new one."

"This one isn't new. See? The cover is coming loose."

"A new one. Take it or leave it."

The churlish utterance "Take it or leave it" has always irritated
me, but for the sake of Fantastic Four # 25, I endured without
comment. The barber smirked when I returned with a new comic
book to trade, thinking he'd gotten the best of me. But in exchange
for what is considered a half-century later as one of the finest
graphic novels ever written (and worth hundreds of dollars on
eBay), I traded him a brand new issue of the Harvey comic *Wendy
the Good Little Witch*. I picked that one out expressly for the scorn
every red-blooded future boy customer would feel at the sight of it,
but of course the dullard barber wouldn't know the difference. *Sic
Semper Tyrannis.*

Returning to my account of a free-spending afternoon, I bought
the Marvel titles I didn't already own and also stocked up on liquor
store snacks, sparing no expense for chocolate-covered cherries,
Hostess cupcakes, and other delicacies. Following this near-toxic
sugar dose, I felt a yen for real food, so I rode on to Biff's Coffee
shop. After parking my bike by the door I strolled in through the air
conditioning and space-age, parabolic décor to my usual seat at the

counter. The high-school-age waitress with beehive hair and heavy mascara came over with an order pad and a smile.

"Hi, Cutie. What can I get you?"

As with next-door-neighbor Cindy and her teen friends, this young lady's assessment of my cuteness did not exactly constitute the straightforward admiration I preferred. But in my best man-of-the-world manner I smiled back and ordered a hot beef and gravy sandwich with mashed potatoes. I washed this substantial meal down with a large coke and chose a hot fudge sundae for dessert. While waiting for the sundae, I stepped over to peruse the giant jukebox. With its robot arm record-changing mechanism, state of the art hi-fi sound, and updated art-deco chrome and electric pastel plastic design, the device could be appreciated as both an advanced engineering marvel and a work of modern art. The playlist featured mostly old-people's stuff — Frank Sinatra and his pals — but I pushed the appropriate red Bakelite buttons for Elvis's "Return to Sender" from the critically unacclaimed 1962 film, *Girls Girls Girls.*

The song's catchy-but-poignant, spurned-lover soliloquy spoke directly through the hi-fi speakers to my heart, for Elvis's girl troubles sounded remarkably similar to mine. All singers seemed to suffer so, with the possible exception of Dion, who, in the narrative song "The Wanderer," traveled around in his hot rod, beating up other guys with his iron fists and having relations with girls who didn't even know his name.

I sighed as I dug into my sundae. In some ways I related to Dion, for I could have my pick of girls at Springdale — or at least I could choose from Roberta, Gwen, and Junie, the three rather plain young ladies who let it be known publicly that they "liked" me. But I continued to carry a torch for Delia Thornton, and my devotion remained unrequited. The morning cookie scene demonstrated that the object of my affection remained enigmatic, monosyllabic, and everything but enthused by my chronic courtship.

Try as I might, I couldn't understand Delia's maddening indifference. By all rights she should see me as her one true soul mate, but she stubbornly resisted the script written in my heart. Life can be an existential trial, I mused (though without that specific articulation). To the other customers' irritation, I sent "Return to Sender" rocking through the restaurant twice more as I continued to muse. Somewhere in much later readings, I came across *Weltschmertz*, the German term for "world weariness." I definitely suffered from a case of junior *Weltschmerz* that day.

After scraping the last of my hot fudge sundae from its crystal dish, I left the waitress a ten-cent tip and made my exit, then retraced my route down Westminster Boulevard, dispersing cash as I went. I bought a few more candy bars and comic books at the liquor store, and at Grant's I splurged $2.98 plus tax on the Polaroid wrap-around sunglasses I'd considered earlier after my shooting gallery session. These modern items further hindered my weak vision, but they radiated too much style to pass up.

In the Grant's music section, I picked up a couple of new forty-fives, including "The Old Crowd" by Lesley Gore. The song, a B-side of "She's a Fool" from the year before, charted modestly as a re-release the following summer. The bittersweet Carole King / Gerry Goffin ballad of a high school graduate who longed for her former companions filled me with empathy. Hadn't I, too, been forced by cruel time and circumstance to leave behind many true friends and companions?

Feeling as sorry for myself as possible with all pockets stuffed and my bike rack packed to capacity, I returned to my lair. But while I lounged on my bed, eating a few candy bars and listening to Lesley Gore, I began to cheer up a bit. Like many a materialist before me, I understood that money wasn't everything. But I still appreciated the plenty of cash I could pour, like hot fudge, over my *Weltschmerz*.

CHAPTER FIFTY

~ Striking Out ~ Many Knives, None Sharp ~ Recess in High Heels
~ Cruel Youth ~ Drowned Hubris and a New Weltanschauung

"Strike one!"

The fastball smacks into the catcher's mitt before I can register it coming at me.

The catcher, a stocky thirteen-year-old, snarls, "Whatta punk — you can't hit!" I squint at the pitcher. Something familiar about him, but my nearsighted eyes can't make out his face from this distance…

For most people, the social drama of teenhood — intense identification with peers, status awareness, conformity with ephemeral fashion, first heartbreaks, and all the rest — begins late in junior high and peaks in the senior year of high school. But during my junior high years the family moved even more often than in earlier days and I missed whole months of school. By the time I made it to twelfth grade, I lived with a group of dropouts in a decrepit rooming house and intermittently attended courses at Apollo Continuation High School. Many of my peers at Apollo were juvenile hall veterans and the girls mostly underage and/or unwed mothers. We could smoke in class and leave when we felt like it, but we had no dances, organized sports, senior shows, or sophomoric political discussions. So my closest brush with high school social experience took place during my fifth and sixth grade years at Springdale Elementary, where, heaven knows, I tried my best to be a Classic American Teenager.

Through fifth grade all unfolded well enough: mostly good grades, well-read, active in sports, peer-group leader. In extra-curricular considerations, I remained the pop music authority and sharpest dresser on campus. Further, to paraphrase the Beach Boys in that year's big hit "I Get Around," the tough guys respected me enough to not bother me.

But then came sixth grade, where I began to learn that being a quick study takes one only so far. As other kids began to focus and excel in various endeavors, I became a young man, as the Asian proverb goes, with "many knives, none sharp." Thus and sadly, this chapter, and my sixth grade passage in general, is a tale of painful initiation into actual adolescence. I hasten to add that the year should by no means be rated a complete debacle; amusement and triumph also threaded through the fabric. As will be related, I went steady with two girls (though not at the same time) and learned the rudiments of guitar.[43] I also joined my first rock band and appeared on stage as a solo act. Furthermore, I became active in a national political campaign and saw my writing featured in a widely-distributed publication. But the overriding theme of sixth grade became "Learning humility the hard way — through humiliation."

The first lesson arose toward the end of the summer, before sixth-grade classes began. While I focused on building up my paper route, playing high-stakes poker, and collecting comic books, most of my peers spent their days at the school field playing catch and three-flies-up, honing their skills, making the transition from softball to hardball. I didn't pay much attention at first, but when I learned Bobby Verdiman had joined an intermediate hardball league where teams wore uniforms — not only tee-shirts, but real baseball pants with stirrup socks and cleats — I knew I must get back in the game.

Unfortunately, the games had been underway for at least three weeks by the time I signed up. Nonetheless, the league office accepted my enrollment fee and I arrived at the field slightly late for a Thursday afternoon game in my hastily purchased $12 uniform and $18 left-handed glove. Better late than never, I thought, but the coach seemed less than glad to meet me. He gave me an irritated glance, then waved vaguely at the bench.

Bobby Verdiman sat next to the last open spot. By way of greeting he snarled, "What are YOU doing here?"

I gave him the cool stare that always infuriated him, and I resolved to put him in his place, as I had in boxing, poker, and scholastics. I based my confidence on past baseball achievements: captain of the softball team in the fifth grade after-lunch league and the MVP of the Padres in last year's Park and Recreation summer league.

---

[43] My repertoire consisted of "Peter Gunn" on the bass E string and the theme from the TV show *The Outer Limits* (a *Twilight Zone* knockoff) on the high E. I didn't need the middle four strings at all.

But this hardball was something else again. At first I couldn't even figure out the stirrup socks. During the pre-game practices, everyone seemed to ignore me except Bobby, and I could have done without his attention. He grimaced and whispered to the other guys while pointing at me. The only breaks from this treatment came when the coach assigned Bobby to warm up the relief pitchers and play outfield a couple of innings each game. My nemesis was on the fast track to becoming team catcher when the current catcher moved up to the ninth-grade Babe Ruth league, and he seemed to have both the skill and acerbic temperament for it.

The rest of the team's eleven-year-olds rarely left the bench, but finally came a game when we scored so far ahead that the coach felt he could safely play us. I manned right field with no incident; then a string of hits from our side put me at bat.

Definitely something familiar about the pitcher of the opposing team ... I squint mightily, then feel a chill of recognition. Could it be that now, in this first time I've officially faced an overhand hardball pitch from an opposing team, the hurler is ... Archie?

Sure enough. The giant throwing fastballs at me was my old nemesis from Schroeder Elementary who, in a foaming rage, shoved me around the playground eighteen months ago. Despite my nearsightedness, I recognized his body language, a unique expression of insane malice, as he stood on what seemed like a twelve-foot high pitcher's mound and glowered down at me. Assuming his promotion from junior high, Archie would soon be starting ninth grade and had fulfilled the promise he'd shown as a large sixth grader: he stood close to six feet tall and probably double my weight. I felt like a first-grader all of a sudden.

When the next strike fanned by, the catcher murmured, "That's two. You hold your bat like a girl."

In an if-only fantasy I entertained for years whenever I remembered the incident, I step into the next pitch and smack it over the fence for a homer, or in darker musings, hit a line drive into Archie's teeth and take out the catcher with my backswing. In real life, I struck out after two more pitches, left two men on base, and slunk to my ignominious place in right field. The other team rallied and scored six runs—two because I fumbled a ground ball to the outfield. Never had I beheld such glaring as I drew from the coach; never had peers radiated such silent scorn. The next time at bat I drew a walk, but got picked off in a double play. We lost the game.

The glaring and silent scorn ramped up. I endured all for another week, then quit the team, to Bobby Verdiman's evident satisfaction.

The baseball fiasco was a harbinger for several more humility lumps to come. Mrs. Taylor's class split when we moved to the sixth grade, with some going to the cheerful young woman teacher in the end room facing the playground, and some to Mr. Everett, the dour new male teacher in the adjoining class. As current luck would have it, I wound up in the latter.

Prompted by Southern California's exploding school population, young men and women with freshly-minted teaching credentials poured in from across the nation, lured by relatively high salaries and a chance to make a start in the Golden State. Mr. Everett, a recent graduate of Washington University, contrasted in every possible way with Mr. Washburn, the last male teacher I'd experienced. Built like a football player, Everett wore a butch haircut and the same blue suit every day. He demanded neatness, piled on homework I didn't have time for with my afternoon and evening work schedule, and gave tests I couldn't finesse with my reading comprehension skills. And I seemed to get on the bad side of him quickly. One day he reprimanded me for reading during classwork time. I began to explain away my offense, but he didn't follow my logic and abruptly ordered me to the principal's office.

To Principal Hysler I presented myself as a victim of a nervous newcomer to the teaching profession, but the principal focused more on my turtleneck and Beatle boots than my alibis.

"Mr. Hill, every day I see you, you're wearing those high neck sweaters. Are you hiding a scar on your neck?"

"Uh, no, it's just ... I just always wear turtlenecks."

"Exactly what I said in the first place. And what kind of shoes are those? Some sort of orthopedic design? Do you have a bunion or a hammer toe, Mr. Hill?"

"They're just ... boots. Lots of kids have them."

"Not that I've noticed. In any case, yours are a hazard. You may either switch to sensible shoes or sit on the side bench at recess."

"But—that's not fair—"

"No, it's perfectly fair. We don't allow young ladies to wear high heels either."

No playground at recess constituted a serious social deprivation—a clear cue to forego the Beatle boots and resist the rising tide of conformity in a more subtle manner. But Mr. Hysler and the rest of the busybodies overestimated my emotional maturity. I determined to show them all that I couldn't be pushed around. After my paper route that afternoon I rode to the shoe repair shop in Westminster, where I paid the old proprietor three dollars to raise my boot heels another inch. I spent my recesses reading for the couple of months until Mr. Hysler relaxed some of the school dress code for girls and boys (more on this development later).

However, my increased reading stopped short of textbooks, so my test and homework grades remained static at best. Within a few weeks, I slipped to fourth in the class rankings. Frank, a short kid with two silver front teeth, held the number one spot; Morris Slatney, my new friend from New York, ran a close second. Number three, and just ahead of me, was Kara Morgan, a girl from the new tract across Springdale.

To compliment her brainpower, Kara demonstrated style and charm to rival Delia Thornton. She wore her sheath skirts tight, her eyebrows plucked, and her hair in a combination beehive puff in the back and shoulder-length flips on either side of her face. She looked like a wanna-be highschooler—my kind of girl—but her handwriting demonstrated a grownup flair and she took her studies seriously, thereby staying ahead of me in all subjects except reading. Like a WW2 Pacific Theatre soldier suffering years of recurrent malaria, I remained chronically lovesick over Delia. But I resolved to get to know Kara better at the first opportunity.

To continue the account of taking my lumps, social and otherwise, I must dredge up many uncomfortable memories. Outside the classroom, my old baseball team members now played fast-pitch hardball exclusively during lunch recess, which let me out, even if I'd been willing to give up the Beatle boots. Formerly I ranked among the best in tricks on the gymnastic bars, having mastered the pullover early, but Nick, a little guy even shorter than Benjy Allard, could do it all—even giants and dismounts. Nick perfected a wicked foursquare serve, too; even before my suspension from the playground, he had the edge on me.

All my knives were getting duller. Once tough guys on campus feared me; now several of those year-older hard cases far surpassed me in height and girth, prompting them to respect me less than in fifth grade. They seemed mostly content to fight among themselves, but Bobby Verdiman not only actively disliked me, he now outweighed me by fifteen pounds. I knew I wouldn't be able to ignore him for long.

Wayne Marshal, a chunky kid who lived across the street from Morris Slatney in the new section of the Springdale tract, loomed as another potential challenger. I'd beaten Wayne in a recess boxing match at the beginning of fifth grade, but over the summer he too passed me in height and weight. Moreover, he developed a formidable new windmill punching style focused on the midsection of his opponents—he would bend over almost double and go in swinging. I witnessed the efficacy of this method on the first day of school when he chose off a new kid in the other sixth grade class. Four or five rapid punches in the belly and the kid ran away crying, as I had done when Wyvernwood Eddie used the same technique on me back in second grade. Besides the unpleasant memories this display evoked, it irked me to learn that Wayne was bullying Morris Slatney. After deliberation, I didn't order the big windmill puncher to cease picking on my friend (and thereby challenging him to say, "Who's gonna make me?"). It seemed common sense to avoid starting fights I might not be able to finish, but the need for common sense can be a bitter epiphany.

Alas, I wasn't even the school's undisputed Beau Brummel anymore. Classmate Tommy Astrid bore a name worthy of a teen idol and looked the part with his perfectly-coiffed hair, sharp-creased slacks, turtleneck sweaters, and half-Beatle boots (with low-enough heels to exempt him from the playground ban). In a 1965 fashion show I may have edged out Tommy on technicalities, but he possessed a natural savoir faire I seemed to lack, and worse, he seemed to know it.

I found all the above disappointments hard to endure, but spurned love brandished the club that laid me lowest. One of the darkest moment of my lifetime relations with the opposite sex occurred soon after school took up in the fall. I felt no foreboding as I rode my paper route that afternoon. The cloudy and slightly cool weather felt perfect for biking. My *Daily Pilots* hefted at thirty pages, exactly the right throwing size (while fewer pages made for a lighter bag, they also engendered unstable missiles).

At my usual break at the gas station near Westminster and Springdale, I'd bought some chocolate-covered Raisinettes and poured them in my Dr. Pepper, a new taste treat I'd recently discovered. I finished the last chewy drink as "The Name Game" by Shirley Ellis came on KFWB via my transistor. The song, an instant hit, featured a catchy tune and the lyrics rhymed names in a structured pattern: "Tony-tony mo-mony, banana fana fo fony," "Shirley-Shirley, bo-burly, banana fana fo ferly," etc. My age group found it diverting to think of names that would lead to obscenities, like "Chuck, Chuck, bo-buck, banana-fana fo-fuck."

I finished the route singing to myself, and all the world seemed copacetic as I turned onto Oasis Drive. Approaching my house, I noticed someone sitting on a bike in the driveway. A female to be sure, and though I couldn't make out the details, I deduced correctly from the lanky shape and curly hair that Pattie, my Girl Scout cookie connection, was waiting for me.

When I pulled up next to her she said, with an odd smile, "I have something for you." After a short dramatic pause she added, "From Delia." She then thrust an elaborately folded piece of notebook paper at me and rode off as fast as her skinny legs could pedal.

With an odd sense of dread I unfolded the lined sheet. I recognized Delia's handwriting, having seen it on notes passed in class, usually a simple "No!" in response to my latest invitation to go steady again. This one was longer. I don't remember the exact wording, but the content exceeded all my wildest hopes. Essentially, Delia had decided to confess how much she "really ~~liked~~ loved" me. It said more, to the effect that she thought me the handsomest boy in school and wanted to go steady with me again no matter what her mom said. And she signed it thus: *xxx 000 xxx Delia.*

In my later teen years I would do my best to present the world, even when the world wasn't looking, with a low-affect. At this moment I presented anything but. My heart pounded and I felt blood rush to my head. I dumped my route bag on my front lawn and pedaled full speed to Delia's house.

When I turned the corner onto Casino I could see Delia in her driveway, hitting a foursquare ball against the garage door. A thrill of anticipation shot through me, tempered by the same undercurrent of dread I'd felt when Pattie handed me the note. No doubt I blushed furiously; my cheeks actually throbbed. I rarely if ever sought supernatural help, but now I said a prayer to whatever force might be in power: "I know it can't be true, but oh please let it be."

As I pulled up next to Delia's driveway, she shot one furtive glance sideways. I knew she'd noticed me, but she continued to hit the ball and wouldn't meet my gaze.

"This note ..." I began, as my heart began to sink and my cheeks grew hot.

Now she looked at me and looked away quickly. Before she turned I could see that she was blushing, too. She put her head down and hit the ball hard. It caromed off the garage door and into the bushes along the driveway. Then she turned again to face me. "It was Pattie's idea," she said. "She wrote it out and I copied it. She thought it would be funny."

I could detect no apology in her voice. If anything, she seemed defiant—taking the same sort of "I won't be blamed for this stupid thing" attitude I'd assumed when, back at Sylmar, I'd heaved the rock and bloodied the kid's head.

"I thought ... I just wanted to ..." I began, but my throat seemed to be closing. I gave up trying to say anything coherent and looked at her mutely.

She retrieved the ball from the bush and began hitting it against the garage again.

After a few long seconds, I rode for home, understanding that nothing productive could come from further conversation. My brain raced in several directions, all negative. How could this happen to ME? Or had I always been a loser? Yes. Clearly star-crossed and jinxed for life from the very beginning.

Recently I'd read a comic book rendition of the Atlantis legend, a fanciful account of an ancient island that flourished in the temperate ocean between Africa and South America. The second and fifth books in the Tarzan series corroborated this history: La, the High Priestess of Opar, directly descended from Atlantians, though her countrymen had in recent years began the unsavory practice of mating with apes. But the books all agreed: original Atlantis natives enjoyed a glorious civilization—until an earthquake, a mindless shifting of tectonic plates, drowned them all. The cream of the earth's scientists, philosophers, poets, and artisans went down wondering "Why us? We were doing so well!" I now understood with complete certainty that, like them, everything I would ever achieve or hold dear would henceforth be smashed, or withheld by the purblind doomsters who ran the universe.

I retrieved my route bag from the lawn, then trudged to my room to lie on my bed, boots and all. I considered playing a record, but all my favorite songs seemed fatuous now. I felt a sudden urge to smash all the records, but I didn't have the energy to rise from the bed. It didn't matter. Nothing really mattered.

After a few minutes, I rallied a bit. No wave could drown me. I would not be cowed by Mr. Everett's or Mr. Hysler's standardization tactics. I would keep up my Beatle boot boycott of the playground and fight Bobby Verdiman, Wayne, anybody who crowded me. I would wisecrack brilliantly about Pattie and Delia's little joke if— when—the story became public.

But life as I had known life was over; I would merely go through the motions from now on. As the evening shadows fell, a large chunk of my hubris broke off and sank, like glorious Atlantis, into warm salt water.

CHAPTER FIFTY-ONE

~ Walkin' and Talkin' National Politics ~ One of the Seven Wonders
~ Girls, Girls, Girls ~ Ice Cream and Tomato Juice ~ Eternal Spring

The mature reader will correctly surmise that the profound sorrow and alienation described in the last chapter decreased substantially as the school year progressed. The elasticity of youth helped much, and in the months after my low moment with Delia I found many distractions, including other girls and, of all things, politics.

Affairs of state hung in the air that summer of 1964, both in the neighborhood and across the nation. By Labor Day the intense presidential race engulfed all other media fodder, and everyone who hadn't already done so chose sides. Accordingly, Jane caught fire for underdog Barry Goldwater, the conservative Republican Arizona senator running against President Lyndon Johnson.

Johnson's campaign team played hardball with their most popular bumper sticker slogan "Goldwater for Halloween." Then they ran an infamous television commercial featuring a little girl picking flowers. A nuclear bomb detonates and the camera lingers on the mushroom cloud. "Vote for President Johnson this November," the voice over solemnly intones. "The stakes are too high for you to stay home."

Considering the dog-eat-dog political climate, the Goldwater team responded feebly. They took the high road for the most part, choosing "In your heart, you know he's right" for their slogan. The Johnson team immediately coined a rejoinder: "In your guts you know he's nuts." The Goldwaterites were obviously out of their depth in modern campaigning,[44] and the polls predicted a landslide.

---

[44] Some creative (though unauthorized) campaigning for Goldwater actually did take place during that season. As reported by Tom Wolfe in *The Electric Kool Aid Acid Test*, novelist Ken Kesey and his LSD-inspired Merry Pranksters drove their psychedelically-painted bus backward through the streets of Phoenix, with American flags flying out the windows and a large sign which read "A Vote for Barry is a Vote for FUN!"

Despite the dim outlook for Goldwater, Jane became an active campaigner. Jay also leaned toward the Republican ticket, but his Nixon bumper sticker in 1960 marked the last time he publically aired his views. According to his sources, Kennedy stole the election from Nixon in Illinois (and thereby won the Electoral College) using all forms of political skullduggery. So, as he said, "There's no sense getting excited about a fixed game." But he smiled indulgently when Jane tacked a large poster on our garage door consisting of Barry's name and forthright, horn-rimmed visage. Jay's only comment: "You're looking for trouble, Bubbles."

He was right. Members of blue collar unions predominated in the neighborhood and the unions campaigned fervently for Johnson. To prove their allegiance, they (or their children) promptly drew horns and a devil beard on the Barry poster. But Jane put up another one and glared so malevolently at smirking passersby that the vandals left it alone.

One day in September she took me with her to the local Republican campaign headquarters. There we met the precinct captain, an earnest young fellow who lived on Croupier Street, one of three gateways to the Springdale tract. Thanks to his influence with his neighbors, their entire block became a giant campaign poster: each house propped a five-foot tall golden plywood letter on its lawn, all the letters together spelling out G-O-L-D-W-A-T-E-R.

Jane called me over from the display of mock soda cans with "Goldwater" on the label and introduced me to this wunderkind of politics. He grasped my hand in a manly grip. "We need to get the truth out on the real issues," he began.

I nodded politely and Jane put her hand on my shoulder.

"If people have the facts," the Captain continued, "they'll vote for the good of the country. I need someone trustworthy to help distribute our fliers. Are you with us?"

He spoke as if I were a fellow adult voter. Perhaps that explains why I accepted his proposition. Or maybe I still sought distraction after the Delia debacle, or I didn't want to disappoint Jane. Whatever the reason for working without pay, I woke up at 5:30 the next three mornings and dutifully put the Goldwater / Miller [45] fliers in every mailbox in the Springdale tract. With school and the paper route and the sales canvassing, I pulled some long days, as the union members for Johnson might have said about their work schedule.

---

[45] New York Congressman William Miller was Goldwater's running mate.

On the third morning I met Morris Slatney walking to school. Moe, a short, skinny, New York City immigrant, always wore suit pants, short-sleeve plaid shirts, and high-top tennis shoes. Despite these unfashionable vestments, we became good friends, for Moe was smart, well-read, and enjoyed sophisticated humor. His parents, always warm and welcoming when I came over for marathon Monopoly games on rainy Saturdays, typified salt-of-the-earth, East Coast Democrats. Moe seemed to be following in their political footsteps; at the sight of my fliers, he stopped and shook his head, aghast that I engaged in campaigning for the Nazi Republican war monger. And he showed no reluctance in telling me so.

By way of rejoinder, I offered a few pat phrases I'd picked up at campaign headquarters — all about the perfidiousness of Lyndon and the purity of Barry.

Moe snorted. After a few years in California, he had begun to assimilate the West-Coast front-drop drawl, but whenever he became excited, he reverted to straight Bronx: "Whaddaya tawkin about? Look, you wanna tawk ISSUES?"

Picture two skinny eleven-year-olds, toe-to-toe and chest-to-chest, repeating the third-hand, biased talking points we'd heard from our parents.

"Johnson's a crook! Him an his union friends stole Texas blind!"

"That's oll right-wing propagandar! Golwadda is crazy! He sees a commie undah every bed and he'll geddus all blown up!"

The school bell rang as if signaling the end of a boxing round, and we proceeded to class. Unlike many adults I know whose heated political disagreements can derail longstanding friendships, we presently agreed to disagree and resumed playing Monopoly the next Saturday. But I'm wondering, Moe: do you still argue the ISSUES every election season with precious little real information to go on? Me, too. But I'm trying to cut down.

On Tuesday, November 3, Johnson won in the predicted landslide. According to the after-campaign editorials around our house, corrupt unions duped all the blue collar democrats like Moe's parents. Democracy, the noble experiment, would succumb to the welfare state as opportunists realized they could vote themselves government benefits. Mob rule would follow, and the shining dream of individual liberty would die. This grim view seemed to match my weltanschauung, for as previously noted, my own influence and power were diminishing on the local stage. But speaking of stages, all of this noble doom and gloom was (at least temporarily) swept away by my show-business debut.

"WanTwoTreeFaw!" This shout, my version of Beatle Paul McCartney's intro to "I saw Her Standing There," began the historic first rehearsal of Johnny and the Seven Wonders, Springdale's sixth-grade sensations. I came up with the band name myself, having read about the Seven Wonders of the World in Richard Haliburton's books. Classmate Brent beat out the rhythm on his snare (the first installment on a real drum kit), and group leader Johnny's guitar intro rasped through his little tube amp. He gave me the nod, and I stepped forward to where the microphone stand would be if any of us owned a microphone. As the band's front-man, I gave my soulful, cracked-voice best on the Ray Charles standard "What'd I Say." With no audience to play to, I focused on Johnny's cousin Lannie, the standout in our four-chick chorus who yelled "What I say!" back at me every time I belted it out. In keeping with the song lyrics, Lannie busied herself with "shakin' that thing," albeit modestly.

"What'd I Say" qualified as a rock standard, but to my developing critical sensibility it seemed like a thin number trying too hard to be soulful. But Johnny picked it, and I had to admit it worked well for this band, providing plenty for everyone to do. As we played through several takes in preparation for our first engagement at a classmate's birthday party, I kept noticing Lannie. She reminded me of someone — yes, she looked like Meredith MacRae, the quintessential sexy-yet-wholesome sixties teen who played supporting roles in the Beach Party movies with Frankie Avalon and Annette Funicello, as well as in *My Three Sons* and other TV sitcoms. And as I, resplendent in my black turtleneck, zipper-pocketed white pants, and Beatle boots, performed my best Elvis-meets-Ray-Charles imitation on "What'd I Say," I could see, even with the greasy blonde hair falling over my eyes, that Lannie was checking me out, too.

To skip ahead a bit, Lannie and I finally became an item in late March 1965.[46] In that season civil rights marches headlined the *Daily Pilot*, and the Alabama of my childhood seemed worlds away. As I glanced over the news while folding my papers, I wondered fleetingly if Corina the subservient maid and the grocery boy I'd known in my toddlerhood were marching with Martin Luther King

---

[46] Lannie was actually the second of my official steadies in sixth grade, the first being the aforementioned Kara Morgan, whom will be discussed presently.

singing "We Shall Overcome." Maybe they joined the marchers in Selma, the ones set upon with fire hoses and dogs. Or were the dogs in one of the other Alabama civil rights confrontations? Difficult to keep them all straight, and besides, I faced more pressing concerns. For instance, right after Lannie accepted my Christopher medal, she accompanied her parents on a spring break visit to grandparents in Arizona. I became a lonely bachelor again until the Monday we all returned to school.

That morning I sent her a note, passed from hand to hand across the classroom. Upon receipt, she gave me a surreptitious nod, and we met at first recess by the tetherballs. After exchanging smiles and shy greetings, she said, "Look! No socks."

I gazed downward. Sure enough, her legs were absolutely nude from her knee-length skirt to her stylish dirty white sneakers.

As she proceeded to outline, the previous school dress code forced Springdale girls to wear socks at all times, an edict bitterly resented by the sixth-grade girls. Thanks to an empathetic PTA mom who lobbied Principal Hysler, he finally relented after spring vacation, and the girls of my generation shed their foot underwear with the same abandon they would shed their bras a few years later.

"The new rule says we're supposed to wear peds," explained Lannie with her mischievous Meredith MacRae smile, "but nobody really does."

The word "peds" sounded clinical, like "brassiere" and "sanitary napkins," whatever those were. I sensed that we might find better topics of conversation after our long separation, but curiosity got the better of me. "Uh, what're peds?"

"Really dumb short socks you wear inside your shoes. They're supposed to keep your feet from smelling or something. They don't show, but they're still dumb."

Our talk eventually shifted to the Beatles, where I felt much more solid. She and her girlfriends worked out a parody of "All My Lovin'" that went, "Close your eyes and I'll bug you / Tomorrow I'll slug you." We could have played tetherball or foursquare while we chatted, since Mr. Hysler also lifted the ban on Beatle boots on the playground, but by this late stage of the school year, we had burdened ourselves with too much sophistication for elementary school games.

At several points in the conversation Lannie gave me the boys-are-so-clueless look we males were lately seeing more often among the co-eds. I also received that look from Junie, a fifth-grader with a desperate crush on me despite my attachment to Lannie. Janie practiced more aggressive affection than Roberta and Gwen, my two-member fan club still going strong from fifth grade days. They limited their adoration to looks and giggles from afar; Junie actually made bold to talk with me.

Looking back, Junie would have been a fine girlfriend for someone interested in a friendly relationship with the opposite sex as opposed to an extroverted introvert like me seeking drama and status. Junie even fit the correct age group—going on twelve and only a few months younger than I. But for some reason she had lost a year of school. Marooned in the social backwater of fifth grade, doomed to wear socks all year, she was unthinkable as an official steady.

Nonetheless, Junie followed me about the school grounds, walked by my house often, and always happened to be in her front yard when I rode by with my papers. As a rule I ignored her, but one Friday afternoon, I pedaled right up her driveway and favored her with a friendly smile.

My motive was of course impure. By way of background, all the fifth- and sixth-grade girls had marched to the auditorium for an hour after lunch that day with lady teachers flanking them. A couple of boy sleuths observed a projector going into the building, so a movie complicated the mystery. But what kind of movie? The girls provided a unanimous, obviously coached answer to our queries, delivered with the aforementioned patronizing look: "It was about ice cream." We tried every inducement, but the girls stubbornly held out. Most of them, anyway. I knew Junie could refuse me nothing.

She tried the ice cream dodge when I asked about the film, but her resolve melted when I leaned close. "C'mon. Just whisper it," I coaxed. I then added, with all the seeming sincerity I could muster, "I'll never tell, swear to God."

With the conflicted expression of the helpless thrall, she looked around to be sure no witnesses lurked in the vicinity. Then she mouthed a small whisper in my ear, "It was about menstruation."

"Huh?"

"It was about menstru*ation*," she whispered a tiny bit louder. Then, blushing furiously, she ran for her front door. She turned before she entered the house, with a look both anguished and imploring. I suspect that she spent an anxious weekend lamenting her weakness and dreading she would be exposed as an informer and traitor to her gender.

She needn't have worried. I refrained from telling anyone that I'd uncovered everything about the mystery — except what the mystery actually meant. We boys knew all about sex and babies and such; we learned everything from unimpeachable sources like older siblings and dirty jokes. But "menstruation," both the term and the process, orbited outside of our (or at least my) ken. It never occurred to me to look the word up in the dictionary (I'd already ascertained that "fuck," "shit" etc. weren't listed), and I remained in confusion about that biological process for at least the rest of the year.

I didn't quite get it even when Marlene, a classmate and resident of the Springdale Avenue apartments, practically drew me a picture. If Lannie were the twelve-year-old version of wholesome Meredith MacRae, Marlene recalled a more erotic film ideal — the Clara Bow / Carole Lombard type, only updated with a sexy, raspy voice like the lead singer of the Angels on "My Boyfriend's Back." Her residence in the low-rent apartments up by Westminster Boulevard (our local Other Side of the Tracks) only enhanced her allure.

While delivering to three or four apartment customers, I'd seen Marlene on site, but she always seemed to be hanging out with the tough variety of male junior high school residents of the building. But one day I found her by herself, chewing gum with a distracted air. I rode near, seemingly oblivious to her presence, intent on artfully hook-tossing a paper to the top floor.

"Hi, Ricky! Hey, come here!"

I stopped the bike and dismounted.

She looked me up and down. "I like your sweater."

The sweater was the same red one I wore almost daily, but why nitpick?

"Thanks," I replied. "Uh, have you seen *Hard Day's Night* yet?" The Beatles movie, released in mid-August, still played on weekends in some theaters.

"Oh Yah. Me and my girlfriends screamed all the way through it. Mary wet her pants."

"Huh." I paused, groping for a witty reply. None occurred to me, so I anticipated today's hipsters: when in doubt, show off your arcane musical taste. "You like the Rolling Stones? I got their album."

"Really? My dad says the singer — "

"Mick Jagger."

"Yah. My dad says he has Ubangi lips."

"So does *my* dad!"

We gradually edged away from her front door, chatting about music and school events. Then, after a long glance at the window of an upstairs apartment, Marlene launched into a story about a seventh-grader who thought she was so big, but she was really just a big whore who let boys come in her bedroom and feel her up when her parents were at work.

I found this a fascinating tale, but unfortunately we were interrupted by her little brother, who began taunting us from behind the locked screen door of her apartment. Marlene hissed, "You little shitass," at him, but this only encouraged more outrageous faces and kissing noises. I wondered if he knew Delia's tomboy sister Bonnie. Or, I mused, did they offer special sessions nowadays in the lower grades to teach younger siblings this kind of harassment? Trish and Greg wouldn't dare!

The conversation resumed as we strolled away. Finally alone in the field behind the apartments, we sat down on a strip of cardboard below the weed line. Not total privacy, but close enough.

"So," Marlene said, smacking her gum, "you know any dirty jokes?" I instantly recalled Linda, the neighbor girl who took off her clothes in front of me, way back in ancient Wyvernwood days four years before. Marlene approached the matter with slightly more subtlety than her predecessor, but new opportunities seemed to be arising.

Approaching age twelve, the desire for physical contact with girls came upon me as naturally as freckles or breaking the five-foot height barrier. Telling dirty jokes seemed like a step backwards in the quest; the better move would have been to do some "making out" (closed-mouth kissing), which I and other members of my set had lately begun to explore at parties. But it was broad daylight, so perhaps a bit of ice-breaking humor would be in order. The problem was, I'd never told a dirty joke to a girl, and I felt shy about beginning.

Marlene suffered no such reluctance. "I've got one," she said. She then proceeded with a variation of "For a Nickel I Will." Inflation had set in since I first heard the joke; now the imbecilic servant said "For a quarter I will" at each request. I then told a somewhat expurgated version of "Chimes" and she followed up with an earthy number about an interloper caught by an irate husband and forced to swallow menstrual blood. The penultimate line, "What're you drinkin'?" set up the punch: a gulping noise and the interloper replying, "Tomato juice."

I chuckled knowingly, but once again I was baffled. It seemed bizarre and inconceivable that females would bleed routinely, especially from their sexual organs. How could those fastidious creatures endure such a thing? Something along those lines apparently took place, but I just couldn't connect the dots.

The brother made an inconvenient appearance at this juncture. Smirking, he announced to Marlene that their mother had returned home from work and expressed disappointment with Marlene's performance of afternoon chores. Furthermore, "Ma says she's gonna blister your butt if you don't get right home NOW."

Thus did the quotidian thwart amour, but I felt confident the setback would prove only temporary. The next day I zoomed through the first two-thirds of my deliveries, then took the time to comb my hair in the gas station rest room before I continued to the apartments. I'd brought along my transistor and a good supply of gum and candy, and my anticipation pitched high. IF we could find a private spot and IF Marlene were as willing as the Wyvernwood girl... But though I searched and stalled and lingered about her apartment, Marlene never showed. When I finally rode away I saw her across the boulevard, leaning on a parked car with one of the junior-high juvenile delinquents.

I could connect these dots at least. Recently I'd read Sherlock Holmes for the first time (the sanitized edition for boys, that eliminated all mention of Holmes's cocaine use), and this case seemed elementary, Watson. Marlene acted mad at someone the day I saw her ... and the same guy she consorted with now had been walking downstairs (and giving us a decidedly hostile look) when I accompanied her home after the jokefest. Thus I easily deduced a love triangle in progress, with (1) Marlene, (2) the older guy, and (3) the older girl who let boys feel her up, as the participants.

Shifting to the inductive mode, I concluded that I was in over my head socially. A love rectangle would be far too tangled. But after my initial disappointment, I took the setback philosophically. After all, I suffered no shortage of female company that season, and hope (among other things) sprang eternal.

CHAPTER FIFTY-TWO

~ Capitalist Dupes at Play ~ A Social Union ~ Mr. Charisma ~ Love's Misfires
~ Tahitian Treat Meets the Plaintive Frontier ~ Flash Trumps Talent

By the beginning of 1965, the popular understanding of "The Sixties" as a time of social and political upheaval was beginning to gel. On the federal front in Washington, Lyndon Johnson put together his transition team to launch the Great Society. In California, Mario Savio had recently given his impassioned Berkeley speech urging campus radicals to fight the oppressive capitalist society by "throw[ing] your body on the gears of the machine to prevent it from working at all!"

This address could not have been better scripted to irritate Orange County residents, and the *Daily Pilot* reported it with great indignation. As I learned many years later, Savio and his followers in the Free Speech Movement elucidated the radical theories of Herbert Marcuse, a San Diego State College professor and so-called Father of the New Left. Marcuse postulated that the seeming affluence of America's middle class was a snare employed by Capitalist Masters to enslave the Modern Proletariat. According to the theory, these new wage slaves, blinded by Detroit dream cars, tract houses, K-marts and eight-hour workdays with vacations and health benefits, were completely ignorant of how covertly oppressed they were. And all that Capitalist bait threatened to leave them unfit for the necessary and inevitable worldwide Socialist struggle.

The Hill family could have been cited as a good example of Marcuse's theory. Steaks for dinner three times a week, pink Cadillac in the driveway of their four-bedroom home, affordable goods and services, freeways, drive-in movies, seven-channel TV programming for the price of a set and a roof antenna — things would seem, at least to those ignorant of the modern socialist dialectic, to be looking up for these survivors of the depression and World War.

Certainly the Hills played in their capitalist fool's paradise with gusto. Jay's new manager's pay made overtime and second jobs unnecessary, especially since his ex-wife hadn't been able to track him down lately. He and Jane delighted in their home projects, continuing their lush landscaping and interior decorating. Mirrors and/or paneling now graced every wall in the house, including those of the new rumpus room, and the exterior featured enough tropical plants to film a Tarzan movie.

In keeping with the high times, the Hill family's ring-in-1965 holiday celebration unfolded with the relative opulence of a Vegas stage show, with even more presents than last year, a bigger flocked tree, gallons of booze, and a dinner buffet for all comers. Automation meant progress in the space age — Jay's bar tools this year featured a battery-operated drink stirrer. Though unfulfilled according to Marcusian theory, Jay seemed to be glowing with satisfaction as he got all the grownups uproariously drunk and watched us kids open our presents.

I too felt more cheerful that season, having recently gotten over the worst of my torch for Delia Thornton. I didn't even buy her a Christmas present, though had she provided the slightest encouragement, I would likely have showered her with cheap jewelry and the latest Paul Petersen oeuvre. But I remained temporarily free from heartache through the spurned lover's age-old method of becoming interested in someone else.

That someone was Kara Morgan, my official steady between Delia and Lannie and the one girl in class who consistently earned better grades than I did. We first met outside of school right before the Christmas break. While delivering papers in the new tract across Springdale, I heard from an open garage the strains of *Beatles 65*, the Fab Four's latest release, just in time for holiday sales. Having purchased the album the weekend before, I had already memorized all the lyrics. Further, thanks to assiduous perusing of all the teen and movie magazines, I knew more press-kit factoids and schlock-journalist fodder about the Beatles than anyone in my neighborhood. My would-be authority even impressed Cindy, the teenage Drolet next door.

Thus I rode confidently up the driveway toward the sound of John Lennon singing "Rock and Roll Music," the ancient Chuck Berry oldie from five years ago. I recognized some kids from school running and jumping around the garage, doing a sort of proto-punk-rock pogo to the music—though of course I didn't recognize that classic dance at the time. To my surprise, Kara stood among the revelers—not exactly dancing (too much self-possession for that), but definitely smiling and bobbing. As I learned later, she lived right across the street. Her standard school uniform consisted of pencil skirt, starched blouse, and cashmere sweater; if I thought of her after school, I pictured her in the same outfit, doing homework at a neat desk. But here in the flesh she wore pedal pushers and a striped tee-shirt, and she looked more alluring than ever.

I knew an opening when I saw one. "You like the Beatles?"

"Uh-*hummm*." She said in an encouragingly playful parody of Beatlemaniac fans.

"Who's your favorite?"

"I like George."

"Really? Me too! How about the Rolling Stones? I've got their—"

"Yuck."

I steered the conversation back to the Beatles. "I'll Follow the Sun," written by Paul McCartney as a teenager and retooled for this album, concluded and "Mr. Moonlight" played next. I thought that number rather sappy, so I commandeered the phonograph and prematurely turned the record over. Side two runs only twelve minutes and fifty-nine seconds, and before the final song "Everybody's Trying to Be My Baby" concluded, I asked her if she wanted to go steady.

She assented, and I presented her with my yellow and white St. Christopher Medal, the same one I'd given Delia the year before. By that solemn act, we became an instant sixth-grade high society item.

Alas, we never kissed or even held hands; our short-lived relationship lacked even the one-sided ardency I'd experienced with Rebecca or Delia. Part of the problem was exterior: her parents kept a tight rein and we could only see each other after school at her house. I would stop for a visit in the middle of my route, but focusing on romance was difficult when I knew that if I stayed too long, *Pilot* customers would begin to call the office, wondering what happened to their papers. But the main reason for the truncated relationship was simply a lack of real affection: we operated more on a social contract than on genuine romance. Kara, stylish and intelligent, made me look good. On her part, she wished to advance in sixth-grade society, and I fit the bill as an established businessman, social leader, and old-line blueblood, one of the first Springdale tract settlers. Of course no one ever articulated, or even sub-articulated, this social anthropology. But the relentless status seeking and social paring which animates adult societies was well underway by sixth-grade.

So we had a few laughs, as the saying goes, but whatever mild limerence we felt went dim by late January. Kara offered to give the Christopher back, vaguely citing her parents' view that young people should avoid committing themselves. Her folks always seemed a bit stiff when I spoke with them, and from their body language I suspected they saw me as part of the daughter-raising problem, wholesome paper route notwithstanding. In any case, the breakup didn't overly surprise me, and I nonchalantly took back the Christopher.

After a month or so of bachelorhood I recycled the handy medallion to the aforementioned Lannie, my third official steady and a thrice-distinguished young lady. I already noted her resemblance to Meredith MacRae. Further, at 5'4", Lannie (in the 93rd percentile for twelve-year-old girls) stood taller than all the boys not yet turned twelve, including me. Thirdly, she happened to be first-cousin of Johnny Garrison, the undisputed leader of the sixth grade.

Johnny is worth a digression. He arrived that summer from his family's military posting on Midway Island, of which he talked much. Of average height and build, he had medium-length brown hair, brown eyes, sallow skin, and rather large lips. In academics and sports, he demonstrated general competence. He excelled at guitar, playing much better than Tommy Astrid or I, but he wore nondescript, mother-chosen clothing like most of the other sixth-graders. There seemed nothing extraordinary about Johnny except the guitar playing, but he provided a first, up-close encounter with someone my own age who exhibited the phenomenon of charisma, the ineffable charm that make those who come under its sway believe they have found a best friend and soul mate.

I knew Jane and Jay both exuded a certain magnetism: people wanted to be their friends even when they weren't passing out the liquor. My wife and son also have a fair share, and I've known several other even higher-degree charismatics, to borrow a term. Wayne Laguna, a Ute Indian friend of my teens and twenties, survived a near-fatal car accident at eighteen, which left him with many facial scars and a drooping eye. He looked like an ethnic Frankenstein, which never made a positive first impression. Yet after a few minutes in his presence, everyone—including police officers who detained him on suspicion, otherwise irritable parents, even

Nanny and every other grandma he met—all warmed to him and delighted in his company.

Johnny possessed this same uncanny charisma. His approval made trends; his indifference doomed them. Guys could be hanging around the playground feeling too much ennui or pecking-order confusion to get a game going; Johnny would arrive, appoint team captains without seeming to be presumptuous, and we'd be on the field. All the girls seemed captivated, including Mrs. Dayton, our new sixth grade teacher who took over our class in January when Mr. Everett didn't return after Christmas break. The official story is that through some miscommunication, Everett couldn't produce the clear teaching credential he needed to continue. But rumor has it that the district fired him. In any case, when Johnny asked that high-strung and usually contrary lady to let us out early for recess one day, Mrs. Dayton actually consented. When he announced his intention to form a rock band, every aspirant dropped everything and showed up at his house that afternoon. As near as I could tell, Johnny did nothing special to earn his high social reverence; he simply had It, like Bill Clinton had It, like Ronald Reagan and the Kennedys and Hitler and Elvis and Clara Bow and Marilyn Monroe had It, and like the last salesman who sold you something too expensive for your budget, but somehow you didn't mind, had It.

Johnny and I never became real friends—never hung out playing records or rode bikes to the store like I did with Kenny or Gary Hallideaux or Benjy Allard. My feelings for him mixed respect and envy in the sort of complex attitude lesser mugs in a 1940s Warner Brothers film displayed toward Humphrey Bogart or Edward G. Robinson ("What's wit him? I oughta be runnin' dis mob.") But however little I actually bonded with the shot-caller of the sixth-grade aristocracy, Johnny profoundly influenced my social life for a few months. He gave his cousin Lannie tacit permission when I asked her to go steady. He organized my performing debut and I found myself naming the band "Johnny and the Seven Wonders" without him having to suggest his name go first. And he was the first person I sought out to show my enhanced Beatle boots. "Hey, Johnny! Check these heels!"

A postscript on Johnny: in 1978 I hitchhiked trip to Coarsegold, California (near Yosemite) to visit the aforementioned Wayne Laguna, a recent immigrant to the area. En route I met, by sheer coincidence, a classmate from Springdale. The last time we'd seen each other, I had been a junior sixties slickster, he a total square with a military haircut and stay-pressed slacks up to his belly button. But in the strange social turnings of the era, we had both morphed by the mid-seventies into seasoned hippies with ponytails and wispy beards. And though we barely remembered one other, we both clearly recalled Johnny Garrison:

"Dude was always talking about living on Midway Island —"

"All the chicks went for him —"

"…guitar at the talent show —"

"… bossed everybody, even the teacher —"[47]

For years and especially after that conversation, I've expected to see the charismatic Garrison appear in the media as a congressman, or a CEO of a company making millions or going spectacularly bankrupt, or perhaps a rock star. Thinking about the last possibility, it occurred to me while watching a Super Bowl halftime show in 2001 that Steve Tyler of Aerosmith could have been Johnny in sixth grade. The general features were there and the lips definitely matched. However, Tyler is not a guitarist, and he was reputedly born in 1948, which would have put him in high school in 1965. And the clincher, according to all available sources, is that Tyler has never set foot on Midway Island.

Yet I'm confident: wherever Johnny is now, if through bad breaks he failed to achieve celebrity, he is nonetheless radiating charisma in some office, factory, or sales route. If there's a company softball or golf team, he's the captain; if he's a junior high teacher, he also coaches the debate team and serves as union steward. And his peers and friends, new and old, undoubtedly seek his approval. Hey, Johnny! Check this book!

In recalling such an interesting fellow, I've drifted from the account of my relationship with Lannie, my second steady girlfriend. But there's little to tell. As with Kara, our association never blossomed into much physical affection, though we did have one delightful closed-mouth make-out session at the party where the band made its debut. Lannie and I were both enamored with the idea of kissing and going steady like the big kids, but the real magic wasn't there. Another reason for our breakup also may be that Lannie's cousinly devotion to Johnny finally became too irritating. In any case, we demoted ourselves to "just friends" before my birthday in

---

[47]This fellow also told me the story of Delia Thornton running off with a biker boyfriend.

April. When I later read Mickey Rooney's autobiography, I could empathize with his quickie marriages and abrupt divorces. If the fire doesn't spark, it's best to move on, as I learned the hard way with Delia.

Speaking of separations, perhaps my underlying chafing at Johnny's natural leadership also led to the breakup of Johnny and the Seven Wonders. After only a few performances we dissolved the band. However, we did share the stage once more, albeit in different acts, at the Springdale talent show, a major end-of-school-year event.

The talent show program follows, with annotations:

1. A comedy duo from the other sixth grade class who also served as MCs for the show, one tall and thin, one short and fat. They wore matching outfits: blue button-down shirts with red ties. With their good stage chemistry, they came off as a sort of junior Martin and Rossi, then-current favorites on the Ed Sullivan show. Between introducing acts, they pantomimed struggles with a large, imaginary dog, then served up lots of jokes about overweight people, including the fat guy doing the twist and shouting "There's ALWAYS room for Jell-O!" They also introduced some edgy elephant riddles, including this two-parter:

> Q. What did Tarzan say when he saw the elephants coming over the hill?
> A. Here come the elephants over the hill.
> Q. What did Tarzan say when he saw the elephants coming over the hill wearing sunglasses?
> A. Nothing—he didn't recognize them.

2. An untitled instrumental duo composed of Johnny Garrison and Brent, our former Seven Wonders drummer. They wore matching maroon shirts and, with guitar, tiny amp, and one snare drum, performed a tight instrumental version of the Beatles' "And I Love Her."

3. The former chick chorus of the Seven Wonders, singing an a Capella version of the Toys' "A Lover's Concerto," the then-current top forty song with melody adapted from a Bach piece. The girls wore matching pink and white jumpers and harmonized perfectly. Lannie looked great, but she seemed to have grown another inch since we broke up—much too tall to invoke nostalgia for our spent romance.

4. An energetic sister act dancing a Tahitian hula. Their parents served as missionaries in obscure South Sea islands for most of the girls' lives. Elder sibling Adrian sat near me in class all year, but I'd never heard her say a word. Prior to the show, I would have described Adrian as "weird" for her almost complete silence and seemingly pathological shyness, and "funny looking" for her high cheekbones, almond-shaped eyes, full lips, and shaggy hair. But somehow she looked much better as she swayed her lithe form in a sarong and bare feet. The hula was so naturally erotic that some parents later condemned it as unsuitable for an elementary school stage, but it certainly seemed a delightfully edifying cultural presentation to me. I sought out Adrian after the first rehearsal, hoping to make up for lost time in getting to know her.

"Your dancing was, uh, really neat," I began.

Never had I observed a person so visibly distressed by a compliment, but I pressed on. "So, you lived in Hawaii?"

"Tahiti," she murmured, staring a hole in the floor.

"Huh. How long you live there?"

"Eight years."

So alluring and professionally composed on stage—but now her eyes darted about wildly in the manner of a World War II movie heroine right before she goes into hysterics under Nazi interrogation. A movie hero might have stilled her trembling lower lip with a bold kiss then and there, but I've never felt comfortable with shy women. I decided to enjoy her performance at the second show and try talking with her later. But as it turned out, there wasn't enough later to pursue the matter.

5. A pale, diminutive fourth-grade girl in a frilly white dress singing the old folksong "Five-Hundred Miles," accompanied on piano by her mother. Mr. Washburn introduced me to folk music's eerie depths, and in the little girl's plaintive rendition I could feel the bittersweet distances of America in frontier times, when five-hundred miles meant definitely far, far from home. This number left me almost as spellbound as the performance of the Tahitians, but I wasn't about to chat up a fourth-grader.

6. Three or four less-impressive but no-less well-rehearsed acts, including mine. My bit showed more audaciousness than talent: the curtain opened to reveal me in black suit pants and a shiny red shirt

with sleeves rolled up to the bicep, fifties style. My face locked in a studied Elvis smolder and my pose came straight from his best performance scenes in *Loving You:* I held my guitar slung from my shoulders behind me with my right hand while my left leg jutted forward.

Backstage, James, a bespectacled classmate who always ran the projector for our class science movies,[48] dropped a phonograph needle. I swung the guitar into position. As "Blue Suede Shoes" (the opening number on Elvis's first LP for RCA records) blasted over the auditorium speakers, I proceeded to lip-sync the song while strutting around the stage, swiveling my hips, and pretending to play the guitar.

This exhibition took place in the days before air guitar and lip-syncing came to typify slackers who never actually *do* anything difficult—they only fake it. Jay and Jane gave me the guitar for my birthday, and they paid for lessons at the music store in Westminster on the condition that I keep up with the practice. I could have followed Johnny's good example in practicing more, but I preferred to spend evenings in my room spinning "Blue Suede Shoes" over and over until I internalized every nuance of the recording.

My show prep also included the studious avoidance of Jay, who might at any time order me to get a haircut. Unfortunately *he* went for haircuts in three week intervals, and his quirky outlook—that a sharp appearance required well-trimmed hair in addition to shined shoes—began around this time to escalate into a seriously divisive issue between us. By junior high I would become adept at avoiding Jay and his haircut edicts for weeks at a stretch. We would have a final showdown right before I turned sixteen, and I subsequently let my hair grow for over a decade.

But at the end of sixth grade, Jay's word remained Law. Unfortunately, he seemed to be around the house more often lately, which made dodging him more difficult. But I managed to go on stage for the talent show with an elaborately upswept pompadour and hair combed down from my temples into sideburn facsimiles.

---

[48] I am aware that James probably seems like a two-dimensional character, the typical techno-nerd in a young adult novel. But not only did he actually exist in real life, he seemed ubiquitous. Every class in every school I attended from fifth grade to high school seems to have been staffed by a bespectacled lad who resembled James and shared his fascination with technology. But according to the pop-culture template, they all now enjoy Silicon Valley millions, early retirement, trophy wives, and the last laugh.

If, instead of a talent showcase, the event had been an actual talent competition and I the judge, I would have given top prizes to the Tahitian dancers and the young folksinger, but as it turned out, my performance received the loudest ovation. A dozen or so girls, trained by repeated group viewings of *Hard Day's Night* and its recent imitators, even screamed. While I exulted in this outpouring, I felt a vague inkling my act didn't compare to the real accomplishments of the others. But justly or not, I was back on top again—admired and/or envied by my peers and even smiled upon by grownups, who thought Elvis a nice boy now that they'd seen the Rolling Stones.

My unexpected triumph seemed like good momentum for seventh-grader status in the fall, when we would move to the new junior high school now under construction across Springdale Street. But as they say in the melodramas, fate had a surprise in store.

CHAPTER FIFTY-THREE

~ 1929 Redux ~ More Elephants ~ First Publication
~ The Return of Grandma Glasses ~ An Early "October Surprise"

Readers will recall that in the Redondo Beach fight with Brian, I compared the incident to the Cuban Missile Crisis and myself to Nikita Khrushchev. Continuing to strum this self-referential chord, during the first few months of 1965 and the personal tribulations that followed, I'm reminded (as perhaps a few other history buffs who read this chapter might also be) of the state of the USA in the months prior to the stock market crash of 1929. Most people expressed surprise at such a financial cataclysm, but many signs foretold its coming. Stock prices had risen exponentially with no economic basis for expansion; meanwhile, significant sectors of the economy, notably U.S. agriculture, had been sinking since the early twenties. In hindsight, the warning of something unpleasant about to happen should have been obvious, but thanks to wishful thinking, the signs went largely unheeded.

In spring 1965, my life followed a similar pattern. After what now seemed a temporary recession, my fortunes took an upswing. Triumphs included the talent show, the San Francisco trip, my expanding paper route empire, relationships with two lovely girls and dalliances with others. My twelfth birthday party, an extravaganza compared to the previous year's low-key event, provided merriment worthy of pre-crash 1929 and featured everything a 1960s teen party could boast of: cases of Shasta Cola, cake and snacks, the latest English band hit records, live music (thanks to Johnny Garrison who brought his guitar and played "Apache" over and over), dancing, and kissing games.

During all the parties that season, the majority of sixth-grade boys expressed willingness to join in the last activity. But some of the girls balked, Delia Thornton prominent among them. She who would in four years be allegedly cohabitating with a biker boyfriend even presumed at my party to apprise my mom of the indecencies occurring in the rumpus room. Jane, who seemed much amused when we discussed it later, calmed the girls down and we proceeded with the festivities.

Encouraged by these highlights, I looked forward to junior high. But as sixth grade entered its concluding months, a 1929-style bust and depression lurked just over the horizon.

Two new activities and a new friend occupied me during this period. At home I began to pick at my guitar and, as previously related, even took a few lessons at the music store. At school, during periods assigned for working on class assignments or listening to the teacher, I developed a series of graphic novels, to use the current term for stories comprising cartoon drawings and word balloons.

Creation is a lonely pursuit, and it is the fortunate artist who encounters a kindred spirit. I found mine in classmate Daniel Redding, who arrived from New England in February. At first Daniel affected a sort of condescending East-Coast manner, as if he found Californians amusingly unsophisticated. If someone called him "Dan" or "Danny," he would firmly insist on his full name, as do most Daniels, Jonathans, and Jameses of the post-millennium.

This approach initially served to ostracize him from most society, including mine, but once we discovered mutual interest in comic drawings, our friendship developed quickly. *Mad* Magazine satire shaped my comedy forte, while Daniel became a disciple of Johnny Hart, whose caveman strip *BC* was the height of sophisticated newspaper-comics-page humor. Soon Daniel and I began collaborating on a graphic venture incorporating all our influences. In a series of full page drawings, we featured ourselves as main characters, usually making sardonic comments on the stupidity of teachers. The action took place on an imaginary secret island, and the series gradually developed a supporting cast of elephants roughly human in size and possessing human skills, including walking upright, talking, and driving. This aspect demonstrated the pervasive influence of the elephant joke fad then in full media bloom. As everyone had once owned a hula hoop and Silly Putty, everyone now knew several elephant jokes. I will rest my case with two more:

Q. How do you tell if an elephant has been in your refrigerator?
A. Footprints in the Jell-O.
Q. How do you stop a charging elephant?
A. Take away his credit cards.

After Daniel and I became better acquainted, I admired both his humor and his indifference to societal pressures. No tough guy nor cute girl nor intrusive teacher could perturb him; he seemed to float serenely above the sixth-grade jungle. So he surprised me one Friday afternoon in May by exhibiting a definite state of agitation. En route from school to home, I heard my name shouted. I stopped and Daniel ran to meet me, panting from the exertion. Without a word he handed over a stapled sheaf of mimeographed pages. I recognized the document at a glance—the monthly PTA newsletter for Springdale school, usually full of cheery exhortations and announcements. Our teachers left them in a stack by the classroom exit and ordered students to take them home to our parents. Sometimes we remembered to do so, but I had not collected one that afternoon on my way out.

"Look in the back," he gasped.

I leafed through rapidly. The final page contained no announcements, chatty news, or calendar reminders. Instead it was a blue mimeographed copy of the latest drawing I'd done for our collaborative comic series. Somehow, one of our most inflammatory anti-teacher pieces had fallen into the hands of the Enemy, who then diabolically presented it to the adult public.

We stood close, silently beholding the mimeographed print. As usual, in the bottom right corner of the page, figures meant to represent the two of us stood talking via word balloons. Recognizable by his cowlick and "DR" written on his chest, the Daniel character is saying, "We gotta buy more planes! The company can't keep up with the customers' demands!"

I could be identified by the turtleneck with "RH" on the front. "Look on the bright side, D.R.," I'm saying. "We cornered the market. Let's raise our prices!"

Most of the page was filled with an enormous pile—a mountain three or four stories high—of dead teachers. Various body parts protrude from the amorphous mass: an arm here, there a leg, there a head with the caricature teacher curly hairdo and glasses. In the sky above, an elephant is flying an open-cockpit airplane which tows a banner proclaiming: "R.H. & D.R. Dead Teacher Supply—We

Deliver!" From the plane dangles a steam-shovel bucket in process of scooping up a big load of body parts.

I don't recall any authorial thrill at seeing this first publication of my career, only a strong presentment that certain readers — namely our parents, the entire Springdale School faculty, and its principal — would view my artistry out of its proper cultural context. I sensed it would be difficult to explain that Daniel and I were simply artistic practitioners of sophisticated "sick" humor, a branch of wit that emerged in the late1950s. For example, the cover of Lennie Bruce's 1958 album *The Sick Humor of Lennie Bruce* features him having a picnic at a cemetery. Though his earlier work seemed mild compared to ours, Bruce led the Avant Gard for much of the edgy stand-up comic routines and sick humor that would follow. *Mad* Magazine also provided a seminal influence, and two *Mad* clones (*Sick* and *Cracked*) crowded the market. But even if I were permitted to give a mini-lecture on the topic, the authorities probably wouldn't understand.

My apprehension cranked into high gear: a copy of this newsletter page might even now be speeding via airmail to Dr. Max Rafferty, State Superintendent of California Schools! I knew of Rafferty as a famous conservative whose column appeared regularly in the *Daily Pilot* and read his screeds often as I folded my papers. Lately I had been amused by his assertion that subversive pop music was rotting the souls of America's Youth. Now I imagined Rafferty seeing my drawing and deciding to make an example of me: instead of seventh grade with my classmates at the new junior high, I would be sent to some desert reform school.

My only comfort was of the misery-loves-company variety: Daniel convinced himself (with no protest from me) that, since his likeness and initials were featured in the drawing, he would be held equally culpable. After a tense conference, we determined a plan of action spurned by most cutting-edge Avant Gard artists, but which seemed wisest at the time: we would go forth resolutely and beg for mercy, immediately and in person.

Thus we returned to school and waited tensely outside the fifth-grade classroom of Mrs. Karmon, the young teacher who, according to the newsletter masthead, served as editor in chief of the publication. Coincidentally, we found the Friday afternoon faculty meeting in progress in that very classroom. Retreating hastily to the end of the building, we peeked from around the corner until all the teachers except Mrs. Karmon filed out. After a further and seeming interminable fifteen minutes, she emerged. I knew her from choir and wished I hadn't skipped the last scheduled practice.

"Uh, Mrs. Karmon…"

"Hi, Ricky!" she said, smiling brightly, then turned to Daniel. "Hello! You must be the famous D.R.! What's your real name?"

Daniel asserted later that he almost said "Wiley," a reference to the water-hating poet iconoclast in the BC comic strip. But my recollection of him stuttering "D-D-Daniel R-R-Redding" doesn't support the claim. Both of us stammered, hemmed, and hawed as we explained that we were…sort of… responsible for the illustration on the back page.

"I know!" Another bright smile. "Mrs. Dayton showed me several drawings by both of you."

This blow seemed to seal our fate. How could our teacher have found our secret files? I'd stuffed mine so far back into my messy desk that even *I* had trouble finding them.

"Everyone in the meeting thought this one was really cute!" Mrs. Karmon continued. "We all had a good laugh. Send us another drawing for our last issue of the year. But use a black pen — the ditto machine will pick it up better." She glanced at her watch. "Well, I have to run and get my daughter from the babysitter."

As she hurried toward the parking lot, Daniel and I turned to one another in silence. Our look bespoke our mutual thought: grownups remained, in the final analysis, inexplicable.

Of course we discontinued the series immediately. First of all, you never knew when the inexplicables would turn on you. Plus, if teachers actually liked the drawings — or even worse, if they thought our efforts were "cute," we weren't achieving the sick, vicious satire at which we aimed. What if Max Rafferty laughed them off, too? That would be downright depressing.

A more serious letdown occurred soon afterward from an old quarter. At the talent show I had, with a sort of horror fascination, marveled at the jokes the grossly overweight kid made at his own expense. I knew my old friend Harald the Norwegian would die before he would present his fatness as an object of mirth, and I related more to Harald than the jolly comedian. My own deepest dread boiled down to eventually becoming so nearsighted that I would be forced to wear my glasses. I would become a stigmatized, (and incidentally astigmatic) four-eyes, on a social par with fatsos, shrimps, and other pariahs. Classmate James, the projector tech and talent show backstage manager, seemed to take his crippling visual handicap in stride, but the "Grandma Glasses" jibe from the kid in bygone third grade continued to burn in my soul. Nothing, not even Jay's periodic admonitions, could induce me to wear corrective lenses.

The trauma began when Mrs. Dayton observed me squinting at the board.

"Ricky, are you supposed to wear glasses?"

"No!"

"Well, have you EVER worn glasses?"

"No!"

"Then we'd better have the nurse check your eyes."

"Uh, I mean, yeah, I used to wear glasses, but I don't need them anymore."

"Well, let's get them checked, just to make sure."

She wrote an eye test referral to the school nurse, on which I neglected to follow through. When she asked about the test results, I became so evasive that she referred the matter to higher authority. Thus followed one of my most acutely painful moments in sixth grade: the day Mr. Prine, the young vice-principal, sought me out in the cafeteria for his idea of a man-to-man talk.

"Hi, Rick!" Mr. Prine sat down across from me at the lunch table. He smiled and leaned forward, holding his coffee cup in both hands. "How's it going?" He usually affected this friendly, we're-all-pals manner, but he also exhibited a fierce temper when aroused and had official license to give swats.

"I'm okay," I ventured cautiously.

Kids around us began rising with studied casualness and strolling for the exits, as if the cafeteria were on fire but they didn't want to start a stampede. Within a minute, Mr. Prine and I had the long table to ourselves.

"So, I hear you don't like to wear your specs."

I frowned and looked around warily, then stared down at my plate. I didn't want anyone to know I even owned glasses, much less talk about them in public. Bringing up the subject at all mortified me as much as "I heard you don't like to wear your diapers" would sound to a seventyish self-made businessman having his first trouble with incontinence.

"Look, I know how it is," Mr. Prine continued, seemingly unfazed by my silence. "I don't much like to wear mine either. But don't you think it's better to be able to see than to worry about what other people think?" He pulled a pair of brown, fade-to-clear hornrims from his shirt pocket and put them on with a flourish. "Not so bad, eh? I wear them for driving and distance. No big deal."

To my great shame, I felt the tingle of forthcoming tears. I had last cried before others when I scraped off many square inches of skin in the flexible flyer incident a few years back, but nothing since the first grade "May I be excused" standoff with Jay had brought me so close to tears of mortification in public. How dare this unknowing fool, with all his authority and subtle menace, confront me? "Driving and distance!" The fool had *no* comprehension of my situation — that I was already blinder than he would ever be! And if I were seen wearing glasses for *five minutes*, my self-esteem and social image would be instantly destroyed! But I could summon no cool riposte; I couldn't even speak for fear of my voice cracking. So I listened to him prattle until he whipped off his glasses and replaced them in his pocket. He then patted me on the shoulder and said, "Give the specs a try, eh?" Then a subtle order: "Stop by my office and let me see how they look." With that, he rose and strode off to handle some other trivial problem.

And I went home to face a monumental one. When I entered the house after finishing my paper route, Jane asked me to sit down with her in the kitchen. Then she confirmed some vague suspicions I'd felt lately, but dismissed as unlikely, given our family's long-term stability. But sure enough, the gist of her long story was that Jay had lost his job and we would be moving again. They had located a new place and were already transporting dishes, linens, and other unobtrusive items.

Like a stock market speculator applying 1930 hindsight to the great 1929 crash, I should have seen this disaster coming. The pink Cadillac had disappeared a few weeks before, replaced by a nondescript hand-me-down Ford from Jay's parents, who recently purchased a beautiful new '65 Thunderbird. When I'd asked about the shuffle, Jay dismissed both the T-Bird and the Cadillac as "kid cars" and changed the subject. Also, he had been around the house much more than usual, and he and Jane often "went shopping" in the afternoons and weekends. For these jaunts they parked Greg and Trish with the Drolet family next door and left me to my own devices. Like a trusting fool, I applauded this arrangement as an acknowledgment of my almost-junior-high-school maturity and a fine improvement over sitting in the car for hours while they shopped.

But my new maturity now deserted me under stress. "Do we really *have* to move?"

"We really do, Honey. And you can't tell anybody about it."

"Why? *Why* do we have to sneak off?"

She winced at the "sneak," but explained patiently that they hadn't paid their mortgage in two months and were in arrears on many other bills. We could be ruined—they could be arrested!—if the word got out. Jay even admonished her and me to not mention the move to siblings Trish and Greg. In his reasoning, if the younger ones were informed, they would say something to their playmates, who would tell their parents, who would either unwittingly or maliciously betray us to the authorities.

After the initial shock I could grudgingly appreciate the trust involved in at least giving me advance notice. Trish and Greg would be playing with their little friends one day, and the next day they'd wake up in a completely new environment with no explanation at all—shades of the junior *Twilight Zone*.

But I wondered privately if I could manage to keep such a secret from everyone I knew. I now faced weeks of pretending to be a normal kid looking forward to starting at the new junior high school with my class. I couldn't even say goodbye—no Keith-style farewell party for me. By next semester I would be a stranger in a strange schoolground and only a fading memory to my current friends.

In short, I was living my local version of October 29, 1929: the market had crashed, and my very own 1930s-style depression was upon me.

CHAPTER FIFTY-FOUR

~ Kubler-Ross Plus Peter Gunn, with a Pinch of Walter R. Brooks ~ A Final Battle
~ First Draft of this Chronicle ~ Autographs ~ Overdosing on the Big N
~ "This is the Way the World Ends"

Speaking of the junior *Twilight Zone*, I ask readers who remember the TV show to imagine host Rod Serling's stylized voice-over for the italicized segments of this chapter:

The final weeks of settled life in Huntington Beach are playing out. You're going through the motions of school, paper route, and home life, always hyper-aware that everything you do is "the last time" you'll ever do it here.

As I learned later, Jay was not actually fired from his job at the market. Rather, when the ex-wife's salary-attachment order caught up with him once again, he invited the supervisor to either ignore it or lose him as an employee. When the boss expressed concern at this choice, Jay quit on the spot.

Unfortunately, this development came about at the same time their prodigious spending on credit caught up with them. They had so many easy monthly payments that they lacked enough easy money to go around, even if Jay had been employed. Not to worry, though—even as we packed and prepared to leave all obligations behind, Jay lined up a job near the new house. No one knew him there, so he could employ an alias. But first we had to exit the present situation, leaving as little to trace as possible.

Over the next few days, you begin to feel something like what Elizabeth Kubler-Ross, in her 1969 book already accessible here in the Twilight Zone, will call the Five Stages of Grief: Shock ("This can't be real! They can't really do this!"), Anger ("If Ed and Eileen are as stupid as Jay always says, why do they have a house and a T-Bird and Jay can't hold on to anything for long?"), and all the rest. Whichever stage incorporates silent pouting is

the one you linger on: "From now on," you resolve as you flip a paper onto
a porch on Calneva Street, "I don't trust nobody."

However, fully investing into the "I'll walk alone" mood proved difficult. One reason may be that I had been reading Freddy the Pig books on a regular rotation since second grade, and author Walter R. Brooks took his porcine protagonist's penchant for melodrama less than seriously. A passage from *Freddy Plays Football* provides a perfect example:

> Freddy had been thinking a good deal about what was going to happen to him ... He would indeed be a wanderer on the face of the earth. But the more he thought about it, the more the idea pleased him in a mournful sort of way. It made him, he felt, a romantic figure who led a sad, gipsy life, a lonely pig, with a secret sorrow in his heart.

Such tongue-in-cheek wisdom tended to undercut my most self-righteous moments. Nonetheless, my working assumption had been that the "sad, gipsy life" of my early childhood lay far behind me, so this evasion seemed terribly unfair.

It also proved difficult to hold on to my secret while shutting down my business empire. When Mr. Simmons came by with the papers the next Saturday, I gave him a week's notice.

"What for, Rick? I was gonna put you up for paperboy of the month this summer. And the office is setting up a trip to Catalina."

I shrugged. "I'm starting junior high and I gotta keep up my grades and stuff." The lie, a variation of my predecessor's reason for quitting, came automatically. And so did this thought: *I'm just like Jay, conning another boss.*

So clear in my memory that the scene unfurls like a movie in rapid sequence and present tense: I shake off the voices and assure Mr. Simmons I will recruit a replacement paper boy. Like the Spanish kings in my history books dispensing land grants in the new world, I carefully consider candidates for the largesse I have power to bestow. But none of the guys I ask jump at this chance to be rich beyond a dozen allowances. Some think the huge coverage area is too much work and responsibility. Some can't imagine the everyday responsibility of running a business by themselves: "You have to do it *every* Saturday, too? And pay a *bill* to the paper?!" Their main problem seems to be lack of imagination: the job and its compensation must be too good to be true. Either the route doesn't really pay so much or their parents will make them put it in a college fund. In the end the paper route splits between Carl Verdiman and another kid who applied directly to Mr. Simmons through other channels.

I throw the last paper on the last working day. The next few afternoons seem either unnaturally long or strangely short. Because I'm not reading the news while folding papers, I miss hearing about the first draft card burnings in Berkeley. I catch something on the radio about Astronaut Edward White's first walk in space, but I don't get the full story. My world tightens down to my own thoughts and perceptions.

Standing by yourself at the edge of the playground, watching the carefree little fourth-graders. Back home, looking in the mirror, you seem like an adult to yourself, even with the freckles. You've grown up here in this house — several inches. You've been in this neighborhood, this town longer than you've been anywhere. But not much longer, not much longer.

When I quit the route I also retired from the night subscription crew. But instead of catching up on my TV watching, I spent evenings in my room, listening to the radio or playing guitar. The few weekly lessons I took at the Westminster music store had seemed uninspiring, but the guitar teacher did do me one great favor: he started me playing right-handed, i.e. fretting with the left hand and strumming with the right. Since both tasks are new to those completely unfamiliar with the instrument, it shouldn't matter if the dominant hand does the fretting — if anything it seems an advantage, especially at first. Yet many teachers, in a perhaps misguided respect for left-handers' rights, will subject a left-handed pupil to the awkwardness of turning the guitar upside down and the difficulty of learning chords that way (as did Dick Dale, the King of the Surf Guitar) or the hassle of custom restringing (Jimi Hendrix and Paul McCartney) instead of having them simply start like the right-handers (Paul Simon). From a practical viewpoint, left-handed guitar players who play left-handed have even more trouble finding playable instruments than left-handed baseball players have finding mitts they can use, so in future guitar borrowing years, I never regretted my acquiescence to right-hander coercion.

Johnny Garrison teaches me the Peter Gunn theme on the bass

string, a more diverting practice than note reading and scales. "Peter Gunn" is strangely comforting as I sit on my bed and play it over and over. I spend even more time on a special school project, a sixth-grade capstone from Mrs. Dayton. The assignment is a ten-page autobiography designed to demonstrate our best penmanship on a clear exposition of our life story so far. I classed Mr. Everett as one of my least favorite teachers, but Mrs. Dayton proves the adage "There are hells below hells." A nervous woman, probably in the throes of menopause, she usually wears a neck brace, supposedly for chronic pain from an auto accident. Apparently she also takes pain medication; some afternoons we are subjected to a rambling monologue on her troubles with her husband and teenage daughters. And woe to a member of the captive audience if his attention wanders.

You have now crossed over to…the Secret Sorrow Zone. Last time you'll see Kara. Or Lannie. Or… Delia. Last time, last time, last time …

"Ricky! If you want to sit next to Delia so you can stare at her all day, I'm *sure* Randy would be happy to trade seats with you!"

I remember the Randy she is referring to chiefly because his last name was Doulia. Classmates often teased Delia Thornton that if she married this lad, her name would become Delia Doulia. Since volunteering for such a name would be inconceivable, Randy is at least one boy in class I don't have to burn with jealousy toward. But at the moment I feel great irritation with Mrs. Dayton.

However, even villains have good points, as I have learned from Freddy books. Simon the Rat is smart and no coward. Doty, the con man impersonating Mrs. Bean's brother to extort money, is full of fun and good stories. Likewise I can appreciate this autobiography assignment as Mrs. Dayton's one good idea, and none of her annoying pronouncements discourages my enthusiasm for the project. I am already plunged into nostalgia by the impending move, so the writing is a welcome outlet and I go at it with fervor. I do three drafts, two in pencil and one in pen, and when I finish, my life story spans twelve whole pages.[49]

Nostalgia is probably as unusual among twelve-year-olds as

---

[49] Unfortunately, the manuscript disappeared when we moved. How much of the past I recalled then has dissipated from my current memory bank? This book could have been even longer!

is heroin addiction; nonetheless, I have a bad case. Sitting in my back yard in the long evenings, I even romanticize flora and home building components.

Those ash trees along the back fence, those banana trees around the house ... you'll never see them again. And the white fence in the front, with the posts Jay sunk three feet deep in cement to last a lifetime. And the paneling and smoked mirrors and tile... you provided unskilled labor on most of these projects; your sweat helped to bring forth the stately beauty of this homestead.

Perhaps the stress of having to keep my secret brings on the last installment of the feud with Bobby Verdiman, the final showdown that has smoldered since fourth grade. For months he's been working up his nerve and looking for an excuse to do battle with me. But like a champion prizefighter in no hurry to put his crown at risk, I've avoided a rematch. Then one day in a mood of sheer perverseness I accuse Bobby of something I knew he didn't do, and I pick something guaranteed to infuriate him. A neighbor girl's skates are missing, and I charge him with the pilfering.

"That's so pitiful, Verdiman. Stealing from a girl!"

Of course Bobby instantly loses his temper, and the fight is on. He charges me; I sidestep and swing a roundhouse at his ear, the same decisive punch I used in our first fight back in '64. But this time my fist bounces off his hard head. He moves in to wrestle, bringing his heavier weight to bear. But I'm quicker, and twenty months of pedaling thirty pounds of papers has given me a wiry strength. As we struggle I maneuver for leverage, and we hit the ground with me on his chest, fist raised to smash his face. The battle is mine!

But suddenly, loyal little brother Carl jumps into the fray. He grabs my arm and twists it behind my back. Outrage! In 1965, Southern California suburban elementary school fighting etiquette is ultra-orthodox — kicking, biting, scratching, sneak attacks, and two-on-one are considered unmanly and downright un-American. In violating the taboo, Carl has disgraced both himself and his brother.

Of course the modern reader could consider Carl's act less harshly through the lens of cultural perspective, for his Native American background mandates loyalty to tribe and family over dominant culture proscriptions.[50] Nonetheless, in the heat of battle, I think him

---

[50] To be fair, my own Alabama cultural heritage makes similar allowances. One example would be the story Uncle Don used to tell about the 1954 Cotton Bowl and

a rat, a snake, and a fink. I consider him monstrously ungrateful as well, since I have just presented him with a lucrative paper route.

Bobby V should, in following the neighborhood code, immediately disengage, take Carl to task, and formally arrange to meet me later to continue the battle. But Bobby is in a state of blood rage and presses on. With Carl continuing to twist my arm, Bobby is able to shove me over and climb astride me. With great effort I manage to twist myself face down before he can get all his weight on my chest and pin my arms. Now he is sitting on my back with no soft places to punch except the arms protecting my ears. As in a chess game where one player has the strategic advantage but is unable to maneuver to victory, we are at stalemate.

Under these circumstances most neighborhood fighters would let the opponent rise, either to face a second round or concede defeat. But Bobby stays put, punching ineffectually at my arms and proffering queries of the "thought you were so tough, huh?" variety, interspersed with claims of victory such as "I'll kick your ass AGAIN, you blame me for some bullcrap YOU did."

Playing to the spectators who invariably gather at such events, I point out that he is begging the question: "Before you can kick my ass again, you're gonna have to kick it once without your baby brother's help!"

Abruptly, he stops punching, but continues to sit on me. Affecting unconcern, I don't bother to struggle. Instead, still playing to the audience, I feign boredom, pretending to yawn and wondering aloud what my family will be having for dinner.

The crowd, mostly on Bobby's side at the onset, now seems to be turning my way. Cries of "C'mon, Bobby, let him up!" resound from even the most partisan of his supporters. After a minute he complies, but takes no threatening second round stance. His expression is hard to read, but he looks more confused by events than otherwise. It's starting to dawn on him that he has not acquitted himself with honor. I give him no help with my stony, self-righteous glare.

Finally he walks away. His little brother follows, with what could be a half-ashamed, half-defiant glance back at me.

---

an excitable University of Alabama football player named Tommy Lewis. While Lewis stood on the sidelines, he saw Rice University player Dicky Moegle break away and dash for his second touchdown in only six minutes of play. Lewis, unable to bear the spectacle of the enemy making a fool of his team, jumped from the bench and ran onto the field, where, with a vicious block, he stopped Moegle's touchdown run. Alabamian football fans always sympathized with Tommy Lewis.

I am relieved to see them go. My twisted arm is throbbing; I doubt I could box effectively if Bobby pressed the matter, and the self-righteous glare was strategy borne of necessity. I walk away myself, giving the spectators a jaunty wave with my good arm. Of course I am less sanguine than I appear. From a neighborhood legality standpoint, since I was on top when the family cheating started, I have won the match. But nothing is really decided. I feel like a fool for egging-on my unstable opponent in the first place, and I am chagrined at having been on the ground, no matter what the circumstances.

I gird myself for the inevitable rematch, but to my surprise, Bobby doesn't press the issue. If not exactly contrite, his manner seems markedly non-belligerent. Since I have more weighty matters on my mind anyhow, this water-under-the-bridge approach is fine with me. A few days later Bobby even signs my sixth-grade graduation autograph book when we pass them around during recess.

Elementary school yearbooks don't yet exist in 1965 and autograph books aren't universal, but during the last week of school many sixth graders circulate little blank books we purchase for a dollar at Grant's department store. I write my name in filigree script on my first page, followed by the declaration: "The Greatest Bunch of Guys in the World!"

This intro seems a little overwrought even at the time, but between living with the secret of the impending move and the memories stirred by the autobiography assignment, I am awash in melancholy. The Springdale scene and my elementary school years are winding down without flourish or fanfare; all will end, as I heard quoted on a TV comedy show (and later identified as a phrase from T. S. Eliot's "The Hollow Men"), "not with a bang, but with a whimper."

And then what for your autobiography? More of the same. New kid, new kid, new kid.

I found my little autograph book recently in the oldest-memory box on the top shelf of my garage. It's my most ancient personal written artifact, my own Book of Kells. And as I flipped through the signatures I thought of that last week at Springdale, of my friends at all the places we'd lived, of Jane and Jay always packing or unpacking. And again I felt the old melodramatic ache of nostalgia, the longest-acting and sweetest of poisons.

CHAPTER FIFTY-FIVE

~ Countdown ~ Looking My Last (Again) ~ More Autographs ~ No Satisfaction ~
"The Blob is Coming" ~ Report Card, Schmort Card ~ Performance Eve
~ Five Hundred Miles from the Deer and the Heather

Last Week of School: Monday Morning

My horseshoe taps echo on the walkway between empty classrooms, for I have arrived at Springdale Elementary unusually early, a full hour before lineup time on the blacktop. The sky is a crisp blue with none of the June-gloom beach town overcast typical this time of year. On the almost deserted playground, a boy and girl are murmuring together at a foursquare court, each in a separate square. The only other person in sight is a girl playing tetherball by herself. When the ball rises in its circumscribed arc, the chain against the top of the pole clinks like a broken church bell. As I stroll restlessly in slow, looking-my-last mode, I can't distinctly see the pigeons huddled together on the eves of the classroom buildings, but I hear them muttering. Back on the blacktop, I'm the first one at our room's lineup spot—probably the only time in my entire school career I've had that distinction.

After time for extensive meditation, a classmate named Dean joins me. We travel in different circles and have rarely conversed, but now we exchange autograph books. On the first page of mine he writes, "When you get married and live in a hut send me a picture of your first little nut." He adds, "D-Liver D-Letter, D-Sooner, D-Better."

Monday Afternoon

After lunch Mrs. Dayton collects our music and health texts, and while she inventories these tomes in the official ledger, we clean our desks. Mine is so messy that the crumpled papers and general refuse (including, alas, all of the dead teacher comic series) take up most of the trash container assigned to our row. We spend the rest of the afternoon reading from our autobiographies, punctuated by occasional breaks wherein Mrs. Dayton relates recent misunderstandings she's gone through with her doctors. While she talks we pass around our autograph books. Daniel Redding disdained getting one of his own, but he writes "Zot!" in mine. "Zot!" is a sound effect from the B.C. comic strip that usually occurs when Wiley, the peg-legged, iconoclastic caveman, is struck by lightning. Johnny Garrison scrawls "Don't panic" below his curiously plain signature. Tommy Astrid writes: "Roses are red, violets are blue, throw-up is yellow, and so are you." This is prime sophisticated sick humor, nothing one should take personally. In his book I write, in the same vein: "To a punk. Get well soon."

Monday Evening

For the past several nights, Jay has been unloading flattened cardboard boxes from his car trunk. Several reconstructed units are allotted to me as I work in my room. Jane hasn't set a limit on what I can take to the new place, but she encourages me to throw away anything I don't really, really want. She has already picked through my clothes, culling everything I've outgrown.

On my little white table radio, the edgy KFWB nighttime DJ plays the Byrds, the Rolling Stones, Them, and other less-wholesome longhair groups that I am beginning to prefer over Herman's Hermits, The Dave Clark Five, and the others that parents think aren't so bad. I put *Journeys Through Bookland*, my Beatle posters, and my BB pistol into a box together. I'll have to wrap my guitar in a blanket, since it doesn't have a case. Looking around, I decide to let go of the kid stuff: Hardy Boys books and dartboard and pennants from Disneyland and Knott's Berry Farm. I'll also leave behind the baseball bat and glove, the bow and arrows, and the tonette flute from fourth grade. They want light packing? I'll give them light packing.

Tuesday Morning

We hand in our social studies books. Mrs. Dayton passes out a state progress test, and we fill in our Scantron answer sheets using number 2 pencils. I find the long multiple choice sheets a welcome distraction from looking-my-last over and over. Mrs. Dayton says these assessments don't count for our grades, but we should still do our best. This is all Bobby Verdiman, Cliff, and a few other guys need to hear. They fill the little bubbles in randomly, put their heads down on their desks and pretend to snore. Mrs. Dayton looks up from logging the social studies books. "Act your age," she hisses, but of course they are doing just that.

At lunch recess, Roberta, my unrequited admirer these last two-and-a-half years, seeks me out on the playground and thrusts her autograph book into my hands. With her limp hair and lean frame, she still reminds me of Olive Oyl on the Popeye cartoons, but I notice she's filling out a bit, and she meets my gaze without the usual blushing. I write, "I.L.B.C.N.U., Ricky." Someone else had written that proto-text-era signoff in my book, and I've used it often since then. Roberta spends a long time thinking. Then she writes, in purple ink, "To a real nice Elvis. Your firend always, Roberta Brown."

Tuesday Afternoon

During afternoon recess, I find Kara Morgan in the playground sector where sixth-grade girls used to jump rope at the beginning of the year. Now the jump ropes have disappeared; the young ladies are standing around in their invisible peds, chatting, listening to their transistor radios, and signing autograph books. Most of them are wearing either white or pink lipstick. I hand Kara my book and she signs her name in beautiful script. She then adds "Repent!" and a few large asterisks. We chat for a few minutes. Delia Thornton is nearby, chewing gum and talking with a girl I don't know. I haven't spoken with her since April.

"Wanna write in my book, Dee?"

She takes the book, signs her name, and returns it without a word.

Wednesday Morning

Both sixth grade classes leave Springdale for a walking field trip to the new junior high school. After a block or so, I feel a strong sense of déjà vu. My memories have been stirred recently by the autobiography assignment, and from the depths of time I recall the Alabama nursery school walks eight years ago. As in those ancient days, we now stroll down the sidewalk two abreast, with one teacher in the lead and the other policing the rear. Daniel Redding is a few rows up. My designated, alpha-order partner is Gary Hallideaux, an immigrant from Louisiana whose dad insists that he play Pop Warner football even though he'd rather collect troll dolls. We all trade sardonic comments and engage in general goofiness, but my attention is fixed primarily on my transistor radio — I'm waiting to hear the latest Rolling Stones song, as promised by the DJ every few minutes for the past hour.

And here it comes: "(I Can't Get No) Satisfaction." The song continues to play all the way down Croupier drive and across busy Springdale Street. I recognize a brilliant hook when I hear one, but in my seasoned music critic view, the song is more repetitive than necessary. Even Daniel, who doesn't bother with pop music, notices the lack of compression. "That," he remarks at what seems like the fifth run of the "I have tried tried tried" bridge, "is a LONG song."

As we pass through the new-school gates, our group instinctively moves closer together. Some older students, seventh graders who will transfer from the old junior high to this one closer to their homes, are also touring. A year at this age can make a real difference: some of the seventh grade boys have shot up to stringy adult size and several of the girls wear beehive hairdos and black eyeliner, or surfer girl bleaches and thick white lipstick. Some look almost like grown-up women, with pronounced hips and breasts. Of course these soon-to-be eighth graders either pointedly ignore our group or stare at us with utter contempt — a reminder that we who constituted the royalty of the elementary school will soon be the lowest in the secondary-school pecking order.

Mrs. Dayton and the other sixth-grade teacher pull the lines together as a Junior High counselor comes out to welcome us. "Ladies and Gentlemen," he begins, then chatters on about homerooms and class schedules and different teachers for each subject. He informs us that we will wear gym clothes in P.E. and take showers during the school day. It occurs to me there's no need to listen to him. Why bother? I'll never see this place again, or any of these people. Might as well plug in the transistor's mono earphone.

Less than a half hour has passed since "Satisfaction" played, but the KFWB DJ is spinning it again, a sure sign the Stones are headed for the top ten at least. Looking like a dour robot in her neck brace, Mrs. Dayton frowns at my inattentiveness. Report cards are yet to come, as she now threatens us almost hourly. But so what? The covert Hill family move is scheduled for Friday night, a few hours after school lets out. I've already stopped worrying about Mr. Prine and his suggestion (wrapped in veiled threat) that I should wear my glasses, and he is apparently too busy to follow up himself. Now I can blithely drop my report card in the street—Jay and Jane will be too busy to ask for it. And they'll never call the school for a duplicate.

Some people may be having troubles: Delia Thornton is icy calm, but, to my studied observation, obviously piqued at the junior high girls giving her superior looks. Mrs. Dayton is sweating profusely, and Mick Jagger seems to be complaining a lot. But I for one can get some satisfaction in knowing (a) there's nothing anyone around here can do to me anymore and (b) they'll all be getting a surprise soon.

Wednesday Evening

Except for a mattress and Blue Chip Stamps sleeping bag on the floor, nothing remains in my room to show habitation. The dismantled bed frame and boxes are stacked against the wall. I sit on the mattress counting my money: a little over ninety dollars. I'd been closer to a hundred a week ago—a hundred and twenty the end of last month. Where does it all go? Collecting Marvel comics runs over two dollars a month … record albums are three dollars each (with tax) at K-Mart for mono and three-fifty for stereo … at least a half-dollar a day on candy and soda. I've been drowning my sorrows with a lot of candy and soda lately. So how will I be able to keep up my independent lifestyle in the new place without a paper route or a big spender like Kevin to play poker with? When the savings run out, how can I possibly make it on a pathetic seventy-five-cents-a-week allowance?

Suddenly I recall past moves when Jay and Jane cleaned out my savings. They usually paid back such "loans," and they seem to be in less-desperate straits than in previous evasions … but you never know. I lock the bills and change in my steel cashbox and stash the cashbox at the bottom of one of the larger boxes full of clothes. I'm learning a rule of modern society: the more one has to lose, the more one has to worry about and the fewer people one can trust.

Thursday Morning

During what used to be our math hour at school we turn in the rest of our textbooks for inspection, after first erasing the most offensive pictures we'd penciled in them. Only a fool would draw in pen—parents are promptly billed for defaced books. Mrs. Dayton then pulls the curtains, and James threads a film into the projector. We settle down as best we can to run out our last state-mandated full day of the prescribed school year, milking the clock with monologues from Mrs. Dayton punctuated by grainy science and history films. All sorts of commotion simmers in the semi-darkness: whispering, imitation flatulence, giggles, and scuffles, until the undertone rises above the soundtrack. During a scene of crowds running in terror from a Chinese flood, I yell, "Big sale at K-Mart!" and someone else counters with, "The Blob is coming!"

Mrs. Dayton stands up periodically to belabor us. "If you want to be held back while everyone else goes on to the seventh grade, just keep it up!" She is shriller than ever and fans herself furiously with a handwriting skills book. We quiet down a few decibels, but more from conditioning than fear. Outside the sun shines warmly and summer stretches to infinity. Our anticipation is palpable; we are like lifers pardoned by the governor after forty years in stir, and there's nothing the warden can do about it except show his spite by prolonging the release as long as possible.

Thursday Afternoon & Evening

I take a circuitous route from school, stopping first at Tibbet's market for snacks and then dawdling through the Springdale streets for more than an hour. *That's where we used to line up for the bus to Schroeder ... that's the corner where I stood and talked with Delia that time ...* It's warm out, but when I finally get home all the front windows are closed and the curtains drawn. But the TV is plugged in and the five o'clock news drones something about the new "ground offensive" in Viet-Nam. The military term catches my attention, but I haven't been much interested in the news since I quit reading it in the *Daily Pilot.* I turn on the radio in my room and catch the sax solo bridge of the Four Tops' "Sugar Pie Honey Bunch," a plaintive musical phrase destined to join "Five Hundred Miles" and the Scottish folk song "Loch Lomond" in their ability to evoke bittersweetness for the rest of my life (so far), whether it be via scenes of deer and heather, railroad tracks to the horizon, or a mild sun going down above a quiet street of tract homes.

I lie back on the mattress and stare at the popcorn ceiling. Jane and Jay are moving back and forth in the hall, but no one is talking much. At seven, Jane takes a break to cook and serve the final sit-down meal in this kitchen: steak, broccoli, twice-baked potatoes — the last contents of our late-model refrigerator's always-well-stocked freezer. We're leaving the new 'fridge; several payments on it are overdue and the new rental place already has one.

I eat in silence as Greg and Trish chatter happily. The last move took place before Greg's conscious memory and Trish has only the dimmest recollections of anything prior to Huntington Beach. They know something momentous is underway, but they don't associate all the boxes and activity with leaving their home and friends. Jane is lost in thought and Jay clearly distracted; he's machinating this latest installment of his famous disappearing act, his lifelong performance art. Tomorrow he hauls away the stage.

CHAPTER FIFTY-SIX: THE LAST

~ Final Countdown ~ As If Pursued by Demons ~ Silent Protest
~ No Friends He Can Trust ~ Moon Through the Ashes ~ Goerke's Neat-O Invention
~ How Low Fall the Mighty ~ Despair and Resolve

Friday morning. D-day, Departure Day, Dread Day. I rise from the mattress on the floor of my former trophy room and dress carefully, choosing items from a final laundry load: white slacks, yellow oxford shirt, white turtle-neck dickey folded over at the exact middle of where my Adam's apple will one day protrude. I wipe off my Beatle boots with a clean white sock, pick my way through the house full of boxes, and go forth into a lovely Orange County June morning.

The shortened school day passes in a blur. One more movie: *Our Mr. Sun*, the 1956 Frank Capra-directed, *Gone with the Wind* of science movies and a perennial favorite since third grade. Midmorning party with cake. Report cards in manila envelopes with metal clasps. While Mrs. Dayton takes some paperwork to the office, I glance over my grades, heedless of her injunction to bring the envelopes home unopened. A in reading, B- in social studies, C in Math. C- in Science—I've had trouble with those lima bean diagrams since fifth grade. C-minus in penmanship. S (Satisfactory)-minus in deportment. This card falls well short of my twenty-three-dollar, Manhattan Beach triumph.

I could argue subjective grading by an unstable teacher, but why bother? The folks will be too preoccupied to ask about the card tonight, and it will disappear by tomorrow. Next September they'll enroll me in some strange school somewhere, and security-minded Jay won't give them the right address to send for my records.

Dismissal at noon—no school lunch today. I want to cement everyone in my memory, but it is difficult to memorize faces when most students are running for the school gate as if pursued by demons. I had planned to look my absolutely final official last at Delia before she left the classroom, but she slips away while I talk with Daniel.

So I poke along home, looking my last, my last, my last at everything else. I notice that all the little five-gallon boulevard trees planted by the tract contractor in late 1962 are now twice my height. At least half the cars parked along the street were leftovers from the 1950s when we moved in; now most of them are 1960s models. And here's our house, the one we'll abandon in a few hours.

On a whim I enter the back yard through the side gate, with its inside peppered with BBs I'd shot at a target pinned there last summer. I hear Marci and Jeanie Drolet playing next door in their deluxe pool. Our doughboy model, the one in which I learned to swim, sits empty in the corner of the yard, its plastic covering half-hanging on its caved-in aluminum sides. The new rental house supposedly has a real pool, a below-ground cement one, like the Drolets'. I took this news with a grain of salt, but what if it were true? A real pool … Jay might lie about a thing like that, but Jane corroborated it under cross-examination earlier in the week.

"If we're so broke," I'd asked pointedly, "how do we afford a house with a pool?"

As Jane explained, rent on the new place is only $110 a month. The bargain price is because the neighborhood is scheduled to be razed by the state highway department to make way for a new North San Fernando Valley freeway. The state buys all the houses in such neighborhoods under eminent domain statutes; then, while the vast construction project gears up, the condemned houses are rented cheap on one-year terminal leases. No problem for the Hills, I thought when I heard this. The state will be lucky if we stay six months.

As I enter the house via the sliding glass back door and make my way through the maze of boxes, a faint hope begins to stir in the atrophied optimism sector of my brain. Perhaps there is a slim chance something even more can come from the impending evasion than a pool (though of course a real below-ground pool is nothing to sneeze at). I recall moving from Redondo and other towns where I'd experienced disappointments or failed expectations, and feeling as we left those places that I was shaking the dust from my feet and starting fresh. The Huntington Beach years have been the closest the Hills have ever come to looking like the normal families on TV, but on the other hand, I have made mistakes, missed opportunities, and suffered disappointments and embarrassment here. Maybe at the new school I can achieve a perfect first impression and somehow sustain my momentum. Perhaps I can pull off being all things to all people and never make a foolish move.

Jane looks up from her packing with a distracted smile as I pass their open bedroom door. For the next hour she is in high gear — the last boxes, then the last dinner on paper plates for us kids — baloney sandwiches on Wonder Bread and a can of the new Franco-American SpaghettiOs split between us.[51] Greg chirps, "Uh-oh, SpaghettiOs!" from the ubiquitous product jingle. When Jane laughs at this exclamation as she pulls the last pots and pans from a cupboard, it occurs to me that she hasn't laughed much lately.

"Sit down and eat something, Bubbles," says Jay, standing by the door with a cup of coffee in his hand.

"I'm too busy to eat."

Jay shrugs, then leaves to meet Eddie and Freddie in the San Fernando Valley, where they will pick up the rental truck. I consider asking whether I can go along, but I am maintaining a certain level of reserve as a silent protest against the move. I am new at silent protests but will continue to perfect them over my early adolescent years.

Relations between Jay and me have cooled over the past few months. His exasperating opinions on personal grooming compelled mw to avoid him in order to maintain my hair length for the talent show. And another incident further distanced us: I'd forgotten to get Jane a present on her thirty-eighth birthday. The following Friday evening we loaded the car in preparation for a drive-in movie. Perhaps the bill that night included *Lord Jim*, during which I set the record for quickest falling asleep to a film. Or it could have been *A Thousand Clowns*, one I stayed awake for wishing I too had a nonconformist uncle like Murray Burns (played by Jason Robarts) for a guardian instead of an insensitive stepdad like Jay Hill (played by Darrell Depew).

In any case, Jay and I brought out the pillows and snacks while Jane gathered Trish and Greg in the house. I had settled into the back and was daydreaming about something, when suddenly Jay turned

---

[51] Later research revealed that canned-food marketer Donald Goerke, who later created Campbell's chunky soup line and many other gastronomical innovations, invented this interesting pasta product.

from the driver's seat and said, "I've got a bone to pick with you, Charlie."

I couldn't think of anything I'd done wrong — at least not anything he would know about. "What?"

"You didn't buy your mother a birthday present."

He was correct; I hadn't. The special date had not even registered.

"I forgot." I said with a combination of wonder and defensiveness. I was usually conscientious about presents; the last two Christmases I took great care in choosing a wallet for Jay and perfume for Jane — quality items in the three- to five-dollar range. I had also bought birthday presents for her the past few years. But with the talent show and other concerns, her birthday slipped my mind.

Jay proceeded to jump to several conclusions about my motives and general self-centeredness. I fumed inwardly. Who was he to tell me anything about my relationship with my mom? She and I did fine before he came along, and we'd be around long after he disappeared into history, if the past provided any indication.

So Jay and I have been less than cordial lately and I don't ask to go along when he leaves to get the moving truck. Jane is glad to have me home to help and provide company, but I am less than garrulous. Unlike the last move, we are well-organized and ready to go early. But the Valley is a three-and-a-half hour round trip, and anyway it isn't dark enough yet. The June evening stretches on … seven-thirty, eight o'clock. Still light outside. Jane tucks in Trish and Greg on pillow pallets in their bedrooms. The living room TV still occupies its usual spot, but it's disconnected from the antenna cord. I sit on the floor, back against the paneled wall, reading sections of Aladdin and Robinson Crusoe in *Journeys Through Bookland.* Almost immediately after his shipwreck, Robinson Crusoe began construction on his island home. When Aladdin found the magic lamp, he wished one of his earliest wishes for a jeweled palace of his very own.

Darkness falls at last and the truck arrives at nine-thirty, right on schedule. Jay is driving the rental and Freddie follows in our car, with Eddie bringing up the rear in his Ford Econoline van. The entire moving crew will be the three brothers and me. Jay Hill has no friends he can trust.

"Let's get it done." Jay is all business; no jokes and encouragement like last time. The new approach works for me; it makes my pointed reserve easier, and I feel more like a grownup crew member. I help the brothers load some bigger pieces: couch, console stereo, beds, and dressers; but mostly I bring along the lighter items: end tables, kitchen chairs, disassembled bed frames. We leave much miscellany behind in the garage, on the back patio, and scattered about the lawn.

Jane drives off and returns with two pink boxes of assorted donuts. Freddie and Eddie come forward to help themselves and drink hot coffee from paper cups. Currently the twins are both the same extra-large size and I'm having trouble telling them apart, but she calls them by their right names. Jay gulps some coffee and grabs a smaller box of kitchenware, his signal that it's time to fill in the gaps with little stuff. I repack Crusoe and haul out my valuable treasures box, placing it where I'll be able to find it quickly when we get to the other end. I continue loading boxes into Eddie's van while they pack the next layer of large items in the truck.

No doubt the Drolets, the Kalanis, and the Verdimans are peeking out their windows as it dawns on them we're leaving. They wouldn't think of embarrassing us by coming over: sneaking out like this could only mean we are facing imminent foreclosure, not unheard of in this credit-overextended neighborhood. But the Hill's? He always seemed so self-assured and well dressed; she so lovely and elegant. They drove a Cadillac and voted with the Republican fat cats. How low fall the mighty.

While the grownups take a smoke break, I step through the sliding glass door to the backyard. A waning gibbous moon peeks through the ash trees. Those trees were little one-gallon sprouts two years ago; now they're spindly adolescents, already higher than the roof. I stand in the moonlight until I hear an engine start, then rush back through the house, only to find the truck pulling away. They've left me to help Jane with the last odds and ends. Eddie's car is parked near the new place so they can unload and go — both twins lived in the Valley, near Eileen and Ed, only a few miles away. When Jane fills me in on this geography later, her expression suggests she is less than happy with the proximity to her in-laws.

I help situate Greg and Trish in the car, and then we drive down Oasis drive for what I must assume will be the final, final time. I glance back at the tract entrance once more as we turn onto Springdale Street. Jane looks tired, but when I ask if our impending abode is old and crummy like the houses in the Tibbet's Market neighborhood, she begins, somewhat dutifully, to promote the good points of the new place.

"Well, it is an older house, but you'll still have your own room. And we'll even have a party line phone!"

She inquires whether I know what a party line phone is. Yes, I've seen them on TV comedies featuring hicks and hick towns. But since we haven't had a home phone in years, I have to acknowledge, to myself at least, that a party line is a step up.

We continue north on old Highway 101 then up through Long Beach in the maze of Los Angeles freeways. Since Jay is unavailable to appreciate my silent protest, I have with pre-adolescent logic, transferred it to Jane.

KFWB Channel 98 plays softly. The home of the KFWBeatles is also on the cusp of change, for 93 KHJ, an upstart that debuted in April with its "Boss Radio" format, will soon eclipse my old favorite as the coolest teen station in the Southland. I lean with my back against the passenger door, my feet stretching to the middle of the floor hump between seats. Jane sighs, lights a Tareyton, and drives on. Her expression is hard to read in the dim dashboard light.

I wonder now, from seeming eons in the future if, like me, Jane felt the ache of leaving behind something more than a house. Raising a family in a home of her own must have given her a sense of stability after the dysfunctional upbringing in Bessemer, the wild show business career, the gypsy celebrity in Mexico and the rootless evasions of the past several years. She could have done much more in the land where everyone is from Somewhere Else: gone further in show business, used her people skills in business, maybe even have become a lawyer like her brother Kirby. Certainly she could have married money like her friend Fran Faye.

But for all her brains and charm, Jane again and again followed her heart instead of her head. Al Landry, the married older man; then Luke Langston, the handsome youngster; then Jay Hill, the most charming, charismatic dreamboat loser of all, who finagled her into the middle-class facade, then ran away from it exactly as he'd always run before. She should have known. She probably did, at least on some level.

I doze while we traverse the Pasadena, Golden State, and Hollywood Freeways (in the 1960s they have names instead of numbers). As we exit the Van Nuys boulevard off-ramp, I sit up, looking around sleepily at the used car lots, the gas stations and liquor stores open late. A few blocks north we drive past Tiara Street, where Jane and Jay first cohabitated in 1959 and I'd collected out-of-state license numbers and bowling pins. I stood on that corner a block down, discussing Dick and Jane stories with my tall friend. Half a lifetime has passed since then: six whole years.

We make our way through the synchronized traffic lights, down Van Nuys Boulevard to Panorama City, past Kaiser Hospital and other tall buildings around Roscoe Boulevard. Nothing urban like this in Huntington Beach. As we turn right on Nordhoff Street, Oasis Drive already seems like another epoch. I look over and catch Jane's profile in a street light.

A half-century later I can see her expression in my mind's eye: an odd mix of despair and resolve. I don't know, but I think she may have met the world with the same expression when her Mama abandoned her to her grandmother's begrudging care and when her Daddy's former colleagues escorted him to prison — and when, en route from Alabama in 1952, she rode west on the Greyhound bus, alone and pregnant with me.

EPILOGUE

1965–Present

1966: Proto Hipster disgruntled by hornrims and a mandated haircut

1969: From Midget EP to Junior JL

Late '70s: Ten years since my last haircut

2010, no more lenses: with Judy in Venice, Italy, while writing Chapter Forty-Four

EPILOGUE

~ A Brief Synopsis of Family Events Beyond the Scope of This Book, Provided for Readers Like Me Who Remain Curious About What Happened Next, Even After a Suitably Resonant Conclusion

When it comes to story structure, I prefer the classic Aristotelian pyramid model where, in the finale or dénouement, the reader finds out what happened to everyone mentioned in the tale just told. What's-his-name became a successful businessman. So-and-so got drafted and died in Vietnam. This young criminal is now a district attorney; that wild girl became a cloistered nun. But the problem with my story is that we always moved fast and didn't look back.

If this were one of those enhanced, "based on a true story" memoirs I could announce that Charlie from Sylmar actually did sell the world's most expensive comic book and bought a sheep ranch with the proceeds; that Bear from San Pedro returned to Indonesia, where I saw his campaign poster in my recent visit to Bali; and that Norman the 16-year-old anti-adolescent clip-on tie achiever became a Grateful Deadhead. But this account is genuine nonfiction (except for the name changes), and with few exceptions, I have no reliable evidence on what happened to anyone outside my immediate family.

I did attempt some online biographical research, but Social Media's main platforms go back only to high school, and my posts to the smaller entities elicited no responses. Free Internet searches availed almost nothing, and I balked at paying for those unsavory services that provide arrest records and credit scores along with the search object's current address and phone numbers. But all failures aside, I am able to supply the reader with a reasonably complete account of the family epilogue (to which generations of creditors would have loved to have been privy to before the statute of limitations ran out).

❈ ❈ ❈

As Jane probably suspected, the Huntington Beach years were a high-water mark in our family quest for the Southern California good life. Almost immediately, Jay and Jane's return to marginal citizenship and willful poverty would rival and in some ways surpass their early history together.

To begin with, the escape from Huntington Beach did not actually take us to Panorama City as Jay had reported, but rather to within the border of Pacoima, a city widely considered the worst slum in the San Fernando Valley. About the time the Watts riots became a TV sensation in August 1965, Jane found out that school district boundary rules required me to attend Pacoima Junior High, an institution notorious for racial violence. Jay quieted her fears by enrolling me across town at Sepulveda Junior High, using his parents' address on Langdon Avenue near the school. We had resumed 1959-style machinations, but at least this time I didn't have to remember a new last name to go along with my fake address.

But I faced more serious social concerns than ethnic turf battles. At the beginning of summer, I made a decision to experiment with wearing my glasses to help navigate the new environs. While so bespectacled, I met Dave, a fellow Marvel comics fan from Texas, who also wore glasses. Since I didn't know anyone else in the neighborhood, I conformed to the prevailing look all summer. But on the first day of junior high, I discovered to my horror that I could no longer function without the disfiguring appliances — my eyes had adjusted to the prescription and my coping skills no longer sufficed. I actually got lost on campus and had to put on the glasses to find my way to my sixth-period class.

In my sensitive perception, the hated lenses brought immediate social disaster, making me invisible to girls at a time when my already active interest had taken a sharp upturn. I also became a target for school bullies. I was a lowly B-7, so most of these antagonists were older and larger than I; moreover, bullies always assumed that a smaller guy with glasses would be easy to conquer (hip clothing notwithstanding), so compensatory psychological ploys proved inadequate.

I was unable to take such setbacks philosophically or acquiesce quietly, so each day at junior high brought its trials. The academic atmosphere was similarly unsatisfactory; most of the overstressed teachers at Sepulveda seemed like functionaries in a Kafka story (or did so in retrospect when I read Kafka several years later). In short, social and scholastic triumphs lay behind me, and junior high realized all my worst sixth-grade nightmares.

In early 1966, Jay executed what would be termed a Hail Mary pass in football. Using all his evasive skills, plus forged income documents and his spare social security number, he signed mortgage papers for a new tract house in Simi Valley, then on the outer fringes of possible L.A. commutes. The scheme came off in part because the Simi tract was also a Hail Mary for the developers; the remote location discouraged sales so alarmingly that mortgage officers were anxious to believe in the sincerity of all comers.

We seemed to be back on the mid-sixties prosperity track, but in late summer 1966, in a sort of hard-luck synchronicity, Jay and Jane both broke their left legs in separate accidents. Jay's job income had been already insufficient to keep up with overdue payments, so we lasted only a month or two on the workman's compensation dole. Right before the sheriffs came in November (the ever-popular evasion month), we abandoned another mortgaged house, skipped out on our new Chevrolet Impala car payments, and fled to Alabama in the Impala.

Jane instigated this farthest move to date, her final return to the Ross native land. We first tried a pay-by-the-week mobile home in Fultondale, right outside Birmingham. Jay's Minnesota/California roots failed to transplant in Dixie; he avoided looking for a job for the duration of our sojourn there. Jane enrolled all three kids in Fultondale Grammar School, where some of my eighth-grade classmates were seventeen years old and drove their own cars or motorcycles. On weekends I walked five miles to read comic books at the nearest shopping center. I couldn't afford to buy any; my allowance had been discontinued and I had long-since spent my paper route fortune.

The problem with weekly rentals is the landlord will begin to nag after only a couple of weeks, so a mid-January 1967 overnight evasion took us back to the family-historic Cloverdale apartments in Bessemer. Thanks to an emergency Western Union MoneyGram from Nanny, we rented a two-bedroom unit a few doors from the address Luke, Mom, Trish and I left in 1957. I attended Bessemer Junior High, where my homeroom teacher was Barbara Ross, the same cousin Barbara who burned Jane with an iron to encourage learning her play-school lessons back in 1931. Barbara must have learned patience along with her professional training, for she taught both history and English with skill and wry humor. I actually liked her lessons on sentence diagramming, which marked me as a future English major. In her classroom I saw firsthand Alabama's reluctant participation in federally mandated integration: only the two top students in each grade at the segregated "Negro" schools in town were allowed to enroll at the white junior and senior highs. I was a stranger in what seemed a decidedly strange land, and I grew terribly homesick for California, but at least two people in my class felt even less comfortable than I.

All advances, loans, and pawn shop revenue ran out by March; we sold our TV and stereo console right after the Beatles' "Strawberry Fields" and "Penny Lane" videos debuted on the Ed Sullivan show. No solution remained but another rerun of 1957 in which we drove straight from the Cloverdale apartments to Nanny's and John's place on Kenwood Avenue in L.A., sleeping in the Impala and subsisting on baloney sandwiches. Jay promised to look for a job, but a few mornings after we arrived, the Impala disappeared, snatched by a patient repo man.[52] That afternoon Jay and Jane fell into a heated discussion, after which Jay disappeared (presumably on foot).

On April 25, 1967, Jane turned forty with no man, no money, and no prospects. Nothing came of her employment application to the Broadway department store where Nanny worked, and further job seeking without transportation was difficult: a white woman walking alone or waiting at bus stops in the Vermont and Vernon district inevitably garnered negative attention. She never got around to enrolling me in the local junior high, primarily because I would have been the only white student there, but also because she desperately hoped we'd only be at Nanny's for another week or two. But months passed, and I never returned to eighth grade.

With an occasional four dollars earned for helping John load, unload, and sell at the swap meet on Saturdays, I would take the bus from South Central to Hollywood. I spent many hours reading album liner notes at record stores, and when I had fifty cents to spare, I could buy and read the *L.A. Free Press* and *Oracle* "alternative" newspapers, or smoke dried bananas (a short-lived fad inspired by the Donovan song "Mellow Yellow") at the Bizarre Bazaar, a pioneer head shop on Selma Avenue. Since Jay wasn't around to dictate my

---

[52] Apprised of Nanny's listing as the nearest relative on the car loan papers, the repo man must have periodically checked her place for the five months since we'd ceased making payments.

fashion choices and I was not attending school, I found myself with leeway to grow my hair longer than ever, which allowed me to blend in with the other budding hippie customers at the Bazaar. In pursuit of such uniform iconoclasm, I also experimented (thanks to John's miscellaneous junk collection) with antique wire-rim glasses, some of which I could almost see through.

Meanwhile, Jane grew quietly discouraged and spent her days watching game shows in Nanny's bedroom. She seemed quicker with the answers than most contestants on *PDQ* (a forerunner to *Wheel of Fortune*), and the conviction grew that if she could win the big cash prizes on the show, she would be able to start fresh—buy a car, find a job, and move us to our own place. She turned on her old charm in the preliminary calls to the game show screeners, and soon Nanny was taking time off work to taxi her to Hollywood. Live tryouts for *PDQ* took place at a studio a few blocks from where, twenty years before, Jane had been an Earl Carroll girl. She made it up the elimination ziggurat to the penultimate round—then the producers dropped her from consideration. It must have been one of the great disappointments of her life. Nonetheless, she put on her bravest smile when she came home to tell me the bad news. "We'll be all right," she said. "Something will turn up."

That something turned out, as usual, to be Jay. After a couple months' disappearance with no contact, he checked in to announce that he had secured part-time work in the Sears lawn and garden department. Furthermore, he had a plan to put them back on Easy Street. He explained how they could acquire expensive power equipment—mowers, edgers, etc.—using the old run-the-accomplice-through-the-checkstand scheme. Jane would "buy" the equipment, load it in John's van (for he would surely loan it to them for a percentage of the profits), and they could sell the machines at the swap meet.

"I don't think so," Jane demurred. "The way our luck's been going, we'd probably get caught."

"Bubbles, have I ever steered you wrong?"

Despite this compelling argument, Jane remained relatively firm. If they were going to get back together again, he would have to come up with something more reasonable and at least closer to legal. Jay disappeared again, but in late summer 1967 he called to report he had found a grocery checker job in the valley and secured an unfurnished two-bedroom apartment near Sepulveda and Oxnard streets in Van Nuys, about a mile from where they'd rented their first place together in 1959.

After five months of virtual house arrest in South Central, Jane was prepared to forgive and forget, but she had finally learned that her best interests precluded trusting in Jay for security. Subtracting several years from her age on job applications, she found an $80 per week file clerk position in Santa Monica, town of my birth. Over the mountain she commuted in a $75 car purchased on a weekly payment plan from the junkyard. The car was a DeSoto of the same faded hue and vintage as the old Plymouth Jane and Luke traded in for the Dodge Dart in 1960. All we needed for the complete retro loop was a Nixon for President bumper sticker, and those would soon be available when Nixon ran again in '68.

Gifted with people skills and a heretofore unexploited business aptitude, Jane rose from file clerk to secretary, then office manager, then hospital administrator. She had found herself at last. Ascending from her nadir as a game show reject, she continued rapidly up the career ladder to become, by the middle of the 1970s, the regional supervisor of a hospital network.

My own progress took another trajectory. Becoming a guy-in-the-glasses marked only the first of many deflations I was destined to suffer in the post Huntington Beach years.[53] From early childhood I had always been a reasonably pleasant-looking lad (even with the precocious hair styles) but during my early adolescence I lost all potential for becoming a model in K-Mart circulars. Over the next two years I would sprout pimples, my canine teeth would come in crooked, and by early 1968 I would shoot up several inches in height without a corresponding weight gain: at just over six feet tall I weighed only 120 pounds. During this period I found myself sinking into personal Hells that made my sixth grade Weltschmertz seem like the Song of Shangri-La.

My timing was poor for such upheavals. Fourteen is the age when we take our heroes most seriously, and I turned fourteen in the inmates-running-the-asylum year of 1967. My perceptions were validated by the social earthquake of the late sixties, which celebrated peculiar perceptions of all sorts. As Jane steadily pulled the Hill clan

---

[53] But I was not destined to be a Grandma Glasses forever. After only 45 years of various glasses styles interspersed with contact lenses, I had laser eye surgery in 2010 and have since enjoyed excellent vision without mechanical correction. Problem solved!

into surface respectability, I leapt into the counterculture maelstrom. Soon I dropped out of the family picture, living more or less on my own from age sixteen and attending school only sporadically. During this time I could often be found hitchhiking (with occasional freight-train hops) around the country in arcane adventures, such as appreciation-of-nature jaunts to Big Sur's stunning panorama of fifty or more hitchhikers in a two-mile stretch of Highway 1; cultural enrichment forays to San Francisco's artistic, slum-nestled music shrines; and quasi-religious pilgrimages to the Mardi Gras bacchanal in New Orleans.

As a result of such aesthetic explorations and other unorthodox pastimes, I have been accused of wasting my adolescence and young manhood in a hedonist daze. Actually, that period featured several notable accomplishments. For instance, I learned much in the way of practical geography. Furthermore, I taught myself to play the harmonica and several guitar chords, not to mention writing a few dozen unpublished songs. Through these years I also showed a flair for expressive dancing and circumventing authority figures, the former perhaps hereditary and the latter most likely from nurture.

While I remained estranged from societal norms through most of the seventies, both Trish and Greg graduated from high school and joined the Navy. When John passed away in 1974, Nanny moved in with the family until her death 1988. By the early 1980s I had changed direction: shook off the daze; cut my hair; married Judy, the love of my life (as Heaven is to Earth, so is she to my elementary school and subsequent loves); sired two brilliant and beautiful children, and returned to school. After pursuing various degrees for the next ten years, I found myself in a University teaching career that incorporated my love of writing and reading. Such a turnaround seemed like a long shot to everyone who knew me, but Jane said she'd never doubted it would happen. "The Rosses are late bloomers," she explained.

Jay and Jane officially wed in 1991 when Jay's first wife, who had resolutely refused to divorce him, died of cancer. Jay continued to job-hop and ran a plethora of get-rich-quick schemes, and for a few flush years he even held an upper-management position as liquor buyer for a market chain. But he always spent more of his and Jane's earnings than they netted, and he would periodically shut down—do nothing but lay in bed and read westerns and crime novels for months until bankruptcy loomed or actually descended. Still, with

Jane's increasing salary, they zigzagged mostly upward until their sixties. Then in the mid-1990s, after Jay's most elaborately planned and executed run from creditors, he once again landed them in Las Vegas, where a late-blooming gambling addiction returned them to relative poverty in their retirement years.

But through all feasts and famines, Jane and Jay continued to be loving and generous to a fault with their grown children, grandchildren, and great-grandchildren. They also remained (for lack of a better term) young at heart, optimistically shrugging off setbacks until the end. They passed away, six months apart, at ages 81 and 77. Upon their crypt in San Diego, their descendants affixed a plaque on which is embedded a photograph. In this picture, taken in upscale nightclub during their flush times in the early 1990s, they are wearing elegant clothes and smiling like movie stars.

The engraved epitaph below the photo could also serve for the rest of the misfits, black sheep, and go-getters of their generation:

"We did it our way."

Made in the USA
Las Vegas, NV
26 February 2022

44623659R10256